Travel Resources

An Annotated Guide

Stephen Walker

The Scarecrow Press, Inc.
Lanham, Maryland • Toronto • Plymouth, UK
2009

SCARECROW PRESS, INC.

Published in the United States of America
by Scarecrow Press, Inc.
A wholly owned subsidiary of
The Rowman & Littlefield Publishing Group, Inc.
4501 Forbes Boulevard, Suite 200, Lanham, Maryland 20706
www.scarecrowpress.com

Estover Road
Plymouth PL6 7PY
United Kingdom

British Library Cataloguing in Publication Information Available

Library of Congress Cataloging-in-Publication Data

Walker, Stephen, 1948–
  Travel resources : an annotated guide / Stephen Walker.
      p. cm.
  Includes bibliographical references and index.
  ISBN 978-0-8108-5245-7 (hardcover : alk. paper) — ISBN 978-0-8108-6947-9 (e-book)
  1. Travel—Bibliography. 2. Travel—Information services—Directories. I. Title.
  Z6011.W28 2009
  [G153.4]
  016.91046—dc22   2009009483

In memory of my parents, Max and Rosa Walker, and my
sister Susan Villalobos

Contents

PREFACE

What *Travel Resources* Is and Isn't

Despite the mention of "guide" in the subtitle, *Travel Resources* has little concern with typical country guidebooks. Guidebooks have been reviewed by several volumes in the past, so instead I gathered together travel resources that might very well have been overlooked in their larger shadow. However, for something about judging the worth of guidebooks, see the section **Country Guidebooks** in the **Introduction**.

Since so many works treat travel by geographic regions, inclusion of sources within this volume must bow to the practical matters of keeping the wordage within bounds, but making the appeal broad through omitting any geographical unit smaller than continents or multi-country regions. The exception to this is the United States, at whose readers this title is primarily aimed. In this instance, works must encompass the U.S. as a whole, rather than as a state or region. Again, there is an exception, which is travel series, whose individual titles may cover states or countries, but considered as a whole these titles offer the breadth that makes their inclusion eligible.

A literature whose omission that is less likely to be mourned than guidebooks is that produced by the business of tourism. While extensive, it is of limited help to most travelers, and therefore is lightly touched on in this resource.

Selection

This bibliography of sources is not exhaustive nor is it a "best of" collection (as the occasional criticism shows). Although there are quality judgments in some annotations, inclusion of a title, organization, website, or business is not an automatic endorsement. To be included, resources must cover the subject and answer basic questions about it; or they must offer a unique approach; or be one of the few aids in this area. The number of titles under any subject varies in abundance, which usually reflects what is available through libraries, bookstores, websites, or organizations. When push came to shove the newest publications have been favored over older ones for inclusion.

Print titles have been verified either by reviewing the item first-hand or by visiting their websites, a strategy especially true for periodicals. Some important works have not been reviewed because I could not get a proper look at them, notably some reference books

About Time

Usually the latest edition of a title has been examined, except when the title is a serial (see **Serials, Periodicals** below).

In cases where the year of coverage claimed in a book's title differs from its publication date, it is the latter that follows the name of the publisher in the citation. When a work occurs annually or otherwise periodically, its rate of appearance is identified ("quarterly," for example), and the year of the edition under examination is provided at the annotation's end. A book with a second or later edition has been denoted, since a work that has gone through several editions suggests that it is reliable and popular.

Particularly in the cases of government publications, where there is both a paper copy and an online one, the newest is chosen for review; and if they bear the same date, the review is usually of the online version. However, be warned that government websites in particular frequently change their addresses (URLs).

Websites have a unique relationship with timeliness of information. Unlike book publication dates, those for websites may not appear, or may not reflect the currency of the updates. As a result, the year when the site was observed accompanies its annotation.

The Entries

With a few exceptions annotations have been based on direct perusal of the work. In the case of organizations I have heavily leaned on their websites for information and have occasionally consulted the *Encyclopedia of Associations* (see **Introduction**). In the instance of books the citation information (title, author, publisher, and year) should be sufficient for the reader to identify them in a library or to order them through a bookstore or their publishers.

In the entries is first the title or name and immediate supplementary information. The annotations summarize the contents of a publication or characteristics of an organization, even when a title anticipates it—for example, *Traveler's Health Sourcebook* (see in **Health**), which gives what seems the whole table of contents in its leviathan subtitle. The most common entries are for books, their typical elements being the geographic range covered, the format or arrangement of data (directory, guide, etc.), purpose, samples of the general contents, and noteworthy features. The ability of the eye to find types of information on a page is important. Therefore, I have noted such matters of format as use of bolded headings and words.

Travel Resources is print oriented. A website has received inclusion only as a result of its containing a document, although there are a few exceptions. Websites have also been recognized due to their association with a title or organization.

Serials, Periodicals . . .

In the bibliography one kind of printed material comes out repeatedly with the same title and scope each time, but has changing contents, and may accept subscriptions. This is called a serial or, more narrowly, a periodical. Newspapers, magazines, and newsletters fit in this category, as do books with scheduled updates (according to months or years). In those instances the rate of frequency is presented in the entry. A few of the terms can be confusing: biennial (once every two years), biannual (twice a year), and bimonthly (every two months or twice a month).

. . . And Series

Publishers must love travel series, for they make so many of them. Series are different from serials. The former have individual titles as well as a second shared title. Words in the series often begin the title, as with *Let's Go, Culture Shock!*, or *Fodor's*. Alternatively, the title may be separate in such series as *Michelin Green Guides, Charming Small Hotel Guides, Footprint Handbooks*. Also, some series share a special theme (for example, *Roadside Geology*).

A majority of series are guidebooks to countries, regions, cities or, in the United States, states. A series lends depth and breadth to guidebooks by multiplying coverage beyond a single physical volume. It seems feasible that guidebook series are popular because a traveler who likes one book in a series will more likely return to others rather than its competitors, for a trade brand loyalty has been indoctrinated. Also, a series cultivates familiarity since it is more likely to be consistent in features, format, treatment, and tone than a random group of books on a topic.

In the entries the word "series" appears in parenthesis after the title.

Library of Congress Subject Headings and Their Uses

In a library catalog one way to search for a book is by subject. Subject headings on records originate from a subject authority list, such as the *Library of Congress Subject Headings* (available in print and online), which has an approved heading along with synonyms and variants of it; for example, the term "hotels" is used instead of "inns." It also directs a reader through cross-references that are either related ("boardinghouses"), narrower ("motels"), or broader ("hospitality industry").

Consulting a subject authority list is one way to begin a subject search in the library's catalog. Or you can search for the title or author of a book, and upon finding its record determine its call number, which will establish the place on a shelf where that book and others like it are located. Alternatively, see what subject headings are used on the record and do a subject search on that basis.

One or more official terms from the *Library of Congress Subject Headings* has been supplied at the end of an introduction to each list for the benefit of those who might wish to search their library catalog by subject. (However, some library catalogs derive subject headings from other authorities.)

Subject headings have also been supplied because in part they may be applied beyond a library catalog's records. Any electronic search with Google or similar web search engines requires the best words to focus a search, and these headings might do the trick. Interested or ambitious parties can electronically explore beyond the lists in *Travel Resources* and locate helpful websites and other sources.

Subject Categories in *Travel Resources*

This book's subject categories at times differ from Library of Congress's, since they should accurately and familiarly describe the contents of each list and be convenient for the traveler. Starting with **Accommodations** and ending with **Work**, each section that reviews travel resources commences with a general discussion that may mention resources that are not included in the accompanying annotated list.

As with library practice, at the end of section introductions I have occasionally plopped in "see also" references. **Motorcycle Touring**, for example, could be related to **Automobile and Recreational Vehicle Travel** or **Budget Travel**.

One issue that plagues library catalogers is where to fit an item that straddles more than one subject. To moderate this difficulty, besides cross references in the text there is a title index at the back.

Since one purpose of this work concerns the means of finding information, a few headings refer to media—**Magazines and Newsletters**, and **Video, DVDs, and Television**. These are not travel subjects themselves.

Books other than this one have taken a subject approach to travel. For example, *The Traveler's Sourcebook* (Omnigraphics, 1997) is in alphabetical order and is heavy with directory-type information. By contrast, *Travel Resources* is an annotated bibliography that includes directory titles, but no addresses.

On occasion a resource has received a star (*) before its title. This indicates I have found that it is of particular use or interest.

Acknowledgment

Thanks to Bob Libbey for bringing me all those travel sections from many newspapers.

INTRODUCTION

Are Guidebooks Necessary?

Consult enough books and other media and you will get an outline or overview of a varied subject. When the subject is travel the coverage can broaden travelers' interests and knowledge. More importantly, information can be used for a traveler's comfort or security. At least by perusing significant resources in one place the reader may conveniently gather a greater clarity of possibilities and extend his or her travel choices.

Conventional country guidebooks are made up of a wide range of subject categories. The *Eyewitnesses*, the *Frommers*, the *Insights*, the *Lonely Planets* may be relied upon to contain information about accommodations, places to dine, the practice of travel, and sights. Their coverage of such interconnecting areas as work abroad, local laws, and special interests is more problematical. Yet, look and you can find books and other resources that concentrate on just one of the subjects crowded in the general guide; the specialty title will surpass in comprehensiveness, detail, and hopefully, authority that of the guidebooks' treatment, especially of those aspects that in some instances are understandably marginalized or omitted by them. The enterprising traveler will wish to find the specialty works in order to supplement or even replace the guidebooks.

Even if the information sought is in a guidebook, it could be hidden. Can it be located in the index or will the table of contents point to a likely chapter? Consider the larger subject or the area it may fit into. At worst, you will need to do a brute search by plowing through the text. Should you be daunted by that, perhaps you should try another guidebook, or look for the subject under different terms, or look for something related—or change your subject.

The concept of travel and traveling is a microcosm of life. It is about how we live and the surroundings in which we live. It concerns people, economy, law, customs, health, and other rules that make up our existence. A restaurant guide is, after all, an updated version of how our ancestors found food. Like education, travel is change or transition and it involves the fresh, or perhaps an acquaintance with what has been vicariously experienced. The essence of travel is experience, which is most obviously mediated through the guidebook, but may also come from a tourist agency, a traveler, or an organization. This is how to prepare for travel. However, there are those who prefer to improvise as they go, getting advice from locals at the place they are visiting, struggling with a foreign language, and learning about the identity of an area's attractions through postcards and brochures. They may find this work superfluous.

Broadening Travel Opportunities

The purpose of *Travel Resources: An Annotated Guide* is to broaden the reader's knowledge through an extensive, varied menu of major and minor travel opportunities and the means of taking them. Use *TR* as a starting place to find out about a book, magazine, website, or association, or learn the means to consult them. After learning about the variety of travel opportunities, concern yourself with increasing the *quality* of your experience.

Once you start discovering you may come across ideas to supplement old interests or awaken new ones. A lover of English literature can travel to those places in Britain associated with writers, using guides designed for that purpose. Or a beginning traveler may discover a love of fine food. Take a walking vacation, a cruise, or mingle with the natives through public transportation.

Finding Information, Especially Online

In the following early sections the summarizing discussion and explanations about searching and the selection of titles have been very general and elementary. The reader should keep in mind that there are exceptions and conditions that have not been taken into account, while others who are informed might justly dispute my suggestions and interpretations. Above all, I've covered a great deal of information in this guide, so inevitably there are mistakes, inaccuracies, inconsistencies, and omissions, which I regret, but acknowledge as mine alone.

While *TR* categorizes travel subjects and describes relevant sources under them, it also provides assistance for those who wish to go beyond the contents and get some clues about the way to search for information about travel. The difficulty used to be the paucity of resources and discovering what they might hold. Today, especially with the web, you risk drowning in a glut of unrefined search results. Learning how to harvest *relevant* information is a skill in itself. Whether your goal is seeking facts about travel or about any other subject, there is the same method in searching for information.

You should have rudimentary skills in searching for information, which in this internet age is now a common activity. "Information literacy" (as it is called) can be grouped with readin', writin', and 'rithmetic for those who wish to cope with this information age, especially in the matter of electronic searching. To put it briefly, you should as clearly and precisely as possible determine what information that you wish and recognize what sources may help you in accomplishing this. Being familiar with the concept of and/or/not searching and the characteristics of the database you're using doesn't hurt. There is also the matter of selecting the appropriate words for describing your topic and selecting the results that are relevant. Then figure out how they might be useful to you. Once mastered the ability increases your chances of finding and employing the information wanted. Research is a skill that can be useful in any subject area.

Should one book or article not be available, something on the same topic may be. Use the Library of Congress subject headings to find similar books or do a keyword search through the appropriate database, from general ones like Google to specialty ones to which libraries may subscribe.

Types of Information

The resources that offer information may be print, organizational, technological, or interpersonal. This last may be a friend, acquaintance or somebody found through one of the first three sources, but at any event they can of course not be named here. Traditionally each type of media has its own qualities. Videos and DVDs can be travelogues that may contain tourist attractions and country background, but not have the level of detail of print. Magazines can contain personal narratives, descriptions, and current trends, but generally do not exhaust a topic. Printed books may cover more overall, but they cannot offer the sensory experience of a travelogue or the news updates of a monthly magazine. Even the most flexible of media information types, the computer, can be faulted for the complexity of operating it and the unreliability of internet information it obtains.

Of the kinds of information presented here, the print media of books, serials, and periodicals (magazines, newspapers, etc.) make up the largest. They have been chosen according to their perceived value as an information resource.

Information from the government is available through print publications, agencies, government bookstores, and on the net. In the listing, the name of a government agency is given before the department under which it serves.

Among electronic resources there are subscription databases that may be available through a CD-ROM or through a password via the internet; libraries are common venues for these, which are frequently consulted for research. Yet above all, there is the internet, the 800-pound gorilla for seeking information. It has a convenience and popularity in providing very specific answers and has a tremendous number of free sites about travel.

Anybody who wishes can publish on the internet, which is a gumbo of facts, errors, half-truths and more. While there are measures that can be taken to evaluate a site, that is outside this work. Instead, the sites listed are usually counterparts to organizations, businesses, and government agencies. In some cases they offer services or texts that are unavailable otherwise.

Be aware that the internet is dynamic, with sites disappearing or changing their addresses, so the information in these works is particularly time-sensitive. For books with collections of websites, see **Computers and the Internet**.

One trend that is rather too new for review is the emergence of the handheld e-book reader which can load scores of electronic text. Such an item is ideal for travelers since it is portable, stores numerous volumes, and is readily searchable.

For further details on types of information, see **Sources of Travel Information** (below).

Reference Works

Reference books are an important resource for those who seek information. This type of writing has been classically defined as a work not intended to be read straight through, but is instead for guidance on a specific point, and so it is arranged in alphabetical, geographical, or other order. Familiar examples are dictionaries, directories, and encyclopedias. Some are created by a team of experts, which gives their contents a particular authority. Reference books may supply the answer to a question or offer a springboard to other sources of information. In this work the most common example, directories, contain addresses, telephone numbers, and sometimes websites; and some specialized ones listed in this book add driving directions, nearby attractions, amenities available on premise, and more.

Reference works need not be directly about travel to benefit travelers. Used in conjunction with a travel work, they can verify or expand on what is there—defining a word on a foreign restaurant menu or giving the history of a town or otherwise offering background facts or an overview.

What to Do about Old Information

Some guidebook information is especially sensitive to change: prices of hotel rooms, hours of an attraction's operation, a calendar of special events. Any of these will be months old by the time of publication and distribution. The timeliness, and so accuracy, of information becomes vital when the traveler is faced with an emergency or needs to know visa requirements.

Websites are another matter, since they can be updated as frequently as their maintainers wish. However, their reliability or authority may be questionable and their addresses can shift. Luckily, the United States government has websites that do supply updated, authoritative, and vital data—for example, the Department of State's "Country Specific Information" (travel.state.gov/travel).

To find the newest print information about a subject there are several possibilities. The current edition of a specific book may be found through Amazon and other online bookstores. The annual mammoth compilation of *Books in Print* (R.R. Bowker) is by title and author while a listing by subject is in its companion *Subject Guide to Books in Print*. The likely habitat for either of these titles is a bookstore or a library, which might have a subscription to their online version. Also consider seeking out a publisher's most recent catalog, whether in print or online.

A serendipitous approach is to go to the library or bookstore and look for the newest books on a subject. In a library acquaint yourself with the uses of the catalog, where book records will contain their dates, and if the catalog is online can likely display its records by year. The physical book itself should display its year on its title page or have it printed on its copyright page.

Some books as a matter of design update annually or so, while others may be revised at the convenience of the author or discretion of the publisher. Any book that continues to go through editions has found its audience and is continuing to give them something they value. A later edition, whether second or thirty-second, may be regarded as an endorsement.

A work that attracts your attention from one of the chapters below may go out of print, in which case be sure to consider a library or used bookstore for it; or be flexible and substitute a work on the same topic.

Reviews of books have usually been omitted when they contain so much information that is out of date, though other advice may be quite useful or interesting, as is the case of *The Airline Passenger's Guerrilla Handbook: Strategies & Tactics for Beating the Air Travel System* (The Blakes Publishing Group, 1989), by George Albert Brown.

All the books mentioned throughout this resource will grow old, but by using them as a starting-off point the interested searcher can find the newest edition or a related work.

Country Guidebooks

To a majority of travelers country guidebooks are the only source from which to learn about a country, region, or city. They tell how to make a country trip more enjoyable by explaining, educating, and reassuring.

Weigh the value of country guidebooks by the following list of features. Not every one of them is in every book and their presence alone does not guarantee quality. Some are not readily observable (for example, reliability of an author). Different guides have their own merits, and you must find the one (or ones) that are right for you. Questions you may have as you travel should be answered by the guide of your choice.

Consider:

- Knowledge and expertise of the author(s). There are ways of checking about a guide's dependability. Is the firm which publishes the guide reputable? Does the author have other titles out, and if so, how were they reviewed? Also, consider verifying some of a guidebook's facts through an encyclopedia or with someone who has traveled to the country or region.
- The number of authors. Some works have a distinct personality since they are written by one or two people, while others might have a team of writers, who may be unidentified.
- The writing style. Some writing is more serviceable than others. Perhaps you have a preference for short, direct sentences rather than long, elegant ones, or for an approach that is serious rather than casual. If the manner how a subject is discussed annoys you, avoid the title. The *Blue Guide* series, for example, is written for the curious traveler and provides an intellectual presentation of a topic.
- Audience. Connected with the previous, this means the work appeals to the type of traveler you are: beginner, advanced, adventurous, epicurean, etc.
- Format. Among possibilities, each page might typically be text heavy; or arrangement may in alphabetical order; or illustrations and boxes may be generously scattered throughout.
- Eye marks. That is, does the text call attention to itself through judicious use of italics, bolding, etc., to make you aware of important issues? Is each section clearly differentiated?
- Related subjects are placed where you expect them to be. For example, you may feel nightclubs are better put with "restaurants" rather than "entertainment," or the address of an attraction should immediately follow the

first mention of it rather than be placed at the end.

- Book's physical features (size, portability, durability, typography). A guide may be coffee table-ready or field-ready. A book's size or bulk should affect your decision to carry it with you or leave it at home. Those who wish to reduce a guide's bulk can increase its portability by ripping out pertinent sections. If the guide is to be carried about and consulted in various conditions it should be durable, sturdy, and resistant to the elements. Font size and contrast affect readability in various levels of light.
- Illustrations. This physical feature can help sell a work. Photographs and drawings serve to pre-acquaint you with sights and after the trip preserve them in memory. Floor plans convey how a building is laid out and where you can wander. Not all travelers like or use maps but for those who do they cause a guide to live up to its name. Maps may be in color and vary in level of detail.
- Specialties. Some country guides particularize a certain audience (budget, business, etc.), interest (art, off-the-beaten-track), or travel aspect (accommodations).
- Geographical coverage. Does it include all or most of the areas where you'll be traveling? And what is the level of detail?
- Balance. Emphasis may be on practical aspects of travel and places to eat, drink, and shop, while some travelers prefer more about sights they wish to see. Find the correct proportion of subjects covered for you.
- Description vs. prescription. A guide falls somewhere in the spectrum of presenting information straight-forwardly or judgmentally. Series guides such as the Michelin rank sights and restaurants with stars, advising the traveler about what it thinks is best. Or a work may be more interested in inclusiveness than selectivity.
- Itineraries suggested. Those who like structure when they travel and want directions from point to point value this.
- Common foreign words and phrases defined. Though this feature cannot replace a phrasebook, it is handy and useful, especially if there is a pronunciation guide.
- Bibliography. A list of related titles can further your reading and knowledge.

- Index. This allows the pinpointing of a subject or location mentioned within the text.

Sources of Country Information

Travel guidebooks are commonly arranged geographically and number in the thousands, as a look at *Going Places: The Guide to Travel Guides* (below) or other bibliographies disclose. A city, a region, several countries, or the world may be the subject of one guide, which can also be theme-oriented (budget travel, "best of," business travel, etc.). Nor does depth have to be surrendered to breadth, as evidence by such a title as *The South American Handbook* (Footprint), though the typography may be smaller than usual and the covers of the book farther apart.

Other sources also offer coverage of countries. There are several publications whose potted country profiles consider population, visa requirements, currency accepted, holidays, social customs, and more. One of the most accessible is *The World Factbook*, which is put out by the Central Intelligence Agency and is available online (www.cia.gov/library/publications/the-world-factbook). Many of the same facts are found in the annual *World Travel Guide* (Columbus Press) and like titles.

Turn to gazetteers for useful but brief data about a place. They are not country guides but geographical dictionaries that are alphabetically arranged by names of cities, towns, rivers, mountain ranges and other places on the globe; pronunciation, history, population, location, and other contents may make up an entry. Two important titles are *The Columbia Gazetteer of the World* and *Merriam-Webster's Geographical Dictionary* (both reviewed in **Maps and Atlases**).

Tourist offices are an obvious source of country information, and their addresses are commonly in guidebooks, newspaper and magazine articles on countries, and in directories.

Day and Weekend Trips

Some guides mix the geographical approach with the idea of short trips from home that last from a day to a weekend, which offers obvious advantages to workers with little or no vacation time or to busy people. Due to the distances involved in these journeys, books on the topic usually assume their travelers go by train or car. Grouped by base city, trips are typically described in terms of the route to take, travel time or distance, and the sights at the destination. Coverage of short trips may also be enfolded in train and country guides.

Among publishers who have produced a number of titles based on these mini-trips have been both Hastings House (*Daytrips New York*, etc.)

and Globe Pequot (for example, the *Quick Escapes Series*, which deals chiefly with U.S. cities).

Sources of Travel Information: A List

Asking somebody, consulting an organization or business, reading, and going online are basic ways that people learn information in general. This work recognizes all these groups, though reading books for information receives chief emphasis.

If there is a dearth of works that have been written on a subject, or those on it don't suit you, alternatives include contacting a relevant organization, whose address can come from a directory, or doing a wide-ranging internet search, which is probably the most convenient way of finding what you seek.

In addition to the annotated titles and organizations that make up the body of this work, more general means and places for finding information have been collected below. A researcher can look here as the first place to turn or the last. Several of the titles mentioned are available both in print and electronically. Keep in mind that an internet search (see number 10) is an additional aid in many of the suggestions on the following list.

1. Try person-to-person. Other travelers give valuable and unique advice, as do the locals. How you go about meeting them varies through design and circumstance.

Your travel agent might be able to suggest a traveler who has been to your destination. If you consider going with a tour company ask for a list of people who have traveled with them. If you have friends who know an informed person, ask for an introduction. Publicize your questions through an appropriate online group or by writing to a travel publication. Once you arrive at your destination there are many opportunities for firsthand information.

2. Travel agents are often the preferred source of information for prospective travelers. Besides doing the housekeeping work of travel— reserving flights and rooms, booking tours and cruises—agents can suggest vacation possibilities. A good agent not only finds bargains but is willing to offer helpful advice. Some agents and agencies specialize in types of travel (cruises, budget travel, etc.) or countries.

Pick an agent as you would a dentist—ask friends, search the telephone book, go online. Those who are concerned about qualifications should determine if the agent or agency has been accredited. Ask either the agent for documentation or contact the accrediting organization. (Locate travel agent organizations in the annual *Encyclopedia of Associations* (Gale/Cengage) or do an online search; several appear under **Complaints**.)

3. The reader can optimize this book by using it in conjunction with a library. Some of the sources mentioned are basic reference material found in almost all but the smallest American libraries. While a bookstore could pinch-hit for some items, and in some cases it will have others that a library will not—or will have newer materials—a library remains the overall best place in which to start a hunt for information. Even a traveler abroad can have access to a library.

For a list of libraries and their locations try the telephone yellow pages, or the latest editions of two annuals, the *American Library Directory* (Information Today) or *The Europa World of Learning* (Routledge, Taylor & Francis Group), which covers all countries. Among online resources, one is Libdex (www.libdex.com).

4. A high-profile source for travel material is the brick-and-mortar bookstore. Some have extensive travel sections, and if you can find a store that specializes in travel, so much the better. However, online mega-booksellers such as Amazon or Barnes and Noble have enormous selections. Beyond books they may sell magazines, maps, and travel gear. For a list of bookstores, try the yellow pages or the annual *American Book Trade Directory* (Information Today). Local chambers of commerce can advise you about locating businesses.

5. At least in the United States a number of major newspapers have a weekly travel section that is a grab-bag of up-to-date travel information. A sample issue might contain destination profiles, news of tours, sightseeing reports, travel advisories, travelers' comments, exchange rates, ticket prices, answers to readers' questions, and advertisements.

To go beyond serendipitous discoveries once required using an index to the papers' contents. However, due to the internet revolution, dailies such as *The New York Times*—containing a substantial travel section, it is one of the most widely subscribed-to newspapers for libraries—now archive their contents and make them searchable, often for a price. Searching may be done at the newspaper's site or through a library or similar source.

6. Travel magazines carry recent information, often have a slew of color photographs, and contain a variety of subjects. Some zero in on single aspects of travel such as cruises. Closely related to these are the magazines that cover leisure and recreation.

If you wish to combine travel with a certain interest, find a magazine dedicated to that interest and there is a fair chance either a recent article or advertisement will address your need; for example, the American Museum of Natural History's title *Natural History* carries advertisements and classifieds for tours, part of them run by the museum. On the other hand, since travel is a popular subject, articles or columns about it commonly appear in numerous general circulation magazines.

Into the gap where broader-based magazines may under-serve certain travel subjects comes newsletters, "zines," and other small circulation titles, including those online. Especially the ones in print can be elusive. They might be mentioned in the travel section of a newspaper or in a travel magazine. If you are an earnest researcher, for a general list try *Newsletters in Print* (published by Thomson/Gale and subtitled *A Descriptive Guide to Subscription, Membership, and Free Newsletters, Bulletins, Digests, Updates, and Similar Serial Publications Issued in the United States and Canada, and Available in Print or Online*); once in print, it is now only online. Another serial is the *Oxbridge Directory of Newsletters* (Oxbridge Communications). For a review of alternative publications try back issues of the bimonthly *Small Press Review* (Dustbooks). In print as well as online, *Ulrich's Periodicals Directory* (ProQuest) is one source that lists magazines and other periodicals.

7. There are numerous organizations related in one way or another to travel, and the *Encyclopedia of Associations* is an invaluable directory for finding them. In the print version—there's also one online—check the index for the word or phrase that deals with your area of travel interest (e.g., "freighter," "study abroad"). The fullest entries offer an address, telephone number, website location, description of the organization, a list of publications, and services.

If you write or telephone an organization with your enquiry you may get a helpful response or none at all; as with tourist offices (see number 8) it depends on their depth of services. Some publish useful pamphlets, magazines, and books that can be obtained nowhere else; these may be noted in the aforementioned *Encyclopedia*.

A business is one type of organization. However self-interested, a business can give travelers valuable information. For example, the exchange rate for a country may be determined by consulting a bank or a specialist in exchanges, such as Thomas Cook. A handy source for types of business is the invaluable telephone directory's yellow pages.

Some businesses produce free publications, but locating a business that has produced a certain pamphlet on, say, renting a car overseas will be a matter of resourcefulness and luck. Although *Bowker's News Media Directory* (R. R. Bowker) produces a catalog of in-house publications, it probably would do little to aid your research.

8. Among organizations, government tourist offices are the standard places for information about their countries, and many have branches in the United States that may be contacted in person, through telephone, by

regular mail, or by e-mail. The depth and variety of information furnished depends on the staff and services of an office.

Some will answer specific questions and some will not. Some will send through the mail free booklets and brochures, which normally cover at least lodging, restaurants, and sights. City and country maps may also be provided. Look in any good country guidebook to locate the address of the tourist office branch in the United States. Newspaper and magazine articles on a country or region may conveniently come with such addresses. They may also be located in telephone directories and in such reference sources as the mammoth *World Tourism Directory* (4th ed.; K.G. Saur in association with the World Tourism Organization and the World Travel & Tourism Council, 1999), whose web presence   is Worldtourismdirectory.com (www.worldtourismdirectory.com).

For the United States, state tourist office addresses may be similarly located. They are also in individual state manuals and are in a reference source such as the annual *CSG State Directory* (Council of State Governments). Tourist office functions can be duplicated by chambers of commerce, for which there are also directories.

According to travel maven Arthur Frommer, many nations promote their culture and image through government "institutes." Locate them through embassies, to which some are attached, or ask about them through tourist organizations. Also, try the keyword index or cultural organizations section in the *Encyclopedia of Associations*.

9. The United States government itself produces many titles that, directly or indirectly, bear on travel. It is the country's largest publisher, and a selection of its publications has been inserted into their subject-appropriate section in this guide. For assistance in identifying and contacting the appropriate government department, use *The United States Government Manual* (Office of the Federal Register, National Archives and Records Administration) which is freely available on a government website (www.gpoaccess.gov/gmanual).

To consult a state's tourism or other office, try the chosen state's government websites or the reference work *CSG State Directory*.

10. Some print titles have electronic counterparts or may come with CD-ROMs, but there is a vast ocean of information chiefly available via the internet. Electronic information can be found much quicker and with less physical effort than print. Very specific questions can be addressed, and information can be current. The traveler is enabled to become a travel agent and locate cheap airfares, reserve a hotel room, book a tour, etc. On the other hand, some information remains based in print resources. For more, see the subject section **Computers and the Internet**.

11. There may be times when you exhaust all your resources at hand.

Some information, printed or verbal, can only be obtained at the place of your visit. It may be the only existing guide to a site or it may be rules governing entry into a monument.

Major Travel References

In this section are travel resources not confined to a subject, but are rather compilations of sources, including organizations that refer people elsewhere. This is a starting place to look for information, so a number of the print sources are travel bibliographies.

Consult a bibliography to find lists of books and other sources of information. Books (and articles) may be bibliographies in themselves or contain one or more, usually at the end, where the authors may create a list of works they consulted in order to write their works; or they may have a collection of recommended readings. Book bibliographies (reviewed below) have a focus. *Going Places: The Guide to Travel Guides* annotates a list of guides, the two volumes of *Good Books for the Curious Traveler* supply background reading, and *The Traveler's Reading Guide: Ready-Made Reading Lists for the Armchair Traveler* has both guides and background reading. Bibliographies may be customized by organizations and businesses; for example, a tour company may include a recommended reading guide for a specific tour.

Although bibliographies age as much as any work, a library catalog can aid in updating their information. For example, should one want to find a novel about Paris too new for the 1993 *The Traveler's Reading Guide* and its lists of non-fiction and fiction, a catalog search by subject with the subdivision of the word "fiction" would help—e.g., "Paris (France)—Fiction."

Lists of travel publications are also found in several basic reference bibliographies or catalogs. Found in libraries and bookstores, the aforementioned *Books in Print* attempts to list all American published books currently available. Arrangement is only by title and author, so for that by subject consult *Subject Guide to Books in Print* or exploit the flexibility of the electronic version of *Books in Print*.

The print and electronic *Ulrich's Periodicals Directory* and the electronic-only *The Serials Directory* compile a worldwide list of magazines, journals, and other periodicals. They can be searched by subjects, travel being one of them. The annual *Gale Directory of Publications and Broadcast Media* (Gale/Cengage) lists American and Canadian newspapers, which could benefit travelers who want to discover something about an area by reading the titles that are available.

Used by librarians, the frequently updated *Magazines for Libraries* (ProQuest) has selective entries rather than a behemoth list. Stating that it is "for the general reader and school, junior college, college, university, and public libraries," the work has a travel section that describes some of the better-known magazines as well as newsletters and electronic journals.

Newsletters are frequently ephemeral and with low circulations, but a newsletter directory such as the aforementioned *Oxbridge Directory of Newsletters* or an online *Newsletters in Print* is a convenient way of finding what is out there. Newsletters are classed according to subject area, one of which is devoted to travel.

Other print sources are directories, which supply addresses, and in the case of many of the specialty travel directories add descriptions of the location. For a list of directories, see the annual *Directories in Print* (Gale/Cengage).

And there are guides and advice books that discuss the many aspects of travel: destinations, means of transportation, practicalities, resources available, and so forth. Some titles have found their way to various subject sections.

Titles

Going Places: The Guide to Travel Guides / Greg Hayes and Joan Wright (The Harvard Common Press, 1988).

Despite its age, this is a major resource for the range of guides that have been written about various countries, and it may lead readers to find newer editions or discover a specialty area. Beginning with "the world," most of the arrangement is geographical, with individual countries under continents or regions. The strength of the book lies in the number of guides—about six per page—and the fact that they bear annotations. The weakness is that the annotations are too brief, and the majority of prices accompanying the titles are probably obsolete. Specialty guides are mixed with the general travel guides, with titles in alphabetical order, so that *Best of Britain* immediately precedes *The Best Pubs of Great Britain*, which is just before *Birdwatcher's Britain*; however, a back section arranges titles according to subject. As many titles are part of a series, all series are collected and described in a separate chapter; though the titles are mentioned again in their appropriate geographic sections. Appendixes include names and addresses of travel bookstores, travel book publishers, and travel newsletters and magazines. 772 p.

Good Books for the Curious Traveler: Asia and the South Pacific / Theodora Nelson and Andrea Gross (Johnson Books, 1989).

Excluding travel guides, this selective bibliography has, for every country, reviews that are placed under a fixed number of subjects, beginning with general works, and typically following with anthropology and archaeology, art, cuisine, folktales, history, nature, performing arts, and books aimed at young people. Unfortunately, some individual countries are at least under-represented by being in chapters concerned with regions, such as that for Southeast Asia; if you were interested in Malaysia, for example, there is no way to find if books cover this country other than going through the chapter, for a geographic index is lacking. The substantial description of a book can be up to a page and may contain quotes from the text. The accompanying bibliographic information is title, author, publisher, year, ISBN number, hardcover or softcover, number of pages, and price, the last of which is almost certainly out-of-date. While overlapping *Sarah Anderson's Travel Companion* (below) with some of the same categories, it covers fewer titles, but provides paragraphs while the other provides a sentence or two. A second volume deals with Europe. 312 p.

Sarah Anderson's Travel Companion / Sarah Anderson (Portobello Publishing, 2004).

The updated version of an earlier edition, it may prove the first of a series to provide reading material on individual regions, in this instance Africa and the Middle East. For those who wish information about a place beyond country guidebooks, this bibliography by area and by country provides titles arranged under topical headings, the number of which varies according to the country examined. Headings include anthropology, art, biography, fiction, food, general background, guides, history, natural history, photography, and travel literature. For each book the author provides the title, author, and date (but not the publisher), and often in just a sentence summarizes its contents. At the front brief views of ten guide book series are crammed into only two pages. For a similar approach, see *Good Books for the Curious Traveler* and *The Traveler's Reading Guide* (both in this section). 199 p.

The Travel Agent's Complete Desk Reference / Sally Scanlon & Kelly Monaghan (The Intrepid Traveler, 2002).

With the convenience of facts in one place, the book has stuff of varying relevance to the interested traveler; so, the codes for the airports are likely to be more consulted than those for the airlines, both groups of which are arranged also by name. Contact numbers are provided for airlines, hotels, tour operators, cruise lines, and more. There is also a small selection of internet sites, and addresses for U.S. and international organizations that supply tourist information. A variety of travel associations comes with a brief description of their purposes. However, close to a third of the volume has a glossary of travel terms and abbreviations which is more for the travel agent. A final selection of information includes brief reviews of individual trade and consumer periodicals and a list of major travel book publishers. 368 p.

"Travel and Tourism." bookstore.gpo.gov/subjects/sb-302.jsp
From the U.S. Government bookstore, find a collection of nearly twenty travel titles, concisely annotated and priced. Examined website: 2009

The Travel Book: Guide to the Travel Guides / Jon O. Heise and Julia R. Rinehart. 2nd ed. (The Scarecrow Press, Inc., 1993).
This is a collection of substantial book reviews for those who want an idea about the number and variety of travel guides. After providing bibliographic information along with price—that will usually be obsolete by now—there is a paragraph about the contents followed by candid criticisms of the guide's strengths and weaknesses. Description and evaluation may take up a page and are typically much fuller than are found in the reviews in *Travel Resources* and in *Going Places* (above), with which the range compares favorably. Guides are arranged according to their countries, which are grouped within broad geographic areas. Unfortunately, no subject index or list of categories in back gathers together the specialty travel titles that are scattered throughout, sometimes in their own subsection. While many of the featured titles are out of print, for some the information remains relevant or unique, and for some newer editions may exist. 397 p.

The Traveler's Reading Guide: Ready-Made Reading Lists for the Armchair Traveler / Maggy Simony, editor. Revised and updated ed. (Facts on File, 1993).
As a guide to the body of writing about places on an itinerary, this work can enhance the experience for the self-educating traveler. Arrangement is geographic, with some countries considered only as part of a region, while others are further broken down, even as far as cities. The United States is treated both by region and by state, and Canada by regions and provinces. Countries or regions have categories that begin with a list of relevant series guidebook titles, which receive no description. Another grouping, "background reading," consists of various types of non-fiction, such as memoirs and travelogues. "History" and "novels" are the most common additional categories. Author, title, publisher, and year of publication accompany about one sentence depicting a book's focus,

sometimes with a quote from a publisher, from a review, or from the text itself. 510 p.

The Traveler's Sourcebook: A Practical Guide to Information on Recreational and Business Travel in the United States / Darren L. Smith and Nancy V. Kniskern, editors (Omnigraphics, Inc., 1997).

Although having an updated edition is desirable, this older volume is still worth consulting. Types of information and format vary according to the focus of the more than eighty headings. They are in alphabetical order, running from "Air Travel," "Airline Clubs," and "Airlines," to "Wildlife Viewing," "Wineries," and "Women and Travel." One topic may consist of tips followed by brief annotations to publications (e.g., "Children and Travel"), while another ("Convention Centers") is exclusively addresses, after a short introductory paragraph. Likewise, organizations may receive full annotations in addition to their address. Sometimes the book combines plain lists of contact addresses with overviews of a subject or material about attractions. There is an overlap of some same headings with *Travel Resources*, though the former is often more specific. 306 p.

World Chamber of Commerce Directory. Annual (World Chamber of Commerce Directory).

Every two-column page has dozens of entries, typically with address, an official's name, e-mail, URL, and the numbers for telephone and fax. State chambers of commerce precede the directory's largest section, those in the United States, which is arranged by state and community. Elsewhere there are collections of locations for state boards of tourism, convention and visitors bureaus, economic development councils, Canadian chambers of commerce, American chambers of commerce abroad, foreign tourist information bureaus in their own countries, foreign and ethnic chambers in the United States and in their own countries, and various addresses concerned with the U.S. government. Another way to find a chamber of commerce is to look up information about an individual city or town in, for example, *City Profiles USA* (Omnigraphics). Examined: 2002; 422 p.

World Travel Dictionary: The Dictionary for the Travel Industry. 2nd ed. (Columbus Publishing Ltd., 1999).

A word or phrase is followed by a simple definition, but there is no pronunciation guide, etymology, or other features of a typical dictionary. The scope is unclear, with a random browse revealing words selected from the travel business, geography, recreation, forms of transportation, meteorology, foreign terms, eating, health, etc., but inclusion is not exhaustive, and one is never sure what term will turn up. Among the appendixes are those that list nationalities and languages, world tourist attractions, and travel associations in the United States, United Kingdom, and elsewhere. As the subtitle suggests, its target audience is the travel professional, but it could appeal to the curious traveler. 256 p.

Organizations

Destination Marketing Association International. www.OfficialTravelInfo. com

The world's largest association of convention and visitor bureaus has a consumer travel portal that provides country and city access to those bureaus so that travelers can find general travel information about accommodations, dining, attractions, etc. Examined website: 2007

AN ALPHABETICAL LIST BY SUBJECT

ACCOMMODATIONS (Bed and Breakfasts, Home Exchanges, Hostels and Dormitories, Hotels and Motels, Rentals, and Resorts)

There are many types of lodgings, from colossal hotels to small bed and breakfasts. The subsections represent the common varieties.

General guidebooks often concentrate on accommodations of the hotel variety, with perhaps a look at one or two other types. They also vary in the selection, number, and detail of lodging listings.

Directories are a mainstay in this subject, some specializing in a single category. Minimally directories should give addresses, telephone numbers and, when available, websites. Better, they should also describe price range, atmosphere, amenities, location, and features of the establishment (restaurant on the premises, etc.), and provide a location map and a rating for quality.

Tourist authority offices of many countries offer free accommodation lists, suggesting the offices have vouched for them.

The following accommodation headings may have titles that encompass several categories.

(Those who prefer to stay at places associated with health or have a religious affiliation should check under the headings **Health Resorts, Spas, and Healing Centers** and **Religion**.)

Bed and Breakfasts

The room that includes a breakfast may be in somebody's home or in a small hotel. North America is well-covered by B&B directory titles. Besides listing individual bed and breakfasts, directories may include telephone numbers for reservation services and addresses for bed and breakfast associations that could also help the traveler book a room in other countries. Tourist bureaus are another aid.

Subject Heading: Bed and breakfast accommodations

Titles

The Annual Directory of American and Canadian Bed & Breakfasts: Includes Puerto Rico. Annual (Barbour Publishing, Inc.).

Under the town of a state or province is a lodging's name, address, telephone and fax number, and electronic contacts. They precede a paragraph that the B&B hosts have fashioned to sell the merits to the prospective visitor, so the directory is not objective. An additional block of formatted information supplies the names of the hosts, the number of rooms along with price range, the presence of a full or continental breakfast, the types of credit cards accepted, and a collection of notes presented as numbers that are decoded at the bottom of the pages; they convey such matters as the permissibility of smoking, nearby recreations, and accessibility for the handicapped. Many of the entries on the two-column pages come with pen-and-ink drawings of the houses. Outline maps show highways and the location of each town mentioned. Examined: 2002; 768 p.

The Bed & Breakfast Book: Australia 2005. Annual (Pelican Publishing Company).

Coming with an attractive color photo, an entry consists of several groupings. Added to a physical address is the B&B's direction and the number of kilometers from a nearby town. Telephone, internet, and other forms of contact are provided together, followed by costs of double and single rooms, sometimes the Australian dollar amount of meals, whether credit cards are accepted, and kinds of beds and bathrooms. The hosts or owners limit their description to a paragraph when, customarily, two properties share a page, while entries on a single page receive more attention. Among the potential accompanying icons are those indicating accessibility; the acceptance of smoking or of children or of pets; availability of a swimming pool; and the accreditation of tourism agencies. Arrangement is by each of Australia's states, which are represented through shaded maps with points for the nearest town to the lodging. However, a road atlas would be an important supplement. Examined: 2005; 336 p.

Bed & Breakfasts and Country Inns / Deborah Edwards Sakach. 16th ed. (American Historic Inns, 2004).

Under state, and town or city, on two-column pages, an entry has a block for name, address, telephone and fax numbers, and electronic contact. As a way of establishing a building's historic credentials, its smallish-type description starts with its approximate date of erection; and several sentences typically contain upbeat observations about the architecture, décor, amenities, and surroundings. Smaller print identifies the innkeepers, price range, credit cards accepted, types and numbers of rooms, types of meals, bed sizes, room and inn features, recreational activities (shopping for antiques is popular), etc. Small, attractive drawings of the structure accompany many of the listings. A letter/number serves as a key to its general location on a full-page, black-and-white state map, which has major roadways and physical features along with a mileage and kilometer scale. An index categorizes inns in assorted ways, such as those built prior to 1800. Puerto Rico and Canada have a limited presence in this valuable, full directory. 450 p.

The Complete Guide to Bed & Breakfasts, Inns & Guesthouses in the United States, Canada, & Worldwide / Pamela Lanier. Annual (Lanier Publishing International).

While other directories are selective, this seeks to be inclusive. Almost 90 percent of the substantial work concentrates on the United States—by state and town or city, with six entries laid out horizontally across each full page. After lodging name, address, telephone and fax numbers, and the names of the innkeepers, are a column for the price ranges; the included meals; the number of rooms and private baths; the credit cards that are accepted; whether rated (by AAA, etc.); concerns about children, pets, smoking, and handicap equipment; foreign languages that are spoken; and times of year when open. Another column of notes suggests the meals and food provided, the amenities, and possible recreation. In a sentence or so the innkeepers boost their property to the customer, after which is included an e-mail address and a website. This is a classic instance of cramming in a large number of listings at the expense of details, maps, and photos, which are absent, though there is an occasional drawing of an accommodation. Examined: 2006; 773 p.

Europe's Wonderful Little Hotels and Inns: Continental Europe / editors, Adam and Caroline Raphael. 27th ed. (Steerforth Press, 2004).

Thick but able to fit in a glove compartment, it provides for every entry a name, address, telephone, fax, and electronic contact information. To describe and judge the site, a paragraph has scraps of quotes from guests whose praises are occasionally tempered by criticism, giving a sense of balance and candor. A third section has bolded headings preceding facts about whether a habitation is open all year, number and types of rooms, the facilities available (e.g., elevator, restaurant, garden), locale, the credit cards accepted, and the price ranges. Labels signify "new" and "budget," while one symbol identifies when a discount is available. Coordinates indicate an inn's location on a country's road map, which bears a symbol of the general position. A popular work that has gone through many editions, it omits Turkey, in contrast to many volumes that embrace it as part of Europe, though the title includes countries that other directories may not. 600 p.

The Official Bed & Breakfast Guide and Cookbook for the United States, Canada & the Caribbean. 8th ed. (The National Bed & Breakfast Association, Inc., 2002).

The book says that it lists only privately owned homes and inns whose rates cover both lodging and breakfast, either full or continental. Arrangement is by state in a volume that allots Canada and the Caribbean just five pages. Under a city or town there is an address, telephone and fax, and frequently e-mail and website. Amenities are presented as numbers 1 to 25, whose meanings are in small print at the bottom of the page, while breakfasts are with the letters "c" (for continental) or "f" (full). The room price is according to the number of occupants. A descriptive paragraph of varying length may be supplemented by a biography of the hosts, and many of the entries have a small black-and-white photograph or illustration, usually of the outside. An occasional note points to the substantial section of recipes at the back. Usage directions for the directory and its appearance could be better. 425 p.

Home Exchanges

If you know someone who is willing to exchange homes, you can work out details between yourselves. Others will probably have to turn to a home exchange organization, such as HomeLink International www.homelink.org and International Home Exchange Network www.homexchange.com. Despite a fee for joining, frequently no money passes between the home owners. They must work out conditions of exchange; for example, whether an exchange need be reciprocal.

Exchanges are different from homestays, whose purpose is the experience or camaraderie of sharing another's domicile.

See also **Homestays**.

Titles

The Home Exchange Guide: How to Find Your Free Home Away from Home / M. T. Simon and T. T. Baker (Poyeen Publishing, 2003).

After an introduction, the authors begin with a review of reasons to exchange. They also cover what to look for in another's home and what your own has to offer, with the understanding that the nearness of groceries, shopping, etc., figure into marketability. Participants may be influenced by how long they want to stay, the time of year, the destination, and the like; while another factor is feeling that their home will be secure. As for ways of judging home exchange organizations, the authors advise determining whether they are non-profit or commercial, the freshness of their listings, their handling of communication between members, etc. Another aspect is negotiation between prospective exchangers, which could involve such points as the acceptance of smoking and of pets, and if cars are included in the exchange. The exchange itself might involve readying necessary documents and preparing the home. Near the end of this how-to work there are comments about the experience of arriving at another home, and what to do when it is time to depart. 186 p.

Home from Home. 2nd ed. (Central Bureau for Educational Visits & Exchanges, 1991).

The first category of the British directory deals with homestays, which separate themselves into European countries, British isles, and the rest of the world; the next, hospitality exchanges or reciprocal homestays, are listed just for visits between Britain and Europe; stays arranged by academic term are gathered under European countries, then every place else; and there are a few listings for home exchange organizations whose scope is worldwide. Taking up a page, each entry is strictly formatted, with icons instead of headings that identify name and address, telephone number, what the organization is (in a sentence), locations of the stay, conditions for a group or individual and their age, knowledge of a language, outings and activities, lodging and board, transfers and travel, and whether insurance is provided. A select number of countries have a few basic facts about them, and a short space is devoted to practical advice about lodging in the residence of others, but the book is at its most useful as a directory. A later edition is available. 216 p.

Hostels and Dormitories

These accommodations for budget travelers traditionally are rooms with beds, while the showers and toilets are down the hall. On the other hand, furnishings may vary from spartan to in-room baths and color televisions.

For hostel locations contact American Youth Hostels or the YMCA. The *Let's Go* series and other budget guides give hostel addresses. During their seasonal breaks some universities and colleges rent dormitory rooms to travelers. Use available directories to find academic institutions or alternatively, contact them using such titles as *The Europa World of Learning, The College Blue Book*, one of the *Peterson* guides (e.g., *Peterson's Four-Year Colleges*), or tourist information centers.

See also **Budget Travel**, **Camping and Campgrounds**, and **Homestays**.

Subject Headings: Tourist camps, hostels, etc.; Dormitories

Titles

Discover America, Hostels in the USA (Hostelling International-USA; American Youth Hostels, 2003).

Limiting itself to Hostelling International hostels, this portable booklet looks like it is designed for a back pants pocket. Contents of an entry are a name and address above bolded headings for mail; phone number; e-mail; number of dorm beds; dorm rates; number of private rooms; dates when open; the office hours; daily times when the hostel is open to hostellers; symbols for such facilities as kitchen and laundry; degree of importance of reservations; the ways to make reservations; the credit cards accepted; and transportation directions. Usually a simple street map shows the position of the hostel in a community, while on a broader scale a simple state map does the same. Two entries may fit on a page in the volume, which has ads related to hostelling scattered throughout. A possible alternative title is *USA Hostel Directory*, available free through membership into Hostelling International-USA. 126 p.

Great Hostels USA: An Inside Look at America's Best Adventure Travel / Colleen Norwine (Sedobe Travel Guides, 2005).

This title is for those who want an in-depth look at selected hostels in selected states along with color photos in a graphically astute package (for those who prefer the plain and non-selective, see *The Hostel Handbook for the U.S.A. & Canada*, below). The two pages dedicated to each hostel begin with a block of contact information and several paragraphs about the lodging as well as a description of the location from a tourist's perspective. A group of separate facts include dorm rates, the number of private rooms, the credit cards accepted, the affiliation, types of mattresses, presence of a kitchen, things to be aware of, etc. A final section considers how well it meets the needs of potential guests according to whether they fall into the categories of solo women, party animals, over 30s, over 50s, couples, families, and groups. Separate maps that show main highways locate the approximate position of a hostel in a state or a Canadian province. 259 p.

A Guide to Monastic Guest Houses / Robert J. Regalbuto. 4th ed. (Morehouse Publishing, 2000).

Listing religious accommodations open to any faith, most entries take up two pages that include a line drawing of the house. The bolded labels following name and address are for telephone and fax numbers; e-mail and internet site; the title of the contact position; the religious order; the kind and number of accommodations; the number of meals served; the costs;

driving directions that can be expansive; and a paragraph on the history of the house and another providing a description of it and its grounds. There may also be words on points of interest, and a special note for details that fit nowhere else. Covering the United States and Canada, arrangement is alphabetical by all states and by all provinces, respectively. An outline map of the two countries has page numbers indicating the general location of a house. 291 p.

The Hostel Handbook for the U.S.A. & Canada / Jim Williams, editor. 10th ed. (The Hostel Handbook, 2002).

About the size and shape of *Discover America* (above), it includes not only the hostels in that work but many others. However, the trade-off is a severe restriction of directory information. Name, address, telephone number, hostel affiliation, and price range are it, though some entries have a few random notes that might relate to freebies, amenities, or nearby attractions, and add a website. There are no maps, and much more space is devoted to advertisements than to the hostel listings. For a polished package that gives detailed coverage of select hostels, see *Great Hostels USA*, above. 104 p.

Hostels European Cities: The Only Comprehensive, Unofficial, Opinionated Guide / Paul Carr. 2nd ed. (Insiders' Guide, 2004).

Covering only hostels in major cities, the directory uses a writing style that is slangy and familiar, while the judgments for each establishment are candid and can be very critical. Expanding an entry are summaries of facts that consist of bolded labels for physical and electronic contacts; rates; acceptability of credit cards; number of beds; presence of private or family rooms; availability of a kitchen; season of operation; the office hours; the time of curfew; the hostel's affiliation; and the extras to be found (e.g., TV, restaurant). Icons designate safety, hospitality, cleanliness, and partying, while there is guidance about how to get to the hostel by bus, car, and train, with the first two generally coming with the unimaginative recommendation to contact the hostel for directions. A city map shows the location of the hostels. Though thick, this could fit in a backpack. A later edition is available. 448 p.

Organizations

Hostelling International. www.hihostels.com

Under the auspices of the International Youth Hostel Federation, it produces an annual directory to hostels throughout the world. Its site includes online bookings and answers to a list of frequently asked questions about the hostelling experience. Examined website: 2008

YMCA www.ymca.int
This organization offers a link to worldwide lodging through its members; for booking exclusive to the U.S. see the site www.ymca.net. Examined website: 2008

Hotels and Motels

With their large compilations, hotel directories may be geographically specific or worldwide in scope. Some also include motels or restaurants.

Businesses such as travel agents and booking agencies will do the locating and reserving for you. Hotel brokers are able to book rooms at discount prices. Or you can act as your own travel agent and book online.

To find hotel or motel chain locations search for the chain's website, write it, or call its toll-free number for a free directory. For a list of chains try an internet search, the yellow pages, or the toll-free telephone digests with their large section on hotels.

There are a variety of hotel directories. One emphasizes rating—the "best of" sort which are aimed at the discriminating (and non-budget) traveler—while another targets business travelers.

In some titles inns and small hotels may be considered distinct.

Subject Headings: Hotels—Directories; Motels—Directories

Titles

All-Suite Hotel Guide / Pamela Lanier. 10th ed. (Lanier Publishing International, 1999).

Suites are at least two rooms with a door between, and this unique directory specializes in hotels with these, rather than with single rooms. The widely published author comments that suites appeal to businesspeople, those who want space, families, and others. Within the simple outline of a state map are shown the locations of the towns and cities noted in the entries, which have name, address, telephone and fax numbers, and total number of suites, while bolded headings are before the hotel's approximate location, minutes or miles from airport, area attractions, what is in walking distance, price range, credit cards accepted, hotel and room amenities, facilities for recreation and business, and the complimentary meals, services, and freebies. A few concluding lines are the stuff of advertising copy. Although the largest space is dedicated to the

United States, several countries are represented. Yet more hotels are briefly listed in the back. 288 p.

America's Best Cheap Sleeps / Tracy Whitcombe (Open Road Publishing, 2004).

Beginning with an overview about the topic, this directory is not fancy, but has a lot of budget lodgings. Pages are laid out in two columns, with listings for both chain and independent motels and inns under state and city or town. The entry block consists of a bolded name and price range, address, telephone number, number of units, and several notes, such as the restriction for pets, and presence of a pool or laundry facility or cable television. Mention of AAA and senior discounts is common, and all entries acknowledge credit cards, sometimes giving their names via initials. An asterisked note indicates the times when higher rates are in effect. For some states and cities a traveler advisory warns about expenses, or about high room demand during certain months, in which case it may suggest alternative towns where to stay. 431 p.

America's Best Hotels and Restaurants: Mobil Four-Star and Five-Star Award Winners. Annual (Exxon Mobil Travel Publications).

Listings for hotels (and restaurants) are by state and city or town in this regularly revised, oblong volume, which could fit comfortably in an average-size car's glove compartment. A hotel icon and either four or five stars precede hotel name, website, address, and telephone number. While excellence of every property is assumed, a few sentences do give a complimentary overview, and are followed by a large block of short facts that would have been better if set off from one another by bolding, spacing, or identifiers. Among the details are the number of rooms or suites and their cost; pet policy; presence of TV, cable, and VCR; pool types; children's programs; bar hours; coffee in rooms; and shopping and recreation availability. Credit cards accepted at the hotels are presented as mnemonic letters (for example, "V" presumably stands for Visa), but there is no key provided for what they signify. At the end of an entry comes recreational and amenity icons, which could potentially be over a dozen. Note that *Mobil* guides such as this one have had a high profile for a long time. The title varies. Examined: 2002; 276 p.

Asia's Best Hotels & Resorts (APA Publications, 2003).

According to the editors of this fine example in the *Insight Guides* series, customers made the selections that cover twenty-one countries (some of which are not part of Asia, such as Australia and New Zealand). One or more color photographs show the inside or outside of the property.

The descriptive paragraphs have a greater thoughtfulness than in most accommodation guides and a willingness to be critical, all in a polished prose. Except for e-mail address, the conventional contact information is here. The same twenty icons representing facilities (babysitting, beach, business center, etc.) always accompany an entry, with those that are present highlighted and the remainder dimmed, as on a website. A box displays beginning costs, a listing of mostly five stars for the hotel or resort, a bellhop rating, and a number up to 10 for the categories of value, staff, location, cleanliness, facilities, restaurants, and families. For each country there is a map and an introduction. 320 p.

Elegant Small Hotels: A Connoisseur's Guide / Pamela Lanier. Annual (Lanier Publishing International, Ltd.).

A sizable page dedicated to each hotel holds a black-and-white photograph of its inside or outside accompanying several paragraphs selling the merits of the residence, from its efficiency and amenities to its architecture and surroundings. A side column provides the address; phone, fax, e-mail and website; rates of rooms and suites, and their number; the credit cards accepted; attractions; the services and amenities, such as parking, library, balconies, and cable TV; restrictions (e.g., no pets); concierge; room service; hours for restaurant and bar; business and sports facilities, conference rooms, and spa services (when present); and the hotel's general location in part of a city or elsewhere. Over three-quarters of the listings are in the United States, with some states omitted, while the remainder are in around a dozen countries and the Caribbean. Examined: 2005; 250 p.

Fodor's Escape to Nature without Roughing It / edited by Constance Jones (Fodor's, 2004).

The specialized listing favors U.S. and Canadian resorts, inns, lodges, and ranches according to their wilderness setting, condition of serenity, degree of seclusion, harmony with the environment, and meals. Organized by state or province and name, a place is commended for several paragraphs in terms of its surroundings, activities, décor, amenities, and similar qualities. Then an italicized "tip" highlights a particular aspect. A block of facts intermixing icons and bolded headings includes the number of rooms, tents, or cottages, the dining facilities, kinds of recreation available, services, classes, room amenities, and price range; while a separate block has contact information. Back matter has categories for types of accommodations (e.g., romantic retreat), ecosystems (e.g., lakeshore), and activities and programs (e.g., mountain biking). 358 p.

Great Places to Stay in Europe (DK, 2004).

Western Europe, that is. A collection of small hotels, bed and breakfasts, and county inns; of the eight entries on a page four have photos and several lines of description that customarily have such laudatory words as "beautiful" and "excellent," since by the fact an accommodation made it within the book means it is "great." The other four entries receive shorter shrift through omission of photos and fewer words, though the same symbols or headings apply to both types for address, telephone and fax numbers, presence of a garden, when closed, credit cards accepted, number of rooms, price range in local currency, etc. Able to fit in a glove compartment, the handsome and well-designed volume has slick pages, and the photos and illustrations are in color, along with the country maps, though for city maps only London and Paris are represented. The arrangement is by country and town. 432 p.

*Hotel & Travel Index. Quarterly (Northstar Travel Media). www.hotel andtravelindex.com

This standard resource is used by travel agents and others for its two-column list of hotels, resorts, and motels, most of which belong to chains. Over half of this large volume covers the United States by state, and the remainder fits in the rest of the world, with Canada, Mexico, and the Caribbean receiving their own sections. The trade-off for the vast number of listings is their brevity, with just name, address, telephone and fax numbers, meal plan type, room rates, and a few other things. Yet the directory still omits some accommodations as well as the towns where they are. An airplane symbol that may appear under a town indicates the distance to the airport, and the word "weblink" indicates that a link to that lodging is available at the *Hotel & Travel Index* website. Street and regional maps in color help show where some of the major hotels and places of interest are located. In front is a world time zone map, currencies and exchange rates for the U.S. dollar, and a table with the number of air travel hours between select world cities. Tabs on the book's fore edge mark some of the most popular locations. It appears that a later version is titled *Hotel & Travel Index Worldwide*. Examined: issue from 2005; approximately 1400 p.

Lodgings and Restaurants for Less (Mobil Travel Guide, 2004).

The trim design by the reliable and long-in-business *Mobil* guides is by state, then town or city. Low cost is a factor contributing to inclusion, while quality ranking for entries is from zero to three stars. The summaries avoid sentences in favor of plain facts with name, address, and electronic contact information followed by (for lodging) number of rooms, seasonal rates, availability of crib, acceptance of pets, presence of restaurant, checkout time, credit card abbreviations, etc. Furthering this, over a dozen symbols identify forms of recreation, convenience of a nearby airport, senior citizen rates, and more. For restaurants expect to learn about menu specialties, hours of operation, cost of meals, décor, and acceptable credit cards. A handful of listings for Canadian provinces are at the end of this solid work. 256 p.

Main Cities of Europe. Annual (Michelin).
    The geographically widest ranging in the *Michelin Red Guides* series (which has expanded from Europe to cover other destinations), this directory of hotels and restaurants is the only one to have any Eastern European countries, though the Western are far and away the majority. Arranged by country, then by city and its environs, the highest ranked hotels come first in the list, designated by an icon picturing up to five hotels, meaning "luxury"; the lowest, the single figure for "quite comfortable," may be followed by a different icon that stands for other recommended accommodations. Since up to a dozen or more listings can be compacted on each page, the space for information is crammed in each entry. Hotel name, address, and telephone and fax number precede a variety of descriptive icons for amenities such as a sauna, television in the room, non-smoking areas, modem availability, and accessibility for the disabled. Credit cards accepted are presented through symbols, and there is also the number of rooms and suites and their price ranges. When a hotel has a restaurant, its name appears along with its meal price-range, while a paragraph of rather fulsome phrases considers the hotel's atmosphere, style, etc. Every entry has a letter code that corresponds to a section of a separate city street map in color. Places of interest and practical information about each city are just marginally noted. For an evaluation of the restaurant portion, see this title under **Eating (and Drinking)**. Examined: 2003; 882 p.

Top U.S. Hotels, Resorts & Spas: Zagatsurvey. Annual (Zagat Survey).
    The compact, oblong directory for chains and individual businesses rates them according to five categories: rooms, service, dining, public spaces and facilities, and cost, the last of which is rendered as a dollar amount or given a letter signifying a range. The scale is from 1 to 30 but almost all categories fall within 20 to 30 (from very good to perfection), so the separation in points between competing hotels, retreats, and spas is not large. The "top" in the title suggests some exclusivity in admission, which is based on voting by the guests of these services. In an entry the name precedes address and other contact matter, plus the number of rooms.

Identified through quote marks, evaluative words contributed by travelers are stitched into a block of descriptive text, and when there is criticism it is signaled by a half-solid box icon. Spas have their own section and index apart from hotels and resorts. An online version is available for this well-realized and deservedly popular title. Examined: 2001; 284 p.

Rentals

Those wishing to stay in a place for a while might consider the convenience and savings of renting a house, apartment, or villa. Local newspaper ads and real estate companies are two sources, as are the companies that handle rental properties abroad, a number of which are on the internet.

Subject Heading: Vacation homes

Titles

European Vacation Rentals / Steenie Harvey (Avalon Travel Publishing, 2003).

The countries covered have been chosen from Western Europe, along with Greece, Cyprus, and Malta. Much of the work has information typical of a general travel guide in its discussion of a limited number of cities and destinations as well as in the presence of sightseeing photographs. For each country, sections on short rentals, long rentals, and rental agreements are the book's *raison d'être*; they gather observations on the types of accommodations, the availability of rental agencies, payment procedures, possible length of stays, and costs, while adding contact details for the agencies. Especially for those interested in going native for a while, sample prices for items give an idea about the daily cost of living. There are few competitors for books on this topic, and therein lies much of its value. 268 p.

Outside's Wilderness Lodge Vacations: More Than 100 Prime Destinations in the U.S., Canada, Mexico, and the Caribbean / Kimberly Lisagor and the editors of *Outside* (W. W. Norton & Company, 2004).

Entries on the two-column pages consist of blocks of short facts and paragraphs. Contact information precedes bolded headings for closest airport, activities (wildlife watching, canoeing, etc.), season of operation, guides and the instructions offered, services (e.g., conference facilities), accommodations (number of rooms and guests), and rates. After an overview, upbeat descriptive sections concentrate on the lodge, and give the sports and activities, the food and ambiance at mealtimes, and road directions to drive there. Another group of bolded headings contain the acceptability of pets, kids, and types of credit cards, concerns such as bears, the nearest medical aid, and a characterization of typical weather. In the book's middle, a group of color photos show various lodges or their surroundings, as do the black-and-white photos scattered about the rest of the directory. 292 p.

Vacation Rentals in Europe / Michael and Laura Murphy (Interlink Books, 2001).

Covering somewhat fewer countries than *European Vacation Rentals* (above), the book is chiefly a collection of chapters that are devoted to Western European countries and are in two sections, with the first describing regions along with the price of rentals and the seasons for booking. The second is a mixed listing of rental properties along with rental agencies in the United States and overseas. Contact details are in a gray box while descriptions are of varying length and depth. Comments about rentals may refer to their location, length of stay, price, etc., while those about agencies may include their length of time in operation, evaluations of their efficiency, the range of the offerings, and the way that they work with their customers. Short, opening chapters offer generalizations that concern renting and means of transportation in Europe. 446 p.

Resorts

Resorts are destinations in themselves. Whether it's a Club Med or a stately hotel, they offer a community of diversions and luxuries. Find listings for them in hotel directories (above) and in resort guides, which should describe accommodations, activities at the resort, and nearby sightseeing opportunities.

Titles

100 Best All-Inclusive Resorts of the World / Jay Paris and Carmi Zona-Paris. 2nd ed. (The Globe Pequot Press, 2002).

A more lavish-looking product than the same publisher's *100 Best Family Resorts in North America* (below), it is replete with color photos. On one fair-sized page is text that, better than many lodging titles, is able to hold back adjectives such as "breathtaking," while a second page has two different shades to divide kinds of information. In buff are name, address, telephone number, e-mail, and website; target group (e.g., families); type of getaway (e.g., the category "sports & fitness");

substantial detailing of the accommodations; its particular strong points; when open; the length of a minimum stay; the rates; a frequently asked question; what to be sure and bring; favorite side trips; and the nearest airport. The blue is for all-inclusive services and activities that make up a package, but also contains things not included or are available for a fee. The coverage is in five geographic sections, with Europe omitted by the authors. An appendix consisting of a table provides additional names with telephone, fax, and words on special features. 244 p.

100 Best Family Resorts in North America / Janet Tice and Jane Wilford. 7th ed. (The Globe Pequot Press, 2004).

In this professional-looking package, the observations on a resort are in five sections, properly beginning with an overview. The accommodations section contains a description that may encompass rooms and their rates, while that about dining offers some of the food to expect. While both also often relate their subjects to the needs of children, the next section notes activities and programs designed for them as well as the costs associated; under a final heading the recreational opportunities for parents and adults are discussed. At the end a box provides name, address, telephone, and URL. Arrangement is by geographical area of the United States and by province for Canada, the two countries that consist of North America in this title. For its target audience, this work should answer their questions. 244 p.

Stern's Guide to the Greatest Resorts of the World / Steven B. Stern (Pelican Publishing Co., 2002).

After introducing each of the geographically arranged resorts, the author devotes several descriptive paragraphs apiece on two-column pages to sections describing accommodations; restaurants, lounges, and entertainment; sport facilities; a miscellany that often mentions shops and nearby attractions; and ending with a block of postal and electronic addresses. To this mix are added numerous photos. An appendix rates eleven categories, including those in the aforementioned headings as well as swimming pools, the appeal for singles, and others. A second appendix provides the high season room prices for standard double rooms, and suites and apartments. Its selection of the "greatest" is geographically biased since, for example, out of five states picked from the continental United States, four of the five have multiple listings. The 2002 edition is apparently the eighth. 384 p.

ADVENTURE TRAVEL

Adventure travel is an umbrella term for types of physical activity that suggest a touch of excitement. Examples of these are backpacking, camping, mountaineering, skiing, ballooning, rafting, and experiencing primitive cultures. The following list includes only those titles that encompass a variety of adventures. For specialty adventures and recreation, see such appropriate headings as **Bicycle Touring** and **Recreation, Sports, and Ranch Vacations**.

Some companies offer worldwide trips or concentrate on certain regions or activities. A company often rates the level of a trip's physical demands.

Outdoor organizations that champion recreation may overlap this area. For example, the Sierra Club emphasizes natural places in a series that begins with the word "Adventuring," as *Adventuring along the Lewis and Clark Trail* and *Adventuring in Australia* (see **Parks, Safaris, and the Outdoors**).

The leisure traveler will have little interest in forming his or her own expedition, although the information is obtainable from The Explorers Club www.explorers.org and the British organization-publisher Expedition Advisory Centre www.rgs.org.

Subjects: Adventure travel; Outdoor recreation

Titles

Adventure Travel Tips: Advice for the Adventure of a Lifetime / Suzanne Swedo (Falcon, 2001).

For those curious about tramping through out-of-the-way places, the small and rather unsubstantial book looks into "adventure" travel. Among its contents is a comparison of group and independent travel, plus advice on using your own interests and limitations to find an outfitter, as well as the kind of questions to consider. All of its subjects are rudimentarily treated, some more than others, such as sensitivity to other cultures, ethics, and safety. If lacking depth and extensive treatment, comments are generally sensible, but can suddenly become over-specific, as in warning about an airline's refusal to take a backpacker's stove that smells of fuel. An occasional, recurring section is called "My Adventure," a personal anecdote of an episode or misadventure and how the author dealt with it. 92 p.

Adventure Vacations: A 50 State Guide to Rock Climbing, Horseback Riding, Spelunking, Whitewater Rafting, Snorkeling, Hang Gliding, and Ballooning / Stephanie Ocko (Carol Publishing Group, 1995).

The title is misleading in two ways. It is questionable whether every state is mentioned with the activities, which are much more varied than the subtitle notes, the chapters ranging from astronomy and birdwatching to Las Vegas and women's adventures. Nothing is covered in depth and may be treated in little more than a page, such as father-and-son adventures, while other topics are broken down by certain states. Sometimes there are only names and addresses accompanied by advice about the reason to contact them for further information, or there may be a paragraph's worth about either a company or an organization that hosts a visit; or about a packaged tour. The author has written several other works on specialized vacations, such as *Adventure Vacations for Animal Lovers* (below), which can be taken as an offshoot of this one. A geographic index would have been useful. 286 p.

Adventure Vacations for Animal Lovers: Exploring Nature on Unforgettable Getaways / Stephanie Ocko (Citadel Press, 2004).

Information gleaned from other sources is brought conveniently and sometimes haphazardly together here. Each chapter gives a general introduction of interesting, though not always authoritative, facts and asides about its subject, which is either a region (Africa, coral reefs, etc.) where a variety of wildlife exists or an animal group (apes, jaguars, etc.) itself. If there are parks and similar zones set aside to protect animals, they are described along with tours and programs offered through companies and organizations; though for some there is only the name, address, telephone, and electronic contacts. There is a single index and no separate geographic one that would have helped a traveler determine all the countries mentioned in the text. 304 p.

The Big Book of Adventure Travel / James C. Simmons. 4th ed. (Avalon Travel Publishing, 2001).

Designed for those who seek packaged adventures, arrangement is first by the land activities of backpacking, trekking, cycling, wildlife trips, cultural expeditions, and research journeys. Water activities are river rafting, canoeing, kayaking, sailing, and expeditionary cruising. Both types are included under a chapter of family adventures. Activities are sub-divided by country (additionally by state or province for the United States and Canada). In addition to the paragraph that describes the experience are groupings that begin with the name and contact information for the operator of the package. The price range is designated inexpensive, moderate, and expensive, according to the cost per day. Period of operation is in terms of named months or the complete year, while length in number of days is given. Types of accommodations are identified, and some come with discount coupons in the back. Geographical and operator indexes enhance ways of searching, and scattered throughout are profiles of a few of the people in charge of the adventures. 389 p.

Gordon's Guide to Adventure Vacations: Getaways for the Unique Minded: The Definitive Guide to Adventure Vacations / Timothy E. Gordon, Ana Bela Oliveira (TAG Publishing, 1998).

The big catalog with two-column pages offers to recreationists eighteen outdoor categories, some of which are closely related, as with cross-country ski lodges, heli-skiing, snowcat skiing, and top-rated ski areas. There is name, address, telephone and often fax number, but no electronic contacts. A paragraph intent on selling the experience to the reader favorably describes the services of the business, the lodging, or the outfitter and, as appropriate, the locales where the activities take place. There are a variety of supplementary formats, from the breakdown of details involved in a trip to the distance of the nearest airport. A mid-section has a number of publicity-type color photos. The presence of a geographic index would have added to the volume's value. 495 p.

How to Choose an Adventure Vacation (Fodor's Travel Publications, 2003).

This compact paperback is arranged by outdoor activity, with some wearing the word "adventure" more readily than others (as wilderness and survival schools vs. golf schools or tennis camps). For each vacation a few pages explain what to expect, then questions and answers address basics that aid in determining the standards for choosing the right trip or school. Several of the same questions are re-worded from chapter to chapter, as about the qualifications of the instructors, the accommodations, and the physical demands. Other questions are determined by the activity (for example, the sailing section asks about the type of boat used). Each ends with a mention of relevant organizations, periodicals, and books. A limited selection of camps, outfitters, and other providers are assembled and sub-grouped by subject headings in a back section where the name, web and physical address, and telephone number precede the description. At the top of a page the lack of a running head keyed to the activity makes it difficult to find where one ends and another begins. 292 p.

Ultimate Adventure: National Geographic Ultimate Adventure Source-book / Paul McMenamin (National Geographic Society, 2000).

This is a polished, large book with a plentitude of attractive color photos amid multi-column texts. Coverage is alphabetical, beginning with "alpine mountaineering" and ending with "windsurfing," with related subjects grouped together (e.g., the chapter on "freeflight" comprises paragliding, hang gliding, and soaring). Other activities are ballooning; cycling; family adventures; fishing; horseback riding; kayaking; motorized adventures; outdoor skills; rafting; safaris; sailing; scuba diving; skiing; skydiving; snowmobiling; surfing; trekking; and wildlife encounters. Conventionally, a chapter selects a few geographical areas that are especially suitable, noting places there associated with the particular adventure. Then it provides comments about individual operators, online sites, videos, etc. Overall, the resource is a fine choice for those curious about adventure travel. 384 p.

AIR TRAVEL

The majority of the abundant sources about air travel deal with airports, airlines, passengers, or flying.

To assist in getting to and from the airport there are guides to ground transportation. At the airport passengers can minimize confusion by consulting terminal layouts placed for orientation at strategic intervals (similar diagrams appear in the back of airline magazines that are free to passengers and in such works as the OAG series).

Publications with diagrams of various plane types show the seating arrangements, so the passenger can learn the location of a bulkhead (for more leg room) or the number of seats across. Plane routes and air distances are covered in some sources, but of most practicality are airline schedules, which include connections. Schedules and other reservation information also are available through the internet, including on-time arrivals and departures.

Books about how to fly sensibly consider different kinds of passengers: occasional passengers, frequent flyers, business travelers, those with disabilities, parents and children. For the dedicated budget passenger there are such sources as a knowledgeable travel agent, newspapers advertising bargain fares, and bucket shops. Among money-saving strategies are booking a charter or becoming an air courier. Courier companies are in the yellow pages under "Delivery Services" or "Messenger Services." If none is in the local directory, try cities on the East Coast, since many of these companies are located there.

The passenger afraid of flying or concerned about jet lag will find advice from books or a doctor. Some airlines have offered seminars.

Finally, all types of passengers should know their rights and the organizations that lobby for them. They may find the appropriate resources below.

Look for this subject also under **Budget Travel** and **Travelers**.

Subject Headings: Air travel; Airlines—Rates.

Titles

Air Travel Consumer Report. Monthly (Aviation Consumer Protection Division, Office of Aviation Enforcement and Proceedings, U.S. Department of Transportation). airconsumer.ost.dot.gov/reports

For those who might be curious about the on-time arrival record of airlines at U.S. airports, this is the place to explore. Tables show percentages of flights that were prompt and those that were late, with some adding the time of day and denoting the cause. Categories are also switched around by carrier, airport, and time of day. Of several appendixes, one presents tables of mishandled baggage reports arranged by airlines, from those with the best record to those with the worst; and another is for passengers who were denied boarding, subdivided into the voluntary and involuntary. Final tables are for consumer complaints, arranged by airline and in other ways. Examined: issue from 2008 (online)

Air-Ways: The Insider's Guide to Air Travel / Laura E. Quarantiello (LimeLight Books, 2000).

The material is certainly more introductory than such a work as *Fly Safe, Fly Smart* (below), though somewhat as broad, so *Air-Ways* is useful for those who want to get some facts about air travel and basic commentary about such things as how often an airline loses baggage and what to do upon learning that a flight has been canceled. While saving money is a topic, it does not receive a disproportionate amount of space. The sequence of chapters follows a logic that begins with choosing an airline, then looking at ticket costs, shopping by computer for one, selecting an appropriate airline seat, preparing for a trip, arrival and check in at the airport, being comfortable aboard, types of emergencies, and the processes that begin with deplaning at the destination airport. 144 p.

Airfare Secrets Exposed: How to Find the Lowest Fares Available Anywhere! / Joel Leach and Carey Christensen. 3rd ed. (Studio 4 Productions, 2000).

Another work on finding ways to save on flying, the first part of it consists of rudimentary discussions sometimes followed by relevant addresses. Thus, consolidators, bucket shops, and discounters are introduced, and then under state individually listed with just their name and telephone number. Brevity means that some chapters are as short as two pages, such as the one about airline ticket auctions. Air couriers, air passes, bumping, frequent flyer programs, etc., help fill out the coverage. Appendixes account for nearly half the volume and are a miscellany of facts and advice chiefly about various aspects of travel in general rather than airfares. In **Air Travel** are other reviewed titles on airfares that are much more thorough. 189 p.

All You Ever Wanted to Know about Flying: The Passenger's Guide to How Airliners Fly / Julien Evans (Motorbooks International Publishers & Wholesalers, 1997).

Contrary to the title, this is more about flying an airplane from a pilot's perspective, but the interested passenger should learn about a plane's functional basics. There are chapter descriptions of the hardware, parts of the flight deck, the physics of flight, the means of taking off and landing, how the autopilot works, pre-flight preparations, and so forth. *The Flying Book* (below) covers some of the same territory, but not to the extent about flight itself, nor with as much detail or jargon, though perhaps with greater clarity. Color photos are used throughout, as are diagrams. 132 p.

Arrive in Better Shape: How to Avoid Jet Lag and Travel Stress / Farrol Kahn (HarperPaperbacks, 1996).
    Alternatively, the paperback could have been called "A-Z of Aviation Health," the title of the section that takes up most of the volume. There are more than forty entries, from aerophobia (fear of flying) to "the wonder juice" (carrot juice), which the author feels is the best remedy for oxygen deficiency. The alphabetical order allows a quick lookup. In general, discussions center on suggestions for psychological comfort and for control of health through dietary means; as well as about onboard things such as seating, cabin air, and pressurization. Also, children, women, and those who are afflicted with diabetes, fainting, and other conditions receive attention. There is an introduction, and in back is a supplement with several short lists—for example, the alcohol contents of various drinks. 169 p.

The Courier Air Travel Handbook: Learn How to Travel Worldwide for Next to Nothing / Mark I. Field. 8th ed. (Perpetual Press, 1999).
    Though it doesn't designate itself as such, this is a directory, except for the abbreviated front matter offering advice about being a courier. However, the chief value of the book for would-be couriers who seek employment is its information about eligible companies, presented in ready-reference format and arranged by areas of the world. A graphic box introduces the name of the company, destinations it sends couriers to, flight cost (now out-of-date), range in number of days the courier can stay at the destination, and the days on which flights depart. A few details among many are the year the business began, the airline used, luggage restrictions, and whether there is an annual fee. Little electronic contact information appears, and the personal names of points of contact are very unlikely to be accurate any longer. The author recommends that the courier use youth hostels and offers pages of addresses for them. 159 p.

Domestic Airline Fares Consumer Report. Monthly (Office of Aviation Analysis, U.S. Department of Transportation). ostpxweb.ost.dot.gov/ aviation

Prompted by the interest arising from *Air Travel Consumer Report,* the Department of Transportation brought out this publication about domestic airline prices. This is another of those government titles full of tables with rows, columns, and statistics. In table 1, cities are arranged under distance blocks (e.g., 101 to 150 miles), across from which are, among other figures and abbreviations, the exact nonstop distances, the largest carrier, and of most significance, the lowest fare carrier, along with its percent market share and its average cost *one*-way (not round trip). Other tables list increase or decrease in average fares and highest and lowest fare markets according to distance. Doubtlessly mundane travelers will happily omit this from resources on which they rely. Examined online: issue from 2008

Fly Cheap! / Kelly Monaghan. 2nd ed. (The Intrepid Traveler, 2001).

Monaghan is very knowledgeable about ways of saving money when it comes to taking flights. He introduces and judges more than a dozen ticketing ploys, supplementing them with usage examples, some of which he admits may be frowned upon by airlines. (The security that has increased after the book's publication no doubt makes several strategies even more suspect and perhaps illegal.) More conventional suggestions touch upon tracking sales and fare wars through the media, using a travel agency that gives rebates, buying tickets at reduced price from overseas, exploring senior membership programs, and so forth. Several chapters include collections of businesses amid their discussions of low fare airlines, air pass programs, consolidators, and air couriers, while others concentrate on frequent flyer miles, possibilities through the internet, and even becoming a travel agent. 253 p.

Fly Easy: Experts Share Their Secrets How to Get There Safely, Comfortably, and Hassle-Free (Fodor's Travel Publications, 2002).

Besides ideas for finding tickets at cheap prices, the compact book gives helpful and plain advice on other topics of importance to passengers. When it comes to baggage, considerations revolve around what to carry on, what to pack, and what to do in case of damage, delay, or loss. One chapter begins with arrival at the airport, then on to check-in, security, options if things go wrong, and suggestions for filling the extra time that can come with waiting for a flight. Also receiving attention are seating, food service, travel with children, safety, jet lag, going through customs, etc., though the depth could be better. Scattered throughout are first-person experiences from passengers. The coverage is comparable to the superior *Fly Safe, Fly Smart* (below). 250 p.

Fly for Less: The Ultimate Guide to Bargain Airfares!: Consolidators, Travel Agents, & Airline Loopholes That Can Save You Up to 65% on Your Airfare! / Gary E. Schmidt (Travel Publishing, Inc., 1998).

While the author does outline cost-saving strategies, the biggest chunk of the book is a collection of data about travel agencies and the top 25 air travel consolidators. Though not obvious, arrangement of travel agencies is by state, and there are bolded labels for physical, telephonic, and electronic contact information preceding that about the company, including its years in business, association membership, the number of agents on the staff and their experience in years, and areas of specialty; a heading of "special options offered for finding the lowest fare" covers the internet, use of consolidators, and tracking software. There are examples of now dated city-to-city discount fares and details about a company and its offerings. Consolidators are separately cross-indexed by airline and by destination along with their toll-free numbers. 262 p.

Fly-Rights: A Consumer Guide to Air Travel (Aviation Consumer Protection Division, U.S. Department of Transportation, no date). airconsumer.ost.dot.gov/publications/flyrights.htm

Rights and responsibilities of the traveler are the general theme. Advice is usually basic, though not always, as with the suggestion that the prospective customer ask for the on-time performance code from an airline. Yet the few observations on airfares cannot compare with the money-saving tips tackled by books like *Fly Cheap!* and others in this section. Otherwise, contents give an idea about what to do in cases of delayed and canceled flights, overbooking and, in particular, "bumping." There are also statements about checking luggage and the problems that may result from damage, delay, and loss, plus discussions about smoking; passengers with disabilities; frequent flyer programs; contract obligations between the airline and the passenger; spotting and avoiding travel scams; facts on health and on safety; and making complaints. The latest printed and dated issue is 1999, but this year is not on the online version, whose 58-page equivalent is available from the Federal Citizen Information Center. See also the section **Government Publications** as well as the entry for the Aviation Consumer Protection Division under "Businesses and Organizations" below. Examined website: 2008

Fly Safe, Fly Smart: The Insider's Guide to a Hassle-Free Flight / Sascha Segan (Hungry Minds, 2002).

Written with advice that is clear and decisive, the volume is compact enough to be comfortably carried along, should the traveler wish. Readability is solid, with the occasional bulleted comments and bolded phrases, capitalized headings for chapter subsections, and several shaded boxes. The coverage of subjects is broad as are the details supporting them. Expect to learn about the ins and outs of airline travel, from the real meaning of the words "on time" and traveling with your pet to maximizing frequent flyer miles and minimizing the costs of buying air tickets. There are also explanations about the fear of flying when its sources are thunderstorms, terrorist attacks, etc., and staying healthy, with a special look at jet lag. For someone interested in air travel, this is an excellent introduction. 322 p.

Fly Smart!: Tips from Behind the Counter / Sandra Yearwood (Hats Off Books, 2003).

"Frequently asked questions" is a category found on a number of websites, but this book has adopted the format, with questions arranged by topic and followed by the answer. The reader may well feel very comfortable gathering compact information in this convenient way, where there are often several answers to a page. For example, the seventeen questions under the heading "ticket refunds" fill just six pages. As appropriate, there are bulleted lists as a way of making details stand out or showing things to do and to bring or not to do and not to bring. Occasional real-life situations serve to illustrate a topic. This is not the place to search for advice about cheap flights (see, for example, *Fly Cheap!* [above]), but rather learn about airline rules concerning reservations, special meals, pets, baggage, dangerous goods, special assistance, oversold flights, children on board, etc. 157 p.

The Flying Book: Everything You've Ever Wondered about Flying on Airplanes / David Blatner (Walker & Company, 2003).

Explanations aimed at the curious lay person range from how airplanes are able to fly to how they are manufactured, with much else. If there is an interest about the reason for banning the use of cell phones during a flight or what a pilot does in the cockpit, this supplies the answers in chapters arranged in general subject areas. However, since there is a section about why airplanes occasionally crash, this is a book that might best be read on the ground, though the reader is given instructions about handling in-air emergencies. What not to look for here is advice about finding the cheapest air ticket and other matters found in many travel books. 248 p.

International How to Get out of the Airport!: Find the Best Way to Your Destination from the World's Airports / Howard Wendland (Natalto World Publications, 1995).

Conveniently pull this small-sized volume out of a back pocket to look under a city name (from Abu Dhabi to Zurich) to find its airport, which comes with its number of kilometers outside the city or its center (the distinction is unclear). The presence of an information office may be noted, and there are bolded headings for the varying types of transportation to take from the airport to the destination, in particular taxis, where there is stated at least approximate cost and time span of a journey. The other types most frequently included are buses, which have hours and intervals of departure, and rental car companies. As appropriate the author adds trains, limousines, shuttles, and services that may be particular to an airport, and he intermittently advises the best among them to take from the airport. 127 p.

Jet Smarter: The Air Traveler's RX / Diana Fairechild (Flyana Rhyme, 1999).
    The same author of *Strategies for the Wise Passenger* (below) has an older, fatter title. Omitting the topics of safety and security in favor of healthy flying, the book offers discussions about jet lag spread through several chapters that look at causes, symptoms and remedies, time zones, magnetic fields, and meta-jet lag. It also considers how passengers are affected by air quality, radiation, dehydration, etc. There are reports on actions that can be taken to alleviate some issues, such as managing how much light is received and how best to sleep aboard, as well as reducing stress through exercise and diet. As in her other book, she wields her pen as an advocate who is alerting the reader that the airlines deliberately put their interest ahead of those that they serve. At the end a question and answer format covers subjects already mentioned. A later edition is available. 399 p.

Safe Air Travel Companion / Dan McKinnon (McGraw-Hill, 2002).
    The area of safety here does not address acts of an atmospheric nature or being struck by an object from an overhead bin, but the criminal intent of individuals. Within the content there is a bit of background on hijackers and hijacking and the preventive measures government and airlines take. To the average traveler the tone may veer into the paranoid, since there is a fair amount about what to do if taken as a hostage; and, McKinnon's assertion to the contrary, the work seems to take for granted the likelihood or inevitability of an attack in any circumstance, as when the author advises passengers to stay away from the crowds at luggage carousels. When addressing other than air passengers, there is coping advice for those who live in a foreign country. The oblong, small size means the book

could be stuffed in a rear jeans pocket, though it doesn't seem necessary to take it on a trip. 153 p.

Salk International's Airport Transit Guide. Annual (Salk International Travel Premiums, Inc.).

   This is a work that lists ways of getting to and from the airport. Alphabetically arranged by the name of the city, regardless of country, an entry has in its preliminary grouping the local time zone based on Greenwich Mean Time, the airport's name, code, and distance from the city; and for airport information a telephone number and web address. In the remainder most entries have a few symbols chosen from a group that signify taxis, shuttles, limos, vans, public bus, rail transport, helicopter, rental car agencies, short and long term parking, and wheelchair readiness. Under these kinds of transportation expect to find the charge, plus there can be advice about where to board, frequency of departure, and destinations. The booklet is portably sized to fit in a pocket. Examined: 2004; 144 p.

Strategies for the Wise Passenger: Turbulence, Terrorism, Streaking, Cardiac Arrest, Too Tall / by Diana Fairechild (Flyana.com, 2003).

   Drawing on her experience as a flight attendant, the author devotes a chapter to each of the subjects in the subtitle. Scattered throughout in graphic boxes, coping or survival strategies are listed. For example, when turbulence strikes there are brief suggestions about what the passenger can do if standing, sitting, eating, etc., and ways of protection from objects that could fall out of the overhead bins. However, much of the short, small book concentrates on the issues' histories along with anecdotes, which may not do much to reassure you about the current flying conditions. Writing on behalf of the consumer rather than the airline, she adds several pages concerning the contents of a "Passenger Bill of Rights," goals for getting the airlines and the government to ensure health and safety. There is more to flying for travelers than is included in this title, and for that other books need to be consulted. 127 p.

Stuck at the Airport: A Traveler's Survival Guide / Harriet Baskas (Simon & Schuster, 2001).

   Here are a few airports in European and Canadian cities, but the vast majority are American, though the list is not comprehensive. The name of the airport, its city location, airport code, and web address comes with a paragraph of background history. A section goes into the cost and availability of luggage, the presence of self-service lockers, and above all the airport's layout, which unfortunately lacks the advantage of diagrams or plans. Other sections concern places to eat, nap, exercise, or smoke. For those with business in mind, there is notice about such things as faxing, making copies, and finding ATMs. Alternatively, the passenger can shop; discover art, architecture, and views; or learn what entertainment is available for children. If your preference is not to be stuck at the airport, the book has the distance from the city, cost of going there, and the means. The title is most useful if carried along, but whether the amount of information for any one airport is worth the effort is another issue. 287 p.

Survival Tactics for Airline Passengers / Ken Cubbin (Avionics Communications Inc., 2002).

Those passengers and flight attendants who feel they might need to know karate or rely on various physical maneuvers to disarm either hijackers or disgruntled people who might put a plane in jeopardy should find chapters that will assist them, along with illustrations. There are also ways of handling oneself in evacuating a plane due to fire or smoke, or acting with the appropriate knowledge when the cabin decompresses, or staying afloat when the plane has ditched in the ocean. The book also addresses more mundane concerns connected with keeping comfortable and healthy on board (e.g., staying hydrated), and examines how the plane operates. An appendix has diagrams of seat configurations in various craft. 184 p.

Traveler's Rights: Your Legal Guide to Fair Treatment and Full Value / Alexander Anolik & John K. Hawks (Sphinx Publishing, 2003).

Assuming no prior knowledge of your rights, chapters tackle familiar categories of travel—air, car rentals, lodging, cruises, tours, international travel—while others have advice on dealing with travel agents and related sellers, using money (such as buying on credit) and travel insurance, crimes and scams, and the rights of those with disabilities and other travelers. Law cases are cited on occasion, and legal terms are carefully and clearly explained, as are the situations that might be the result of a company's rules. A re-occurring box labeled "travel tip" has elaborations about what to do to avoid or moderate problems, or provides additional facts. A larger variety of potential difficulties and a step-by-step guide to remedying rights that have been wronged would have added to the further worth of this title. 290 p.

Businesses and Organizations

Aviation Consumer Protection Division, Office of Aviation Enforcement and Proceedings. U.S. Department of Transportation. airconsumer.ost.

dot.gov

The agency fields complaints about aviation issues from members of the public and makes available to them publications of pertinent information. A list of over one-dozen titles is under the heading "Travel Tips & Publications" (airconsumer.ost.dot.gov/pubs.htm), including *New Horizons: Information for the Air Traveler with a Disability* (reviewed in **Travelers—Disabilities**), *Getting the Best Air Fares*, and *Baggage Tips*, aka *Tips on Avoiding Baggage Problems*. Examined website: 2008

Federal Aviation Administration. U.S. Department of Transportation. www.faa.gov/passengers

Responsible for safety regulations and other things, this agency supplies the air passenger with handy facts about airline travel and provides online status checks for airport conditions. Several categories at the site are similar to that found as headings under **Travelers** (see in this work), while some links consist of advice and facts, such as an averaging of wait-times at the security check-points. The site also carries toll-free consumer and safety hotline numbers for problems, concerns, and complaints. One tab links to a collection of airline on-time statistics and accident reports that are not designed for the casual browser. Examined website: 2008

OAG. www.oag.com

Having produced titles in the past that have undergone several word changes, OAG (Official Airline Guides) continues to have numerous print and electronic works that provide airline timetables and other relevant travel information. *OAG Flight Guide North America* is a twice-monthly timetable of connections taking place within North America, while its monthly companion is *OAG Flight Guide Worldwide*. The twice-yearly *OAG Flight Atlas Worldwide* shows global air routes on maps, and *OAG Executive Flight Guide* is a periodical series that collects flight schedule timetables by regions of the world, such as Asia Pacific or North America. Examined website: 2008

AMUSEMENT PARKS AND FAIRS

A popular family destination, amusement parks and fairs have their own directories, which contain addresses, prices, seasons of operation, and evaluations. For travelers who may wish to take in nearby sights, also bringing a guidebook is prudent. There are several individual guides to the world's number one amusement park, Walt Disney World.

Subject Heading: Amusement parks

Titles

AAA Guide to North America's Theme Parks (American Automobile Association, 1997).

The book's broad size, numerous color photos, and two-column layout make it eye-catching. In addition, major headings are one color and subheadings are another, but this has no significance beyond looks. A selection of states are represented and a few Canadian provinces, presumably because they are the only ones with *theme* parks. After the park name and an introduction the sections typically have directions; accessibility information; parking costs; hours and season of operation; guest services such as availability of ATMs and stroller rentals; details on don't miss rides; entertainment and shows featured; restaurants; kinds of souvenirs; admission prices (now out-of-date); possible discounts for members of certain groups; and a block for name, address, telephone number and, occasionally, the park's internet site. Considering the publisher, it is ironic that no highway maps with park locations are here. 248 p.

The Amusement Park Guide: Coast to Coast Thrills / Tim O'Brien. 5th ed. (Globe Pequot Press, 2003).

The most comprehensive of the guides in this section, it is by state and by Canadian province. An entry begins with a name, address, telephone number, and URL. Typically at least two paragraphs' worth of park highlights and practical matters are given by the author in his enthusiastic way. A few extended entries follow their description with icons for the season of opening; operating hours; admission policy (e.g, pay one price vs. pay-as-you-go); top rides list; the roller coasters available; how many hours to stay; the best way to avoid the crowds; and road directions. Front matter includes ten tips about dressing for the outing, and another ten for making the day safer and more enjoyable for kids. There are also lists for the top non-roller-coaster rides, theme/amusement parks, and more. Numerous parks both big and small are here. 325 p.

Amusement Parks: An American Guidebook / John Norris and Joann Norris. 2nd ed. (McFarland & Company, Inc., 1994).

The arrangement under state provides the name of the amusement or theme park and the town where it is located, with a paragraph or more that may talk about its surroundings, history, entertainment available, rides, shops, and restaurants. Separate, bolded labels are for the season and hours of operation; best days to attend; ticket costs according to age; additional conveniences and attractions; other sites of interest nearby; and the address along with telephone number. There is seldom evaluation that considers a park's strengths or weaknesses, and of course the prices, if not the time of operation, are outdated. Occasional black-and-white photos appear throughout. 158 p.

The Cheapskate's Guide to Theme Parks / Steven J. Urbanowicz (Citadel Press, 2004).

This limits itself to seven parks apiece from the Northeast and the Midwest, six from the South, and five from the West Coast. Heading an entry are name, address, telephone number, website, admission cost, and months of operation. A paragraph is devoted to the park's history, followed by a list of its major attractions; directions for getting there; advice about planning for passes and the time to go; parking and other things to prepare for at the beginning of a visit; and taking up the most space, a guide to the rides, with comments on avoiding the longest lines and the path to the rides. A simple park layout shows the main entrance and the relative location of named rides. The "cheapskate" in the title appears chiefly in suggestions about getting the best admission costs. For the twenty-five parks presented in this volume there is more depth than in *The Amusement Park Guide* (above), but the latter has many more entries and includes Canada. 212 p.

AUTOMOBILE AND RECREATIONAL VEHICLE TRAVEL

A good car touring manual should contain routes, maps, distances, sights, services, unfamiliar traffic regulations, and if need be, car-related foreign phrases and a list of international road signs.

Those who will be driving abroad should get the International Driver's License (IDL), which was sanctioned by the UN in 1949 and allows its possessor to drive in all countries that recognize it. It is available from the American Automobile Association and the National Automobile Club, and from organizations that offer travel services.

For touring advice and for vacation literature consult the Association or its equivalent in other countries, such as the Automobile Association in Britain. The associations publish a wide assortment of travel works as well as offering other services. When weather affects a state's road system, the highway patrol and department of transportation can alert the traveler.

A travel agency can help with car rental, or a car can be rented at the destination's airport or the nearest town. A car rental agency can be a source of information, not only about renting but also sights, routes, and other tourist interests; and it may offer maps or driving guides. Car rental agencies are mentioned on various internet sites, appear in the yellow pages and as airline magazine ads, and they have counters at larger airports. Some country guide books give addresses and advice about car rentals.

Especially for overseas visitors who do not care to rent, one option is purchasing a car from a dealer then, at trip's end, either selling it back to the dealer or importing it back home. Or visitors could go to the bother of shipping their own vehicle abroad. Bringing a car into the United States will involve the purchaser with U.S. Customs, the Department of Transportation, the Environmental Protection Agency, and Internal Revenue Service (IRS) regulations, so contact them for advice.

Visitors may hire a taxi for a day tour by negotiating either directly or through a hotel. For a free trip, deliver a car to a destination. Drivers are engaged by auto transporter companies, whose addresses are found in the yellow pages under "Auto Transporters & Drive-Away Cos." They can also ship a car overseas.

Available online as well as from motor clubs or from software stores are route planning programs. They suggest a variety of routes to a destination and calculate the length of the drive. Some programs create charts with routes, cities, mileage, and directional information, while others create maps. The vehicle itself may have Global Positioning Systems (GPS) instrumentation and other fancy technologies.

On the internet are such services as lists of international traffic signs (as www.travlang.com/signs) and prices for gasoline (www.petroprice.com, etc.).

As applied to travel, the word "overlanding" is relatively uncommon. Apparently a British concept, it may be popularly defined as budget travel in a rugged vehicle over a challenging distance and route; camping out or staying in cheap lodgings is usual. Appealing to the adventurous-minded, an overland trip begins in, say, London and ends in France or South Africa or Nepal. Distances and the time it takes to cover them vary according to destination. A traveler may hook up with such an activity through adventure companies or undertake it independently.

See also **Distances** and **Maps and Atlases**.

Subject Heading: Automobile travel

Titles

Digest of Motor Laws (American Automobile Association).

The facts for drivers are clearly and thoroughly presented in an easy to find framework. Within a state, U.S. territory, and province of Canada, headings deal with motor vehicle registration; various taxes; the driver's license; traffic rules; towing; passenger car trailers; motorcycles and mopeds; liabilities; accident reports; bail bonds; chemical testing; motor vehicle inspection; the nonresident violator compact; and contacting the state police or highway patrol. Several subject headings come with subheadings, such as "traffic rules" which elaborates its text under "speed limits," "speed checking devices," "radar detectors," "child restraints," and many others. The reference is small enough for a glove compartment. Newer editions are available. Examined: 1999; 580 p.

Drive USA / Andrew Vincent (Vacation Work Publications, 2002).

The British publisher has designed this for the driver unfamiliar with American ways and loaded it with lots of thought-out detail. For example, a discussion of "driveaways" (delivering a car belonging to someone else) delves into the origin of this practice, levels of service, the reasons for enlisting as a driver and the responsibilities, the expected costs, documentation and formalities, choosing the right vehicle, procedures, the possibility of repairs, etc. Yet there are many other subjects, major and minor, found in the work, such as driving licenses and plates; the driver with disabilities; getting deals with rentals; the reason for buying a car; insurance costs; city driving; road etiquette; parking; the handling of various traffic offenses; police impostors(!); checking over the car; experiencing the elements; and the reliability of mechanics. Several itineraries for interstate routes are compactly covered. Bullets, shaded boxes, and numerous subheadings facilitate the ability to locate facts in the text. 219 p.

Frommer's Driving Tour Guides (series) (Wiley Publishing).

Series titles begin with the name of the European country or a part of the United States followed by the words *Best Loved Driving Tours*, as with *Britain's Best Loved Driving Tours*. Graphically impressive with color photos and maps, the very efficient layout suggests separate itineraries after introductory comments about the region. On the three-column pages driving directions accompany the numbered and described sights along each route, whose duration in days plus distance in miles and kilometers are shown. A constant sprinkling of gray boxes gives information on recommended walks, natural history, history, things of interest to children, scenic routes, and an attraction unique to the area. The directions from one point to another often omit mileage, and those who want something about service stations and other practicalities should look elsewhere. Examined: *Britain's Best Loved Driving Tours*, revised 6th ed. (2004; 176 p.)

How to Take a Road Trip / Wayne Hoffman (Fodor's Travel Publications, 2003).

A compact and sensible "how to" guide is composed of six chapters that consider: the choice of destinations (though little on destinations themselves), preparing a route, and the responsibilities for duties during a drive; the type of vehicle to use—your own car, a rental, an RV, or a motorcycle; the luggage to use for a trip, the stuff it will contain, and where to put it all in the vehicle; passing time, taking breaks, and traveling with children or pets; handling car breakdowns, hazardous driving conditions, and other problems; and types of places to stay. An appendix has an interesting division by state of capsule information about license requirements, rules for right turn on red, laws related to wearing a seat belt or helmet, and typical speed limits. Interspersed through the text are short first-person accounts from the experiences of drivers as related to the subject then under discussion. 191 p.

Importing or Exporting a Car: Guidelines for Permanent and Temporary Purposes (U.S. Customs and Border Protection). www.cbp.gov/ linkhandler/cgov/newsroom/publications/trade/importexportcar.ctt/import ingacar.doc

The online text concentrates on government regulations. Major areas of interest for those who might wish to import a car into the United States are related to documentation; avoiding the introduction of foreign pests; shipping; dutiable and free entries; purposes of importation; standards (safety, bumper, theft prevention, and emission); federal tax; and driver's plates and permits. A minor section addresses ownership documents necessary for exportation. Examined website: 2008

Moto Europa: The Complete Guide to European Motor Travel / Eric Bredesen. 1.3 ed. (Seren Publishing, 1996). www.ideamerge.com/moto europa

An introduction debunks myths about the difficulties of driving in Europe, while chapters deal with obtaining a car in terms of renting, leasing, buying, shipping, and importing, especially as related to expenses. There is general advice about driving in a foreign country, parking, breakdowns, and the like. Varying in depth are country-by-country facts that have, when applicable, lists of toll routes, non-toll mountain passes, fuel concerns, the meaning of road signs, driving laws and behavior, cautions about parking, and breakdown and emergency contacts. When there is ferrying to be done, the appropriate companies receive coverage. Travel advice skews toward the budget end in a useful volume designed for a large glove compartment, with its width more than its height. The text is also available online. 317 p.

The Next Exit (The Next Exit, 2004).

The large volume in two-column pages gives extremely detailed accounts of the services available at the pull-offs from interstate highways of the continental United States. Within each state arrangement is by the interstates and their exit numbers, which are related to the nearest mile markers. Find at the exits lettered, numbered, and named roads and nearby towns, and there are bolded categories for the businesses offering gas, food, lodging, and "other," which may include hospitals. For a few exits there are "no facilities." If the business is RV or truck accessible the color red is used, and occasional notes indicate the availability of diesel, 24 hour presence, etc. Red is also used to show routes on a shaded state map that may be referred to on every right-hand page. The book is of most relevance to the driver and riders on cross-country trips or those frequently on the interstates. A later edition is available. 542 p.

Overlanding: How to Explore the World on Four Wheels / John Steele Gordon (Harper & Row, 1975).

Few works have been dedicated to overlanding, which may be generally considered as adventuring long, rugged distances by land in a sturdy vehicle for an often lengthy time, possibly with a group of people, and often on a budget. Due to the age of the publication some information is out of date or dated (such as that about political situations, costs, photography equipment, and the list of overlanding companies), and some is also covered in various books about travel, but the title nonetheless supplies some particular glimpses into this style of nitty-gritty touring. Also, there is still useful advice about what to look for in a vehicle, the social interaction among members on the expedition, the practical presentation of who is responsible for what chores and their importance, selecting food in Third World markets, etc. 328 p.

Passport's Let's Drive Europe: The 10-Language Phrasebook for Motoring Travelers (Passport Books, 1989).

The book is wider than it is tall to accommodate its ten columns in English, French, German, Spanish, Portuguese, Italian, Dutch, Danish, Swedish, and Serbo-Croatian. To keep its appeal broader than the word "drive" in the title, the first part has translations for traditional travel subject areas in matters relating to eating, shopping, emergencies, etc. Its second half, for the motoring tourist, has words and phrases related to its heading "garages and breakdowns." Also, shaded illustrations of a car's engine parts and other innards are numbered and cross-indexed to the group of multi-language columns, which is useful for communicating with a mechanic who doesn't know a part's name in another language. 96 p.

RV and Car Camping Vacations in Europe: RV and Car Camping Tours to Europe's Top Vacation Destinations / Mike and Terri Church (Rolling Homes Press, 2004).

In this attractive package a general introductory chapter about European camping and campgrounds notes what to expect from camps (e.g., plumbing, electrical service) and, along with general travel observations, tells what to take along. The bulk is devoted to route directions and descriptions of sights chiefly in Britain and Western Europe, accompanied with collections of campsites that begin with a block for name, address, telephone number, fax, website, e-mail, and GPS position. Over a dozen symbols signify such relevancies as the acceptance of reservations or credit cards or tent campers or pets, and if the campground has laundry facilities or telephones. This is elaborated upon in a narrative. Numerous black-and-white maps show the routes to be taken, and there are extra comments about roads and driving in various countries. 319 p.

Organizations

American Automobile Association. www.aaa.com
    Besides road atlases, it has published state guidebooks and advice about travel. Examined website: 2008

Automobile Association. www.theaa.com
    This British counterpart of the American Automobile Association has produced numerous British and European road atlases and a variety of publications about motoring, accommodations, camping, and touring, particularly in Britain and Europe. Examined website: 2008

Energy Information Administration. U.S. Department of Energy. www.eia. doe.gov
    Here is available data on current gasoline prices at the pump from various U.S. regions, including weekly prices from select states and cities. Examined website: 2008

BICYCLE TOURING

Whether for a few hours' exercise or a few weeks' touring, a bicycle ride encourages close contact with the out-of-doors. Books on touring take into account preparation, equipment, maintenance, route difficulty, and other matters.

Group and independent tours are offered by bicycle touring companies and by some adventure companies, which may be discovered in biking and travel magazines.

The traveler who gets the urge to cycle while on vacation can consult the usual suspects for finding bicycle rentals: the yellow pages, a hotel desk, or a local tourist office.

Subject Heading: Bicycle touring

Titles

Bicycle Touring Made Easy / Lise Krieger (Vitesse Press, 2002).

Concentration is on preparation for a trip while keeping the bicycle and oneself in good working order. The author is also interested in ways of riding comfortably, what to outfit on the bicycle and the rider, maintenance, safety, health and, in short chapters, nutritional food and camping out. By keeping its focus it gives more information on these aspects than the manuals that are more expansive, such as *The Essential Touring Cyclist* (below), which has the advantage of adding information on tours themselves, transportation of the bike, and other concerns. Photographs throughout of people biking, of equipment, and of repairs enhance the text. 159 p.

Bicycle Touring: The Complete Book on Touring by Bike / Patricia Vance (Van der Plas Publications, 2000).

There is a lot of good, sound advice in this clearly written work, the chapters divided into smaller subdivisions. Subjects include touring with a group versus going it alone; the importance of finding a good route book; the nuts and bolts of planning a route; how separate parts of a bicycle contribute to touring; performing repairs on the road; clothing; panniers and other equipment; some rules of riding a bike; the means of transporting the bike to the place where the tour commences; staying healthy and safe; and general travel concerns. Vance explains not only what to take but also why to take it, and in addition to relating personal cycling experiences gives lists of what were brought on two tours, one in the United States and one in Turkey. 224 p.

Bicycling Magazine's Guide to Bike Touring: Everything You Need to Know to Travel Anywhere on a Bike / Doug Donaldson (Rodale, 2005).
    Early on a columnar chart is supplied to guide cyclists in their choice of tours based on numerous preferences, and this is logically followed by chapters on picking a tour company and planning one's own tour. Individual features of a bicycle receive compact commentaries, while advice on riding skills encompasses practicalities, etiquette, and safety. Among other subjects are riding off-road and mountain biking, ways to train (illustrated through exercise photos), adjustments to riding in the elements, and making repairs on the road. "Dream trips" offers brief facts about ten cycling destinations. Near the end are packing checklists, keyed to the length and distance of a cycling trip, from weekend to cross-country and international. 237 p.

Cycle Europe: 20 Tours, 12 Countries / Jerry Soverinsky (MBI, 2004).
    Though the slick-paper and color photos seem to make the book a bit too attractive to take on a bicycle trip, that is nonetheless where it should be used. After a short introductory section about bikes and travel, there is the collection of routes. Self-touring directions for a day or more are put in a shaded box, where numbered miles mark the distance at arrival points, while the capped and bolded words "left," "right," and "straight" tell the cyclist what to do. Outside the box, accompanying text is broken into sections that give the region, addresses for tourist information, the location of bike shops, advice about the sights to see and the restaurants to stop at, and other practical observations. The cyclist author also provides thoughts about riding in various countries as well as anecdotes of his experiences. Large-scale maps trace the paths in mostly Western European countries. Somewhat weighty to be portable, this is intelligently and well designed. 400 p.

Cycling the USA: Bicycle Touring Nationwide / John Smith (Motorbooks International, 1997).
    Like *Cycle Europe* (above), the chief concern is not in the preliminary bit about how to prepare for a tour but in the routes taken. The division of the book is into regions of the country, with Alaska and Hawaii treated separately. Grouped under a state is the trip's name; distance in miles and kilometers; duration of the journey in days; its rating (easy, moderate, strenuous); whether it is a loop or one way; a description of its beginning and ending and sometimes the means of getting there; the geographic area where accommodations are available; and in the most substantial section, the things to see and directions about riding the route. The major tour is followed by others that may be a distance away, and they usually receive

briefer treatment. Clear maps show the road number(s) that the cyclist will take. For those cyclists who want more of a challenge, there is a collection of long tours. While the oblong work is portable, the text could do with more details, such as naming names of hotels, and it should have had a breakdown by mileage of significant spots along a route. 224 p.

The Essential Touring Cyclist: A Complete Guide for the Bicycle Traveler / Richard A. Lovett. 2nd ed. (Ragged Mountain Press, 2001).

The first half of this sensible and to-the-point narrative addresses in particular the touring beginner, giving chapter basics about bicycles and their equipment, wear for the rider, maintenance, hazards and trials of riding—described in the second part with more variety—and training for day tours. The last half discusses longer trips, which range from organized tours to those with decreasing degrees of logistical support but with more schedule flexibility and independence. The adventurous will find suggestions about outdoor equipment to carry and repairs and replacements for the bicycle. The author sizes up appropriate destinations, stopping places, navigation, and camping out, as well as the challenges of hills, wind, tunnels, etc. There are also short bits on transporting bicycles and traveling internationally. 160 p.

Organizations

Adventure Cycling Association. www.adventurecycling.org

Its magazine, *Adventure Cyclist* (9 per year), has accounts of journeys plus advice, reviews, and news of interest to cyclists. Once a year it also publish *The Cyclists' Yellow Pages*, a directory of worldwide bicycling organizations and tour operators that includes sources for books and maps, how-to information, and more. Examined website: 2008

BOOK REVIEWS

Find out what's new and what's relevant from reviews of travel books. Reviews can be found in both travel and non-travel publications.

To locate book reviews on any subject use the basic library resource *Book Review Index*, which indexes the contents of periodicals that entirely or selectively contain reviews. Or browse those travel magazines, newspapers, and websites that carry book reviews.

What follows is a collection of some of the more popular library-oriented periodicals dedicated just to reviews, including travel works. All are also available online.

Periodicals

Book Review Digest. 10 per year (H. W. Wilson Company).

Arranged by author, this periodical excerpts book reviews of both fiction and non-fiction works from some of the popular magazines and newspapers. Among the terms in the subject index is "voyages and travels." Conveniently, issues may be gathered together into a yearly cumulation. The *Digest* is also available electronically. Examined: 2008

Book Review Index. 3 per year (Gale/Cengage).

Containing citations only, it arranges them by author or title in this largest source for current book reviews. Unfortunately, there is no subject arrangement, so before conducting a search be prepared with an author or a title and, hopefully, a year. *BRI* is also available electronically. Examined: 2008

Booklist. Semimonthly (American Library Association).

With capsule reviews arranged by subject, this is a major book review magazine for librarians who buy books for public libraries. Examined: 2009

Library Journal. Semimonthly (Reed Business Information).

Containing many current reviews, the magazine puts its short reviews of travel guides as well as travel writings in a section called "Travel & Geography." Examined: 2009

BUDGET TRAVEL

Budget travel books explain how to save money on transportation, dining, lodging, and other particulars. Some emphasize one area over another. The subject of transportation—air, rail, and ground—receives a lot of space, from cheap tickets to passes. There are also directories of budget lodgings, which include budget motel and hotel chains. In this vein, many guidebooks class lodgings according to price.

Budgeting is relative. There are budget travelers who wish to save money without sacrificing much comfort. Then there are budget travelers whose lack of money obliges them to rough it. For them are hostels and cheap food. The most indigent of this group may be attracted to budget guides with words like "hitchhiking" and "vagabonding" in their titles.

"Free" is a word every budget traveler recognizes. There are books that provide lists of free attractions as well as sources for free information. Another form of enticement is coupon books, which have discounts on retailers, lodgings, restaurants, airlines, theaters, and tourist attractions.

Two segments of budget travelers for which there are guides are the aged and the student (or young) traveler. For both groups travel discounts exist. Since the young have a greater tendency to travel at the expense of comfort and safety, the best budget guides for them have a nitty-gritty practicality.

Industries have been built on ways of saving travelers money. Some may specialize in airfares, in accommodations, in tours, or in cruises; or like some travel "clubs," they may offer several of these services. Occasionally the subject of newspaper or magazine articles, the clubs offer bargain prices on cruises and package tours.

Some travel businesses, such as Trailfinders (headquartered in London), produce publications that may both promote their services and offer budgeting advice.

Besides this section, look in this book's appropriate categories for titles that have information about traditionally cheaper forms of transportation and accommodations—e.g., the bus and the hostel—or about discounts on the more expensive forms—as flying and hotels.

See also **Hitchhiking and Car Sharing**

Subject Heading: Travel costs

Titles

Backpacking and Camping in the Developing World: A How-to Adventure Guide for Travelling on Your Own or with a Group / Scott Graham

(Wilderness Press, 1988).

Traveling cheaply in the Third World presents special challenges and opportunities. Despite the words "backpacking and camping" in the main title, this book is mainly about the subtitled "travelling" in these countries. The book covers the same territory as regular travel advice books, but with an eye toward the twin special circumstances of traveling cheaply—avoiding the privileged tourist position—and adapting to non-Western countries. After short sections about Latin America, Africa, and Asia, there are looks at money, health, receiving mail, dealing with natives, ethical travel and all the other subjects that are part of this most basic form of traveling. 144 p.

The Cheapskate's Guide to Vacations: How to Save Thousands of Dollars No Matter Where You're Going / Stephen Tanenbaum. Revised and updated (Carol Publishing Group, 1999).

This is full of the author's first-person accounts about ways he discovered for traveling on the cheap or about experiences that he had. The text is interrupted by tips related to whatever subject is under discussion. The first quarter of the work offers advice about finding bargains (e.g., through promotions) and ways of saving money. The remainder discusses types of vacations (cruising, safari, package) and mentions a variety of destinations that the author has enjoyed. Whether the destinations are London, Tahiti, Israel, or other countries, there are suggestions about where to stay and what to see and do, with references to saving dough. The age of the book means that using the internet receives only a few pages, while specific tours that are named probably no longer exist. 299 p.

Consumer Reports Travel Well for Less / Editors of *Consumer Reports Travel Letter* (Consumers Union, 2002).

Very clear and level-headed in its explanations, the book amounts to a manual on how to travel and is based on an understanding of what the consumer should know and the working of the travel industry, along with its special words and abbreviations. In addition to money-saving tips, background facts could help the consumer in the management of travel plans or the consideration of less familiar options such as, say, charter airlines or extended stay hotels. Mostly canny advice on planning, using the web, airfares, accommodations, land transportation, tours, cruises, and other typical topics are supplemented through separate boxes and tables, such as the one where prominent guidebook series are evaluated by "personality," plus their strong and weak points. Plenty of bolded headings make for scanability (e.g., subdivisions are easier to find). A likely counterpart in Britain is *Which? Holiday* (Which Ltd.). A later edition is available. 340 p.

The Encyclopedia of Cheap Travel: 1,000 Companies, Consolidators, Agencies, and Resources / Terrance Zepke (Infinity Publishing, 2002).

A first chapter is on planning a trip and several consider best deals for tours, independent travel, airline tickets, cruises, and accommodations, plus there is a collection of fifty ways to travel free or receive payment for travel. The subject can be as narrow as, for example, solo travelers on tours, ground transport for the independent, air passes, hostels, and the vacation as a tax deduction. Overviews and discussions are supplemented through basic annotations to bolded names of businesses, organizations, and services on lists that should assist the traveler's quests. Not an encyclopedia in terms of alphabetized headings followed by a description, its broad size allows for a number of sources that would be of use to any traveler, besides the one seeking a cheap trip. 185 p.

Fly Free, Stay Cheap! / Vicki Mills. Revised (Platypus Publications, 1998).

In the heart of this slender work strategies are laid out for manipulating frequent flyer program miles in order to travel "free." Some of these deal with using credit cards for miles, where methods can be complicated or may not meet the approval of the credit card companies or may land the careless user in financial problems. Also, there is generic advice about budget travel, with some personal anecdotes, while several of the more expensive destinations are singled out with ways to enjoy them without spending a bundle. One stylistic gimmick is that the author bolds and capitalizes the word "free" whenever it appears in a sentence. 72 p.

Free U.S. Tourist Attractions: A Directory of Free Family Entertainment in Every State of the Union. 1998/1999 ed. (Pilot Books, 1998).

The plain directory by state has minimal information. Under the name of a town is the name of its attraction, the address, perhaps a very few words of description, general times when open, and a telephone number. Among the places are museums, historical sites, churches, houses, cemeteries, parks, companies that provide tours, and educational institutions. The completeness of the listings is unknown, and why a tourist would find it worthwhile to visit any of the facilities beyond the fact that they cost nothing is a question that will require a more informative travel book to answer. Also, it would have been helpful to have had maps giving an idea where in a state a town is located. 218 p.

Guerrilla Travel Tactics: Hundreds of Simple Strategies Guaranteed to Save Road Warriors Time and Money / Jay Conrad Levinson, Theo Brandt-Sarif (AMACOM, 2004).

The major theme of the book is saving money, with a secondary that of getting value for the same. Well over one-half is devoted to reducing the costs associated with airline flying, where advice might enlist such specialized terms as "open jaw ticketing," "code sharing," and "consolidators"; there are also thoughts about getting the most out of frequent flyer mileage and searching for bargains on the internet, which is additionally a resource in the part of the book about reserving hotel rooms. Extended stay and loyalty programs are among the accommodation strategies. Further coverage concerns car rentals and the advantages of complaining as a way for the proactive customer to protect his or her rights. Small gray boxes scattered throughout the text offer either tips about what to do or alerts about what to watch out for, though the distinction can be blurry. 273 p.

Insider Travel Secrets You're Not Supposed to Know! / Tom Parsons. 2nd ed. (Best Fares USA, 1998).

In a direct style the author explains many ways of saving money on travel, especially when it comes to flying. With familiarity he looks at keeping an eye open for air bargains, creative ticketing, investigating tour packages, usage of frequent flyer miles as applied to individual airlines, etc. In other chapters there is the expected advice on saving when it comes to hotels, car rentals, cruises, and train rides, as well as use of coupons and discounts. Details may be outdated when they include prices and address various rules specific to a business. Not all the themes involve the bottom line, for there are a large number of tips, both general and special, about traveling itself. The format of two columns per page enhances readability by surrounding paragraphs with white space and beginning them in bold. 447 p.

Pay-Nothing to Travel Anywhere You Like / PayNada.com editors (Great Pines Publishing, 1999).

Written in a slangy style and with an inside-dope attitude, a pay-nothing approach on each page (or occasionally more) comes with advice and contact information. The idea of traveling without cost may be true some of the time, but the authors appear to minimize the inevitable effort or trade-off, which may mean being a skilful complainer when things go wrong, performing lectures for board, or even stretching the truth. Despite the title, much space is based on the idea of reducing expenses, which may require trying airline or hotel consolidators, joining frequent customer programs, traveling at the time of hurricane season, taking cruises at the last minute, using coupon books, etc. A number of possibilities are different enough so that they will not be found in other save-money travel books. 94 p.

The Penny Pincher's Passport to Luxury Travel / Joel L. Widzer (Travelers' Tales, 1999).

In a quest to reduce expenses on luxury travel, the author has a discussion about off-season and other destinations where the supply of tourists is less than the demand, and follows with other chapters about getting your money's worth, the strategies of tipping, being fairly compensated for mishaps, etc. Throughout first-person travel experiences are used to illuminate a subject, while at a chapter's end is a summary of the points made in the text. The suggestions are sensible, well-represented, knowledgeable, and not lacking ethical conscience. The reader who seeks savings on basics rather than luxuries might prefer to consult *Consumer Reports Travel Well for Less* and other titles in this section. 242 p.

Travel Smart. Monthly (Communications House). www.travelsmart newsletter.com

In addition to its general features on travel, the newsletter reports on deals in air, accommodations, and car rentals as well as other means of saving money. Examined website: 2008

The World's Cheapest Destinations: 21 Countries Where Your Dollars Are Worth a Fortune / Tim Leffel (Booklocker.com, Inc., 2003).

The author profiles seven countries in Asia, the same number in the Americas, three in Africa and the Middle East, and four in Europe. There are introductory remarks about a country and its cheapness, then separate sections have several paragraphs on accommodations, locally available food and drink, travel within the country, and more. This is not a resource for addresses of hotels or restaurants, but expect general advice on the kinds of accommodations or eating, always with the cost in mind. Street-smart warnings are issued about hassles and other problems that the individual may have to accept if traveling on the cheap, but the addition of how-to specifics would have been welcome. A revised, larger edition is available. 113 p.

You Can Travel Free / Robert Wm Kirk (Pelican Publishing Company, 1998).

Besides offering more options and more advice than many competitors, the thick, professionally accomplished book also devotes chapters to its subjects where others may have a subsection. As with them, the use of the word "free" is relative, since strings of some kind—joining a club for a fee, making trades, etc.—are attached. There are several bargains that apply only to specific places, as free things to do in London or free flights from Los Angeles. Some of the travel opportunities are illustrated through different personal experiences, though it is not always clear if they are accounts of real life cases. Names and descriptions of organizations appear in chapter discussions on free accommodations; cruising; staying in someone else's home; hosting group tours; sightseeing; volunteering; grants and scholarships; working vacations; travel careers; teaching overseas; teaching your own language; and others. 492 p.

Publishers

Entertainment Publications. www.entertainment.com
So far as travel is concerned, it offers book titles containing restaurant, hotel, and amusement discounts for a selection of American and Canadian cities. Examined website: 2008

Frommer's Travel Guides. www.frommers.com
A name long associated with the idea of traveling on a budget, Frommer's has a web presence that offers a variety of services and advice, plus a broad series of guidebooks (e.g., *Arthur Frommer's $-a-Day Guides*). Examined website: 2008

BUS TRAVEL

Reasons for choosing the bus can be its relative cheapness, its ability to go where no plane, boat, or train does, and its convenience as a form of public transport. Also, bus travel can be intracity, intercity, or international. Especially in Europe, international boundaries may be frequently crossed, so it is convenient to choose among the bus lines that function like Eurail, allowing on and offs throughout the continent, such as Busabout (www.busabout.com) and Eurolines (www.eurolines.com).

Like trams and the subway, buses are a major type of public urban transportation. Some guidebooks are so helpful as to list bus numbers to popular tourist sites. Tourist information counters and bus depots or headquarters are likely distributors of bus schedules and routes (which may also be available online). Other good bets are hotels, bed and breakfasts, and hostels.

Subject Heading: Bus travel

Titles

Russell's Official National Motor Coach Guide. Monthly (Russell's Guides).

Covering the United States and Canada, this standard arranges its long-distance timetables by bus line, with Greyhound Lines taking up the largest space. The means of finding departures and destinations is to begin by either locating table numbers on major lines' accompanying route maps or checking the alphabetized town and city index in back of the volume. Too typical of such displays, reading and interpretation of what is there require effort, especially where there are many stops. Had there been alternating white and shaded areas across, the eye could follow relatively effortlessly. Among other details are codes for days of the week and many symbols encompassing types of stops and agency services. Examined: issue from 2003; 352 p.

CALENDAR INFORMATION

Events, festivals, and historic anniversaries furnish purposes for visiting another state or country. Conversely, an unforeseen holiday or event may mean closed shops or otherwise seriously thwart travel plans.

Practical country guidebooks present a yearly sequence of important dates, while individually published books consisting of dates in calendar arrangement supplement the coverage. Dates in books may designate festivals, fairs, holidays, anniversaries, and performing arts events. Also, newspapers may periodically carry a calendar of activities that can be local or a day trip away.

Calendar publications such as the bimonthly *Association Meetings* are aimed at the convention planner and business traveler. They cover dates for meetings, conferences, and trade shows, and they may describe the site of the event.

Calendar information should be current, though older material can have some use. Anniversaries and holidays may re-occur predictably, but festivals can move around, and events may be once in a lifetime.

Titles

Holidays, Festivals, and Celebrations of the World Dictionary: Detailing Nearly 2,500 Observances from All 50 States and More Than 100 Nations . . . / edited by Helene Henderson. 3rd ed. (Omnigraphics, 2005).

The main section of this large reference presents short histories in an alphabetical list of holidays, festivals, and celebrations, though details from a tourist point-of-view are omitted. Contact information for a country's travel, tourism, or other relevant agency concludes some entries, and later a select number of addresses are gathered in appendixes, one of which has legal holidays by country. The appendixes and many indexes, sizably contribute to the bulk. Among the latter the most important to the traveler are two arranged by month—with events on fixed days or within a recurring time period able to provide when-to-go information for a trip. Additional indexes offer a subject approach by categories, while a general index includes countries and states. Further facts about some of the obscurer holidays are available in another reference work, *The Folklore of World Holidays*, edited by Robert H. Griffin and Ann H. Shurgin (Gale, 1999), though it lacks a geographical index. 906 p.

CAMPING AND CAMPGROUNDS

Camping is here treated as a function of travel, not as a part of woodlore.

There are books on camping by train and especially by various types of four-wheel vehicles. Most camping-travel books concentrate on Europe and the United States.

There are camping directories that describe both public and commercial campgrounds, while campground chains (such as KOA) may have directories in print or online. Summer camp directories inform about recreational and learning opportunities for the young, while other directories look at different styles of camping, such as by recreational vehicle. (Note that recreational vehicle clubs are among those listed in the *Encyclopedia of Associations*.)

The U.S. government has agencies with jurisdiction over its camping areas. The Bureau of Land Management (www.blm.gov) has the greatest amount of acres, while the Fish and Wildlife Service (www.fws.gov) offers few chances for camping at its National Wildlife Refuge System. The Forest Service site (www.fs.fed.us) can be searched for camping information, and the National Park Service's parks are the subject of several commercial directories (see **Parks, Safaris, and the Outdoors**). At its website the U.S. Army Corps of Engineers (www.usace.army. mil/visitors) provides searches for lake recreation areas.

Subject Headings: Camp sites, facilities, etc.; Camping; Trailer camps

Titles

Backpacking with Babies & Small Children: A Guide to Taking the Kids Along on Day Hikes, Overnighters, and Long Trail Trips / Goldie Silverman. 3rd ed. (Wilderness Press, 1998).

That so much can be written in intelligent detail about this special issue is a testament to the author's knowledge. The interested parent will find advice in chapters which deal with a spectrum of topics, among them the age to start a child on a hike; the clothing to choose based on weather conditions; diapers; shoes; packs to carry kids or for kids to carry; food and cooking; entertainment; hygiene; and safety. While there are general comments about camping, the focus is always on the care of the child who is outdoors. Photographs are with the text, which is designed for reading through rather than for quick reference. 166 p.

Camping Europe / Carol Mickelsen. 2nd ed. (Affordable Travel Press, 2001).

Arrangement is by country, with each receiving an overview of its history, scenery, transportation system, and camping status, and what follows that is arrangement by region or city. For the tourist an idea of a place's attraction can be from a few sentences to a few paragraphs. Asterisks set off information about nearby camping, with clipped phrases about where the site is and driving directions; and perhaps something about the amenities, the dates when the campground is open, and a price range vaguely signified by the number of $ signs. Most pages have simple shaded road maps that encompass large areas and signal the location of campsites. In covering so many Western and Eastern European countries and Turkey, much is omitted about the sights, so a country guidebook would be one worthwhile supplement. There is a small amount of preliminary matter about the practicalities of camping. A later edition is available. 348 p.

National Park Service Camping Guide / William C. Herow. 2nd ed. (Roundabout Publications, 2004).

After its name and address, a national park (or recreation area, monument, etc.) is typically described in three paragraphs, the first giving its location in the state, date of founding, its features, and entrance fee; the second something about its visitor's or information center; and the third an overview of the campgrounds. A chart of park activities is represented through icons, from biking and hiking to birding and skiing, while a separate set of symbols for each NPS campground shows such sometime amenities as RV capability, showers, swimming area, and equestrian trails. While contributing to the book's convenience, the icons do require flipping to the front in order to decipher them. Under a campground's name short comments include its relative location, months when open, its number of sites, cost, and the maximum length of stay. The states where the parks are located are rendered in black-and-white maps that trace the major highways. 240 p.

Trailer Life Campgrounds, RV Parks & Services Directory. Annual (T.L. Enterprises). www.tldirectory.com

Affiliated with the Good Sam Club (which is for RV owners), the large and thick directory is similar in design to *Wheelers* and *Woodall's* (below). Arranged by state or province and town, entries contain such information about a campground as its elevation, dates when open, driving directions, condition of interior roads, direction from town, and a collection of details related to sites, facilities, and the recreation available.

Also referenced are last year's rates, credit cards accepted, and contact means. Three separate ratings (up to 10) measure completeness of facilities, cleanliness and physical features of restrooms and showers, and visual appeal of the park. A group of state highway maps in color precede those for Canadian provinces, and there is one for Mexico; coordinates to the maps are with the entries. Here and there tourist areas within a state or province may be spotlighted, while ads for certain campgrounds supplement their entries. Examined: 2004; 1932 p.

Traveler's Guide to European Camping: Explore Europe with RV or Tent / Mike and Terri Church. 3rd ed. (Rolling Homes Press, 2004).

Much more attractively arranged than *Camping Europe* (above), this good-sized book also presents much more information about the campgrounds themselves, which are arranged by country or country groups. Campground entries adhere to a fixed format, with the bolded name followed by bolded headings for address, telephone, fax, website, e-mail, and GPS. By the side of this group a small road map shows nearby towns and the campground. Dates of opening precede a flurry of icons signifying reservations, tents, handicapped access, restaurants, swimming, pets allowed, telephone, bus, etc. The remainder of information composes several paragraphs that describe the camp's location, its facilities, its closeness to a town or city, and its route for drivers. The city, town, or area close to the campers separately receives just a few lines covering its touristy features. Introductory matter considers buying or renting a camping vehicle, driving in Europe, various aspects of a campground, and other things. The treatment is intelligent and useful. 639 p.

Wheelers RV Resort & Campground Guide. Annual (Print Media Services).

Reminiscent of a large yellow pages directory, the three-column pages include advertisements among the entries. Arrangement under a state or Canadian province is by city and town, though in the few pages dedicated to Mexico, it is simply by city and town. A division determined between private and public parks encompasses a range of classifications (e.g., recreational vehicle park, Bureau of Land Management), with the private also receiving a star ranking of from one to five, the highest being for the parks that are "above the norm in many respects." Name, telephone number, highway location and driving directions precede a list of possible amenities and activities (dump, flush toilets, showers, boating, etc.), the cost range, seasons of operation, and mail address. A code references a town or city on a road map for every state and some provinces. Examined: 2002; 767 p.

Woodall's North America Campground Directory. Annual (Woodall's Publications).

Not for those who wish to travel light, this thick directory divides the U.S. and Canada into east and west parts, with Mexico among the latter. Introductions to states and provinces briefly profile their attractions by region. The directory principally lists campgrounds (private, public, and military), but there are also tourist attraction sites and RV sales and service locations. Under a town or city is an entry's name; driving directions; particular campground facilities rated by a combination of type, number, and quality; and recreation opportunities separately rated. Other information includes seasons when open, telephone number, and perhaps rates in dollars and e-mail address. Letter/number coordinates refer back to black-and-white state or province maps, which show major and secondary roads along with lakes, waterways, and parks. Ads large and small are amid the three-column pages. Consider this title a companion to *Woodall's Tenting Directory* (below). Examined: 2004; 1952 p.

Woodall's Tenting Directory. Annual (Woodall Publications). www.woodalls.com

It covers the United States, Canada and, very lightly, Mexico. Introducing a state or province is a relatively detailed road map followed by an alphabetical, quick-reference chart of the parks that shows map coordinates, total number of sites, and various activities. Under state or Canadian province and town or city, the entry is a private or public park or campground typified by name, compactly worded driving directions, and a section for facilities (number of sites, hookups, presence of cabins, laundry, groceries, etc.) and for recreation (lake swimming, boating, hiking, basketball, playground, etc.). Other facts encompass handicap access, times when open, and telephone number. Ads are among the entries, which omit icons and websites and go easy on abbreviations. A front section on diversions such as bicycling, birding, hiking, rafting, and campground activities describes some of the localities where these can be enjoyed. See also *Woodall's North America Campground Directory* (above). Examined: 2007; 528 p.

COMPLAINTS

First, deal directly with the entity (airline, tour company, or whatever) you hold responsible for the problem. If that is unsatisfactory learn from consumer directories the appropriate governmental or private agency that handles complaints. If that finally proves disappointing there remains the option of hiring a lawyer.

Different problems require different approaches. In instances where there is a dispute over a credit card payment, contact the issuer of the card, while safety concerns may be an issue for the National Transportation Board, which fields complaints and supplies information about travel by land, water and air. Concerns about air travel—other than safety or security issues—are the province of the Aviation Consumer Protection Division of the U.S. Department of Transportation (see **Air Travel**). A dispute with a travel agent might be arbitrated by travel agent organizations, and a tour operator who presents problems might better be dealt with by one's travel agent or the agency's owner.

To find which federal government agency handles a specific complaint, call toll free the Federal Citizen Information Center (pueblo. gsa.gov) or contact the Department of Justice's Office of Consumer Litigation (www.usdoj.gov/civil/ocl/index.htm), which deals with consumer protection statutes and will refer consumer complaints to other departments. These may have their own consumer affairs section, such as the aforementioned Department of Transportation's Aviation Consumer Protection Division.

For state assistance speak with your state's attorney general office, which oversees consumer complaints, though remember that if the company that is the cause of your concern is located in another state, it is there that you must apply. Another agency is the state's consumer affairs department, whose address, besides being available online, is in the state's official manual or *Consumer Action Handbook* (below).

Subject Heading: Consumer protection

Titles

Consumer Action Handbook. Annual (Federal Citizen Information Center, United States General Services Administration). www.consumeraction.gov

A small part of this work deals with the subject of travel, where there are tips on the means of resolving air travel problems, advice about protecting the customer's valuables, and a short list of sources that contain travel safety information. Two-thirds of the book's content is a directory that includes addresses of state, county, and city consumer protection offices as well as that of federal agencies that handle complaints, plus Better Business Bureaus and national consumer organizations. One means of finding those groups that relate to travel is to turn to the index, where "travel" is a heading with several references. The title is available online and in print. Examined: 2007; 174 p.

Organizations

American Society of Travel Agents. www.travelsense.org/consumer/index.cfm
    The world's largest travel trade association will investigate complaints from customers about its own members and will try for a solution. The site with which it is associated also contains travel tips. Examined website: 2008

Attorney General Offices.
    Contact the Attorney General Office of the state where the business in question is located. Online, find the addresses from the National Association of Attorneys General at www.naag.org/ag/full_ag_table.php or the state's official manual, which may also be in paper form. Among other sources a list may be found in the *Consumer Action Handbook* (above) and in the annual *CSG State Directory*.

Better Business Bureau. www.bbb.org/alerts/Travel.asp
    The Bureau facilitates communication between disputing parties and may make mediation available. At the online site is advice for travelers. One resource for BBB state addresses is the *Consumer Action Handbook* (above). Examined website: 2008

United States Tour Operators Association. www.ustoa.com
    One means that a traveler has of gaining some protection from companies that become insolvent is to limit himself or herself to those who are part of this professional group, which promotes a code of ethics, member accountability, and attempts to resolve complaints. Examined website: 2008

COMPUTERS AND THE INTERNET

Sit down at an internet computer terminal and browse the numberless travel websites. While there are travel databases available only through subscription, most of them are free. A shopper may compare prices and then reserve an airplane seat, a hotel room, a cruise berth, or a rental car. More than travel books, sites range from an everything approach to a single aspect of travel (work abroad, adventure trips, security, etc.) to highly specialized interests.

A credible starting place is the Yahoo! travel section (travel.yahoo. com). Also, look for publisher websites, such as Lonely Planet (www.lonelyplanet.com) or Moon Publications (www.moon. com).

Online searching is a craft that cannot be realistically covered in the following few sentences. Briefly, three general rules should guide the searcher: (1) Pick the "right" database—one that includes the subject sought. (2) Pick the words that best describe it. If necessary experiment by substituting related words, or words that are more specific or general. (3) Determine how the database handles search commands. For example, it may or may not default to the operator "and," which instructs the computer to combine terms. To find out about online searching, look for books about the topic or ask a librarian.

Offshoots of the computer are used for activities other than database searching. There is a crop of dedicated, handheld devices that will translate languages, determine money conversion rates, provide GPS coordinates, or contain electronic "books." Buy them from electronic dealers and at travel shops. These small computerized devices and their big brothers will continue to expand their abilities.

Keep in mind that due to the volatile nature of the internet, website addresses may have changed or disappeared by the time a book containing them has been published. If the address given doesn't work, as an alternative try to search by the title of the website through Google or a similar search engine.

Subject Heading: Travel—Computer network resources

Titles

The Incredible Internet Guide to Adventurous & Unusual Travel / Marc Dauphinais & Michael L. Sankey (Facts on Demand Press, 2001).

This title highlights an area relatively skimped on in works about electronic travel sites, though they do list a greater number of URLs. Varieties of outdoor activities and those of particular interests compose the substance of this book. Among the categories are adventures associated with water, fishing and hunting, the yesterday years, rugged challenges (such as paragliding and llama trekking), cultural journeys, sports, and theme camps for children. There are also listings for tour operators and a small amount related to aspects of traveling. In the summaries of varying lengths there is little about navigation or design and seldom evaluative comments about the websites, which are occasionally reproduced as they appear on the computer screen, thereby adding to information about them. 241 p.

Online Travel / Ed Perkins (Microsoft Press, 2000).

Despite the word *Online* in the title, this is chiefly a book of knowledgeable travel advice that has a supplement of reputable sites. Breaking the text throughout are graphic boxes plus bordered remarks that discuss special aspects of the subject covered in a chapter. The expected suspects are treated: destinations, activities, air travel, accommodations, cruising, vacation packages, trains, problems, etc. An appendix contains a list of subject-divided sites, some repeated from the text, but none with annotations. Since the author has written in the past from the view of the consumer, this bias shows itself in the emphasis on using money with prudence, knowing the rights of a traveler, and protecting oneself from rip-offs. For those who would like a better balance of travel advice with surfing websites there is *Sams Teach Yourself Today E-Travel* (below), which similarly comes with various illustrations of web pages. 272 p.

*The Rough Guide to Travel Online / Samantha Cook and Greg Ward (Rough Guides, 2002).

With a British bias, this list of travel-related websites is in three large parts. Before plunging into the basics of traveling, the first begins by spending several knowledgeable pages on how to use search engines. Then there are reviews of sites of guidebook publishers, airlines and air ticket sellers, bus networks, insurance, weather, etc. The second part highlights particular activities or themes that travelers might seek out and the requirements of particular types of travelers, while the third is arranged by country, Antarctica to Zimbabwe. The intelligent summaries describe what is on a site and how navigable it is for the searcher, and an inclusion in this book serves as a recommendation of a site's stability and content. Though much is crammed into this small but thick *Rough Guide*, the design is friendly, with a blue banner highlighting the site name, its address printed below in the same color, and the text in black- and-white. A later edition is available. 432 p.

Sams Teach Yourself Today E-Travel / Mark Orwoll (Sams, 2000).
Blending a travel advice guide with coverage of online travel resources, the book identifies the familiar types of information helpful to travelers and tells them where to find the information and how to use it, as in booking a hotel, airline seat, or train reservation. The sites highlighted are of quality, but the continuous bantering tone and joking asides will likely be an annoyance for some readers and may cast a suspect light on the author's judgment. At the beginning of every subject chapter there is a useful summary in the margin of major points to be explored, which are repeated with different wording at the end. There is also a little instruction about such technology matters as finding a search engine, arranging bookmarks, and testing the reliability of sites, plus observations both about bringing a laptop and taking digital photographs. A list at book's end groups some of the websites mentioned in the discussions. For those who care to skip "how to" advice and prefer annotations of serviceable websites, see *The Rough Guide to Travel Online* (above). 302 p.

The Software Encyclopedia. Annual (Bowker).
This large, two-volume work can be consulted as a general print source that lists various programs for the computer. Look for a subsection on travel guides under the heading "Transportation and Travel," where each title comes with a summary along with the name of the publisher. Arrangement is by system (Apple, IBM PC, etc.). Examined: 2007; 2 vol. (3118 p.)

Travel Planning on the Internet: The Click and Easy Guide / Ronald L. Krannich, Caryl Rae Krannich (Impact Publications, 2001).
Well beyond the pocket size of some similar titles reviewed in this section, on the one hand *Travel Planning on the Internet* outclasses them in wordage about the sites it chooses to describe, and on the other scatters numerous lists of addresses throughout the volume without any annotations at all, particularly noticeable under the destinations chapter, contrarily the most expansive subject for the other books. Additional major areas come with discussions and with URLs concerning gateways into travel, types of travelers, interests and activities, basics for traveling, guidebooks, media, forms of transportation, accommodations, and online buying and booking. Some of the sites mentioned are no longer available and some are of questionable merit. The beginning is an elementary introduction to web searching and a short look at newsgroups and lists. 260 p.

The Traveler's Web: An Extreme Searcher Guide to Travel Resources on the Internet / Randolph Hock (CyberAge Books, 2007).

The collection of websites that are mostly free to use is categorized by their subjects, the most substantial two dealing with travel guides online and with reservation services for flights and hotels. Other subjects concern resource guides; trains, cars, and ferries; cruises; finding a place to stay and what to eat; adventure, outdoor, and educational travel; special groups (e.g., families) and special needs; countries; and practicalities. A paragraph or more may include the purpose, content, or features of the site, and sometimes there is a consideration of how to navigate through it. Sections of advice about researching and discovering the particular thing that is sought appear strategically in the chapters. Each topic area concludes with a list of discussion groups and forums. This is a title that encompasses a lot of information. 400 p.

The Traveller's Internet Guide / edited by Jonathan Lorie and Amy Sohanpaul. 2nd ed. (WEXAS, 2002).

In this collection of websites, over half are in a chapter arranged by destination. Presented in a plain layout, they are briefly glossed in terms of what each offers or its purpose, sometimes with a few words on its usefulness—but usually the view is non-evaluative. A few countries, like the U.S., are under both general entries and subdivisions by state, province, or other administrative unit. Another section, on trip preparation, rounds up sites about the weather, health, safety, red tape, maps, booksellers, travel journalism, travelogues, equipment, food, drink, etc. A few frontal pages devote themselves to explanations about searching and buying online, and in the back there is short advice on computers and their use as a way to augment traveling. 208 p.

The Virgin Internet Travel Guide: Version 1.0 / Davey Winder (Virgin Publishing, 2000).

More substantial than *The Traveller's Internet Guide* (above), its early portion explains what is special about the internet, and then deliberates on ways of performing searches. The chapters on travel provide lists of online addresses whose annotations typically mix brief but astute description with evaluation. Although the chapter focusing on traveling considers exchange rates, health, packing, working abroad, etc., a number of categories are lacking, and in some instances a sprinkling of quirky sites stand out as unnecessary amid a finite number of general ones; for example, a dozen electronic language references include "Cockney Online" and "Survival Maltese." The longest chapter concerns destinations while another offers types of activity holidays. There are also URLs for travel by air and other means, for accommodations, for going in luxury, and a miscellany for what this small, portable book calls "the seasoned traveler." A later edition is available. 247 p.

You Are Here Traveling with JohnnyJet.com / Eric Leebow with John E. DiScala (Yahbooks, 2003). www.johnnyjet.com

Unlike *The Rough Guide to Travel Online* and *The Traveller's Internet Guide*, there is very little about destination websites. Instead discover a stimulating variety of online sources that offer something about traveling or about activities that may be enjoyed on vacation. Links are in such usual categories as saving money on fares; lodging; ground transportation; enjoying the outdoors; health; and travel for the family, for seniors, for students, and for those in business. Yet there are also some detours, as ways of fighting hotel room boredom, sources aimed at flight crews and pilots, and facts on frequent flyer and other mileage programs. Entries consist of site name, URL, and a short description, which evaluates neither content nor design. The title assumes at-hand access to the internet, which is more of a challenge to the traveler on the road. The book is a counterpart to its website, which likewise carries links to featured web pages. 531 p.

DISTANCES

Knowing the distance from a destination has both a practical and intellectual attraction. Practically, distance plus speed determines the hours of a trip and figures in its cost; the distance a car will travel affects how much money must be set aside for gas, and while gas cost is hidden in a plane ticket, knowledge of flight distance can inform a passenger how many frequent flyer miles may be accrued. Apprehension of distance also gives an educational perspective on how near or far a place is, and it satisfies curiosity.

While the scale on general maps allows for calculation of approximate distance, road maps have mileage figures marked along their routes or on charts of distances between important cities. Most detailed are book-length distance tables that cover the world. Additionally, distances may be contained in air, land, and water timetables. For example, the railroad schedules put out by Thomas Cook contain distances, as do some Eurail guides and books about day trips.

On the internet a number of sites can calculate the distance between two points. Find them with a search engine by trying such a phrase as "distance between cities."

See also **Railroad Travel**

Subject Heading: Distances—Tables

Titles

Direct-Line Distances: International Edition / Gary L. Fitzpatrick and Marilyn J. Modlin (The Scarecrow Press, 1986).
Direct-Line Distances: United States Edition / Gary L. Fitzpatrick and Marilyn J. Modlin (The Scarecrow Press, 1986).

The small print tables in kilometers (*International Edition*) or miles (*United States Edition*) that fill the volumes are twenty columns across and one hundred rows down, the latter bundled in groups of four with a blank line on either side so that tracing to the horizontal and vertical intersection is easier. Table headings are alphabetized place names preceding numbers that answer the shortest distance between two points. Both books repeat most of the same locations, though some will be found in one and not in another; yet either claims in its introduction that it cites "1001 cities, towns, islands, and other places around the world." Line-drawn maps show the location of places that are used in the tables. Designed as a reference, their hard-cover and large size make them less than mobile. Both are 275 p.

Rand McNally Dist-O-Map: Travel Distance Finder (Rand McNally & Company, 1995).

A simple red and blue road atlas of the continental United States has been sectioned into six regions. Behind each map is attached a rotating wheel with city names on its perimeter that allows the viewer to "dial" a distance between points. While the only routes drawn are principal highways—interstate, federal, and state—this is still a handy way of simultaneously getting a sense of where the destinations are physically located and the numbered miles to them. Some smaller communities have also been marked on the maps themselves, but their mileages are not on the wheels. A final coast-to-coast map with a wheel contains the interstates and the largest cities. A newer edition is available. 7 p.

EATING (AND DRINKING)

Travelers have common questions about eating: Where do I find a good (or cheap, or any) place to eat? Where do I find local (or American, etc.) food? How do I understand the menu?

To answer the first two questions, look for help at tourist offices or see the restaurant sections in city guides, such as complimentary ones found in some hotels. Chapters on eating and drinking appear in general guidebooks, while several specialty guidebooks are dedicated to the subject. They may group restaurants by specialties served, such as vegetarian dishes. Also, accommodation guides often discuss restaurants, telephone directories contain listings for them, and locals will give advice.

The most detailed information is found in restaurant guidebooks which commonly rate food, service, and atmosphere; these guidebooks may be multi-country, country, or city. The *Michelin Red Guides* series is better publicized for its restaurant evaluations than it is for its hotel ratings. American counterparts are the *Mobil* series and the *Zagat*, which uses patrons rather than critics as judges.

Descriptions of cheap eateries are in budget guides. Although they may not name the McDonald's and Kentucky Fried Chickens of the world, these chains may be found most conveniently by wandering through a city's commercial area. A dedicated chain lover can search online for locations, preferably before a trip. Or see if the destination's telephone directory contains these brand names, which will offer the taste of the familiar, though perhaps with a local twist.

When a foreign restaurant does not have a menu with parallel English text or an employee who is bilingual, translate a menu with specialized and general language books or with an electronic translator.

There are alternatives to eating in a restaurant. Buy food in a grocery store or, keeping in mind potential health risks, a meal from a street vendor. Find them through serendipity or ask for information.

Should *drinking* not be described with the restaurant section in country guides, see if there's a section about bars and nightlife. Fodor's guides and others treat this separately.

Titles

America's Best Hotels and Restaurants: Mobil Four-Star and Five-Star Award Winners (Exxon Mobil Travel Publications).

A more exclusive counterpart to *America's Top Restaurants* (below), the *Mobil* annual uses professional judges rather than a survey and has a little more detail. It also features many less restaurants, while including hotels. In the listing a restaurant icon precedes four and occasionally five stars, below which are name, web and physical address, and telephone number. Several sentences may discuss the restaurant's décor and food. Another grouping is a variety of short facts, which typically designates the type of cuisine, hours, days closed, if reservations are accepted, the price range, parking, and credit cards that are honored. Common icons identify if there are facilities for people with disabilities and if smoking is allowed. Similar to hotels, restaurant entries are under state and city. In one form or another *Mobil* guides have been around for a long time. Also see this title under **Accommodations** and its subdivision, "Hotels and Motels." For later editions the title has undergone changes. Examined: 2002; 276 p.

America's Top Restaurants (Zagat Survey).
　　The Zagat Survey has produced many city and regional guides, especially for the U.S., using feedback from the customer as the means of arriving at a judgment. This oblong, compact title appears regularly, with evaluated eateries grouped under names of cities or areas. The plain and effective format shows the restaurant name, address, and telephone number before a brief review that assembles together customer quotes, which lean typically, but not exclusively, to the laudatory (since the restaurants entered here are supposed to be "top"). Supplementing and quantifying the description are numbers based on a 1 to 30 range, with the higher the number the better the quality; they rank food, décor, and service. A fourth category, meal price, bears a dollar amount or occasionally a letter for an amount range. Among the few symbols are those for highest ratings and for serving hours. Restaurants with top food rankings also appear, by area, in a front separate section, as do those judged to be the most popular. An end section arranges area restaurants by cuisine. This is a solid and democratic resource. The title has had various changes. Examined: 2007; 348 p.

The Artichoke Trail: A Guide to Vegetarian Restaurants, Organic Food Stores & Farmers' Markets in the US / James Bernard Frost (Hunter, 2000).
　　Arranged by city and state under each region of the country, the larger half of the work concisely flies through a number of vegetarian restaurants in its discussions, parenthesizing their street addresses and telephone numbers. However, a few restaurants are highlighted, where in a separate block they are rated from "fair" to "must visit," priced, labeled by cuisine, and marked for days open; additional paragraphs consider their atmosphere, choice dishes, quality, and the like. Small and simple state

maps show the relationship of major highways to the restaurants. Although there may also be brief observations on the presence of tourist attractions, the title should not be mistaken for a general travel guide. The second, substantial half of the book is a plain alphabetical-by-state listing of farmers' markets, with just name, address, telephone number, and the days or season when open. 435 p.

Eat Smart in . . . (series) / Joan and David Peterson (Ginkgo Press).
    While not billing itself as a series, all titles by the same authors begin *Eat Smart in* and are followed by a country and the subtitle *How to Decipher the Menu, Know the Market Foods & Embark on a Tasting Adventure. Eat Smart in Mexico* commences with a historical survey concerning the cuisine, which is then considered in terms of regions and their specialties. Numerous recipes are provided plus a brief section of tips on shopping. A few pages of useful phrases for restaurants and markets are translated into Spanish, beside which are phonetic pronunciations. Taking up the most space, a menu guide defines each restaurant dish, usually mentioning its ingredients and as appropriate observing where it is a specialty. A more succinct second list of food, spices, kitchen utensils, and cooking terms often functions only as words for translation. Travelers who wish to learn about native food rather than have just a quick translation of keywords will find this is the resource to consult. Examined: *Eat Smart in Mexico* (1998; 142 p.).

European Menu Reader: For Eating out in over 25 Countries. 2nd revised ed. (Berlitz Publishing Company, 1997).
    This is about the same size as the *European Menu Translator* (below), but more polished and over twice its thickness, containing translations in an alphabetical arrangement of fifteen languages, from Czech to Swedish. Each language section begins with a guide to pronouncing individual consonants, vowels, and diphthongs, though there is no phonetic guide when it comes to the words. Useful or common words and expressions are grouped under the headings of "hungry," "asking," "ordering," "the bill," "complaints," and "numbers," with the English given first. However, a food glossary gives the native term before the English, and may elaborate the definitions or cross-index the English words and expressions. Greek and Russian are given in their non-Roman alphabet, and then parenthetically re-spelled. This work has the proverbial fault of trading depth for breadth, through omitting a considerable number of food words from the various languages in order to put what it offers in a manageable compass. A later edition is available. 320 p.

European Menu Translator / Whitney H. and Anne T. Galbraith (Creative Minds Press, 2002).

The countries of France, Germany, Italy, and Spain receive a little over twenty double-columned pages apiece of food-related translations. The bolded native word or words are simply translated into their English equivalent, yet may be left undefined; for example, "pastis" is stated to be a "Pernod," but what is a "Pernod"? Words for numbers, days of the week, the months, and expressions of courtesy are also among the translations, though not for every language. Besides being used to clarify a restaurant's menu, the *Translator*—small enough to fit in the back pocket of a pair of jeans—could also assist a shopper in a food market. Front matter gives a few words of advice about dining out in Europe in general and the four countries in particular. There is no guide to pronunciation. 120 p.

Main Cities of Europe. Annual (Michelin).

Arrangement is alphabetical by Western European countries, with a little of Eastern thrown in, and then by major cities, where hotels are grouped before restaurants and the latter are ranked from luxury (represented by five forks and spoons) to quite comfortable (a single pair). Every page squeezes in numerous brief entries that are heavy on numbers and special markings. Taking between one to two lines is the name, address, telephone number, fax, and symbols for types of credit cards and a few other items. The next line may have days or dates closed and the price range for a set menu or one that is à la carte. There are one or two lines of description and sometimes a collection of menu specialties, but those expecting more in-depth judgments should seek elsewhere. A color map presents a large view of each city, and lines "square" the city into sections that are designated by letters, which are used both by an accompanying street index and as location keys in the restaurant entries. The cover has a convenient flap of the symbols and their meaning. Though not including every European country, the title is the geographically broadest among the *Michelin Red Guides* series, known for its multilingual ratings for restaurants and hotels of Europe, beyond which it has recently expanded. See another review of this title under **Accommodations**. Examined: 2003; 882 p.

Menu Reader's Dictionary (Peter Collin Publishing, 2000).

French, German, Italian, and Spanish are the four languages where food words are translated into English and vice-versa. If the diner doesn't know what a food term means or is confused by the occasional British terminology—as with "mushy peas"—there is seldom an elaboration, and absence of phonetic pronunciation invites mangling of a language if real life ordering is attempted. Launching each language segment is matter that has types of its country's eateries, how a menu is divided, the times when meals are usually eaten, the symbols representing a restaurant rating, expressions categorized under a few headings (such as "ordering" and "complaints"), and a translation of numbers one through ten. Of handy size, there are two columns per page, with each headword bolded. 215 p.

The Non-Connoisseur's Menu Guide to Ordering and Enjoying French, Italian, and Spanish/Latin American Cuisine / David D'Aprix (Living Language, 1999).

Like a lighter version of the *Eat Smart in* series (above), the oblong, portable guide—mostly annotated lists—does some educating of its reader about food and drink, which are grouped under headings that may be unique to a country; so pizzas are only under Italy and tapas are only under Spain and Latin America, though in a few cases (aperitifs, entrees, desserts) the same headings apply to all the countries. The foreign item, usually of several words, is followed by a clear phonetic pronunciation and a short explanation of what it is. Words appearing here may afterward be repeated in a simple translation section that is a glossary of ingredients and techniques that divides itself into related food groups. The lists are readable thanks to plenty of space between terms. There are also a paltry number of suggested meal menus—some of which are regional specialties—and a tipping chart that calculates fifteen and twenty percentages of dollar amounts. A newer edition with a different title is available. 192 p.

The Vegetarian Traveler: A Guide to Eating Green in over 200 Countries / Bryan Geon (Warwick Publishing, 2000).

Arranged under countries by regions of the world, there is an intriguing if brief peek at the native dishes available and, since many are meat, possible alternatives. Restaurants and food stalls are sometimes considered as options, and there may be advice about the acceptability of vegetarianism by the locals. Several sentences summarize the language or languages spoken, and are followed by an English-to-foreign template of a few phrases ("I do not eat ___ ") and examples, such as "meat," "chicken," and "fish," along with a phonetic key to pronunciation; "thank you" is also translated. Those seeking to find more about a country will have to look elsewhere, for everything but the subject of food is excluded in the book, a trade paperback that could come along in the luggage if needed. (Among other sources of information about the non-meat diet provided in this work is the publisher Vegetarian Guides www.vegetarianguides.com.) 240 p.

Where the Locals Eat: The 100 Best Restaurants in the Top 50 Cities / compiled by the editors and researchers of Magellan Press (Magellan Press, 2007).

Since national chains or franchises appear to be completely left out, the title of this oblong volume should be clarified as the best 5,000 local restaurants in U.S. cities. Arranged in alphabetical order, each city has ten restaurants that receive a paragraph apiece. The restaurant's name and its particular cuisine are followed by a description of the features that recommend it. At the end are days open and/or whether breakfast, lunch, and dinner are served; plus address and telephone number. A city section finishes with "the rest of the best," which simply has the remaining 90 restaurant names, only with telephone number and cuisine. Price or price range is unfortunately absent. 312 p.

ECOTOURISM AND SOCIALLY RESPONSIBLE TRAVEL

Some travel with a sensitive conscience. They both wish to enjoy the natural world and realize that the impact which they have on such a world can be decisive. Eco-travelers are especially attuned to the social responsibility of how they influence their destination, whether it is the local economy or the natural environment.

Americans traveling abroad change other cultures for good or ill. Collectively their spending power influences other economies, especially developing ones. Their money has no conscience. It may turn a master artisan into a mass producer of trinkets; profit an international hotel but not the local community; or tempt children into beggary through tourists' free gifts.

Even without their power over income, foreign travelers may offend the native culture. They may ignore customs, exploit hospitality, or pollute the land.

However, socially responsible travelers respect the integrity of a country and its culturally diverse people. They are thoughtful guests in their host's home. They support environmental and other issues through ecotourism (nature or cultural travel with scruples) and patronize the local economy. They have a moral and political sensitivity about their effect on foreign people.

Exchanging thought for deed, some travelers assume their social responsibilities by volunteering to work for non-profit organizations. There are also tours whose sole motivation is political or ideological.

See also **Manners and Customs** and **Volunteer Work** under **Work**.

Subject Heading: Ecotourism (For greater specificity, add the country name, preceded by a space or dash.)

Titles

Arthur Frommer's New World of Travel / Arthur Frommer; assisted by Pauline Frommer. 5th ed. (Macmillan, 1996).

This is full of challenging and at times provocative thoughts of a man whose ideas have helped form conventional travel. Essays offer alternatives to traditional trips as they question values and delve into a wide range of subjects. Several themes emerge. There are advocacies for activities that transform or improve a traveler's body, mind, or spirit, or that promote social commitment; discussions of uncommon or unfamiliar things to do and places to go; and, naturally, a thread throughout about budget-saving possibilities. Jaded travelers and those who want to enhance their time on a trip could profit from this work. Though some of the essays are conventional—for example, a chapter entitled "A Visit to the New Paris" is an endorsement for seeing the Louvre and several other well-known museums—others take on controversial realities, such as slave labor on cruise ships. 378 p.

The Good Alternative Travel Guide: Exciting Holidays for Responsible Travellers / Mark Mann with Zainem Ibrahim. 2nd ed. (Earthscan Publications Ltd., 2000).

The beginning third of the book discusses the significance of ethical tourism and presents a selection of first-person encounters. Most of the remainder is a directory of travel operators who have met the criteria that respects indigenous cultures and ecological awareness. Those in the United Kingdom, Europe, the United States, and Australia are grouped together, and then the arrangement is by country, which is described in a paragraph or so. Next to the name of the local operator is its category of accommodation or activity (for example, rainforest lodge or volunteering), which is indexed later. The operator is concisely described, and there are symbols and their fill-ins for address, telephone, fax, website, and e-mail, which make for a lean but eye-friendly entry. 246 p.

EMERGENCIES

Commonly, travel emergencies are legal, health, or financial. Crime, imprisonment, and terrorism are examples of the first; sickness, accidents, and death the second; and destitution and stranding the third.

When in trouble turn to government agencies or private organizations. Overseas emergencies fall under the jurisdiction of the United States State Department's embassies or consulates, where their Office of American Citizens Services and Crisis Management (part of Overseas Citizens Services) handles problems. Problems customarily fall under one of what have been called the five Ds: Death, Destitution, Detention, Disappearance, and Disease.

The Overseas Citizens Services in Washington, D.C. is under the Bureau of Consular Affairs, which also handles Passport and Visa Services. OCS is the place that notifies the public about the safety of family and friends during disasters or political upheavals. It also arbitrates child-custody cases, helps transfer money, and issues travel advisories.

For a list of U.S. embassies and consulates see *Key Officers of Foreign Service Posts* in the State Department's telephone directory (www.state.gov). A directory of embassies and consulates of every country is at usembassy.state.gov and the commercially produced *World Tourism Directory* (see number 8 under **Sources of Travel Information** in the **Introduction**).

The Department of State's "Country Specific Information" (travel. state.gov/travel) gives a summary of each country's "pressure points" for travelers: entry requirements, safety, medical information, etc. When conditions are such that a high potential for violence and physical danger is possible, "Travel Alerts" or "Travel Warnings" are issued.

In addition, there exists for travelers several private assistance organizations, profit and non-profit. They provide help similar to embassies and the OCS. They can give financial help, provide an English-speaking lawyer or doctor, send messages, and evacuate the sick. They may have a twenty-four-hour service and multilingual employees. Among them are International SOS and Travel Assistance International. Check with your insurance agent for referrals or get in touch with organizations by going online or looking up the keyword "emergency" in the *Encyclopedia of Associations'* index.

Some travel agencies subscribe to a twenty-four-hour service that helps travelers with such issues as itinerary changes, off-hour reservations, and relaying telephone messages. Ask the agency if it is a subscriber.

See also **Health** (for medical assistance businesses and organizations), **Law**, **Money**, and **Safety and Security**.

Titles

The Worst-Case Scenario Survival Handbook: Travel / Joshua Piven and David Borgenicht (Chronicle Books, 2001).

A few pages apiece are dedicated to a predicament, with some appearing to be taken directly from a Hollywood drama of the Hitchcockian or Indiana Jones variety, such as losing someone who is following you or stopping a runaway train. Then there is advice on foiling a UFO abduction, though as with the other problems the treatment is serious and the numbered instructions are straightforward. A variety of experts in their areas were consulted in order to provide authoritativeness. Likewise the accompanying illustrations are clear and aid the survivalist in visualizing ways out. The average traveler is unlikely to find himself or herself in situations covered in this work, but knowing how to deal with these scrapes may give re-assurance and, for the curious, provide entertainment. The book fits easily in one's hands. 191 p.

Organizations

Overseas Citizens Services. Bureau of Consular Affairs. U.S. Department of State. travel.state.gov/travel/tips/emergencies/emergencies_1212.html

Especially this entity's Office of American Citizens Services and Crisis Management section is responsible for U.S. citizens abroad when it comes to death, crime victimization, financial assistance, sickness, and legal difficulties. It administers the Consular Information Program, which advises the traveling public about possible. Terrorist threats and short-term problems can be quickly publicized through the Services' public announcements. Examined website: 2007

Travelers Aid International. www.travelersaid.org

With a presence at select airports, train stations, and bus terminals, this non-profit service is most noted for assisting the traveler who is stranded or in need. Examined website: 2008

GOVERNMENT PUBLICATIONS

Government documents can be easily overlooked despite the vital facts they contain for travelers. Since the items are often free or cheap, and many are available on the web, their treasures ought to be more widely known. The nation's largest publisher, the United States government each year produces thousands of titles on numerous subjects. They are found in libraries, government bookstores (both physical and virtual), and they have an impressive online presence.

Since the government has lawmaking authority, travelers ought to pay special attention to titles that deal with travel and the law. United States Customs allowances and passport requirements are just two of the subjects addressed in this area.

Of the government departments that produce important travel titles, those of State, Interior, Commerce, and Transportation deserve particular notice. From a traveler's perspective, the first deals with matters of going outside the United States, the second with vacation spots in the country, the third with tourism and items brought in from overseas, and the fourth with the movement of people and goods. It simplifies a search to know which government agency has oversight for one's area of interest. That gives a place to begin.

Along with other popular interest titles, a few travel items are available through the Federal Citizen Information Center. For any question about which government program or agency handles a situation, call or write the nearest Center (below). Or if the agency is known, contact it directly.

Several books explain the ins and outs of locating government documents. For example, there is a chapter about travel publications in *Using Government Information Sources: Electronic and Print* by Jean L. Sears and Marilyn K. Moody; 3rd ed. (Oryx Press, 2001).

Subject Heading: Government Publications—United States—Bibliography

Titles

"Catalog of U.S. Government Publications" (U.S. Government Printing Office). catalog.gpo.gov/F

As the *Monthly Catalog of United States Government Publications* this was a paper index to publications produced by the government, and items related to travel were mixed in with all other topics. Transferred to online, the site has a keyword search making it possible to roundup publications scattered through a variety of agencies. Examined website: 2009

Organizations

Federal Citizen Information Center. www.pueblo.gsa.gov

Its National Contact Center handles letters, e-mail, and telephone questions by citizens about federal agencies, programs, and services. The website has a section about travel, which is also one of the subjects of popular government publications that the Center sells—and sometimes distributes freely—through the mail. Online all the titles are available to be read or ordered. Examined website: 2008

U.S. Government Online Bookstore. bookstore.gpo.gov

Its site offers various government titles for sale or for free, but there are no links to the texts themselves. Among the browsable subject headings are "Recreation" and "Travel and Tourism." Examined website: 2008

HEALTH

There is an embarrassment of riches when it comes to resources in this area of travel, with prevention and treatment the two major subjects. Even if not being exposed to exotic diseases in exotic countries, a traveler is likely to be subjected to out-of-the-ordinary physical stresses. The prudent may consult a doctor before going, especially as a precaution against doing so during or after a trip. At any rate, a physician can be a valuable source of information about travel health.

In preparation for a journey determine if there is a need for any vaccinations or booster shots, such as tetanus. If the doctor prescribes pills, learn about their ingredients and effects in a recent *Physicians' Desk Reference*.

Consider insurance. Does your present health policy include overseas coverage—and if so, to what extent? Ask your insurance representative. It is possible to buy travel insurance policies that provide foreign hospitalization expenses or reimbursement in case a trip is canceled due to illness (though watch out about the exemption for pre-existing conditions). There are also assistance companies that arrange for such services as emergency medical evacuation, medical escort, and the presence of English-speaking doctors.

Be aware if the destination country has had any recent outbreaks of disease. Those that are serious enough will be announced in a traveler's advisory issued by the United States State Department (see **Emergencies**). Other government sources of health help are the Centers for Disease Control and Prevention (below) and the United States Department of Health and Human Services.

Travel medicine and tropical medicine have become specialties that have generated their own clinics and their own organizations. Clinics may be located by consulting local health facilities, the internet, etc.

People who suffer from chronic weaknesses, such as diabetes, can get travel advice from organizations that treat the ailment. They may even have a booklet or book on the topic, as with the publication of the American Diabetes Association (below). Also, manufacturers for the treatment of various ills may offer free print or online literature about their area of expertise.

Not least, books on healthy traveling discuss jet lag, diarrhea, heat stroke, insect bites, life-threatening travel complaints, and other problems.

Subject Heading: Travel—Health aspects

Titles and Websites

Bugs, Bites & Bowels / Jane Wilson-Howarth. 3rd ed. (Cadogan Guides, 2002).

There are diverse topics such as travel with children, getting ready, and taking immunizations, but the brass tacks is in the separate chapters describing and prescribing treatments for varieties of diarrhea, worms, bad food, malaria, insects, skin problems, animal threats, and aliments; while situations deal with hot places (especially the danger of too much sun) and cold (e.g., mountains), the water (from drowning to river blindness), and categories of accidents. Those who are expatriates receive individual attention. A handy edition that is readably designed with sections and subsections clearly marked, the main points of every chapter are in a summary box, and there are drawings of many troublesome critters. There are also several maps with shaded risk areas, gray-boxed case histories pertinent to the illness or problem under discussion, and ready reference tables. Hopefully, paranoia for the incipient traveler will not be caused through a perusal of this knowledgeable contribution by a physician. A later edition is available. 344 p.

CDC's Complete Guide to Healthy Travel: The Centers for Disease Control and Prevention's Recommendations for International Travelers / Kent C. Davis (Open Road Publishing, 1997).

With a slightly misleading title, this work is by a commercial concern that has adapted information from the U.S. government's Centers for Disease Control and Prevention. Except for combining Australia and the Pacific, each chapter focuses on part of a continent, naming the countries encompassed. Diseases and health problems of the region are discussed, but since many of them are global, this leads to substantial repetition, sometimes verbatim, from chapter to chapter. Among the ailments briefly covered are malaria, yellow fever, dengue fever, Japanese encephalitis, typhoid fever, cholera, hepatitis A and B, HIV/AIDS, schistosomiasis, and rabies. The text commonly explains what they are, assesses the risk to travelers, and shows measures of prevention. There is nothing about either accidents or a number of health predicaments. Other travel health books are more thorough and up-to-date. 350 p.

Culture Shock!: A Traveller's Medical Guide / Paul Zakowich (Graphic Arts Center Publishing Company, 1996).

Major subjects include examinations of vaccination as part of trip preparation; climate; medical emergencies; diarrhea; stings and bites; skin problems; sun; altitude sickness; and special travelers. Diseases particularly targeted are viral hepatitis and rabies, while others are grouped under the insect induced, the sexually transmitted, the airborne, and those from soil and water. In the appendix diseases are crowded under world regions, but geographic arrangement has been done with far greater expansiveness and thoroughness in other works on travel health. Anecdotal cases concerning stricken travelers and cartoons throughout enhance a friendly and non-technical read, though the information it gives may not satisfy those who want a manual that is both authoritative and detailed. 214 p.

The Diabetes Travel Guide: How to Travel with Diabetes—Anywhere in the World / Davida F. Kruger. 2nd ed. (American Diabetes Association, 2006).

An example of a health travel guide specific to a single condition and published under the authoritative auspices of its medical organization, it contains little of the generic travel advice found in mainstream works. Instead, this addresses such concerns as what the diabetic should wear, the bringing of insulin and related medical supplies on a trip, disposal of needles, food to be eaten or avoided and when, pills that should be taken, and dealing with common illnesses. A multi-language translation of phrases that deal with diabetic situations appears at the end. Chapters come with lists, checklists, and boxes of medical facts, while bolded subdivisions in the text enhance ease of reading and finding, and the book's compactness makes for portability. 221 p.

The Doctor's Guide to Protecting Your Health Before, During, and After International Travel / W. Robert Langue. 2nd ed. (Pilot Books, 1997).

A clearly written book on prevention, symptoms, and treatment begins with recommendations of what to take, health assessments to make beforehand, and comments on medical insurance. Following are chapters on traveling with heart disease, high blood pressure, and other specific conditions; vaccines; problems directly related to traveling (fear of flying, motion sickness, etc.); risks from the sun and other aspects of the environment; safety; food and water precautions; bowel problems; infectious diseases, from malaria to AIDS; handling medical problems in another country; and relocating abroad. The explanations are for the layman, so they shy away from going in depth. 121 p.

Exercises for Airplanes (and Other Confined Spaces) / Janet Diamond (Excalibur Publishing, 1996).

The purpose of the work is to show ways to combat discomfort and keep healthy while sitting on a plane or being in a space where freedom of movement is limited. In order to follow the various instructions, a traveler should have this book on board, but although thin it is too large to fit in most pockets. Only a few illustrations accompany the numbered exercises, which begin with general warm-ups and then target areas of the body, followed by the mind ("visualizations"). The compact discussions of jet lag, dehydration, motion sickness, diarrhea, fear of flying, and the like encompass homeopathic remedies, foods, herbs, drugs, or aromatherapy. A small airplane graphic often serves as a paragraph pointer. 53 p.

Fitness for Travelers: The Ultimate Workout Guide for the Road / Suzanne Schlosberg (Houghton Mifflin Company, 2002).

Find in this volume attacks on excuses that travelers give for avoiding exercise, clues to locating exercise spots (including a list of fitness centers that may be used during an airport layover), what to eat on the go, and what some of the better-known fast food restaurants offer in terms of health food. The author also examines travel concerns such as the effect of high altitude and other environments on cardiovascular workouts, and workouts which may also be adapted to a temporary location (e.g., building stairways). For lifting suitcases, walking, and sitting extended periods the related muscle groups are identified and exercises for them are prescribed. Photos show individuals working with equipment, dumbbells, and tubing in a gym, or in a pinch using either their hotel room or, for stretching, most anywhere. The agreeable tone of the book keeps in mind that the target is the person on the go, and unlike *Road Warrior Workout* (below), it comes with wide coverage and many details. 191 p.

Going Abroad: A Comprehensive Guide to Answering the Call of Nature Anywhere in the World, from Using the Ubiquitous "Squat" Toilet to the Bidet: A Must for Travelers, Wherever They, Er, Go: The Bathroom Survival Guide / Eva Newman (Marlor Press, Inc., 1997).

The majority of the book is a collection of individual anecdotes from the author or from other travelers about the novelty and sometimes misadventures of visiting foreign toilets, especially the squat kind. Almost of necessity the explanations have a heavy tone of levity. That so much could be written about the topic, and kept interesting, is in part because this is one area that most travel guides skip. Stories involve operating the necessities (not always so obvious to the neophyte), their constructions (or, in one case, the vehicle that contains them), the etiquette involved, locating them while traveling, toilet paper or its water system alternative, and a few matters related to showering. Newman contributes numerous drawing of the toilets and how they function as well as diagrams for the stages of squatting and rising. It is educational. 108 p.

Health Information for International Travel. Biannual (Centers for Disease Control and Prevention, U.S. Department of Health and Human Services). wwwn.cdc.gov/travel/contentYellowBook.aspx

Also known as the *Yellow Book*, its target audience is health care providers. Available in print and online, the government publication contains facts about vaccination and quarantine, and goes on to look at yellow fever and malaria by country, while a host of other maladies are briefly analyzed in terms of what they are, the countries where they occur, their symptoms, their prevention, and their treatment. The health hints for numerous threatening situations even include the shipment of human remains for burial, and there is a broad look by continent or region at local hazards. There is also a unit on types of travelers, from those with HIV, or expectant, or with disabilities, to immigrants who might have a greater susceptibility to disease. The substantial part on the child traveler treats dehydration, animal bites, ear pain from flying, altitude sickness, too much sun, etc., and elsewhere provides vaccine recommendations; plus there is information about the health of international adoptees. Examined website: 2008

The Healthy Traveler: A Handbook of Easy Solutions for Common Travel Ailments / Susan W. Kramer (Aspen Press, 2002).

Presented in alphabetical order, the ailments start with altitude sickness and end with stiffness, while those in-between include bleeding, constipation, foot problems, insomnia, missing medicines, and parasites. Summarized at the end of each subject, remedies discussed in the text reflect the knowledge and values of the author, a therapeutic herbalist, and may be as simple as changing a behavior or can be more controversial, such as acupuncture or magnets. In addition, there is a roundup of important things to put in a travel kit. The color green highlights headings and italicized words, thereby making important points easier to spot in the small and portable book. Expect neither facts about immunization nor the scope of health threats found in *International Travel and Health* (below), but if the idea of treating oneself with homeopathy, massages, and the like does appeal, this is a useful title. 203 p.

How to Shit around the World: The Art of Staying Clean and Healthy while Traveling / Jane Wilson-Howarth (Travelers' Tales, 2006).

Whereas *Going Abroad* (above) concentrated on toilets and their usage, here the range is much broader, more medical, and is probably the most complete on the subject. Conditions described are usually away from the Western tourist track and in villages, or out with nature, or any place where customs and facilities are different. Bulleted, practical tips follow the discussions by Dr. Wilson-Howarth about kinds of diarrhea and more serious intestinal ailments, what to eat or prepare against, techniques for doing without toilet paper, the avoidance of worms inside the body or creepy-crawlies around the toilets, and the possible complications of bathing. There are also recommendations for older travelers and for children in terms of diarrhea, rehydration, comfort, etc. Graphical boxes on most pages contain relevant stories, either humorous or educational, from travelers. An earlier version is titled: *Shitting Pretty: How to Stay Clean and Healthy While Traveling* (Travelers' Tales, 2000). 165 p.

How to Stay Healthy & Fit on the Road / Joanne V. Lichten (Nutrifit Publishing, 2001).
    Omitting from her scope diseases and accidents, the dietician author finds remedies through the appropriate diet (and menu possibilities), taking opportunities for exercise while on the go, achieving mental as well as physical health, modification of behavior, staying in touch with important people, and other ways. Instructions are given in terms of straightforward actions that are usually within the reader's control. She logically adds issues in safety to those of health, but detours a bit into some generic travel concerns (e.g., booking a flight, packing). Notably in the chapter titles, she enjoys making comparisons between maintenance of the body and that of the automobile (e.g., "Putting the Brakes on Stress"). The business traveler seems to be the audience directly addressed. Editing problems in this small work reveal themselves through faulty syntax and repeated phrases from the same sentence. 208 p.

International Travel and Health. Annual (World Health Organization). www.who.int
    One of the publications from the World Health Organization, it comes in print and is freely available online in a PDF format. Find extensive advice about what may be done to avoid or treat health problems as a result of air travel or the threats to the body and life when it comes to water, animals, driving, violence, and infectious diseases, which are separately broken down into tabular format. Substantial chapters are devoted to vaccine preventable diseases, and one to malaria, while a few pages deal with blood transfusion. A single list of countries comes with comments about yellow fever vaccination certificates and malaria risks, but omits the other aforementioned hazards. Shaded maps show where a disease is present or prevalent. For those interested in health, this is one of the most detailed and authoritative works to consult, and it is updated by *The Weekly Epidemiological Record*, which is also available online at www.who.int/wer. Examined website: 2008

International Travel Health Guide / Stuart R. Rose, Jay S. Keystone. 13th ed. (Mosby, 2006).

Well-written and well-designed, this major reference resource begins with an overview followed by looks at trip preparation, vaccines, jet lag, motion sickness, safety in food and drink, and treating diarrhea before discussions about individual diseases, which customarily identifies what it is, where it occurs, its symptoms, treatment, prevention and, as available, vaccination. As with several other titles, malaria receives special consideration. Other subjects that garner particular attention include insect bite prevention; AIDS and sexually transmitted diseases; altitude sickness; medical care abroad; travel insurance; pregnancy during travel; and travel with children. On the other hand, accidents and crime, for example, are skimped on, perhaps because they fit less comfortably under the rubric of health. Over half the book contains handy region and country profiles that come with health advisories touching on the risk and prevention or treatment of common and other diseases, thereby repeating some facts offered earlier; the name of one or more hospitals is also part of the commentary. A preface states the book is published annually. View an online version at www.travmed.com. 762 p.

Physicians' Desk Reference. Annual (Thomson Healthcare).

Traveler or not, whenever prescribed a new drug the prudent will check this long standard and mammoth source for information about usage, side effects, and other particulars. However, the reading is not layman friendly. A front section provides color photo illustrations of pills. Examined: 2007; 3482 p.

The Pocket Doctor: A Passport to Healthy Travel / Stephen Bezruchka. 3rd ed. (The Mountaineers, 1999).

Since the book could snugly and perhaps comfortably fit in the back pocket of a pair of jeans, it is portable—yet at the expense of omitting depth to its contents. For example, many diseases are limited to an appearance on an immunization table, where columns give space to the vaccine, its recipients, the primary series and booster, and notes. Another table has details on drugs and their doses. Dr. Bezruchka offers no approach by country or region, so the traveler to, say India, will not know if malaria or hepatitis is to be guarded against. Information that is here has the merit of providing advice for a wide but generic variety of situations (bites, jet lag, colds, allergies, shock, etc.) yet ignores what could be important details. To rely solely on this work for medical guidance could prove a mistake, and it would help a great deal for the reader to have supplementary knowledge or first-aid training as back-up. Or add a bigger book such as *Travellers' Health* (below). 127 p.

Road Warrior Workout / Crunch (Hatherleigh, 1999).

The numerous action photos filling the volume show individuals trying out exercises, especially those for the busy traveler who will be flying in the near future. One chapter consists of a six-day program that involves going to the gym for strength and stretching, with a list for the minutes that it takes or repetitions of action to be practiced. Healthy as it may be, a direct connection to travel appears slight. The two remaining chapters are far more relevant. In the first a model is shown exercising either in an airplane seat, next to it, or by a wall, while in the second she is adapting the hotel room and what is in it for her purposes. The slender book is a most useful accompaniment to a trip. 137 p.

The Rough Guide to Travel Health / Nick Jones, Janet Gray, Charles Easmon. 2nd ed. (Rough Guides, 2004).

The opening section about preparation, coping (immunizations, strategies to combat fear of flying, ingredients of a medical kit, etc.), and travelers with specific needs has several themes linked to the book's bulkiest part, an A-Z listing of problems. That unfortunately lacks a table of contents, though this is moderated by the relevant subject name running along the side of each page, in green letters, and by the book's index. Many of the problems are broken down into introductory comments, a description of symptoms, and the diagnosis and treatment. Dr. Jones and company also devote a few pages of instructions on first aid, and in a compact section by region and country insert charts for vaccinations from local diseases and for malaria prophylaxis. This relatively portable resource may be the champion among its competitors for the number of exotic diseases it recognizes. The *Rough Guide* in the title invokes the practicality and reliability of the brand. 298 p.

Safe and Sound: Healthy Travel with Children / Marlene M. Coleman (The Globe Pequot Press, 2003).

Whereas the title *Your Child Abroad* (below) is plainly truth in advertising, the words in the subtitle by this pediatrician author have fogged their meanings, so the scope is broader and less detailed than might be supposed. Additionally, a number of pages are devoted to facts on safety, as distinct from health. While some of the subject matter is about traveling children, other concerns the dangers that may befall the child at home; likewise, some of the suggestions that focus on the adult traveler could be found in any general travel guide. The work overlooks a great deal that concerns travel to other countries and seems to be designed in terms of domestic trips. A number of suggestions are bulleted for ready reference, and text is usually displayed in a varied layout. 211 p.

Staying Healthy in Asia, Africa, and Latin America / Dirk G. Schroeder. 5th ed. (Moon Travel Handbooks, 2000).

Since the book is intended to be small enough to be packed along, its amount of contents is limited. It serves best as a ready reference source for introductory facts about health and disease, so those seeking details and background should go elsewhere. There are suggested immunizations, a pre-departure health list, cautions about what to eat, basic rules of hygiene and nutrition, guidelines for the use of medicine, and more, which precedes entries for diseases and conditions grouped under such headings as common health problems, fevers and parasitic diseases, and first aid for illness and injury. The disease or problem may have several subdivisions presented, with variations, in a table that flags the likelihood of contracting (e.g., "low," "moderate"), the means of transmission and of prevention, and symptoms. A paragraph concludes with the ways of treatment. There are several drawings, and some maps show the prevalence of certain diseases. 198 p.

The Travel Doctor: Your Guide to Staying Healthy While You Travel / Mark Wise (Firefly Books, 2002).

The author, a doctor, conveys a distinct professional presence in the book's tone, and at times he reveals a wry manner, while supplying lots of information in a familiar and clear style, making this one of the worthier titles on travel health. In contrast with many similar works there are more chunks of text, and fewer page subdivisions and bullets. Except for the singling out of malaria, health risks with something in common are grouped by chapter, such as that on sexually transmitted diseases. A brief survey by region has sections on diseases borne by food, water, and insects, plus the menace of other problems. There is also advice dedicated to first aid, flying anxiety, motion sickness, culture shock, safety, and environmental dangers. Types of travelers who receive attention are businesspeople, women, the young, those with certain medical conditions, potential adoptees, and those who have recently returned home. Cartoons help the more worried reader keep matters in perspective. 303 p.

Travel Fit & Healthy (Fodor's Travel Publications, 2001).

First, there is advice about planning, packing, and taking health measures before leaving home. However, the greatest amount of space is devoted to taking care of oneself aboard a plane, where there is particular attention paid to kinds of food and opportunities for exercise. A shorter chapter is on ways to spend time relaxing in a hotel room or using it for types of exercises, and another about the things worthwhile to eat or avoid, choice of restaurants, and what to guard against. While several workouts are described, there are no accompanying photographs that serve as visual cues, in contrast to *Fitness for Travelers* (above). Text is broken up through spaced headings and occasional insets, and wording and sentences are properly on the compact side, since the health suggestions throughout are usually simple and basic, stretching at times into general travel tips. An overlying assumption appears to be that travel will be in America. The small paperback could fit in the back pocket of pair of jeans. 131 p.

"Travel Health Online" (Shoreland Inc.) www.tripprep.com

The arrangement by country includes immunization recommendations, observations about malaria, and crime warnings. There is also description by ailment and a list of travel medicine providers throughout the world. Registration is required. Examined website: 2008

Travel Healthy: The Smart Traveler's Guide to Staying Well Anywhere / Lalitha Thomas (Hohm Press, 2002).

For the traveler the author offers a method that has been labeled "naturopathy." As the chief means of staying well on a trip she suggests ingesting the right supplements, foods, and drink (grapefruit seed extract, anyone?), as well as taking specialized health mixtures, tonics, or bee pollen, one of several "superfoods." The variety of products is presented with facts about them, what they do, and their effects on which parts of the body. Short sections on providing specific types of nourishment to children are scattered through the text. Except for jet lag, the work is arranged with an eye for treatment or health goals rather than by ailment; however, the back supplies a symptom index. Other practices are described also, such as exercise and use of sunlight. Some ingredient preparations seem a bit much for someone who is traveling, though one need not be in this situation to use them. The precise scope excludes mentions of malaria, yellow fever, and similar diseases. 162 p.

Traveler's Health Sourcebook: Basic Consumer Health Information for Travelers, Including Physical and Medical Preparations, Vaccination Recommendations, Transportation Health and Safety, Essential Information about Food and Water, Sun Exposure, Insect and Snake Bites, Camping and Wilderness Medicine, and Travel with Physical or Medical Disabilities; Along with International Travel Tips, Geographical Health Issues, Disease Risks, a Glossary, and a Listing of Additional

Resources / edited by Joyce Brennfleck Shannon (Omnigraphics, 2000). The work collects in one place reprints of selected contents from both a scattering of U.S. government titles that are free or online and from other groups or individuals that have authoritative information. The text is to the point and has enough bullets and bolded subdivisions within chapters to enhance the location of subjects. While there is sufficient breadth, the depth is less than that found in several other travel health titles, though there are subjects here that are missing from them, such as a discussion and table of life jacket types. Countries are not profiled separately, but rather each is gathered under area chapters, where general advice is repeated verbatim from—in this case—*The World Factbook*, so diseases or dangers associated with a single country may be overlooked. Certainly as a work of ready reference, the sourcebook fits the bill. 635 p.

The Travellers' Good Health Guide: A Guide for Backpackers, Travellers, Volunteers and Overseas Workers / Ted Lankester. Revised and updated ed. (Sheldon Press, 1999).

Subjects are broadly and quickly treated in three stages of travel, beginning with trip preparation, which ranges from immunization and a health self-inventory to mental preparation and handling the flight. Once abroad, the matters are eating, drinking, and diarrhea (and other hygiene-related discomforts). A discussion of malaria goes into greater detail than similar ones about AIDS, stress, the adjustments to some extreme environment, animal dangers, pregnancy, and children as travelers, among others. A section on returning home talks about the possible experience of culture shock, the necessity for a medical checkup, and keeping aware of possible exotic and other threatening conditions, which are described. There are several recommendations that apply only to the British audience, who are invited by the physician author to take his book along on a trip for its advisory value. The style, cartoons, and the judicious breaks in the text contribute to reader-friendliness, but those who want greater depth must consider other titles. A newer edition is available. 230 p.

Travellers' Health: How to Stay Healthy Abroad / edited by Richard Dawood. 4th ed. (Oxford University Press, 2002).

Dozens of doctors and health workers provide authoritative chapters about treating the things that can jeopardize a traveler's well-being. Some larger categories detail hazards coming through food and drink, poor hygiene, insects, air and sea travel, accidents (some resulting from recreational activities), and climactic extremes. Other travel subjects include water that is fit for drinking or swimming in; animal bites and stings; particular groups such as children and those on expeditions; dental problems; and insurance. There is a summary paragraph of a topic with its text broken up by bolded headings, while boxes, tables, and a limited number of maps and illustrations further comprehension throughout the volume. Of the ten appendixes one is a country table tagging the degree of risk from a host of diseases, and another has columns for safety of drinking water. The book is even more wide-ranging than *International Travel and Health* (above), and although at times it veers into the technical, its value as a reference resource is worth the bulk it would take up in a traveler's luggage. 730 p.

Your Child Abroad: A Travel Health Guide / Jane Wilson-Howarth, Matthew Ellis. 2nd ed. (Bradt Travel Guides; The Globe Pequot Press, 2005).

Written by two doctors, the book is blocked into chapters on preventing disease and those on what to do in case of accidents and sickness. The understandable suggestions for taking care of a child's well-being extend from planning a trip to the eventual return home. After a discussion about preparing children for travel and gathering preventative or contingency items, there is a description of possible hazards, from food that upsets the stomach to illustrations of insects and their ilk that bite or sting. A later part sets up hypothetic accidents (choking, burns, broken limbs, etc.) and explains how parents might minimize their effect. While a good part of the commentary sees children as a group, the authors have also sorted them into two age ranges, one month to one year, and beyond one year up to adolescence. Subjects may be treated in just a paragraph, as with "dangerous toys," or they may go on for several pages, as in the case of diarrhea. The viewpoint is British, as revealed in the vocabulary (for example, the use of "nappy" instead of "diaper"). Other Wilson-Howarth books are *Bugs, Bites, & Bowels* and *How to Shit around the World* (both above). 212 p.

Organizations

Centers for Disease Control and Prevention. wwwn.cdc.gov/travel
This authoritative government health agency devotes one area to travel and has links to subjects covered in its *Health Information for International Travel* (above). Examined website: 2008

International Association for Medical Assistance to Travellers. www.iamat.org
Besides offering advice about health risks, this non-profit organization provides a directory of participating physicians and medical institutions

abroad. The physicians must speak English and be trained in Europe or North America. IAMAT also has other publications and services for members, such as a fixed rate for the first consultation of the doctor. Examined website: 2008

The International Society of Travel Medicine. www.istm.org
    The group of MDs and other professionals lists members with clinics, by country and by state. Examined website: 2008

MedicAlert Foundation International. www.medicalert.org
    In instances of emergencies, the non-profit organization can provide personal medical records and offer other services for its traveling members throughout the world. Examined website: 2008

World Health Organization. www.who.int
    The health agency of the United Nations has a section of its website devoted to travel, with links to reports, news, and a key online document, *International Travel and Health* (above). Examined website: 2008

HEALTH RESORTS, SPAS, AND HEALING CENTERS

A healthy body may be the reason for a trip. Build up or lose pounds while staying at a spa. The following are directories of spas and health resorts in the United States and worldwide. Entries contain such basic information as address, cost, and a description of the facility.

There are also directories for those travelers who seek spiritual or mental sanctuaries in the metaphysical rather than the physical. A variety of recreations is designed to nurture healing.

Travel companies may consider locating spas and health resorts as part of their business, or may specialize in it, as SpaFinder, which has a spa locator at its website www.spafinders.com.

Subject Headings: Health resorts; Retreats

Titles

The Cheapskate's Guide to Spas: Over 150 Great Escapes, Romantic Retreats, and Family Adventures / Nathaniel Altman (Citadel Press, 2002).

Spas are considered in two categories, spa towns and destination spas (where a visit to the spa is the *raison d'être*). In the former the town is discussed in terms of its history and natural features that contribute to it being an attraction for spas, though facts about shopping and culture are commonly minimized. A bolded heading marks when to go, and another introduces profiles of less expensive spas, which is the heart of this practical directory. The format in the two categories usually shows bolded name, address, website, etc., before one or more descriptive paragraphs about the spa. There are italicized headings with information about the kinds of facilities available (such as swimming pools); the treatment services; the room amenities and costs, and hook-ups; special deals that allow money saving, as through buying packages or going at non-prime times; the provisions for children or pets; what is nearby; directions for getting to the spa town or the spa; and a miscellany of good-to-know facts. The arrangement is geographic. 303 p.

Fodor's Healthy Escapes. 7th ed. (Fodor's Travel Publications, 2001).

A good-sized oblong directory uses plain and rather small print for its roundup of resorts, spas, and the like in the United States, Canada, Mexico, the Caribbean, the Bahamas, Bermuda, and on cruise lines; although almost two-thirds of the volume concerns the U.S., divided by state. Each spa is named and fitted with one or more categories, such as "luxury pampering" or "holistic health," defined at the book's beginning. Several paragraphs may delve into a history of the property, treatments, the program, activities, and the ambience, without an overkill of marketing enthusiasm. One block of bolded headings compactly contains types of workout equipment, services (e.g., aromatherapy), swimming areas, the classes and programs, the recreation opportunities, and children's offerings. Other segments summarize the number of rooms, whether the meals are part of the package, sample menu items, the nightly rates and the credit cards that are accepted, and the address, telephone number, and URL. A newer edition is available. 346 p.

Healing Centers & Retreats: Healthy Getaways for Every Body and Budget / Jenifer Miller (John Muir Publications, 1998).

By state or Canadian province, the entry is first blocked into name, address, telephone and fax numbers, and electronic locations, which are followed in twin columns by paragraphs that may outline the destination's history, philosophy, daily routines, programs, etc. Then bolded headings precede the hours and days of operation, type and number of accommodations (unless they are not offered), approximate costs, and the credit cards accepted. There are also the meal plans—if included—that are commonly three per day and often as not vegetarian; and services, recreational activities, and facilities that may note the acreage along with the various living, meeting, and workout areas; plus the makeup of the staff, special notes that frequently address the concerns of non-smokers, and the names or at least types of nearby attractions. Facts about getting there often consist solely of the travel time from some major point, as like as not an airport or city. Similar to numerous John Muir products, the design is attractive, but in this case the details could be richer. 229 p.

100 Best Spas of the World / Bernard Burt & Pamela Price. 3rd ed. (Insiders' Guide, 2006).

Starting off in a geographical arrangement with the United States, each spa receives close to two fair-sized, two-column pages. Since the inclusion of a spa marks it as the best, descriptive paragraphs under the spa's name and location are in upbeat terms of what it provides, its setting, and its activities. This is followed by basic information under bolded headings for physical and electronic addresses; seasons open; reservation telephone numbers; details about the accommodations and meals; the facilities available to guests; the kind of services and programs; a rate range as determined by the number of dollar signs; the best (economically?) spa package along with its cost; the credit cards accepted;

how to get there; and nearby places of interest. Frequent shaded boxes give asides on the types or benefit of various health offerings. 195 p.

101 Vacations to Change Your Life: A Guide to Wellness Centers, Spiritual Retreats, and Spas / Karin Baji Holms (Carol Publishing Group, 1999).

The influence of a New Age outlook appears through the division of the contents into earth, fire, water, and air, which seems gratuitous, since the connection between the elements and the renewal centers may be very obscure. After name and place is given, paragraphs may touch on scope, practices, goals, surroundings, amenities, programs, and the participant's experience. Bolded headings precede phrase summaries about the season that the facility is open; scenery and relative location; the accommodations; activities and services provided; any religious affiliation; the costs; and at the end, have physical and electronic addresses that will offer more information. The level of detail varies according to the entry, and while listings are not sorted geographically, there is a topical index. 205 p.

The Spa Directory / Suzanne Duckett (Carlton Books, 2002).

Of a size that could fit in a glove compartment, this oblong book has pages colored according to the broad geographical areas they represent (Europe, the Americas, etc.), with a narrower locality stated in a shaded band across the top of an entry. Name, address, booking details, and website come before an overview and bolded breakdowns where the author chats about a spa's ambience, its regular guests (for example, businessmen, families, celebrities), the available treatments, specialties of the house, the cuisine (and perhaps mention of the restaurant), for who or for what activity or concern the destination is ideal, and a brief suggestion about what to pack. At the start of each geographic section a quick reference chart of spas has columns that contain up to three stars for expense and check marks denoting the presence of luxury, healthy food, gym, pool, outdoor sports, and alternative treatments. 304 p.

Spa Guide / John Segesta & Anne Stein. 2nd ed. (Open Road Publishing, 2003).

The authors consider spas to be of three types and place them accordingly by chapter. A destination spa is a self-contained center that commonly offers an all-inclusive package, whereas a hotel amenity spa is part of a hotel or resort, and a day spa is open for the short-time visitor. With some variation or inconsistency, an entry begins with a block that contains the name, address and other contact information, priced packages and perhaps what they include, the major credit cards accepted, and the location of the airport. Then, one or more paragraphs discuss the spa, after which bolded headings lead to a list of its services, the character of the facility, the meal plans, and something about the accommodations. Approximately twenty states are represented as well as a modest showing from Canada, Mexico, and the Caribbean. 214 p.

Spa Vacations: Your Guide to Healing Centers and Retreats / Annalisa Cunningham (Avalon Travel, 2001).

The author of *Yoga Vacations* (below) aims at a more familiar health subject, and she limits her directory to chiefly the United States, although there is a small bit devoted to Canada, Mexico, and the Caribbean. Arranged by region and state, the entry has a name, a gray box with the health center's physical and virtual address and telephone number, and icons, which may stand for such major activities and treatments as beauty/relaxation (skincare, massage, sauna, etc.), cleansing/nutrition, and meditation. Paragraphs varyingly discuss the spa's history, background, surroundings, special treatments, and routines. Like other health and spa books reviewed in this section, there are groups of bolded headings before brief responses about accommodations; rates; credit cards accepted; the types of meals; the services; recreational activities; facilities; the presence of disability access; special notes; nearby attractions; nearest airport; and directions for arriving at the spa by car as well as the availabilities of rentals. 244 p.

Transformative Getaways: For Spiritual Growth, Self-Discovery, and Holistic Healing / John Benson (Henry Holt and Company, 1996).

The spirit, mind, and body may undergo treatment together or apart through a variety of institutions and centers described in two or three paragraphs that usually refer to their number of acres, their scenery, distance from a city, activities, history, goals, and perhaps a little about the sponsors. A column of fixed, bolded headings come with the corresponding address; telephone number; season of operation; programs (duration and sometimes the type); guest capacity in what form of lodging; rates in dollars; and meals, which are often three per day and vegetarian. Some entries might also note services. Chapters are by single-site, multi-site, journeys to distant places, and wilderness and ocean programs that are grouped geographically. The U.S. has the most entries, although other parts of the world are also featured. Rather confusingly, the program type and special needs indexes in front give the number not of the directory's page but of a preceding, alphabetically arranged getaway list. Among the twenty program types are body cleansing, ceremony, hatha yoga, self-expression, and vision quest. Simple maps have numbered dots that locate the destination. 298 p.

Vacations That Can Change Your Life: Adventures, Retreats, and Workshops for the Mind, Body and Spirit / Ellen Lederman (Sourcebooks, 1996).

Each of the first four parts has two subdivisions. Holistic vacations branch into those that are comprehensive and those that are associated with individual disciplines, while spiritual vacations place discovery and renewal separate from social action and service. Healing and health vacations are featured in terms of mind and spirit, followed by the body, and the subject of self-improvement treats personal empowerment followed by programs that enhance relationships. The last part, learning vacations, tackles a variety of opportunities whose emphasis is in the arts and languages. In one or two pages the entry consists of a name, several paragraphs describing the activities and goals, a cost range signified by dollar symbols, the address, and telephone number—though unfortunately there are no URLs since the publication was before the internet's heyday. The book has as its strong point a unique roundup of services. Order is alphabetical rather than geographic. 411 p.

Yoga Vacations: A Guide to International Yoga Retreats / Annalisa Cunningham (John Muir Publications, 1999).

In this large-paged directory the spacing, as well as the divisions that begin with bolded headings in two columns, make for readability and for ease in locating details. A paragraph or two offers an overview of what the retreat is like before the aspects that are furnished in segments, usually with elaborations: address; air and ground access; a background and (in quotes) philosophy of the teachers; the yoga style practiced; any criteria students must have for acceptance; disability access; clothes and other items that should be brought; a profile of the room or area where the yoga takes place; number of possible participants; description of accommodations and meals; the cost; a sample daily schedule (a good touch); other activities available; an upbeat quotation about the stay by a guest; and a summary. A little more space is devoted to the retreats in the states of America than to those in other countries around the world. The author has also written *Spa Vacations* (above). 253 p.

HITCHHIKING AND CAR SHARING

Car pooling or ride sharing brings hitchhikers and drivers together. Physical or electronic bulletin boards may publicize the requirements of individuals, or matching may be brought about by non-profit organizations (such as www.erideshare.com or www.toshare.org) or by for-profit businesses. These services exist in Europe (in Germany it goes by the name "Mitfahrzentrale" and in France it is called "autostop"). As a gathering point for students and the young—groups likely to contain hitchers—universities and youth hostels may have offices matching drivers and riders, or at least bulletin boards doing the same. Also, these places provide informal networking for those who want either a ride or rider.

Another possibility, at least in Europe, is a (for-profit) central office in major cities that matches driver and passenger going to the same destination. To locate the office ask at the city's tourist bureau.

There is also the yellow pages, which has the subject heading "Car & Van Pool Information."

If wanting to hitchhike in the classic sense of holding a thumb out along the side of a road, gather information from titles below or from any number of web pages that offer advice about the subject. Find them by putting the word "hitchhiking" in a search engine box.

See also **Budget Travel**

Subject Headings: Hitchhiking; Car pools

Titles

Europe on 84¢ a Day / Gil White. 2nd ed. (Gil White, 1995).

In one of the more complete books about the subject, the author sprinkles his advice with anecdotes from his on-the-road experiences and, as with *Vagabond Globetrotting* (below), goes to fairly desperate remedies, such as sleeping in a police station, though he also deals with more conventionally budgeted responses. While he talks about finding free accommodations and free food, elsewhere he considers tactics that do involve spending money, albeit little. The chapter of country profiles is a collection of facts under numerous bolded headings, some about sights and others providing remarks about hitchhiking and forms of public transportation, contact information for youth hostels, and the status of employment for travelers. Another chapter offers, in a number of languages, common words and several group phrases about getting rides, accommodations, and food, plus asking directions, and what to put on hitchhiking signs (discover the Turkish for "home to mom"). Basic country and downtown maps are designed to show the location of youth hostels, either on roads to named towns or on local streets. 423 p.

The Hitchhiker's Handbook / James MacLaren (Loompanics Unlimited, 1995).

The style is slangy, vulgarly humorous, and has frequent obscenity, probably reflecting the kind of vagabond experiences that can come to be part of hitchhiking. After exploring such questions as why people hitchhike and what the driver owes the hitcher (nothing), the manual gives the nuts and bolts about where and how to stand along what thoroughfares, your dress and presenting yourself, lettering signs, and interacting with whoever offers a ride. The author then writes of how to avoid or handle a variety of dangers and annoyances: weather, animals, plants, and humans; and follows this with a chapter on subterfuges for getting a ride. The miscellany of advice at the end is chiefly about hazards and making do. To show when the subject alters, groups of paragraphs are regularly separated by the drawing of a hitching thumb, adding to the readability. 141 p.

Hitchhiking in America: Using the Golden Thumb / Dale Carpenter (Lies Told Press, 1992).

Both a manual of practical suggestions and cultural reflections on the topic, it uses passages from books, magazines, and newspapers to substantiate observations on the past and current conditions of hitchhiking through the United States as well as its popular representation in forms of mass media. The book's personable style and outlook is reflective and even at times intellectual, for the author is curious about such things as the interdependence of humanity as shown through hitchhiking and so, for example, looks into reasons that individuals will hitch or why drivers will or won't give them lifts. He ranges from the issues faced by women hitchhikers to thumbing stances and the relationship and etiquette that is between the driver and whoever becomes a rider. He offers numerous personal anecdotes to make his points. 136 p.

Vagabond Globetrotting: State of the Art / Marcus L. Endicott. Revised ed. (Enchiridion International, 1989).

This book has good and varied advice for those who travel on an extremely limited budget as well as for any traveler who wants an introduction to the range of possibilities about this activity, from conventional comfort to the nitty-gritty. For example, most travel books will omit instructions about how to hitchhike or hop a freight train, though a few more may address working one's passage on a yacht (and most will use a word such as "accommodations" rather than a chapter's more basic "shelter"). Perhaps due to advising about travel that is occasionally on the poverty margin, the author is a believer in having credentials—among those discussed are vaccination certificates, diving permits, letters of reference, and press cards. The 1989 date is a drawback most obviously in matters that might involve technology, for there is naturally nothing about e-mail or the internet in the discussion about staying in touch. 176 p.

Vagabonding in the U.S.A.: A Guide to Independent Travel / Ed Buryn. Revised ed. (Ed Buryn, 1983).

Despite its date much of the narration remains contemporary because it aims at the constants of how living intersects travel. The magical and metaphysical (and marijuana) are here as well as in-depth explorations of the basics of a nomad existence at a budget-minded level. This may take the form of camping—the equipment to have, food to bring and what to cook, sleeping outdoors, etc. Means of travel separately considered are car, bicycle, motorcycle, walking, and hitchhiking. The author shows that economic wherewithal can come from practicing various kinds of trades or skills suitable for those who want the vagabonding style of life. One chapter looks through the eyes of the foreign visitor at North America, chiefly the United States, and thereby points out some national characteristics that might help the reader see his or her country more distinctly. Another is about networking with people, be they relatives, friends of friends, or strangers. The practical suggestions provided can be adapted even for the upscale or more conventional traveler. 424 p.

HOMESTAYS

Intentions make a difference. Travelers can stay in a private home when their object is simply lodging (see **Accommodations**). On the other hand, they may lodge because they wish to learn about the household's outlook, culture, and language (many language courses require homestays). Visitors become, for a time, a part of the host family, thus receiving a privileged perspective of the host's country. Such sightseeing that they do is secondary to being with the host. Homestays, their boosters argue, increase international understanding.

Some homestays are reciprocal exchanges between families or groups, while others are one way. Students of high school and college age are traditional homestay participants, but adults also avail themselves of the opportunity.

Although it is possible for a person to engineer a visit—which can vary from a single day to several months—most people will go through homestay services run by an independent organization, a school program, or a travel company. Some exchanges are confined to occupational groups, such as educators.

Homestay organization addresses are available in directories and from some foreign tourist offices, which can put the visitor in touch with organizations for their countries. There are a few works on the topic, but travel guides may have something for the countries they cover. Likewise, seek information on student exchange programs, since homestays are likely to be part of the package.

See also **Study and Travel**

Subject Headings: Educational exchanges; Exchange of persons programs

Organizations

AFS Intercultural Programs. www.afs.org
It offers secondary students, teachers, and others a chance of living abroad with a host family. Examined website: 2008

Federation EIL. www.experiment. org
This is the worldwide network of The Experiment in International Living, which was founded in 1932 on the premise that people from different cultures should learn how to live together. Homestays are one of the services provided. Examined website: 2008

The Friendship Force. www.thefriendshipforce.org

To promote friendship across cultures, country chapters arrange exchanges for individuals to stay in private homes. The website allows searching for exchanges. Examined website: 2008

The Hospitality Exchange. www.hospex.net

It produces twice yearly directories of travelers who wish to host and be hosted. Examined website: 2008

People to People International. www.ptpi.org

To promote international understanding it offers exchange and other programs for adults and students. Examined website: 2008

SERVAS. www.servas.org

With a philosophy that peace can be sustained through international meetings, this organization has a network of hosts for other traveling members seeking accommodations. Examined website: 2008

LANGUAGE

Traveling where people speak an unfamiliar language can be scary. Travelers may fear they will be helpless in communicating their wishes and understanding the natives. One way around this is to visit only English-speaking countries. Even though over fifty countries have English as their official language, this does not exclude other languages being widely spoken there. For example, in parts of the United States there are communities that have more Spanish than English speakers, while Canada has both English and French-speaking inhabitants.

Still, there is a difference between visiting Canada and visiting France, where English will less likely be understood. Aside from avoiding non-Anglophone countries, common ways of coping are to move about in tours with an interpreter or stay only in international hotels where English is sure to be spoken. Language inconveniences are reduced but the language barriers to understanding peoples and their cultures remain.

A foreign language is not an impediment but an opportunity. If armed with a dictionary and phrasebook travelers are more likely to interact on their own with people who speak another tongue. Travelers will call on new verbal—and old non-verbal—skills.

Even for those knowledgeable about another language or prepared by a language course, portable dictionaries and phrase books are useful. Those who want to travel even lighter can do so with foreign language translation cards, with phrases arranged by situation.

Anglophone pocket dictionaries conventionally have two sections: English to foreign language and foreign language to English. On the other hand, look for phrase books to be arranged by situation or subject. Dictionaries and phrase books that crowd in more than one language are designed for visits to several countries or visits to multi-language countries. Other language works target a type of traveler, as the business-person or the motorist; or collect slang and insults. Some books combine definitions with phrases. Oxford University Press, HarperCollins, and Langenscheidt are among the publishers who produce these pint-size sources. Browse for titles in the language or travel section of bookstores, or bookstores that specialize in languages.

An electronic replacement for print is the handheld translator. Available through electronics and travel stores, they contain one or more languages, and some can even pronounce words for their user! There are also a number of internet sites that will perform translations.

Ambitious travelers will want to go beyond wordbooks. They can independently learn a language through a combination of cassettes and texts. Although there are a few stand-alone self-help books, the majority of language-teaching aids come in kits consisting of manuals, cassettes or CDs, and workbooks; read the manual, listen to the pronunciation, and write in the workbook.

To determine what languages on what cassettes or CDs are available, consult the annual *Books out Loud: Bowker's Guide to Audiobooks* (Bowker) or something similar.

A foreign language is best learned in its own country, where the visitor can attend classes at a school while lodging in a native speaker's home. For a catalog of foreign language programs in foreign locations check *IIEpassport, Short-Term Study Abroad* (see review in **Study and Travel**) or book a program through the National Registration Center for Study Abroad (www.nrcsa.com) or elsewhere. For programs closer to home try the nearest university or language school. Also, discover addresses of language-learning centers from cultural societies of countries with branches in the United States; for example, the Goethe-Institut (which promotes German language and culture) and others with similar goals are in the *Encyclopedia of Associations* and could be online. Also, consulates may be able to supply a list of their country's language schools for foreigners.

See **Study and Travel** for more resources.

Subject Heading: [French, etc.] language—Conversation and phrase books

Titles

Colloquial Series (series) (Routledge). www.routledge.com

Covering a vast number of languages, the series' self-instruction text for beginners comes with audio CDs or cassettes, and lessons include grammar, vocabulary, reading exercises, phrases, and dialogs. There is also matter about culture. Examined website: 2008

Dover "Say It" Series (series) (Dover). store.doverpublications.com

Even smaller and thinner than *A Rough Guide Dictionary Phrasebook* (below), the series covers phrases and words in a variety of languages. Arrangement is by subject, travel situation, or place (post office, etc.) where numbered phrases or relevant words may be used. A simple phonetic pronunciation is underneath them, and under this is the English meaning. As another form of access, an entry's number is indexed in back by its keyword. Nearly one-third of the French volume consists of a supplement with sub-categories concerning food and wine. The publisher's *Listen & Learn* series teaches language through cassette and manual. Examined: *Say It in French* / Leon J. Cohen (1962; 187 p.)

Eyewitness Travel Guides (series): *Phrase Book* (subseries) (DK Publishing). us.dk.com

Translations for a language range between single words to complete sentences, where there are parallel pronunciation sounds. Even if the mini-dictionary in the rear were not just English-to-foreign, there is more of this one-way translation in the book than the reverse, with native words and phrases commonly set off in colored "boxes" under such headings as "things you'll hear" or "things you'll see," dependant on the circumstances. Except for a collection of everyday phrases and some slang, the arrangement is by subjects that travelers might expect. Among them are those dealing with numbers, time, hotels, camping, driving, traveling around, restaurants, menu items, stores, services, sports, telephone, emergencies, and health; and most have short introductions. The small size allows the volume to fit in the average back pocket of a pair of jeans. Examined: *French Phrase Book*. 1st American ed. (1998; 144 p.)

Hugo in Three Months (series) (DK Publishing). us.dk.com

The self-learner will be able to choose a book with CDs or cassettes among many languages. The series name varies, for some titles begin with the language followed by the phrase "in Three Months" (e.g., *Welsh in Three Months*). Examined websites: 2008

Kwikpoint International Translator. www.kwikpoint.com

Cards show pictures instead of words so no foreign language needs to be learned. Examined website: 2008

Language/30 (series) (Educational Services Corporation). www.lang30. com

There are over thirty languages covered, with each accompanied by two audio CDs or cassettes and a phrase book. Including the topics of greetings, business, and emergencies, the courses are based on the accelerated language learning method developed for U.S. government workers. Examined website: 2008

Pimsleur Language Program (series) (Simon & Schuster). www. simonsays.com

The basis of the Pimsleur method is learning by listening, so this series is exclusively audio. Languages taught are from around the world and different levels are offered. Examined website: 2008

A Rough Guide Dictionary Phrasebook (series) / compiled by Lexus (Rough Guides).

This subtitle appears on a group of books encompassing some European languages plus a smattering of Asian and African. Able to fit in the back pocket of a pair of jeans, this is chiefly a bilingual dictionary where more words are translated from English to the other language than vice-versa (similar to *Eyewitness Travel Guides*, above). Pages are separated into two columns with single-word definitions, and there are occasional intervals for travel advice and cultural tidbits in the English-word-first section. Introductory matter provides simple facts about grammar (nouns, verbs, prepositions, etc.) and defines a few essential words in categories such as months, numbers, and basic phrases. At the end a "menu reader" identifies terms for food and drink. In the subject of travel the *Rough Guides* series is associated with practical and down-to-earth advice. Examined: *Swahili: A Rough Guide Dictionary Phrasebook* (2001; 198 p.).

Businesses, Organizations, and Publishers

Barron's. www.barronseduc.com

With a wide coverage, Barron's stresses language-learning through its many language works, though it also produces bilingual dictionaries and phrasebooks. Individual print titles concern verb conjugations, slang and idioms, pitfalls, beginner self-teaching, grammar, the business traveler, visual language guides, vocabulary, and pronunciation. Any of them may come with cassettes or CDs. Examined website: 2008

Berlitz.www.berlitzbooks.com

Besides being a language school with offices worldwide, Berlitz is a producer of travel guides, maps, atlases, and language works for travelers—self-study courses, grammars, bilingual pocket dictionaries, phrase books and phrase cards, menu readers, cassettes, and CDs. Examined website: 2008

Foreign Service Institute. www.state.gov/m/fsi

Under the auspices of the Department of State, the Institute teaches language courses designed for diplomatic and overseas support personnel. Commercial publishers have adapted the courses, which cover many languages. Examined website: 2008

Harrap. www.chambersharrap.co.uk/harrap

This is a publisher of big and little language dictionaries, including specialties such as bilingual business and slang. Examined website: 2008

Hippocrene Books. www.hippocrenebooks.com
    In the language field, this publisher produces an abundant number of bilingual dictionaries (including those for children), plus self-study and phrase books. Examined website: 2008

Langenscheidt Publishing Group. www.langenscheidt.com
    Among its travel-related publications are its bilingual dictionaries, phrase books, and language self-study titles. It is associated with Berlitz Books and Insight Guides, and it is a distributor of the *Insight Guides* series. Examined website: 2008

Language Course Finder. www.language-learning.net
    At this site searching for language schools throughout the world is possible by language, country, and a list of qualifying criteria. Languages taught range from Afrikaans to Zulu. Examined website: 2008

Living Language. www.randomhouse.com/livinglanguage
    The chief concern is providing texts, audio, and online courses for those interested in learning another language either in depth or with just the basics. Examined website: 2008

Lonely Planet. www.lonelyplanet.com
    The publisher of far-roaming travel guides has a series, *Lonely Planet Phrasebooks* that, as may be expected, includes exotic languages (e.g., Hill Tribes, Tibetan). Some phrasebooks come with audios. Examined website: 2008

National Registration Center for Study Abroad. www.nrcsa.com
    Foremost among its activities, the company provides for learning various foreign languages through programs in dozens of foreign countries. Students, teachers, executives, and older adults are among the groups that receive attention. Examined website: 2008

Penton Overseas. www.pentonoverseas.com
    The publisher has several language teaching series that combine audio recordings with printed matter, some at different levels: *Learn in Your Car*, *VocabuLearn*, etc. Examined website:2008

LAW

Beware both ignorance of the law and reliance on dated legal regulations. Otherwise, you may discover that the expensive product you bought abroad is from an endangered species and will be confiscated by U.S. Customs; or that you no longer meet the visa requirements for a country and are refused admission at its border.

A nation's government is the chief and authoritative lawmaking body, and American citizens can turn to theirs for facts, advice, and free publications. An obvious source is the Department of State, responsible for passports and travel advisories. Passport office addresses are in its publications, while passport forms are obtainable from government websites, travel agencies, post offices, and court houses.

Passports are in the domain of the Department of State, but visas must be obtained from a foreign country's embassy or consulate. The visa is a document that conditionally grants a traveler permission to enter a country. Processed through the embassy, there may or may not be a charge for the document. In addition to addresses provided in some travel works, a logical source for locations of embassies is a Washington, D.C., telephone directory, since in this country the greatest number is there. However, the embassy needed could be in your city of residence, so don't overlook the local directory.

To avoid some of the nuisance in attaining a visa, consider visa services which, for a fee, submit visa applications to embassies for processing. The services are a logical source of information about the latest visa requirements. Look for them in the yellow pages under the headings "Visa Services" and "Passport Photos."

Legal problems abroad? Contact the nearest U.S. embassy or consulate. They can replace lost or stolen passports, send a representative to visit an imprisoned traveler, and find an English-speaking lawyer. They also may supply income tax forms. The imprisoned can additionally be helped through such a group as the International Legal Defense Counsel and through various assistance companies.

For those inclined to seriously pursue the subject of law and travel, there are technical treatises aimed at legal professionals and business managers, such as *Hotel, Restaurant, and Travel Law* (Delmar Learning, 2004).

Since laws are the responsibility of a government, there is a preponderance of U.S. government publications listed below. The government has also transferred many print publications to the web, sometimes exclusively.

See also **Emergencies, Government Publications**, and **Health**

Subject Headings: International travel regulations; Travel—Law and legislation

Titles

How to Legally Obtain a Second Citizenship and Passport—and Why You Want to /Adam Starchild (Loompanics Unlimited, 1995).

After giving a background on passports and citizenship, Starchild spends several pages on the advantages and disadvantages of having dual nationality, whether for the United States or other countries. By contrast he later discusses what it means to lose citizenship (expatriation) or deliberately renounce your allegiance to the United States. There is advice about moderating or avoiding U.S. taxes through establishing residency abroad, and comments about forms of asset protection. A sizable proportion of the text doesn't address the why in the title, though there is plenty about the topic of citizenship in different countries that might be interesting without being practical. Since much of what constitutes citizenship is a legal matter, the person who wishes to get the most updated facts will need to contact the relevant governments. 131 p.

Organizations

Animal and Plant Health Inspection Service. U.S. Department of Agriculture. www.aphis.usda.gov/travel

This agency is responsible for protecting the agricultural health of the U.S. through enforcing regulations governing the introduction of plants and animals and agricultural products. Travelers can learn what food and other stuff to avoid bringing into the country. Examined website: 2008

Bureau of Consular Affairs. U.S. Department of State. travel.state.gov
Among the titles that it issues are:

Applying for Your U.S. Passport the Easy Way. travel.state.gov/passport/fri/pubs/pubs_854.html

In a question and answer format, the application process is explained in this online publication. Information also addresses, plainly and simply, such matters as lost or stolen passports and name changes of passport holders. The print version, *Passports: Applying for Them the Easy Way* (Bureau of Consular Affairs, 2003), additionally has addresses of regional passport agencies. Examined website: 2008

Foreign Consular Offices in the United States. www.state.gov/s/cpr/rls/fco

The work is arranged by country, under which are the states where the foreign consular offices are located along with their address and names of officials. Examined website: 2008

International Adoption. travel.state.gov/family/adoption/intercountry/intercountry_473.html

Besides the general information on the subject, there is a list of countries with links to their adoption regulations. Examined website: 2008

Tips for Traveling Abroad. travel.state.gov/travel/tips/tips_1232.html

Contents include looks at travel regulations, passports, visas, immunizations, health and travel insurance, responsibilities of consuls, etc. It also has basic and sound travel advice. Examined website: 2008

Travel Warning on Drugs Abroad (Bureau of Consular Affairs, 2000).

Online this appears to have been absorbed into a short section on drugs in *Tips for Traveling Abroad* (above). Examined website: 2008

Bureau of Consumer Protection. Federal Trade Commission. www.ftc.gov/bcp

Among its documents are those warning about travel frauds and travel scams, such as *Telemarketing Travel Fraud.* Examined website: 2008

Customs and Border Protection. U.S. Department of Homeland Security. www.customs.ustreas.gov/xp/cgov/travel

U.S. Customs oversees what comes into and leaves the United States. Among its titles are:

GSP and the Traveler: Bringing in Articles from Developing Countries (Revised 2005).

Some items are duty free if brought from designated developing countries under the U.S. Generalized System of Preferences. The publication defines GSP and lists popular tourist items eligible for duty-free treatment under it. Examined website: 2008

Know Before You Go: U.S. Customs and Border Protection Regulations for U.S. Residents (Revised 2007).

With an online version amounting to some 60 printed pages, it discusses the obligations of U.S. residents returning from international destinations, what and how much to bring into the United States from other countries, exemptions or duties that may apply, the sending of goods to the U.S., and prohibited and restricted items (e.g., medications, importing automobiles). Examined website: 2008

Office of Law Enforcement. Fish & Wildlife Service. U.S. Department of the Interior. www.fws.gov/le
    This agency offers a number of publications. Among them are:

Facts about Federal Wildlife Laws (U.S. Fish and Wildlife Service, 2000). training.fws.gov/library/Pubs9/wildlife_laws.pdf
    Online and in paper, the laws about the import, export, trade and sale of wildlife—whether alive or dead, including products made from them— are explained for the benefit of tourists, hunters, importers, exporters, scientists, and educators. Examined website: 2008

Tips for Travelers. www.fws.gov/le/Travelers/TipsforTravelers.htm
    This discusses what wildlife and plants are not allowed to be brought into the United States. Examined website: 2008

LIBRARIES

Throughout the world libraries are full of information pertinent to travelers. Provided that rules don't prohibit entrance, the traveler can look there for local newspapers, which have information about movies, plays, concerts, events, etc. (in non-English speaking countries libraries may offer readers access to English language newspapers and magazines). Libraries may also have local histories and even guidebooks. Librarians should be consulted for help in finding things.

There are also pocket libraries (or reading rooms) that are part of resorts, hotels, cruise vessels, clubs, and the like. Of independent reading rooms the most familiar is run by the Christian Scientists.

Libraries may be worth visiting in themselves. Perhaps they are renowned for their architecture, their book collections, or their exhibitions (such as the famous manuscripts displayed in the British Library).

The following directory presents addresses and describes libraries of the world.

Subject Heading: Libraries—Directories

Titles

World Guide to Libraries. Periodically published (K. G. Saur).

For those who wish to discover what libraries exist in the place that they will visit, this formidable multi-volume directory provides the facts. Under country, then library type (national, university, public, special, etc.), entries come with name, address, telephone number, electronic access options, collection breakdown, and somewhat more. Examined: 2005; 2 v. (1308 p.)

MAGAZINES AND NEWSLETTERS

General interest travel magazines are a grab-bag of observations and news on destinations, accommodations, food, transportation, and shopping. The presentation varies. Some magazines are like large glossy travel brochures while others offer critical examinations of vacation spots. Conventional features are reader comments (both recommendations and criticisms), book reviews, and classifieds.

The subject of travel appears also in non-travel magazines. *Better Homes and Gardens* is one example of a mainstream popular magazine that regularly features travel articles. To locate a subject in a popular magazine try the common library title (available both in print and online), *Reader's Guide to Periodical Literature*, an index which also analyzes a few purely travel magazines.

A comprehensive list of travel magazines is under the subdivision containing the word "Travel" in the periodical catalogs *Ulrich's Periodicals Directory* and *The Serials Directory*.

A smaller cousin of travel magazines is travel newsletters, which typically scrimp on photos and cater to a very select audience. They have been indexed most notably by *Newsletters in Print*, which has ceased publication as a print title to be absorbed into a database.

Titles

Condé Nast Traveler. Monthly (Condé Nast Publications). www.concierge.com/cntraveler

Some articles deal with destinations or with special travel subjects such as beach resorts. Departments include a question and answer section and "stop press" news items. Color photographs abound as well as color advertising and advertising sections. The target audience appears to be the traveler who is well-to-do. Examined: issue from 2008.

ITN, International Travel News. Monthly (Martin Publications). www.intltravelnews.com

Whereas *Condé Nast Traveler* is polished, this is a plain, newspaper-like publication with black-and-white photos, and its target appears to be the everyday traveler to foreign places. The bulk of contributions are from readers writing about their experiences or offering advice (where to stay, what to be wary of, etc.). While the longest reports deal with destinations, typically several items can be found on a page, so a lot of news is covered, with such familiar types as attractions, good tour guides and bad, packing, cruising, rail journeys, and health. There can also be book reviews, and at the end is a classified section, though plenty of ads for tour companies are scattered throughout. Examined: issue from 2008.

National Geographic Traveler. 8 per year (National Geographic Society). www.nationalgeographic.com/traveler

The biggest articles come with outstanding photographs of travel destinations throughout the world, while shorter ones deal with the art of traveling as well as special activities that some places offer, or explore a gamut of subjects. The pages offer their share of color ads, like other slicks in this section. Examined: issue from 2008

Travel & Leisure. Monthly (American Express Publishing Corp.) www.travelandleisure.com

The illustrated magazine has articles on vacations spots and places to eat and stay, and regular features for letters, questions and answers, best deals, and so forth. Examined website: 2008

MAIL AND MAILING ADDRESSES

To find the cost of sending mail overseas consult the post office or the *International Mail Manual* (below).

To receive mail when either traveling or with no fixed address, the first choice is probably e-mail. However, there are other possibilities. Mail could be sent to a pre-designated post office in care of general delivery (*poste restante*). And there are mail-forwarding services that rent their addresses where mail is held for a fixed length of time.

Besides the internet, addresses may be found through a telephone directory. For a zip code try the *National Five-Digit Zip Code & Post Office Directory* (also below).

Subject directories collect addresses of businesses, institutions, memberships, etc. Thus, museum addresses will be in a museum directory. To determine if a directory exists, check through *Directories in Print* (also available online) or a library's catalog.

Titles

International Mail Manual / United States Postal Service. Periodically revised (The Service). pe.usps.gov

With an alphabetical arrangement by country, the *IMM* has notes on what mail is prohibited or restricted, custom forms required, size limits, prices for post cards, aerogrammes, insurance, etc. Tables show weights and costs of sending mail abroad according to category of shipment. A simpler version is *International Postal Rates and Fees*. For U.S. rates, see the U.S. Postal Service's *Domestic Mail Manual*, also available at the same web address. Examined: 2008 edition (online)

National Five-Digit Zip Code & Post Office Directory / United States Postal Service (The Service). www.usps.com/zip4

An arrangement by state begins with an outline map sectioned into three-digit zip codes. A list of towns with post offices that have one code is followed by those communities with multiple ones. The breakdown is by the named streets, then the numbered, in seven daunting columns per page. Front matter contains the abbreviations used, and at the back there is a section for military zip codes. In print form the hefty set has been available in many libraries (in its online incarnation the website requires the filling in of address, town, and state in order to locate the code sought). Its print title has changed to the *National Zip Code Directory*. Examined: 2003; 2 vol.

Organizations

Universal Postal Union. www.upu.int
    With the backing of the United Nations, the Union facilitates postal cooperation between countries. Its site has links to foreign postcodes. Examined website: 2008

MANNERS AND CUSTOMS

Some travelers are inadvertent ugly Americans. What they look upon as their acceptable manners may prove indecorous or embarrassing in a foreign social setting. Pointing, speaking slang, gift-giving, and other actions may strain a business deal or offend a host. Understand the pitfalls of another culture to avoid blundering.

In particular the etiquette involved in tipping confuses many travelers, since it varies from country to country. Likewise, tipping conventions within a country reflect various social expectations, as the proper tip for a taxi driver differs from one for a doorman.

Subject Headings: Travel etiquette; Business etiquette

Titles

Behave Yourself!: The Essential Guide to International Etiquette / Michael Powell (The Globe Pequot Press, 2005).

The modest-sized book devotes two or three pages apiece to each of forty-five countries, which are accompanied by color photographs. The categories of etiquette center on meeting natives, conversation, eating and drinking; and general observations on behavior, dress, and giving gifts and tips. Short paragraphs in each category target separate aspects, such as how to perform a handshake in Mexico, or the disclosure that in Taiwan wearing attention-grabbing clothing should be avoided. The tidbits provided are interesting and helpful, but the limited number of them means a lot of examples are left out for the traveler who might find social propriety quite important. 141 p.

Culture Shock! (series) (Graphic Arts Center Publishing Company).

With an entertaining sense of humor and an infusion of personal experiences, the book strives to offer a familiarizing profile of the national characteristics of the people and the country in which they live. Their daily existence is seen in such terms as media (as, what types of television show are popular), politics, social values, attitudes toward work, customs of communicating, and leisure activities. The author also tackles what it is like for a foreign family to settle in. There is a short list of events and concepts that contribute to defining a country, whose politicians and celebrities receive one-line identifications. A few pages have a cultural quiz in multiple-choice format. In addition to the *Culture Shock!* country series, there is the city series with the city's name followed by the words *"at Your Door"* (e.g., *Culture Shock! Munich at Your Door*). Examined: *Culture Shock! Denmark* / Morten Strange (2000; 224 p.)

CultureGrams. Periodical (CultureGrams). online.culturegrams.com
 Formerly called *Culturgrams*, the slightly changed title offers a country in four pages. Major categories are subdivided into subjects, as "Lifestyle" gathers paragraphs on "family," "dating and marriage," "diet," "recreation," "holidays," and "commerce." Among other bolded headings relevant to manners and customs are "religion," "general attitudes," "personal appearance," "greetings," and "gestures." A final heading, "For the Traveler," speaks briefly to passport and visa requirements and has addresses for those seeking tourist information or wishing to contact an embassy. Some of the same details are available from *The World Factbook* (see **Sources of Country Information** in **Introduction**), but presentation and selection makes the contents easy to digest for students and others who want a quick view of what people are like in a country. This title is also available online. Examined: 1999; 2 vol.

Do's and Don'ts around the World: A Country Guide to Cultural and Social Taboos and Etiquette (series) (World Travel Institute, 1998).
 The 1998 series of books explores individual regions of the world such as Asia, the Caribbean, the Middle East, and Russia and its former republics. For each country there is a multi-page table of rows and columns. The heading for the first column asks if the thing under discussion is customary, allowed, permissible, used, or okay; the square beneath will be blank or have a checkmark. The next heading is for not customary and frowned upon, and the third is for what is disallowed, forbidden, or a crime. The last column has the occasional number to a footnote that comes at the end of the table. The do's and don'ts considered in the rows range from giving salutations (or business gifts) to discussion of religion and automobile driving behaviors. A slightly different table has yes or no next to the subject. With this format the many cultural attitudes can be taken in quickly. Examined: *Do's and Don'ts around the World: A Country Guide to Cultural and Social Taboos and Etiquette: Europe* (1998; 326 p.)

Essential Do's and Taboos: The Complete Guide to International Business and Leisure Travel / Roger E. Axtell (John Wiley & Sons, 2007).
 Much but not all of the book concerns manners and customs. The much begins with something on the ambiguity of world gestures, which were treated at book-length in the same author's *Gestures* (below). Following chapters cover general protocol; hosting international visitors;

using English around the world; and things women should know. Customs and manners are also treated through the perspective of eleven popular destinations, from Canada and Mexico to India and the United Kingdom. On the other hand, some of the contents are chiefly concerned with business advice, notably when it comes to using the internet and to exporting. With the same publisher Axtell has produced a number of earlier titles beginning *Do's and Taboos*, which are related to international behavior, using English abroad, and other topics compressed for *Essential Do's and Taboos*. See also *Do's and Taboos around the World for Women in Business* in **Travelers—Business**. 284 p.

Gestures: The Do's and Taboos of Body Language around the World / Roger E. Axtell. Revised and expanded ed. (John Wiley and Sons, 1998).

Sometimes with a humorous tone, the first, rather larger half of this work discusses the importance of gestures, types that are most popular throughout the world and, dividing them into parts of the body employed, what each means in different places. The last half arranges gestures by continent and country, bulleting each fact about them, from a few to dozens. This is the more practical section for travelers, who can look at the countries they may be visiting and learn the significance of their body language. 238 p.

How to Tip (Fodor's Travel Publications, 2002).

Where to tip, who to tip, and how much to tip summarizes this small book, whose concern is chiefly with the United States. The where defines the chapters, which cover bars and restaurants, hotels, in transit, resorts (along with cruises and casinos), and international destinations. The who at these places describes what various workers should be doing to earn their tips, which are provided in dollar amounts and sometimes percentages. For the tipper's convenience a math table shows dollar amounts from one to one hundred and how much 15 and 20 percent make up each. The premise of the title is that the traveler will tip, and at times the advice appears to be generous with its readers' money. 115 p.

The International Guide to Tipping / Nancy Star (Berkley Books, 1988).

Much more of a ready reference than a discussion about how to tip, the majority of the text is alphabetically arranged, with casinos, facials, (human) guides, pool attendants, and taxi drivers among the subjects that are then broken down by selected—largely European—countries, except for the United States, which has its own chapter following the same format. Easily the biggest topics are hotels and restaurants, both subdivided by the type of personnel, then by country. If a tip is recommended, it is given in the national currency, occasionally translated into dollars. A few pages offer advice on tipping proprieties in general or for cruises or on replacing tips with gifts. Those who worry that tipping conventions may have changed since 1988 might feel compelled to consult a newer book. 240 p.

Living in the U.S.A. / Alison R. Lanier; revised by Charles William Gay. 5th ed. (Intercultural Press, 1996).

The book describes America and Americans to foreign visitors. The authors are cautious in generalizations about their subjects, which they treat perhaps a bit simply, as though they were writing a primer for the easily confused. However, those of its readers who are natives may find it refreshing to see their culture pitched through the sensibility of an outsider. The first of the three parts examines values, customs, and attitudes toward such things as the political system, work, and society. The second part tackles the practicalities dealt with in travel guides—for example, what to wear, transportation, medicine, avoiding crime, finding food, and keeping in touch with family. Aiming at those who will stay longer, the conclusion gives advice on looking for a house, what items to buy and where to buy them, obtaining household help, schooling, making friends, etc. A later edition is available. 219 p.

*The Travelers' Guide to Asian Customs & Manners: How to Converse, Dine, Tip, Drive, Bargain, Dress, Make Friends, and Conduct Business While in Asia / Elizabeth Devine and Nancy L. Braganti. 1st revised ed. (St. Martin's Griffin, 1998).

This treats over a dozen countries, including Australia and New Zealand. Beginning with an outline map and ending with key phrases, each country is split into the same subdivisions, which are signaled by graphics; among them are "greetings," "telephones," "conversation," "in public," "meals"—further refined into "table manners," "places to eat" (not an address list), and "specialties"—"private homes," and "money and business" (as in business practices). A raft of fascinating facts and advice are bulleted under these. The authors have also published *The Travelers' Guide to Latin American Customs and Manners* (St. Martin's Griffin, 2000); *The Travelers' Guide to African Customs and Manners* (St. Martin's Press, 1995), *European Customs and Manners: How to Make Friends and Do Business in Europe* (Meadowbrook Press, 1992); and *The Travelers' Guide to Middle Eastern and North African Customs & Manners* (St. Martin's Press, 1991). 352 p.

MAPS AND ATLASES

Both beautiful and useful, maps should identify features of interest to tourists (airports, historic sites, and so forth). One diagnostic of a guidebook's quality, maps should be sufficient in number and they should be practical. Similarly, the relationship between maps and the accompanying texts should be clear and near. Maps are better in color since their details are more distinctly readable.

Maps, of course, need not be attached to guidebooks. They can stand alone or be bound together as in an atlas. There are various types of maps. For example, many travelers think in terms of road maps, which can cover a small region up to a collection of countries. Here look for mileages (or kilometers) shown between points.

Country maps are in the familiar world atlas, though the detail can prove disappointing. As a narrower geographical focus is required, the number of atlases offering this also narrows. However, city maps can be easier to find than regions of a country. Hotels within a city may supply both free city maps and tourist booklets that include maps in their pages.

Finding a city map without being in the city itself may be troublesome. Besides an internet search, sensible actions are to find a guidebook with city maps; or write the proper tourist office; or use a map (or book) catalog to locate works related to the city. Sketchy city maps are in certain OAG publications, Michelin red books and other hotel books and, at least in America, telephone directories. Discovery may be a matter of luck.

Urban bus and subway route maps simplify getting around and, besides some presence online, are commonly available from tourist offices and local transit authorities. Other route maps are designed for the railroad commuter, the cyclist, and the walker. The hiker will seek out topographic maps, and the culture buff literary maps that highlight authors' haunts. Some maps include photos and small panels of text for tourist interests.

Not all maps open alike. The traditional map may have to be totally and cumbrously unfolded before it is useful. Other maps are ingeniously designed to flatten out only in that section sought after, or they may pop-up into three dimensions such as the colored maps by VanDam. Another physical characteristic to consider about a map is the material on which it is printed, which determines its durability and resistance to water.

Obtain maps from such usual places as bookstores (especially those with a large travel section), tourist offices, and hotels. Although few in number, map stores are the best physical source, and some are also online.

There are numerous commercial publishers of maps, and among the non-profit organizations are the National Geographic Society, the

American Automobile Association, and its counterpart in Britain, the Automobile Association.

Two government agencies that create maps are the Central Intelligence Agency and the United States Department of the Interior, whose Geological Survey produces topographic maps, which show landscape elevations, roads, lakes, campsites, and other natural and man-made features.

Rand McNally is probably the most widely known map publisher in the world. Other large publishers, Michelin and Lonely Planet, do both maps and guides. There are also such foreign publishers of road and tourist maps as Berndtson and Berndtson, Cartographia, Falk-Verlag, Freytag & Berndt, Hallwag Kümmerly + Frey (a few maps are accompanied by a sliding distance guide for measuring kilometers from city to city), Hema Maps (especially strong for Australia and New Zealand), Hildebrand, and Nelles. For background on several of the above publishers, see *The Map Catalog* (below).

An atlas may cover the world or a single country such as the United States. An index in an atlas is extremely important, since it gives the coordinates to pinpoint a town or area. An atlas may also have theme maps (for example, population), climate data, time zones, and other features.

Major world atlases are awkward or impractical to take on trips. In the planning stage of a journey they give a sense of where things are and the distance between points.

Pocket atlases are designed for portability. Unless they are sufficiently restricted in geographic scope, their appeal is likely to be more recreational than practical, since they are not detailed enough for good motorist maps. With them you can show your foreign friends where your hometown is or find your position relative to nearby places.

Like other printed volumes, atlases can be listed in *Books in Print*; and they may also be in map catalogs. For an idea of what to look for in atlases, see the critical evaluations of titles in the perceptive but dated *Kister's Atlas Buying Guide: General English-Language World Atlases Available in North America* by Kenneth F. Kister (Oryx Press, 1984).

Turning an atlas on its head, another important source for geographic information is the gazetteer, a dictionary arranged by place name. Unfortunately, it may not have maps.

Not least, technology has had a major influence. On the internet there are maps-on-demand that can pinpoint addresses, and programs that draw up routes. Electronic stores and outdoor companies have Global Positioning System receivers that locate one anywhere on earth. Some cars are now equipped with them.

Titles

AA Big Road Atlas, Europe. 2nd ed. (Istituto Geografico De Agostini S.P.A. and Automobile Association Developments Ltd., 2001).

The publishers and format are identical to *Frommer's Road Atlas, Europe* (below) and the maps appear to be so. It is simpler to note the differences between the titles. *AA*'s pages are bigger, fewer, and are stapled rather than spiral-bound, only English appears (though the map place names avoid Anglicization, as "Venezia" is used instead of "Venice"), and to fit more area in the frame, the scale is usually smaller, so details may be omitted. One advance in this atlas is the use of district names to help the reader locate him or herself within a country. As with *Frommer's,* the distance chart is in kilometers. A newer edition is available. 124 p.

*Atlas & Gazetteer Series (series) (DeLorme Mapping Company).

The topographic map series produces very detailed state atlases where a page equals one rectangle of a customized grid that overlays the entire state. Categorized features such as historic sites and recreational spots have separate lists with brief annotations and with keys to their location on the map, which represents towns, roads, creeks, woodlands, elevations, campgrounds, hunting areas, scenic drives and similar. Global positioning system data is also here. Examined: *Missouri Atlas & Gazetteer* (1998; 72 p.)

Business Traveler's Briefcase Atlas (Rand McNally, 2000).

The gist of this briefcase-sized, spiral-bound combination of destination facts and atlas is the space devoted to twenty-five American cities, which are enhanced by airport diagrams and maps in color of downtown streets and the cities' areas. Columned pages compactly present sections that discuss a city's forms of transportation; and have addresses with telephone numbers for hotels, select restaurants (with several sentences of commentary), leisure time localities, and attractions. The second part of the atlas presents color highway maps for the states, Canadian provinces, Mexico, and Puerto Rico. Since two "address finder" CDs are part of the package, a computer is a necessity if they are to be used, and this may mean carrying a laptop to capitalize on the portability of this work. A later edition is titled *Rand McNally Business Traveler's Atlas.* 208 p.

Collins Mini Atlas of the World (HarperCollins, 1999).

A stripped down version of *Pocket Atlas of the World* (below) both in size and content, it has the same faults, such as hiding the part of the map that is in the book's gutter. It shows maps of the world in terms of physical features, climate, countries and time zones, and population. The main part is the color maps which on facing pages usually include at least two countries, though the scales vary. In another section each gray-shaded continent comes with selective islands on one page and lakes on the other. A list of country names has columns for area, population, capital, languages, religions, and currency, while a back index of place names with their map location also serves as a table of contents. Slightly too thick to fit in a vest pocket, it is still very portable. 253 p.

The Columbia Gazetteer of the World / edited by Saul B. Cohen (Columbia University Press, 1998).

A work that has had previous incarnations, this thick, three-volume set is the most comprehensive of gazetteers. The alphabetical entries cover a range of place names throughout the world, from provinces and regions to rivers and caves. The most common entry is for urban habitations, where details may include phonetic pronunciation, designation as "city," "town," or "village," population, the administrative area it is in, what of prominence it is near in terms of mileage and kilometers, its latitude and longitude, its agricultural and industrial products, and perhaps other things of note, such as historic significance. Especially for the traveler who wants to gather any tidbit about smaller or less known places, the *Columbia* (which has an online version) may be the first resource to use; afterward more specific works may be consulted. A later edition is available. 3 vol. (3578 p.)

Columbus World Travel Atlas. 10th ed. (Nexus Media Communications/ Columbus Travel Publishing, 2006).

Aimed at travel fans and the travel industry, this is a very interesting and useful atlas that is arranged by continent or continent and surroundings. Having red airplane symbols highlighting airports, the country and regional maps are clear if perhaps a little simple for someone interested in detail, but they are especially good in showing mountainous areas. Some areas on earth show more accompanying thematic maps than others. While Europe has the greatest variety, and Africa has separate maps for physical features, climate, languages, Red Sea diving, and wildlife parks, the Australasia and Oceania part has only one (long-distance rail services for Australia). Overview text for the geographical sections has diverting comments on travel trends, problems, popular destinations, and the like. Among the twenty-one appendixes are lists of highest and lowest places on the globe, the longest rivers, a metric conversion chart, a glossary of foreign geographical terms, and a table of countries with statistics. An index chiefly of places concludes the volume. 256 p.

Flashmaps (series) (Fodor's Travel Publications).
    The unique series of city guides is composed of full-paged maps themed to the location of such subjects as airports, subways, and other transportation systems; top attractions; museums; parks; shopping spots; restaurants and lodging; nightlife; and more. Maps that have locations marked with numbered circles are followed by a list of names, addresses, telephone numbers, and the corresponding numbers; when there are restaurants among them, facts include categories of food and price range symbols, while hotels have only the latter. With streets in white, the maps usually have a pale background, making for strong contrast with features and numbers, which a few times are color-coded. A simple, thumbnail-sized map on every page gives the position of the larger map to its surroundings. The series lacks explanatory text, but there are plenty of print-heavy guidebooks that could be used along with it. The small oblong guide can fit partly down a jeans back pocket. Examined: *Flashmaps: New York* (2002; 60 maps and 141 unnumbered p.)

*Frommer's Road Atlas, Europe (Istituto Geografico De Agostini and Automobile Association Developments Ltd., 2007).
    Sensibly spiral-bound so the large pages can lay flat, the atlas shows roads in color on a pale white background with dark shadings (presumably an elevation indicator), while green represents natural areas. The map's legend displays almost two dozen road types, plus various tourist attractions. Rather than country names on the maps, there are ovals containing one or two letters that are defined in a list at the front, where the names have not been anglicized, so "Greece" (GR) is "Hellas" and "Poland" (P), "Polska." A thoroughly practical work designed for drivers in Europe, its brief explanatory text is in English, Italian, Spanish, French, and German. When the map on one page ends it is possible to find its continuation elsewhere through small triangles with page numbers. A separate section contains street maps for major cities, some of which also highlight city centers. There is an index of place names with location coordinates, and a city-to-city distance table that uses kilometers rather than miles. 304 p.

*Hammond Passport Travelmate and World Atlas (Hammond World Atlas Corporation, 1999).
    The full-color maps usually encompass a number of countries on two

facing pages, though Canada and the United States get closer scrutiny with four apiece. Detail has been traded for covering large geographical areas. A small gazetteer section has names of countries, some islands, U.S. and Australian states, and Canadian provinces, along with their area in square miles, population, and map reference. Among the additional contents are travel hints, time zones, addresses, airline distances, weather data from world cities, holidays by country, and conversion tables. Easy to fit in a back pocket, there is a lot of handy material in here that allows travelers to have at-hand a source that will both represent where a place is and answer other basic questions. 127 p.

The Map Catalog: Every Kind of Map and Chart on Earth and Even Some Above It / Joel Makower, editor. 3rd ed. (Vintage Books, 1992).

In a rich, interesting exploration of the subject, a majority of the volume is taken with types of maps. Of greatest relevance to the traveler are the chapters about transportation routes (for bicycles, mass transit, and railroads), recreation, tourism, and specific areas such as counties and foreign countries. After an explanatory introduction, there are groupings under U.S. government and commercial sources. In the former are annotations for both organizations and names of maps or map series; and though the latter is composed chiefly of an increasingly dated list of publishers, it brings useful information about them and the scope of their products. Among the appendixes are the names, addresses, and telephone numbers for both state map agencies and for map stores. 364 p.

MapEasy's Guidemap to (series) (MapEasy).

Artistic city maps of the United States and other countries have as their most conspicuous feature notations of small green squares (for shops), red dots (restaurants), blue diamonds (hotels), and black stars (noteworthy); the name of the establishment is next to each. Sometimes there are a few words of description. At least in the case of central London, other single sheet maps are larger and cover more area on one side than this one does in two but they lack this type of detail. There are several map insets. Examined: *MapEasy's Guidemap to London* (no date; 1 sheet)

*Merriam-Webster's Geographical Dictionary. 3rd ed. (Merriam-Webster, 1997).

Gazetteers are reference works that can verify the existence of a place slighted in a guidebook or expand on a name in an atlas. So long that it is a proper name from a map, it should be listed. Appropriate for a home library, *Merriam-Webster's* is an excellent one-volume gazetteer, thumb-notched for alphabetical groups of letters. Identifying comments that come after a name and pronunciation may include the place's approximate location in a country, distance from a major city, population, basis of economy, and historical events. With a key in the front, abbreviations are constantly used in entries, and symbols are frequent. A pronunciation guide is included at the bottom of most odd-numbered pages, and a short glossary of some geographical terms is located in the back. Gray-and-white maps up to a page in size accompany entries for countries, U.S. states, and Canadian provinces. The only shortcoming is the missing names that appear in the much larger three-volume *Columbia Gazetteer of the World* (above). 1361 p.

Michael Brein's Guide to . . . (series) (Michael Brein, Inc.)
    In the series, maps with routes illustrate how to get around in selected cities through use of public transportation (subway or bus). In the case of London, one side has a much enlarged illustration of its well-known underground (subway) plan, in which some stops are accompanied by numbers that represent particular points of interest. On the reverse these are treated in over thirty close-ups showing streets, placement of the stop, and a route to the numbered attractions, which are named on each mini map's left side along with the big map's reference code, its zone of cost, the names of lines serving the named stop, and perhaps exit instructions and other brief facts. The small maps may be too simplified, for streets are left out and the paths can be much more complicated than suggested. In a list of attractions, "must-sees" are put in red, while all are given a few descriptive words and the indication if there is a cost. Examined: *Michael Brein's Guide to London by the Underground* (1998; 1 sheet)

National Geographic Road Atlas: United States, Canada, Mexico (MapQuest.com, Inc., 2001).
    The large, vivid atlas has such color keys as green for parks and yellow for urban areas, while routes appear according to their type: free, toll, primary, secondary, interstate, etc. Symbols of particular tourist merit include airports, railroads, ferries, public campsites, points of interest, visitor information centers, golf courses, and ski areas; plus there is the symbol for hospitals. Most insets are just detailed enough to show the major thoroughfares through the larger metropolitan areas along with the position and names of significant attractions, though for the largest cities there are downtown street maps. Regardless of size every state occupies at least one page, though several of the smaller Canadian provinces are put together. As may be expected, the atlas has a mileage and driving time map and a city-to-city mileage chart, while another chart shows distances

between national parks and cities. In a front section several parks are highlighted. A later edition is available. 168 p.

The Penguin Encyclopedia of Places / John Paxton. 3rd ed. (Penguin Books, 1999).

If size matters, this gazetteer seems in proportion to *Merriam Webster's Geographical Dictionary* what that title is to the three-volume *Columbia Gazetteer of the World.* The *Penguin's* many fewer entries make for many fewer details. There are neither maps nor pronunciation guidance. In their alphabetical location, the native versions of anglicized names are used to point to the English name (e.g., "Cnossus" points to "Knossos"), where the full entry appears. For the tourist, the book's advantage is its comparative portability, though it is somewhat thick. Also, information may be more quickly discovered due to the shrunken number of places, which one may infer have been selected as the more significant on the globe. And the cost is cheaper. 1031 p.

Pocket Atlas of the World (Barron's Educational Series, 1999).

As portable as a paperback, but just slightly wider, the atlas introduces each continent and renders it in political, physical, and people maps, following with the countries, most being shown with their neighbors as a result of the very large scale. Moreover, the compactness means that only the largest roads and urban areas are labeled, and since a single map is on both sides of the open book, the place near the gutter is a challenge to see. After the maps section is a group of six boxes per page, with each having a short list of ready facts about a country, and as with large atlases there is a name locator index at the back. Use the atlas as an overview or introduction to where's where, and take it along, but for any particular place get a sufficiently detailed map for finding the way. 264 p.

The Road Atlas, Midsize: United States, Canada, & Mexico (Rand McNally and Company, 2003).

About as tall and wide as a sheet of copy paper, the highway atlas varies from one state per page to several states on facing pages, while next to the states are the indexes of their towns and cities with map coordinates (the size of the names on the maps reflects their populations). The treatment is the same for Canadian provinces, but Mexico, Mexico City, and Puerto Rico are crowded on one page. Toward the end of the atlas smaller maps for cities are grouped in approximate alphabetical order. To provide contrast the state or province background is in white, while featured roads are blue, red, orange, or gray. Names of state parks and green shading for nature areas are among the acknowledgments to tourists.

There is a separate mileage chart, and one North American map shows mileage and driving times between cities, while among non-map extras are features about selected itineraries and free attractions. 88 p.

United States City to City Atlas: For the Traveling Professional (American Map Corporation, 2001).

U.S. maps compose three alphabetized sections in this fair-sized highway atlas. The colored state maps that precede the collection show the major thoroughfares that go into and out of metropolitan areas. Then, the major cities among this group are selected and their downtown streets and beyond are featured in blue, white, black, and gray, along with an index of streets (an index of communities by state is in back). For some states a map may encompass facing pages, but the wide gutter margin allows for the visibility of the middle part. There are overview maps for Canada, Mexico, and a coast-to-coast interstate highway system. The mileage chart is for the lower forty-eight states only. Compared with the Rand McNally *Road Atlas, Midsize* (above), this has detailed city street maps, so for downtown driving this would be of more service. 272 p.

World Heritage Map / The UNESCO World Heritage Centre (Map Link, 2001).

As tourist attractions go, the World Heritage group is at the top. To be designated World Heritage, a site must be recognized by UNESCO as having remarkable value to the planet. This large, color world map lists more than one thousand of them on its back, where they are alphabetical by country, with a sentence or two of description for each. On the map side, countries bear the site names beside numbered circles that are colored according to categories (endangered, natural, cultural, historic, and a mixture of the preceding). Due to the proportion of spots found there, Europe rates a magnified inset, and miniature illustrations of a few dozen on the World Heritage list are present. 1 sheet

MONEY

How much will the trip cost? For many travelers the answer solely determines the choice of going or staying. Some costs can be reckoned ahead (airline ticket, tour package) and some are unknown or unplanned (souvenirs, emergencies [see **Emergencies**]). However, costs become problematic in proportion to the independence of a traveler—that is, who neither prepays nor prearranges but travels as the spirit moves him or her.

The U.S. government has sources that serve as guides for daily cost of living here and abroad. For figuring daily travel living costs abroad there is the *Maximum Travel Per Diem Allowances for Foreign Areas*, and for home there is the *Domestic Per Diem Rates* (both below). In the private sector, a consulting firm, Runzheimer International, publishes *The Runzheimer Guide to Daily Travel Prices*, a periodical which deals with cost of living expenses.

Of course banks are a major source of information on money. American banks transfer money abroad, quote foreign exchange rates, and exchange dollars for foreign currencies. So do such businesses as Thomas Cook and American Express.

A well-known source for foreign exchange rates is *The Wall Street Journal*, which has daily quotes for selected countries. Various internet sites offer up-to-date rates or can calculate the conversion from one currency standard to another (for example, see www.xe.com/ucc). When traveling in another country, find rates posted by banks, foreign exchange counters, and hotels.

Worldwide use a credit or debit card to withdraw money from automatic teller machines (ATMs), whose locations may be sought through the internet. Both Visa (Plus) and Master Card (Cirrus) have online sites (visa.via.infonow.net/locator/global/jsp/SearchPage.jsp and www.mastercard.com/cardholderservices/atm) that can find ATMs in numerous countries.

Travelers returning to this country may discover they still have foreign coins, which banks abroad or here will not exchange. This money as well as any currency can be donated to a UNICEF program called Change for Good (below).

Travel may be tax-deductible if job-related or if a result of participation in non-profit responsibilities. To find who qualifies, contact the Internal Revenue Service or consult its publications.

Titles

Domestic Per Diem Rates (U.S. General Services Administration). www.gsa.gov

How much can a visit to a place be expected to cost on a daily basis? For this the GSA has online sites and a downloadable spreadsheet list with columns by state, city destination, county, season begin and end dates, and prices—which are for the amount that will be allotted by the U.S. government to its employees for a city's lodging, food, and incidental expenses, with a final column adding them together for a maximum per diem rate. The title varies. Examined website: 2008

Maximum Travel Per Diem Allowances for Foreign Areas. Monthly (U.S. Department of State). aoprals.state.gov/web920/per_ diem.asp

The State Department's estimate of the maximum daily cost of living abroad for its employees is documented here. When the figures are downloaded as a spreadsheet, the most helpful columns identify country; a location that is often a city; season start and end dates; and expenses for lodging and for meals and incidentals, with a dollar summation of them all. Similar to *Domestic Per Diem Rates* (above), it likewise gives a traveler an estimate of how much to allot for daily expenses. Examined website: 2008

Travel, Entertainment, Gift, and Car Expenses: For Use in Preparing . . . Returns. Annual (Internal Revenue Service, U.S. Department of the Treasury). www.irs.gov/pub/irs-pdf/p463.pdf

Publication 463 is an IRS form that deals with deducting travel and other expenses that are business-related. Examined website: 2008

Organizations

Internal Revenue Service. U.S. Department of the Treasury. www.irs. ustreas.gov

Consult the IRS for questions on deducting travel expenses. Helpful publications are number 463 (*Travel, Entertainment, Gift, and Car Expenses*, reviewed above) and number 970 (*Tax Benefits for Education*). Examined website: 2008

Office of American Citizens Services and Crisis Management. Overseas Citizens Services. Bureau of Consular Affairs. U.S. Department of State. travel.state.gov/travel/travel_1744.html

Among its powers are transfers of funds overseas to benefit U.S.

citizens in need and approval of emergency loans for the destitute.
Examined website: 2008

UNICEF www.unicefusa.org/support/cfg.html
  To help children, UNICEF's Change for Good program accepts
contributions of foreign coins and currency. Airlines have assisted this
organization by distributing donation envelopes to its passengers.
Examined website: 2008

MOTORCYCLE TOURING

Books that address touring by motorcycle typically consider types of motorcycles, their maintenance, clothing for a trip, and routes.

See also **Automobile and Recreational Vehicle Travel** and **Budget Travel**.

Subject Heading: Motorcycle touring

Titles

Adventure Motorcycling Handbook / Christ Scott. 4th ed. (Trailblazer Publications, 2001).

Of the three parts composing the work, the first discusses what it takes to tour with a motorcycle, from showing the steps for fixing a punctured tire (in captioned photographs) to evaluation of the right bike and clothing. In the second part, short sections examine countries and continents for riding through. Since this is adventure motorcycling, some of the featured places are exotic. Boxed insets provide supplemental comments, while one page summaries for each route (e.g., Dubai to Britain) from a single named rider's perspective are formatted in more than thirty headings, such as trip duration, sponsorship, best day, biggest mistake, bike's model, type of baggage, and accidents—a tantalizing amount of information. Riders relate their own travel stories in the last part, and while diverting, it has the least assistance for the reader. A later edition is available. 288 p.

American Motorcyclist Association Ride Guide to America / edited by Greg Harrison (Whitehorse Press, 2005).

Dividing tours into parts of the continental United States, the attractive, polished work that contain many color photos begins with tips on carrying stuff on the motorcycle and riding on the road. Pages of introduction to each region are followed by separate round trip itineraries. At their head are the short features of name, distance in miles, highlights of attractions, and directions measured in terms of the mile reached, meaning the cyclist must watch the pedometer. Each route comes with a clear, color road map laid over a simple topographic background. However, the majority of the itinerary is a narrative about sights, the names of which are bolded. Those who want more trips in the same region are told of relevant titles from this publisher. 286 p.

Motorcycle Touring & Travel: A Handbook of Travel by Motorcycle / Bill Stermer. 2nd ed. (Whitehorse Press, 1999).

This book's largest chapters give advice on choosing a motorcycle, accessorizing and maintaining it, and wearing apparel. The smaller discuss what and how to pack, riding with others, camping, security and safety, clubs, tours and, with material that is far too meager, motorcycling in other countries. Colored boxes among the two-column pages provide extra details about aspects of some topics. Approximately the size of a *Time* or *Newsweek*, the work comes with both black-and-white and color photographs. The contents could have been beefed up with possible itineraries, addresses of pertinent touring companies and organizations, and a section of book and magazine titles. 160 p.

Motorcycle Touring: Everything You Need to Know / Gregory W. Frazier (Motorbooks, 2005).

Large without being thick, the book concentrates on the how of motorcycle touring through a generous use of color photos, sophisticated graphics, and two columns of text per page. An introductory section is a first-person account of traveling, and the remainder keeps this point of view and lessons from the author's experiences as it relates to a number of topics: going by oneself vs. with others; equipment; maintenance and repairs on the road; packing; cycle gizmos and gadgets; keeping warm, dry, and cool; physical hazards, etc. One impression given is that motorcycle touring is for adventurous people willing to live on a tight budget, along with all the circumstances that this implies. 157 p.

MUSEUMS, ZOOS, ETC.

Museums, zoos, and related institutions (nature centers, museum villages, etc.) are major tourist draws. They receive selective mention in general guidebooks, but directories centered on them offer the opportunity for comprehensiveness and detail. Besides name, address and telephone number, expect useful listings to have the hours of opening and closing, entrance fees, available facilities, and a description of the collection.

The majority of museum directories concentrate on North America, though some cover Europe or the world. Books may also be about museums based on their area of concentration (such as archaeology, oddities, war) or category (living displays, historic houses). Such guidebooks that specialize in this area are likely to give the greatest amount of attention to art museums.

Titles

America's Ancient Treasures: A Guide to Archeological Sites and Museums in the United States and Canada / Franklin Folsom, Mary Elting Folsom. 4th revised, enlarged ed. (University of New Mexico Press, 1993).

More at home on a bookshelf or carried in a vehicle, this commanding reference is a must for those who wish to know museums, parks, geographic areas, and sites associated with archaeology that is related to the American Indian and prehistoric people. Each region (Southwest, Great Plains, etc.) has an introduction followed by a state or province with its collection of entries. The name of the place has a paragraph with address, telephone number, when open, the price of admission and, at times (presumably when finding the destination is enough of a challenge), driving instructions. Further paragraphs discuss the history and the remains that are there, the degree of attention being dependant on its importance. An attractive layout usually places entries at the bottom half of the page in two or three columns, while the top half is dedicated to a photograph, illustration, or mini-essay. Maps are omitted. The date of publication means that some information is obsolete. 459 p.

America's Art Museums: A Traveler's Guide to Great Collections Large and Small / Suzanne Loebl (W.W. Norton & Company, 2002).

A state-arranged entry begins with a formatted section of place and name above bolded headings for address, telephone, website, and hours. There are collection strengths (which may be an artist, genre, medium, country, or time); special events (often with the succinct label "temporary exhibits"); a grab-bag of other offerings, such as the presence of a museum shop; activities for children; and whether the parking is on the street or elsewhere. Narrative paragraphs give a history of the museum, its founders, and touch upon several highlights on display, though there is no real discussion of their significance. The directory is undoubtedly selective both in its inclusions and the facts about them, but if the reader is satisfied with an overview, this offers it. To find out about accommodations, eating, other attractions, and so forth, consult a regular travel guide. 426 p.

America's Strangest Museums: A Traveler's Guide to the Most Unusual and Eccentric Collections / Sandra Gurvis. Revised and updated (Carol Publishing Group, 1998).

Arranged by region and state, this could be used as a guide, or simply read serendipitously for entertainment, since it offers no subject index. Each museum chosen receives several pages of narrative background and description of contents set off in a tone of humor and wordplay. Frogs in art and as knickknacks, Elvis is alive, the tooth fairy, and a history of the fur trade are a sample of the variety of this sub-genre of off-the-beaten-path travel. At the end of an entry the practical information comes in a few lines relating to address and telephone number, the general location and opening times (both of which can be vague), and whether there is an admission price. Look for web and e-mail addresses in an appendix rather than with the entries, where they belong. "*America's*" is a small misnomer, since Ontario, Canada collections are slightly represented. 307 p.

American Art Directory. Biennial (National Register Publishing).

Consult a library for this as well as *Museums of the World* and *The Official Museum Directory* (both below). As the *OMD* focuses on U.S. museums, so the *American Art Directory* further focuses its scope, at the same time omitting parts from the other two. Like *The Official Museum Directory*, there is more information than the visitor needs. Notably lacking in all three titles are value judgments on quality, services, and amenities. In the largest section of this work the arrangement of art organizations is by state or province (since Canada is also covered), then town or city, where is displayed museum name, address, telephone number, and fax and electronic data. Among the bolded areas is one giving categories of special subjects and a second expanding a little about the collections. A third, "activities," notes the presence of programs for adults and children, public lectures and concerts, tours, film series, museum shops, etc. A much smaller section provides some similar facts about museums abroad. A subject index proves a useful cross-reference, though the front of it lacks a master list of subjects within, so it will not be possible to know at a glance that there are such terms as "dolls" or "Mexican art." Examined: 2007; 1027 p.

Art across America: A Comprehensive Guide to American Art Museums and Exhibition Galleries / edited by John J. Russell and Thomas S. Spencer (Friar's Lantern, Inc., 2000).

After the state, community, and address, bolded headings are concisely filled in as to telephone number; fax; internet address; administrative head; admission cost; annual (?) attendance; when established; member-ship availability; accessibility for the disabled; parking; days and hours open and closed; facilities (exhibition areas, library, shop, etc.); types of activities (films, gallery talks, lectures, temporary exhibitions, etc.); and if there are newsletters or other publications. After this, a few lines of text describe what is in the collection. Small black-and-white photographs spotlight pieces of art or the building that houses the collection. This big book has a page-sized map for each state showing its interstate routes and locating the names of the cities and towns that are homes to the sites. Not every entry has the full complement of headings, and typically no individual works are analyzed nor are there any museum diagrams. But there are *many* art destinations cited. 898 p.

Children's Museums: An American Guidebook / Joann Norris (McFarland & Company, 1998).

Under a state is the name of the museum and its town or city. After an overview of one or more paragraphs come short sub-areas. One sentence summarizes the museum, often in a few words that commonly have the phrase "hands on"; and another identifies just a general location (e.g., downtown, a neighborhood) without benefit of driving instructions. Other parts note hours and admission costs, unique exhibits, the names of nearby attractions (minus addresses), and where to write or call for more information. Even entries that have all these parts are skimpy in filling them. Maps would have been more use than the black-and-white photos here and there of a museum's outside or inside. In its current edition, it is unsatisfactory because it provides too little. 217 p.

The Essential Guide to Collectibles: A Source Book of Public Collections in Europe and the USA / Alistair McAlpine and Cathy Giangrande (Viking Studio, 2001).

The fascinating and attractive book may be browsed for its own sake, but therein lies its problem as a guidebook, since touring suggests finding attractions geographically. Rather than geographic, organization is by broad subjects—childhood memorabilia, decorative arts, etc.—that are then narrowed down to a variety of categories, from kitchenalia and eating utensils to hunting, shooting, and fishing. An entry is brief, giving the name of the museum or place, the address, telephone, website, the times when open, and several lines defining what is there. Color examples are on most of the slick pages. At the back, the collections are listed by country, but unfortunately not by city, and this is one time when the United States is not sub-arranged by state. However, if there is interest in any of the subjects covered, consider putting up with the book's drawbacks. 640 p.

A Guide to American Zoos & Aquariums / Darcy and Robert Folzenlogen (Willow Press, 1993).

Arranged geographically and with dots marking locations on blank state maps, an entry begins with a brief overview followed by information for visitors (driving directions, hours, admission and parking fees, the presence of a children's zoo, comments on programs and tours, etc.), some of which is inaccurate owing to the book's datedness. There is also the number of mammals and other types of species, special exhibits, animals that are part of a breeding program, research done, seasonal festivals and programs, and an address. Gift shops and amenities are omitted, as are acreage and landscape description. Aquariums make a small portion of the 173 listings, whose quality must be inferred, for there is too little evaluation of the attractions. A newer edition would be welcome. 324 p.

Little Museums: Over 1,000 Small and Not-So-Small American Show-places / Lynne Arany; Archie Hobson (Henry Holt and Company, 1998).

Attractions appear to be selected according to their appeal and interest. While some of the museums deal with traditional subjects, a number concentrate on people, commercial enterprises, aspects of social history, or collections of objects. Tourists who like the surprising or off-beat may be pleased by what they discover here, whether it concerns water skiing, magic, nuts, funeral services, elephants, or farm toys; any of which might be found thanks to the subject headings assigned to museums at the back of the work. Arranged under a state's city or town, the museum and its focus are described in several sentences. A mention of gift shops, tours, programs, libraries, and hands-on comes in colored type, as does separate areas for telephone number and address, locating the museum, and times of being open, along with whether entrance is free or fee (though no prices are provided). 431 p.

Museums of the World. 8th revised and enlarged ed. (K.G. Saur, 2001).
Although in two large volumes, the print remains small, crowded, and in four columns per page to accommodate the contents of this, the largest directory of museums. Under alphabetized country and city or town, the name and address of the museum is in its native language rather than translated into English, and this is followed—with occasional omissions—by telephone and fax number, URL or e-mail address, the head's name, the type (for example, local or natural history), and a few generic words designating what is in the collection. For locating a museum by its holdings, look through the broad subject categories in the back of volume two, where additionally there is a small list of names of noteworthy persons. Found in larger libraries, this reference work has begun to be revised on a yearly basis, so newer editions are available. It is most handy for identifying or verifying museums that exist where one is planning a visit or when one is intent on finding museums that deal with a certain subject. 2 vol.

The New York Times Traveler's Guide to Art Museum Exhibitions. Annual (The New York Times).
The states of the United States and selected countries of the rest of the world—in Europe especially—appear in this oblong book which, though thick, should still fit in an average glove compartment. The concentration on a yearly schedule of exhibitions makes much of the information in an edition very time sensitive, though for the touring art lover this is an important acquisition. The temporary exhibitions are presented in terms of date, name, a short description, and whether they travel, with the remainder of the entry providing more fixed information, which encompasses the museum's name, address, and website; a summary of its permanent collection along with a note of its highlights and the building in which it is housed; its admission price; times of opening; and when it is closed. Icons identify the presence of recorded tours, programs for children, food and drink vendors, museum shops, and accessibility for the handicapped. Front matter is a list of major traveling exhibitions and shows that focus on particular artists. The black-and-white illustrations are chiefly of paintings. The exhibitions are gathered in a convenient form as they are nowhere else, but likewise it is they who make much of the work obsolete when the year ends. Later editions are called *The New York Times Traveler's Guide to International Art Museum Exhibitions*, which apparently ceased in 2005. Examined: 2002; 496 p.

The Official Museum Directory. Annual (National Register Publishing).
The directory of institutions is in the colossal first of the two volumes

where the arrangement is by state and town or city for aquariums, arboretums, historic houses, nature centers, planetariums, and zoos, in addition to types of museums. The range of information under each listing is far in excess of what the traveler will find useful, with the relevant though succinct areas being name, address, telephone number, electronic address, type of museum, collection contents, offerings (guided tours, lectures, films, exhibitions, etc.), hours, and admission prices. One of the sections in back indexes the directory entries by broad subject category, with art, history, science, and specialized museums narrowed into sub-categories. Another section gathers together the URLs presented in the entries. Do not expect to discover names of works or of exhibits, but use it like *Museums of the World* (above). Examined: 1998; 2 vol.

On Exhibit: Art Lover's Travel Guide to American Museums / Judith Swirsky. Annual (Abbeville Press Publishers).

While the scope of *The New York Times Traveler's Guide to Art Museum Exhibitions* (above) is international, this is U.S. only and lacks the other's polish and readability. Under a state's town or city, a listing consists of the museum name and address and, in small print, telephone number, website, and italicized headings—whose number varies with the entry—among which are those for opening and closing times and days, free days, costs for adults and children, group tours, the historic quality of the building, shop, and permanent collection details. A paragraph expands on the museum's holdings, and in the majority of cases is followed by its year's list of exhibits, consisting of dates, names, and often descriptions. The many abbreviations and symbols encompass facts about nationality, media, subject matter, museum services, holidays, and other things that can mean continuous trips from the entry to the explanation of the codes in the book's front or to one of the tear-out bookmarks that contain them. The title appears to have ended in 2002. Examined: 2001; 335 p.

The Zoo Book: A Guide to America's Best / Allen W. Nyhuis (Carousel Press, 1994).

A book that must please those who love zoos, among its zoo-going advice that precedes the regionally arranged entries is the matter of handling children and the characterization (with photos) of interesting animals. Bolded subdivisions supply hours, admission fees, directions, what not to miss, touring tips, and entertainment shows. Then paragraphs compose an introduction, commentary on featured and other exhibits, and something about the the stuff designed for youngsters. Zoos that did not make the first cut get recognized with a single paragraph under "Best of the Rest." After them are zoos recognized only through name along with their city and state. Wildlife parks, special zoos (for reptiles, birds, or monkeys), aquariums, aquatic parks, and theme parks get compact coverage, as does the final selection of worldwide zoos, with upbeat descriptions of their size, quality, and animals on show (animals mentioned in the text are in the index). Maps would have been a plus. The same author has published *America's Best Zoos: A Travel Guide for Fans & Families* (Intrepid Traveler, 2008). 277 p.

NEWSPAPERS

For valuable travel ideas mine the Sunday travel section of daily newspapers. Aside from features on countries and tourist destinations, contents can include news of tours and cruises, air rates, readers' questions and readers' recommendations, travel advisories, articles on types of travelers (business, elderly, etc.), and eclectic travel pieces. The ads, too, are worth noting.

To keep travelers up-to-date, the *International Herald Tribune* and *USA Today* are American English-language newspapers widely found abroad. Look for them and British newspapers on sale in large international hotels; or seek out a bookstore or newsstand with an international section, or an American culture center or club, or even a library. Conversely, those who visit the United States from non-English speaking countries might consider similar courses of action in order to find news in their own language. For a list of newspapers aimed at foreign language enclaves within the United States see the "Foreign Language Newspapers" section in *Bowker's News Media Directory*.

Local newspapers are a keyhole to a specific part of a country. Whatever their language, newspapers of all countries are selectively listed in the *Political Handbook of the World*. For a list of North American newspapers (and broadcast stations) try the *Gale Directory of Publications and Broadcast Media*. The internet offers several sites that list English-language newspapers published abroad, e.g., "Worldwide News in English" at www.thebigproject.co.uk/news

PARKS, SAFARIS, AND THE OUTDOORS

Animals, plants, scenery, and closeness to nature are the universal attractions of national parks and wildlife areas throughout the world. Some travelers extend their visits for days while to others they are a few hours' diversion.

Use park directories to locate information about them. A good directory should have each park's name, location and how to get there, seasons of operation, entrance fees, area size, recognition of facilities, and geographical and wildlife features.

There are numerous guides about America's national parks. The Audubon Society, the Sierra Club, and the International Union for the Conservation of Nature are three major nature organizations that have produced directories for United States national parks. The National Park Service has published a number of titles on both parks and wilderness areas.

If the park is elsewhere, it could be included in the coverage of a country guide, the more likely if it is well known. Individual park directories cover Africa, South America, and the world. Among commercial publishers, the London-based New Holland has produced several books that cover parks in such under-reported areas as southern Africa, the Philippines, and Indonesia.

African parks in particular are popular destinations for tours and safaris. Arrange visits through general tour companies, adventure outfits, and the travel programs offered by zoos, museums, and wildlife organizations. The chief means of finding tours offered by these last three can be through the ads and classifieds in the magazines or newsletters they publish.

Subject Heading: National parks and reserves

Titles

Africa's Top Wildlife Countries / Mark W. Nolting. Revised and expanded 6th ed. (Global Travel Publishers, 2003).

This starts with general advice about the safari experience and the different types, such as game drives and walking safaris. The author now and again borrows on first-person experiences in describing a park or wilderness entry's physical features and wildlife, particularly mammals and birds. The park accommodations are classified by comfort and amenities, with perhaps a sentence giving the number of rooms and other facts. However, omitted are the various details found in the better books on U.S. parks, though this book does come through with an inclusiveness for the seventeen countries treated here, a few of which are admitted as being unsafe to visit; which does not stop Nolting from profiling all of the numerous parks with his enthusiastic point of view. A scattering of black-and-white photos of animals, people, and surroundings are joined by a center section in color. At the head of every country chapter a shaded map shows roads, towns, parks and other areas, and a few of the major parks are also mapped. Although missing from the various appendixes are listings of outfits that provide wildlife packages, this is the book to consult on African park safaris. 688 p.

America's National Wildlife Refuges: A Complete Guide / Russell D. Butcher and others (Roberts Rinehart Publishers in cooperation with Ducks Unlimited, 2003).

The refuges are alphabetized by their names under each state. The lengths of descriptions vary, but many take up at least a substantial page. There is no subdivision of the contents other than with paragraphs, and no bolding of important things, so location of a fact requires reading through until it is found. Frequent themes are waterfowl, their habitat, and environmental endangerment, while the U.S. Fish and Wildlife Service is liberally quoted. Visitor activities and entrance fees may or may not be noted, and places for lodging and food are acknowledged only through brief naming of nearby towns. The end of each entry has one box with access directions and another with name, address, and telephone number. Maps are lacking. The series *Audubon Guide to the National Wildlife Refuges* (below) is a better choice, but it does not have, as this one does, all the refuges in a single volume. 714 p.

Audubon Guide to the National Wildlife Refuges (series) (St. Martin's Griffin).

With several states to a volume, these slick oblong books have color photos and black-and-white drawings of animals. Maps are principally in two shades of green, with blue for water features, and as appropriate they show numbered traffic routes, park headquarters, campgrounds, parking spots, and boat ramps. Within each state, a refuge is introduced, followed by sections on its history and directions for getting to it along with bolded parts for season, hours, fees, etc. Touring the refuge is considered in terms of automobile, walking, cycling, and canoe, kayak, or boat. The largest space is devoted to giving the visitor ideas about the landscape and climate, varieties of plant types, and the animal life (especially, and unsurprisingly, birds, but also mammals, reptiles, and amphibians). The final heading, "activities," may expand into subdivisions for camping and swimming, wildlife observation, photography, hikes and walks, seasonal events, and publications. An occasional inset is dedicated to special subjects, such as the cottonmouth water moccasin or hunting and fishing seasons. Though some refuges receive fuller treatment than others, like the *National Geographic Guide to the National Parks of the United States* (below) this attractive series is very good at what it does and is crisp in its organization. Examined: *Audubon Guide to the National Wildlife Refuges: South Central—Arkansas, Kansas, Louisiana, Missouri, Oklahoma* / William Palmer (2000; 243 p.)

The Complete Guide to the National Park Lodges / David L. Scott, Kay W. Scott. 5th ed. (Insiders' Guide, 2006).

Arranged by state, the lodges are under the jurisdiction of the National Park Service. After a short introduction to the park or equivalent along with general observations on accommodations, there are several substantial paragraphs that offer a balanced and thorough picture of an individual lodge, and may include advice, such as which rooms have the best views. Description is followed up through as many as eleven bolded headings that encompass rooms; wheelchair accessibility; reservations; rates; location as it relates to a road or where it is in the park; the season of operation; food and meals; transportation in the form of air flights, rentals, and bus service; facilities (restaurants, gift shops, etc.); available activities; and conditions for pets. On the large pages a drawing of the lodge accompanies each entry, and throughout there are shaded area maps that may show routes to the lodge and around the park, but omit explanations for several symbols. 246 p.

Fodor's Family Adventures / Christine Loomis. 4th ed. (Fodor's Travel Publications, 2002).

Choose from more than a score of activities in which families may participate: archaeology, biking, canoeing, cattle drives, trekking with llamas and burros, wildlife encounters, etc. Each chapter comes with a suite of sensible questions to ask about trips that are worldwide, though the majority is in the United States and Canada. An entry has the age recommended for the youngest (as, "6+") unless labeled for "all," and provides an overview of the name of the company or outfitter and its offerings, then a substantial description with details of the experience for family members. Contact information, seasons of availability and costs, come in an italicized grouping. For those who want to know more, there are resources in the nature of organizations, books, periodicals, and products accompanied by brief comments. A short geographic list by region of the U.S. or by country shows trip destinations. The work succeeds admirably in hitting its target. 274 p.

The Great American Wilderness: Touring America's National Parks / Larry H. Ludmer. 3rd ed. (Hunter Publishing, 2000).

The regionally arranged parks have sections and subsections along with insets for brief tips and other commentary. After an overview, there are headings that concern getting there, park history, size, admission fee, climate and when to go, and contact information. Auto tours and short stops describe what can be seen, the more prominent features bolded in the narration; then a space devoted to longer stops emphasizes where to hike, while another section of special activities may describe horseback riding or touring by four-wheel drive. Various hotels, motels, and dining facilities within or near a park are separately reviewed in several sentences, but campgrounds are usually put in a table with columns for their name, location, number of sites, and cost per day. At the end of the book are multi-day itineraries that are referenced to the parks. The simple map for each park marks its area in gray, with roads and icons identifying the whereabouts of information availability, restrooms, etc. The binding for the trade paperback should be stronger, and it cannot compete in attractiveness with the Audubon or National Geographic titles (in this section), but its text packs a lot of comments. 506 p.

National Geographic Guide to the National Parks of the United States. 4th ed. (National Geographic Society, 2003).

Among the several strengths of this slick-papered book are, as to be expected, the color maps. For each area of the country and for the individual parks, they clearly mark ranger stations, campgrounds, roads, and trails against a topographic background. Numerous color photos share the two-column pages of park description that comes with subsections about getting there, the best time to visit, and what to do. Giving mileage and time length, there are suggestions for trips on foot or by vehicle that are up to a day or more, with names of the important stops and sights bolded in the narrative paragraphs. Another section has the address for park headquarters and facts about the season and accessibility; visitor centers; entry fee; pets; facilities for the disabled; things to do; special advisories; overnight backpacking; and accommodations, which have a price range. When National Monuments, Forests, and Refuges are close, there is excursion information in thumbnail format. Knowledgeable, thorough in coverage, and extremely well-designed, this is a first-rate work that can be readily taken along in a car or perhaps a pack. A companion volume is the *National Geographic Guide to the State Parks of the United States*. A later edition is available. 464 p.

National Park System Map and Guide (National Park Service, U.S. Department of the Interior, 2006). www.pueblo.gsa.gov/cic_text/travel/parkserv/parkserv.htm

The online site—an earlier version of the title—consists of two PDF links. A United States map with state outlines and routes for interstate highways shows waterways and locations in color to aid readability, and it identifies park systems by names along with abbreviations for type (as "NHS" for National Historic Site). Puerto Rico and other islands with U.S. ties are squeezed in here. The other link is to a table that has a row for a park's name, address, and telephone number, and almost thirty colored columns registering whether there are fees, visitor centers, picnic areas, hiking, swimming, bicycle trails, cabin rentals, accessibility, etc. In paper, the title is a one-sheet foldout, with the map and a list of parks on opposite sides. Examined website: 2008

National Parks Europe (The ENDAT Group, 2000).

America is rich in comprehensive park guides, but Europe is not. This one restricts itself to describing the landscape features, animals and plants, and the associated history, while omitting suggestions for accommodations, eating, and activities, even if the latter are implied. Nor are their fee listings, best time to visit, directions to get there, and all the other facts that are familiar in American park guides. Of moderate size, the book has three-column pages that are interrupted by bolded headings that change from entry to entry; and there is a two-page spread, with color photos, for each of the nearly one hundred parks reviewed from thirty-some countries. The small park maps are chiefly of pictorial rather than practical interest, though at the start of regional sections there are larger multi-country maps with red numbered dots showing relative locations of parks. At the end of an entry is a box containing contact information. 255 p.

The Official Guide to America's National Parks. 12th ed. (Fodor's Travel Publications, 2004).

Grouped by state, the entries in this oblong book hover around the length of a page of descriptions and facts that are to the purpose. An overview paragraph of a few lines is followed by "What to See & Do," which identifies activities and comments about the physical facilities and if there are ranger-guided tours, etc. "Food, Lodging & Supplies" is divided into bolded headings for camping, hotels, restaurants, and groceries and gear. "Fees, Hours & Regulations" may include a pet policy. Another section supplies instructions about getting to the destination, and a final one lists mail addresses, telephone numbers, and URLs. Dependable for planning a trip or taken along in a car, it covers, besides parks, historic sites, monuments, memorials, battlefields, and natural areas. Several appendixes swell the number of entries. A later edition is titled *Fodor's Official Guide to America's National Parks*. 483 p.

Parks Directory of the United States: A Guide to More Than 5,270 National and State Parks, Historic Sites, Battlefields, Monuments, Forests, Preserves, Memorials, Seashores, Trails, Heritage Areas, Scenic Byways, Marine Sanctuaries, Wildlife Refuges, Urban Parks, and Other Designated Recreation Areas in the United States Administered by National, State, and Municipal Park Agencies. Also Includes Canadian National Parks / edited by Darren L. Smith, Kay Gill. 5th ed. (Omnigraphics, 2007).

Despite the descriptive completeness of the subtitle, some more comments may be added about this thick, large-paged book. A number of designations in the title have their own chapters, the largest by far being for state parks (arranged by state). Park and conservation-related organizations also have their own chapter. On the two-column pages an entry begins with name, address, website, telephone number, and fax. Characteristics that are noted depend on the category. In the case of state parks, there are bolded headings for acreage; the location relative to a road or nearby town; facilities; activities; and special features. A simple and effective one-to-two page map for each state marks the position of every park, while several U.S. maps—insufficiently detailed—are for wildlife refuges, etc. A classification index groups the parks by type and a special features index is chiefly keyed to proper names in the entries. A final index is alphabetical by name of park. This is a thorough overview for those considering park vacations. 1101 p.

The Safari Companion: A Guide to Watching African Mammals, Including Hoofed Mammals, Carnivores, and Primates / Richard Estes. Revised and expanded ed. (Chelsea Green Publishing Company, 1999).

This reliable and substantial resource can be kept in a vehicle to consult for additional information about a species being observed. For every species, types of information are grouped under bolded headings. For example, one paragraph identifies the animal (using weight and height range, tail, coat, color, and other markings), while another describes at length where it lives, and a third goes into how it fits into the ecology. Other topics concern activity, social/mating system, how the mammal moves, reproduction, offspring and maternal care, and its predators. For some animals, the largest amount of description concerns elements of behavior. General animal classes, such as carnivores, are characterized in introductory chapters. Each mammal is depicted in a black-and-white drawing. A simple map shows main national parks and game reserves from the southern tip of Africa to as far north as Uganda. 459 p.

Sierra Club Adventure Travel Guides (series) (Sierra Club Books).
    The representative work from the series here examined is the second edition (1999) of *Adventuring in Australia: New South Wales, Northern Territory, Queensland, South Australia, Tasmania, Victoria, Western Australia* by Eric Hoffman, and it comes with more breadth than depth. The Australian states noted in the subtitle are described particularly, though not exclusively, in terms of parks, areas of wilderness, and various other points of interest, plus attention is paid to walks and other recreations within the range of the moderately active. Though reminiscent of the *Let's Go* budget series in format, the book has inconsistencies, with parts headed "accommodations" or "access" disappearing then reappearing from entry to entry. The emphasis is on natural attractions, but the author also looks at dining, entertainment, and other ways of spending time in the cities, the major ones depicted through efficient gray-and-white street maps. In this series a score of titles begin with the words *Adventuring in*, with "adventuring" understood as the enjoyment that is derived from being outdoors rather than the quest for thrills. 514 p.

United Nations List of Protected Areas / World Conservation Monitoring Centre and the IUCN World Commission on Protected Areas (IUCN/UICN, 1998).
    Having a vast scope but a narrow depth, the imposing library reference work should be consulted by the ambitious park visitor wishing to discover the thousands of "protected areas" that exist throughout the world, well-known or obscure. In alphabetical order, island nations and the countries of all seven continents appear with their territories described under a bewildering number of titles: coastal parks/reserves, conservation areas, forest reserves, game reserves, historic sites, national parks, protected landscapes, whale sanctuaries, etc. Across from the site name is its category (labeled I to VI and based on the reason for protection), its longitude and latitude, size, and year of establishment. That's all there is. However, with knowledge of a name and locale, one could hunt down in a gazetteer or elsewhere the details about the landscape, flora, fauna, and if there are amenities for the tourist. At the back of this considerable book are lists of World Heritage Sites, biospheres, wetlands, and bird protection areas. (Aside from its age and brief number covered, the 1972 *National*

Parks of the World [Golden Press] by Kai Curry-Lindahl and Jean-Paul Harroy does provide basics on geology, topography, and plant and animal species.) A later edition is available. 412 p.

Organizations and Publishers

National Park Service. www.nps.gov

This government agency has numerous titles dealing with natural history, landmarks, specific parks, and related subjects, though many are not aimed at the casual tourist. Some are available both in print and for free on the internet, such as *The National Parks: Lesser-Known Areas*. Examined website: 2008

Sierra Club. www.sierraclub.org

Producing publications under its name and offering national and international outdoor programs, its site has links leading to descriptions of them. Examined website: 2008

UNESCO. whc.unesco.org

On this site find a link to *The World Heritage List*, an identification of world-class natural and cultural locales by the United Nations Educational, Scientific and Cultural Organization. Typical examples on the *List* are parks, geographic features, archaeological remains, and historic cities. Examined website: 2008

PHOTOGRAPHY

Commemorate travel experiences with photographs of the trip. But to avoid disappointment take the right camera and be familiar with its operation.

Printed help is available. Photography manuals may have a chapter on travel shots and travel guidebooks occasionally make a nod to taking photographs, but there are complete books about travel photography. They provide advice on equipment, preparation, the mechanics of a good photo, and what to photograph.

(It is also important to know what *not* to photograph. Some countries prohibit shots of airports, railroad stations, and of course military installations; and it is proper etiquette to ask permission before pointing a camera at someone.)

Digital photography continues to gain on film photography, so much so that recent books on digital photography are quicker to age as digital cameras and techniques evolve in leaps.

Subject Heading: Travel photography

Titles

Berlitz Travel Photography / Jon Davison (Berlitz Publishing Company, 1995).

Certainly small enough to fit in a back pocket, the book uses its two-column pages to explain the technique and other matter behind the accompanying color photographs that the author/photographer has taken throughout the world. It suggests ways of looking creatively at the places to which one travels. There's also a little shoptalk about photography. 128 p.

A Comprehensive Guide to Digital Travel Photography / Duncan Evans (AVA Publishing, 2005).

Most of the book is about how to go about shooting travel subjects, with categories for hot (e.g., beaches) and cool places, people, action, animals, types of transportation, and architecture; and a concluding chapter about the use of special digital effects. With examples from a host of different photographers, each pair of facing pages shows a color travel photograph several times and discusses it in terms of an overview, how it was shot and enhanced, whether it is for sale, separate tips about the shot, and perhaps a chart showing contrast levels or other features. The book's blurb states that the audience encompasses both the "experienced photographer" and the "happy-snapper," though in the latter case it is better to assume there is prior familiarity with camera operation. 144 p.

The Digital Photographer's Handbook: Travel / Simon Joinson (Roto-Vision SA, 2003).

Less than a quarter of the book addresses travel photography, which compactly discusses traveling with a camera, types of subjects to shoot, professional techniques, and more. The majority of the work is an all-purpose manual on using digital photography, albeit travel photographs are the examples throughout. There is an introduction to cameras, lenses, scanners, software tools, and printing, and later there are instructions about manipulating the image after it has been downloaded onto a computer, including methods such as removing elements, adding a new sky, and changing color. To reflect its stages of alteration a photographic image is repeated with modifications. 110 p.

Digital Photography Outdoors: A Field Guide for Travel and Adventure Photographers / James Martin (The Mountaineers Books, 2004).

The author states his work is designed for the serious outdoor photographer, whether amateur or professional. As someone dedicated to finding the just right shot, he outlines the resolve and know-how it takes. A number of travel photographs serve as examples throughout the text as it discusses techniques, composition, light, cameras and their accessories, and the like. The part related to digital shooting looks at photo editing programs and file formats, the uses of computers and peripherals, methods of changing the image, etc. The chapter of most relevance to the traveler is the concluding one, which compactly considers approaches to shots as they separately apply to water, mountains, forests, wildlife, and other travel or outdoor subjects. 157 p.

*Digital Travel Photography Digital Field Guide / David D. Busch (Wiley Publishing, Inc., 2006).

For once there is a guide that for most of its content truly integrates the subject of travel with photography. The graphically astute design promotes the reader's ability to find specific facts, with two columns of text broken up by different shades of in-chapter headings, bolded bullets, sufficient white space, and a dispersion of color travel photos throughout. The clear, informed explanations about the technical aspects of digital picture-taking and about the unique artistic opportunities of travel photography are aimed at the beginner, but once the basics are explored subtler approaches are discussed. In the volume's latter half a series of tables present possible photographic situations and analyzes them in terms of lighting, lens, camera settings, exposure, and accessories, the author's work serving as examples for the reader. An appendix has a select annotated list of relevant websites and notes a few books. 236 p.

Great Travel Photography / Cliff Hollenbeck, Nancy Hollenbeck (Amherst Media, 1996).

The depth of coverage is at best average in this tallish, flat book, and one gathers that the audience is the casual traveler who may already be familiar with camera basics. While inevitably some of the information is for the camera shooter rather than the traveler, there is also information that applies to any traveler, with or without camera. In-between is advice on such matters as keeping the camera and film safe and undamaged when on the go, and how to photograph in different environments, from aerial photography to underwater, winter, etc. There are numerous photo examples, both in color and black-and-white. 108 p.

Kodak Guide to Shooting Great Travel Pictures: Easy Tips and Foolproof Ideas from the Pros / Jeff Wignall. 2nd ed. (Fodor's Travel Publications, 2000).

About twice the size of *Berlitz Travel Photography* (above), its principle of letting the color photographs represent individual themes and rules of technique overlaps much of the same territory, as it also does with the Busselle title (below). Broad categories concern people and their haunts; wild things; the uses of light; weather; natural effects; combining it all; the application of existing light and flash; and equipment. Within these, two pages apiece are devoted to related topics. On the first is a double column commentary that comes with a box of a few brief tips (e.g., "Use bold shapes as focal points") and sometimes a small photo. Facing it is usually a full page of from one to several photos which unfortunately do not possess captioning and are not referenced in the text. The amateur makes the most appropriate audience. 214 p.

Michael Busselle's Guide to Travel & Vacation Photography / Michael Busselle (RotoVision, 2002).

This slickly produced work with color photos on each page is itself designed as a work of art. Printed on a background bearing sepia illustrations, several short blocks of text emphasize words meant to be significant by displaying them in different fonts, which to some readers could prove a distraction. The *raison d'être* of this title is the photos which, like a large version of *Berlitz Travel Photography* (above), the photographer author uses to give pointers about. An added line discloses the type of camera involved and other technical details. The photos and the analysis of them are put in four categories: destinations; people, animals, and plants; the employment of composition and light; and equipment used. There is little about traveling. 206 p.

Travel Photography: A Complete Guide to How to Shoot and Sell / Susan McCartney. 2nd ed. (Allworth Press, 1999).

The emphasis is on photography rather than travel, and on the idea of selling the pictures taken, so the amateur would be better served by other works. The author draws on her experiences in looking at the equipment and the technique required to take photos and in discussing travel photographs as a genre, and advising what to photograph. For those with a greater interest in travel itself, the most relevant parts of the book concern shooting on location as well as researching a destination and getting there; plus there are personal and photographic checklists. A collection of visual highlights identifies things to shoot in some of the countries, areas, and cities of the world. The photographs in here are black-and-white. The author has also published the book *How to Shoot Great Travel Photos* (Allworth Press, 2005). 339 p.

Travel Photography: A Guide to Taking Better Pictures / Richard I'Anson (Lonely Planet, 2000).

There are generic considerations of photographic equipment, but only one chapter directly addresses traveling with a camera. After comments on exposure and composition, the author devotes the largest part of the book to classes and sub-classes of things photographed: people, portraits, travel companions, mountains, snow scenes, deserts, cities, special events, markets, food, moving objects, wildlife, aerial shots, etc. A discussion of the subjects comes on every page with captioned color photos that explain the scene being shown and how it was captured. A brief final part is concerned with photos after they have been developed and brought home. The book's size allows it to be carried along on a trip, but the content also provides a means of assessing the photographer's own skills. A later edition by the same author has been published as *The Lonely Planet Guide to Travel Photography* (Lonely Planet, 2004). 222 p.

Travel Photography: How to Research, Produce and Sell Great Travel Pictures / Roger Hicks and Frances Schultz (Focal Press, 1998).

A British team furnishes experienced and canny advice on many topics for the vocationally minded who seek to combine commercial photography with travel, but the point and shoot traveler will discover that most of the information is beyond his or her need. With a personal approach they provide concrete examples from their professional lives and that of their colleagues. The scope encompasses such matters as photography for travel articles or brochures, that involved in reportage (e.g., taking war photos), and the management of a photo tour. Color bands on the page and its fore-edge serve as a code to a chapter's subject, and of the numerous photographs, the majority are in color. 202 p.

The Traveler's Eye: A Guide to Still and Video Travel Photography / Lisl Dennis (Clarkson Potter, 1996).

A slick-paged work most at home on the bookshelf, it is distinct from the other photography books reviewed. It has a more personal and thoughtful approach to its subject, as some of the chapter titles suggest ("Aesthetic Exercises" or "Seeing Color, Form, and Content"). Dennis comes closer to writing essays than a how-to manual, and she frequently quotes other photographers' philosophical views. The fairly substantial captions to the color photographs explain what the author saw and sought, and sometimes the equipment employed. The last few pages provide suggestions about cameras and traveling, but the volume is more concerned with photography as an art rather than a skill. The "video" in the title occupies a single chapter. 192 p.

Vacation and Travel Photography / Sean Hargrave (Amphoto, 1995).

Among the titles reviewed, this point and shoot guide for the compact camera may be the best for the beginner. The color photos on every page have captions that reflect techniques but do not specify geographic location. Often a third of the page has short questions and answers or bulleted pieces grouped as pointers, do's and don'ts, or types of camera skills, and all are related to such topics as time of day, the beach, nightlife, people, movement, theme parks, on safari, and skiing. It is a quick read, yet it is easy to discover specific advice. Though thin, its size does not permit it to fit in a pocket. 96 p.

PRONUNCIATION

To communicate verbally in an unfamiliar language—or in a familiar language with unfamiliar names or words—one must pronounce with care and accuracy. Foreign language dictionaries and phrase books help.

At least learn to correctly pronounce the names of places. In a verbal exchange a native of a foreign country who can recognize no other words than a spoken place name should be able to surmise the speaker is seeking that place.

From a good atlas first discover the appropriate *form* of the place name (for example, in Italy "Florence" is called "Firenze"). Then learn how to pronounce the name approximately as the natives do, unless the preference is to trust to luck. For the pronunciation of proper geographic names try a conventional dictionary, gazetteer, or pronunciation dictionary.

See also **Language**.

Subject Heading: Names—Pronunciation

Titles

Pronouncing Dictionary of Proper Names: Pronunciations for More Than 28,000 Proper Names, Selected for Currency, Frequency, or Difficulty of Pronunciation / editor, John K. Bollard. 2nd ed. (Omnigraphics, 1998).

Place names are just one of the kinds that are here, but unfortunately there is no separation by type, so they must be found alphabetically in the mix. In the first column is the name along with a brief identification of what it is; in the middle column is a simplified pronunciation based on conventions of English spelling; and the last column contains its transcription into the special alphabet of the International Phonetic Association, which can be a challenge to the uninitiated. Some words are provided with two ways of pronunciation. 1097 p.

World Words, Recommended Pronunciations / W. Cabell Greet. 2nd ed., revised & enlarged (Columbia University Press, 1948).

Its approximately 25,000 geographical and personal names, along with a sprinkling of foreign words, are grouped in three columns to a page. The geographical name is followed by its country and, if it is a physical feature, its type (river, mountain, etc.). Once in a while notes are added. The pronunciation is given with special accents and letters, then repeated without either, in familiar alphabetic sounds. Both pronunciations show syllable separation and where the stress falls. Native versions are cross-indexed with Anglicized (e.g., "Firenze" and "Florence"). Coming out three years after World War II, the edition's choice of names was influenced by the theaters of operation during that era, but the coverage is global. Unless pronunciation has done a fair amount of shifting over half of a century, this should remain of use. Much smaller than *Pronouncing Dictionary of Proper Names*, it is likewise a reference book and not something that normally would be toted along on a trip. 608 p.

PUBLISHERS

Some publishers and distributors are identified with travel books or allied subjects. For example, Lonely Planet is a famous publisher that gives its name to its guidebooks, while Globe Pequot produces a wide variety of travel titles. If a book pleases you, see if its publisher (or author) has something similar. This may be accomplished in different ways.

Seek out a website produced by the publisher. Likewise, search by the name of the publisher in library electronic catalogs and websites of bookstores, Amazon.com, Barnes & Noble, and Powell's Books being among the ones with huge inventories.

For vast lists of books by author and title try the standard *Books in Print*, in whose electronic version works may be searched by publisher. One of its print volumes separately provides publisher names, addresses, telephone numbers, e-mail addresses, and websites. *Publishers, Distributors & Wholesalers of the United States* (R.R. Bowker) is another useful title.

An efficient way of discovering publishers' names and addresses is through the bibliographies in reference-type travel resources. In the 1988 *Going Places* an appendix gives names and addresses of all the publishers mentioned in its extensive bibliography. Selective publishers have been collected in *The Traveler's Handbook* and in special issues of *Transitions Abroad* (both reviewed, respectively, in **Travel Advice** and **Study and Travel**).

RADIO, ETC.

There are places and circumstances where internet radio is not available, but traditional radio is. Whether in a car or as a portable, a traveler's radio provides news, entertainment, and company, and it links even the most isolated listener to the outside world.

In areas of political unrest one type of radio—the shortwave—can assume a vital importance, as journalists in world hot spots have attested. Buy a shortwave in an electronics or department store or online. To discover popular magazine articles evaluating radios check the *Reader's Guide to Periodical Literature*.

Use a shortwave with a frequency guide, which supplies listeners with station names, signal frequencies, city locations, formats, and times of broadcasts; among worldwide services that can be heard are the English-language Voice of America and the BBC.

Not radio but a different listening experience is the travelogue in various formats, such as cassette. Those designed to be played in a car along highway routes instruct that they be turned on or off according to location. Others provide a self-guided walking tour through use of a portable player. Numerous museums employ this means of introducing their collection.

For travel and other audio titles the catalog *Books out Loud: Bowker's Guide to Audiobooks* (Bowker) may be consulted.

Subject Heading: Radio stations—Directories

Titles

Passport to World Band Radio. Annual (International Broadcasting Services, Ltd.).

This is a work that will be of most interest to the shortwave enthusiast. This has product reviews, a how-to section, descriptions of individual programs by time of day, station addresses by country, broadcasts in English and in the language of the country, and a large section called "blue pages" that presents a table of frequencies with world band schedules. Examined: 2004; 592 p.

Radio on the Road: The Traveler's Companion / William Hutchings (Arrowhead Publishing, 2000).

Here is a tabular guide to the stations that can be tuned to from a car radio. Each alphabetically arranged state or Canadian province has a summary page of several paragraphs aimed at sightseers, a temperature and precipitation table, and a few quick facts (state nickname, population, etc.). However, the bulk of a chapter is its easy-to-scan rows that distinguish the broadcast city or town, the AM or FM call letters and frequency, and the format, over which two dozen are recognized—such as types of music, ethnic broadcasts, National Public Radio, and talk radio. Unfortunately, there is no format index in the back, nor are there maps to help a driver determine the location of the nearest stations. Separate tables identify stations that broadcast Major League Baseball and the National Football League, talk show hosts, National Public Radio, and as clear channels. The book should fit in a glove compartment of average size. A later edition is available. 343 p.

W.H.I.M.P.U.R. Map (Where Is My Public Radio) (Marjory Lee Enterprises, 2001).

Folding out into a large size and printed in sepia, this map of public radio stations has the eastern half of the continental United States on one side and the western half on the other, along with insets for Alaska and Hawaii. Without highway routes or other features, the states are simple outlines of a jagged, computerized quality, and the station locations are marked with dots by their call letters. In the white space outside the map an alphabetized list of call letters comes with telephone numbers, those for Guam and Puerto Rico being separately listed. A later edition is available.

World Radio TV Handbook, WRTH: The Directory of International Broadcasting. Annual (WRTH Publications, Ltd.).

This directory is not for uninitiated travelers, but if listening to the radio is important wherever one's locality, it provides names, addresses, call letters, kilohertz, kilowatts, etc. for countries from Afghanistan to Zimbabwe. The largest section concerns national radio, followed by another on international radio and a third on television stations. A frequency list for shortwave, mediumwave, and longwave stations has a part set aside for international broadcasts in English and several other languages. Additionally, there are radio receiver reviews and color maps with transmitter sites. The print is small, the columns frequent, the abbreviations unavoidable, and the entries may take some figuring out. Examined: 2007; 672 p.

Organizations

Voice of America. www.voa.gov

The United States government organization offers radio and TV broadcasts, plus webcasts, of news, information, and music in many languages throughout the world. Online program schedules and a list of radio broadcast frequencies are available. Examined website: 2008

RAILROAD TRAVEL

Unlike in America, train transportation in Europe and other parts of the world is heavily used, both by tourists and natives, and the coverage of several guides reflects this usage, with Europe especially receiving much attention.

Guides that deal with Eurail discuss schedules, routes, station facilities, onboard amenities, sights, fares, and passes, and may be illustrated through rail/route maps. Similar details are also presented in other train travel books.

Railway timetables are available from a country's rail authorities and perhaps from its tourist bureau. In the United States Amtrak distributes its own timetables in paper and has them online. Publisher Thomas Cook produces large timetables as well as individual rail maps

Like books about day trips that acknowledge the importance of the train, rail guides describe excursions from base cities to popular destinations, and they give schedule, length of journey, and a description of the place visited. (See **Day and Weekend Trips** in the **Introduction**.)

Rail guides should also discuss train passes, which are a convenience and can save a rider money if used over enough miles. They can be purchased from the rail company as well as some travel bookstores, travel agencies, and tourist offices.

Besides passengers who go on an excursion for the scenery alone, there are train buffs for whom riding a train is an end in itself. They yearn after an old steam engine and antique trains. In North America at least, tourist railroads and railroad museums receive directory attention. If this is not enough, the buff can search out the titles of train magazines and newsletters gathered in periodical directories (*Ulrich's*, etc.).

Taking a rail tour is a style of travel offered by select companies. Look for their advertisements in train periodicals, or consult various online sites.

Subject Heading: Railroad travel

Titles

All Aboard!: The Complete North American Train Travel Guide / Jim Loomis. Revised 2nd ed. (Prima Publishing, 1998).

Assuming the reader has an interest in the subjects both of trains and train travel, this manual for users of Amtrak has details aplenty and convenient subheadings. After a history of railroads, there is matter on preparing for a trip, packing, life on board, and the responsibilities of those who work on the train, at the station, and in administration. Also covered are problems that may occur, a consideration of the various train car types, the mechanics and conventions of operation, trains that carry freight, safety, and taking the train in Canada or Mexico. A selection of itineraries shows them in terms of basic facts (distance, duration, etc.) followed by a description of the journey. Among the appendixes are further itineraries, descriptions of a few hotels for the train traveler, a directory of railroad museums and excursions, and a list of agents who specialize in this manner of transportation. A two-page map shows the Amtrak's passenger system with the major cities or towns through which it goes, while elsewhere is a fare map and a sample timetable. 411 p.

Empire State Railway Museum's Tourist Trains. Annual (Kalmbach Books).

   This directory is undoubtedly something that is designed for travelers who love trains. Alphabetically listed under state or Canadian province, then city or town, the name of the railroad or museum is enhanced by added categorical words such as "train ride," "museum," or "standard gauge." An entry comes with a large black-and-white photograph, usually of a train but sometimes of the museum building. In their own grouping are the mailing address, telephone number, e-mail, and internet URL. The area for "description" usually has the lengthiest details, the others concisely providing facts that cover schedule, admission/fare, locomotives/rolling stock, special events, nearby attractions, and directions. There are also symbols for amenities, association memberships, credit cards accepted, and so forth. State maps and one for Canada are simple. A gathering of blue pages in the center is composed of coupons for some of the featured railroads. Examined: 41st ed. (2006; 454 p.)

Eurail and Train Travel Guide to the World. 28th ed. (Houghton Mifflin, 1998).

   The first part provides general material that includes advice on using rail passes and route charts, planning a rail itinerary, and alternatives when missing a train. Taking up the bulk of the guide, chapters by country—or by groups of countries—have tourist information, perspectives on trains and train travel, a list with English translations of station signs in several European languages, a country's special passes, and sights in major cities and towns. The largest categories in these chapters are devoted to in-country routes, day journeys, scenic trips, and international connections, which are presented as compact descriptions of what can be seen and are accompanied by timetables of departure and arrival, with appropriate notes such as whether snacks are served and exceptions to daily and weekend runs. For Western Europe, shaded country maps show lines with names of stops, some of which are not represented on the selected timetables. Europe does receive the most treatment, both in terms of details and of space (about two-thirds of the book); and for those travelers who are only interested in this area, a companion publication is *Eurail and Train Travel Guide to Europe*, the same as *World*, but without the other countries. Not only because of its contents, but due to its practical layout and convenient size, either guide is welcome aboard. (Unfortunately, there appears to be no newer editions.) 1047 p.

Europe by Eurail; Touring Europe by Train. Annual (Globe Pequot Press).

This long-established source offers remarks about rail travel from cities in seventeen European countries, with additional looks at arriving there by land, air, or sea, transportation, and important sights, along with a little history. A schedule for train and ferry connections to other base cities readily helps the traveler. Simple country maps show town names and rail lines. Sub-chapters on day excursions from the major cities begin with summaries naming the station of departure, distance and average time to the destination, and city dialing code; and for the tourist information office, there is its address, telephone and fax numbers, hours of operation, its website and e-mail, and directions to it. The narration about the excursion is usually no less than a page and as with the base city describes its background and what is worth seeing. This part also has its own timetable of departure and arrivals as well as the train number, and if reservations are necessary. The general appendix of this valuable and hefty work has various short pieces of information. Examined: 32nd ed. (2008; 543 p.)

Europe by Train / Katie Wood. New ed. (Robson Books, 2005).

In thickness, design, and continuity of updated editions this is similar to another budget title, and could be called *Let's Go* with trains. Actually, this is a country guidebook for the backpacker and those who travel cheaply, with the space devoted to train travel rather paltry; so if expecting schedules and similar detail, better check another title, such as *Europe by Eurail* (above). Several pages of generalities in the introductory matter discuss this popular European form of travel, and for each country there is a plain rail map with names along the route, and train and tourist information. Descriptions of major cities include a short section on station facilities, though the majority of this text concerns tourist information services, addresses, sightseeing, accommodations, and places to eat and drink. Well over thirty European countries are treated, plus Morocco and Turkey. 752 p.

Great Railway Journeys of Europe (Discovery Channel; APA Publications, 2002).

This very attractive guide made from slick paper has excellent color photos on every page, occasional color maps showing rail routes, and other illustrations. It is also well-laid out, with small columns by the main text naming major attractions; or providing the Thomas Cook timetable numbers, a journey's distance and duration, and frequency of trains; or a small photo; and contributing a pointer to the page of the appropriate route map. Taking up the chief part of this work, the narration of (bolded) towns, cities, and sights encountered along a route has at times the immediacy of a journal entry and often shows the author's feelings. A limited number of countries—all Western European—are treated in depth, and at the end of each is a listing of their museums and heritage lines, which in addition to the basics gives the nearest station and, for lines, the length of track. Throughout are short articles about aspects of trains, and an introduction provides some history. End matter categorizes country information in digest form. Although lacking town or city maps, it is a worthy choice for the traveler going on the journeys described. 400 p.

The International Railway Traveler. Monthly (The Society of International Railway Travelers). www.irtsociety.com

This slick newsletter with notebook holes contains first-person articles; notes on new routes, updates of amenities, equipment, and stations; announcements of Society trips; tips on train travel; and descriptions of sights. Some articles promote the newsletter or the Society. Examined: issue from 2003.

On the Rails around Europe: A Comprehensive Guide to Travel by Train / edited by Melissa Shales. 3rd ed. (Thomas Cook, 1998).

From departure to destination the emphasis is on sightseeing at various stops, with the names of the appropriate attractions bolded in the text. Mention of places that are of interest away from the rail stop is under the main section of alphabetized European cities—including Turkey's Istanbul and several in Eastern Europe—and the short nod to rail travel is chiefly the inclusion of fastest routes and of locals. Beyond the space devoted to attractions, the two-column pages discuss, under their own headings, tourist information, places to stay and eat, entertainment, etc. The city street maps are shaded and could certainly serve a pedestrian or motorist in a pinch, while the diagrams of rail lines come with the names of stops. A country-by-country section has some of the same information, though with a broader scope, and with more about rail travel. This is one of the *Thomas Cook Touring Handbook* series, whose titles deal with travel by car, train, and ship. 568 p.

Riding the Rails: Tourist Guide to America's Scenic Train Rides / William C. Herow. 2nd ed. (Roundabout Publications, 2002).

In this directory arranged by state, name, address, telephone number, and internet address precede the most substantial part, a few comments on what the journey is like. Then there is a sentence or so for separate sections that have the station where the passengers board and its relative location, the schedule of operation, the fares, notes (which often inform about reservations or group discounts), and a checkmark list of annual special events or excursions. Despite the word "scenic" in the title, there are no photographs or illustrations beyond maps. A state's map shows major highways and several towns, with heavier lines apparently depicting the rail route and, adding to the confusion, the few towns mentioned in the text may not appear on the map. Unlike for example *USA by Rail* (below), there is no detail about stops or places passed along the way. Some states have only one or two routes listed, while several states are wholly omitted. 232 p.

Thomas Cook European Timetable. Monthly (Thomas Cook).
Thomas Cook Overseas Timetable. Bimonthly (Thomas Cook).

These standard titles have rail and ferry schedules, with the latter also providing those for coach and bus services. *European* has separate inter-European and country divisions showing the major lines along with train type, number, and possible amenities. Alternate issues have special features on such subjects as rail passes and tourist railways. National maps are provided as well as station location plans and a shipping section. The *Overseas* title deals with the entire world except for Europe. The two also have an Independent Traveller's edition, which for *European* comes out three times during the year (one time for *Overseas*), and has a supplementary section about rail passes, plus other matter directed at the independent traveler. Vertical and horizontal column lines on the small-print pages challenge the eye to follow along the host of times and abbreviations. The titles are currently known as *European Rail Timetable* and *Overseas Timetable*. Examined: issue from 2003 of *Thomas Cook European Timetable* (560 p.); information also from www.thomascook publishing.com

The Thomas Cook Rail Map of Europe. 13th ed. (Thomas Cook Publishing, 2001).

A large foldout map in color presents rail lines against a white background of countries. On one side is Europe, beginning as far west as Ireland and reaching beyond Moscow, while also taking in most of Turkey. On the reverse is a blowup of the multi-country area from Paris across to Warsaw, and from Amsterdam down to Genoa. Additional routes marked are those for bus, train-ferry, and other ferries. Though the railway lines are in several colors, they can be a challenge to follow with the eye, perhaps inevitable when such a large system covers so much. There are no city maps showing what stations connect to which lines, nor an index to towns along the routes. The map helps in planning a rail trip and giving a sense where one is going and where one has been. A later edition is available. 1 sheet

USA by Rail / John Pitt. 6th ed. (Bradt Travel Guides and The Globe Pequot Press, 2005).

After a history of American rail and advice about traveling by train and in the United States, the majority of the work provides an itinerary of city-to-city routes run by Amtrak. A chapter opens with general route information composed of an overview and bolded headings with brief answers about frequency of departures, duration of trip, reservations, equipment, sleeping, food, the lounge car, and baggage. Major stops receive the longest descriptions among the listed towns, cities, and sights, all of which are marked with the number of minutes from the previous station to the next. Each route is visually represented as a line that has nodes with names of towns and cities that are part of the journey. U.S. steam trains and Canadian trains and routes are separately treated. For travelers with enough interest in the places included, a regular travel guide would be a useful supplement. 338 p.

Businesses

Amtrak. www.amtrak.com

Besides reservation services, the online site has schedules and timetables, routes, and find-a-station. Examined website: 2008

RECREATION, SPORTS, AND RANCH VACATIONS

Some travelers like to sweat. They seek outdoor vacations in foreign places that let them play at their favorite recreation or sport. Designed for these fans are recreation guides listing and describing the places with the activities they seek. The guides may evaluate the quality of the experience, such as the difficulty of a golf course or the conditions of a diving environment. Sports such as golf rate many travel guides, while automobile racing, soccer, and tennis camps are among those that have been singled out with their own directories. There are also sports that have no dedicated travel guides.

In a bookstore these guides are more likely to be in the sports than the travel area. In a library locate them through a subject heading search under the name of the recreation or sport, either as a general heading—for example, "Outdoor recreation"—or a specific one; adding a subdivision such as "Guidebooks" often contributes relevancy. In *Travel Resources* see also under names of specific activities (e.g., **Adventure Travel**, **Bicycle Touring**).

If interested in sport package vacations look for them in magazines or websites covering the individual sport.

Vacations on ranches almost deserve a separate section. They offer various activities to travelers who seek them and could be considered an offshoot of resorts.

Titles and Websites

American Casino Guide / written and edited by Steve Bourie. 2008 ed. (Casino Vacations Press, 2008).

The opening one-fourth of the book has chapters on casino games and provides strategies about playing them. In the directory section for every state there is a local overview of gambling, which may note whether there are Native American casinos, what games are available, and what laws control them. The double-columned entries are ordered with bolded name above a block that has address, telephone number, and website, and then is a second block with, more or less, a toll-free telephone number, number of restaurants, a determination if liquor is served, cost of buffets, casino size in square feet, games played (given as abbreviations), availability of senior discounts, and special features. There is no added narrative to help the player learn more about each casino. State maps show routes with the featured places marked in numbered circles, and a few cities have clear street maps. Coming out annually, this casino directory ends with some 140 pages of money-saving coupons. 496 p.

Farm, Ranch & Country Vacations in America / Pat Dickerman (Adventure Guides, 1995).

The West, Mid-America, and the East are broken down by state, each with an outline map bearing numbers that represent the corresponding farm and ranch names beside it and their approximate geographic positions. The names are repeated in main entries, but unfortunately without their map number. A small subheading (e.g., "a seaside country inn") precedes the bolded name, and then comes the address, telephone and fax numbers, and the names of the reservation persons (now possibly obsolete). The descriptive paragraph about the farm or ranch are as upbeat as a travel brochure, and the praising words of owners and guests are often quoted, so for those seeking something objective, this is not the source. However, the content does particularly address activities and comforts, while at the end are numeric room rates (definitely obsolete). A wide left-hand margin has brief notes about the destination's distance from the nearest major metropolis, its season, length of minimum stay, maximum number of guests, "families welcome," and rate range. Adding to the graphic effectiveness are frequent color photographs of the places or of activities around them. 248 p.

Fodor's Baseball Vacations: Great Family Trips to Minor League and Classic Major League Ballparks across America / Bruce Adams and Margaret Engel. 3rd ed. (Fodor's Travel Publications, 2002).

It takes a specialty guide like this to supply details found nowhere else. Following a geographical arrangement, there are separate tables of capsule facts for about one hundred leagues and their stadiums, with most of the information designed to aid the visitor in seeing a game. It includes the stadium's address; written directions about driving there; the parking situation; address and numbers for tickets; price ranges; game times; tips on the seating; the status of seats for people with disabilities; the type and quality of a stadium's food; the smoking policy; the visiting team's hotel; and tourism addresses. Elsewhere the stadium is discussed along with its history, and attention is paid to nearby baseball venues. There are a few, short recommendations about where to stay and where to eat, and descriptions of some places where families can enjoy themselves. The shaded highway map for every chapter shows major routes to the places, and like other Fodor titles, the layout promotes finding information. 399 p.

Fodor's Great American Sports and Adventure Vacations. 2nd ed. (Fodor's Travel Publications, 1996).

Alphabetical arrangement of subjects begins with baseball fantasy camps and ends with working farms, while in-between are caving, cross-country skiing, fishing camps, surfing schools, and many other interests, several of which have had their own guides (a few are reviewed in this section). After an introduction to the chapter's activity, a sub-area for choosing the right trip (or camp or school) offers answers to frequently asked questions. Next comes useful commentary about major companies in that sport or adventure field, and this is followed by the geographically arranged favorite trips (or schools), whose descriptions in two or more paragraphs lean toward the promotional; addresses for them along with the dates of operation and costs are compactly presented at the end. A section on "Sources" is divided into discussions of organizations, periodicals, and books. The double-columned book is well thought out and arranged, and were it not for its age, would be the first choice for locating information on these subjects. 359 p.

Gene Kilgore's Ranch Vacations: The Leading Guide to Guest, Resort, Fly-Fishing, and Winter Ranches in North America / Gene Kilgore. 7th ed. (Avalon Travel, 2005).

Presenting eleven states and one Canadian province, the attractive, large directory has on facing pages a double-columned entry and its color photos. After an introductory paragraph to a ranch, bolded headings encompass address; telephone; e-mail; website; airport; location in miles from town or city; membership affiliations; awards (e.g., AAA 3 Diamond); nearby medical facilities; numbers for conference capacity and guest capacity; rates and the conditions that may be attached; credit cards accepted; the seasons of operation; activities; children's programs; and entertainment choices. Expect some salesmanship in the details for the remaining headings on accommodations, dining, and the summary. Two well-done maps, chiefly in green and tan, show the interstates, major cities, and the location of the ranches, which have icons according to the subjects in the book's subtitle. Appendixes include special categories for the ranches featured and a calendar of western events. 347 p.

Golf Travel's Guide to the World's Greatest Golf Destinations: The Ultimate Resource for the Discriminating Golfer / Terence Sieg and the editors of *Golf Travel* (Broadway Books, 1997).

This oblong book with its attractive and useful interior design is geographically arranged, with the golfing attractions of select countries and states judged from the traveling golfer's perspective, but also with an eye to the scenery. Sections individually treat the golf courses, golf services, lodging, restaurants, and non-golf activities through verbal evaluations and through numerical ratings of from one to twenty, which are added together against a perfect score of 100; an appendix shows the top twenty golf spots for each of the categories. As "greatest" in the title indicates, the resorts chosen for inclusion in the book are already of high caliber, so the descriptions can swerve into hyperbole, though this may be balanced by occasional carping. Other features are driving directions, small photographs, and outline maps with sites marked. 475 p.

Guide Naturiste Mondial (World Naturist Handbook). 22nd ed. (International Naturist Federation, 1994). www.inf-fni.org

Appearing about every two years, and with a title additionally in French and German, the directory lists hundreds of clubs, campgrounds, and other spots that accept nudity. Usually with two per page, an entry consists largely of a small roadmap and a confusing number of icons whose meanings are in tables at both the book's front and back and are explained in six languages. Occasional notes in French, German, and English accompany a name and address given in the native language, after which is a telephone number. At the top of a page is an outline map of a country, while for the U.S. the state is shown. The order within a region can be puzzling, since the beginning letter of a country in English may be different from the listing in the book, whose very international flavor may make it difficult to comprehend for some readers. Later editions have been published. 721 p.

Jim Balzotti's Custom Ranch Vacations / Jim Balzotti. 3rd ed. (Balzotti Publications, 2002).

The "official book of the Dude Ranchers' Association," the large, heavy work, reminiscent of a catalog, has many photographs, including almost 100 pages of color ones in a center section. A ranch in a selected state or Canadian province receives a page of text that it shares with a photo, and sometimes further photos are on the opposite page. Be prepared for descriptions designed to entice you to visit the ranch. If the slant can be ignored, it is possible to sort out useful facts about the owners, the natural scenery, the lifestyle, the amenities, the interior furnishings, the meals, and the activities, especially horse riding. A grouping at the bottom supplies mailing address, telephone and fax; web and e-mail address; occasionally the relative location (typically in miles from a town); nearest airport; the guest capacity; season of operation; the policy on children and pets; the rate range (via the number of dollar signs); and the credit cards accepted. In the back are articles about riding and the West. 390 p.

Outside. Monthly (Mariah Media Inc.). outside.away.com/index.html
Worldwide outdoor sports and recreation are described for general audiences in this illustrated magazine. Articles are about men and women against the elements, destinations for the adventurous, the environment, equipment, etc. The online site includes a travel section. Examined website: 2008

Recreation.gov. www.recreation.gov
This federal government website gathers together the various agencies responsible for land management and allows a search of their land holdings through different recreational categories. Examined website: 2008

The Sports Fan's Guide to America: The Ultimate Travel Companion for the Avid Fan / Mike Tulumello (Longstreet, 1999).
The arrangement is by American cities that host major-league sports, with Canada left a few pages to itself. Better for the sports fan than the traveler, the book has material beyond the addresses for major-league baseball, basketball, football, and hockey teams—along with their home fields, courts, or rinks—but the travel information chiefly concerns transportation to the arena, the location of sports bars, the "main drags," and author recommendations for places worth visiting. A state directory at the back provides name, address, and telephone number for college and professional teams. Full-page diagrams of the major stadiums with numbered parts can be of help to those searching how the seating is set up; and this is perhaps the best about the guide, whose humor and slangy tone may be at times off-putting. 290 p.

Tennis Camps, Clinics, and Resorts / Joanie and Bill Brown (Moyer Bell, 1998).
Each tennis teaching locale is arranged by state, then city or town. A square box encloses a bolded name and address above a telephone and fax number, website address, and contact name. Six or so parts follow with text, the first of which reckons the destination's distance from a city and comments on its weather, and perhaps other matters. In a second part several instructors may be named and qualifications given, plus the overall number employed. Next are separately treated the learning goals, the contents of the programs, and the types of courts and other facilities. "Costs" supply various dollar amounts attuned to accommodations, meals, services provided, and length of stay. Though double-columned, the size of the book and use of spaces makes for comfortable reading. There are no photographs or maps. 230 p.

Top Rated Western Adventures: Guest Ranches, Pack Trips & Cattle Drives in North America / Maurizio Valerio (Derrydale Press, 2000).

How positively guests answered questionnaires determined whether a business qualified for inclusion, but there are no rating scores. The two pages dedicated to an entry are mostly photographs and graphics, with a block of print giving name, address, contact numbers, and electronic presence. The description of the adventure location is written by the owners or managers who use the normal complimentary adjectives, and there is a quote from a satisfied participant. Icons are arranged in four categories: seasons of operation, western activities, other activities, and services. A small accompanying map appears to be a satellite image with names added. The appendix includes a partial yet large listing of outfitters and others by state or province; but unfortunately, the individual businesses are squashed together on top of one another, making them a challenge to distinguish, and they lack street address, zip code, and telephone number, so contacting them requires going to other sources. The ranches and outfitters are also separately arranged by activity categories. 212 p.

The Ultimate Guide to Marathons / Dennis Craythorn and Rich Hanna (Marathon Publishers, 1998).

The top one hundred marathons average two wide pages, each entry having a quick-to-read part that begins with an overall score totaled according to course beauty, course difficulty, appropriateness for first-timers, race organization, and crowds (these and other categories are individually ranked from first to last in an appendix). The brief data continues with places for address, date of marathon, its start time, number of participants in a recent year, its cost, etc. After an overall view, bolded headings introduce paragraphs that report on the course; the crowd and support for the runner; the logistics of getting there; accompanying activities; awards that may be presented; accommodations available; related events or races; area attractions; and the name and address of local running stores. The entry order is by date that the race is run. The information is much reduced in additional profiles of eighty local marathons, and there are charts showing the elevation above sea level of several races. Attractive and very well thought out, the book only lacks some general travel information (closest airport, driving directions, maps). A companion volume is *The Ultimate Guide to International Marathons*. 345 p.

The White Book of Ski Areas / Robert G. Enzel. Annual (Inter-Ski Services). www.inter-ski.com

Now subscribable online, this popular directory has the resort or area's name, address, and telephone number in a graphic box, then continues with headings that may include a variety of skiing statistics; season rates and instructions; additional recreation possibilities; lodging; restaurants; services (shops, credit cards accepted, child care, etc.); highway directions; and whatever is new for the year. All of this is in the same strict format and with no provision for quality judgments. Separate black-and-white state maps show major highway routes and the outline of counties, which are not named, while marked ski locations are reflected in an accompanying miniature table of contents. Shaded illustrations of mountains may show ski trails. Arranged by state and name, the entries have a confusing layout, for on the large pages in three columns they must be read across, when the instinct is to read them down. Later editions are available exclusively online. Examined: 24th ed. (1999; 326 p.)

Worldwide Riding Vacations: A Global Guide to Holidays on Horseback / Arthur Sacks and John Ruler. 2nd ed. (Compleat Traveller, 1999).

Each geographically arranged entry has a large, two-columned page opposite an arresting color photo. Its top area has the plain facts of the riding company's name, address, telephone number and electronic presence, season of operation, nearest airports, location (though without driving directions), and the price of an excursion along with what it includes. Below, a narrative part has an introduction followed by bolded subsections reporting on children's programs, the accommodations, special activities in addition to riding, the meals, and the rides; a few lines blurb why one should visit. A blue bar at the bottom of the page succinctly names highlights of the vacation, some of which repeats what has been said in the text. Separate chapters offer personal experiences of riding horses in particular countries and regions. 383 p.

Organizations

Bureau of Land Management. U.S. Department of the Interior. www.blm. gov

The Bureau produces numerous guides and maps to the public lands that it manages. Examined website: 2008

The Dude Ranchers' Association. duderanch.org

Part of its website has directory information for ranches chiefly in the American west and two Canadian provinces, presenting a block for name, address, telephone number, and link to the ranch, plus a price range, before moving to more in-depth details. Examined website: 2008

RELIGION

As part of package tours, visits to historic churches are popular and seemingly inevitable. Yet there are independent travelers who enthusiastically seek out religious sites either due to faith, curiosity, or other motivations. Travel guides devoted to culture may make room for places with holy associations but will lack the breadth or depth of the works listed below. Of religions, Judaism has been the subject of the greatest number of travel guides.

As resorts supply distractions, retreats allow banishment of distractions. Often with religious affiliations, they offer a place of retirement from the world and give the opportunity for healing or concentrating on a purpose.

Subject Headings: Christian shrines; Jews—Travel—[country name]; Pilgrims and pilgrimages—[country name]; Retreats

Titles

The Atlas of Holy Places & Sacred Sites / Colin Wilson (DK Publishing, 1996).

Lavish with colored photographs and illustrations, this coffee-table book usually spends, in its largest section, from one-half to one page about both the history and importance of the most significant sites throughout the world. The entries are keyed to a 25-page group of colored and shaded maps whose large geographical coverage of the globe means that the spots marked on them are useful only for broadly relative positions in countries. Shapes and colors specify if a site is still in use, its age, and land heights. There is a listing of several hundred additional places toward the back with name, date, state or country (which sometimes also has the city or town), and a few brief lines of description. The maps have errors and, worse, the locations provided are so general that you must search elsewhere to find an address. Still, the book is attractive and the scope is extremely far-ranging. 192 p.

Catholic Shrines of Western Europe: A Pilgrim's Travel Guide / Kevin J. Wright (Liguori, 1997).

After a brief history of pilgrimages and advice on making them, the author provides a by-country description of shrines, the majority of which comes with small black-and-white photos of their outside or inside. He narrates each one's history with the miracle that consecrated it, and quotes a prayer associated with it. Background is further enhanced with an enumeration of the shrine's most important features. Accompanying addresses are for more shrine information, for the tourist office, and places to stay. Arrival instructions cover car, train, and bus, the first accompanied by route names positioned on a diagram. Viewing tips, plus a piece of trivia or a fact, complete the entry. A companion publication is *Catholic Shrines of Central and Eastern Europe: A Pilgrim's Travel Guide* (1999). 238 p.

The Christian Traveler's Companion. The USA & Canada / Amy S. Eckert and William J. Petersen (Fleming H. Revell, 2000).

It is arranged by region, then under a state (or province) the town or city entries come with a paragraph or more devoted to subjects that take in both the family-oriented and religious, from general attractions such as zoos and outdoor activities to descriptions of noteworthy religious events (including nativity scenes and dramas), monuments, sectarian communities, and individual churches along with their histories. At the beginning of each state a graphic box for tourist information supplies a telephone number, though no address, and several websites about the state and some of its more popular cities. Advice is absent when it comes to accommodations, eating places, and highway directions, nor are there maps marking the towns and cities. A number of towns mentioned are off the beaten track, while a scattering of boxes throughout the volume contain brief suggestions for things to do and places to see. A separate work covers Western Europe. 414 p.

The Christian Travelers Guide (series) (Zondervan Publishing House).

The Christian Travelers Guide to Great Britain (2001) opens with some fifty odd pages, where one part is about British history and a second about English literature, music, art, and architecture. However, the majority of the volume is an A to Z listing of English, Scottish, and Welsh cities and towns. Each has its history followed by a "places to visit" section that has descriptions of churches and other points of interest, both religious and lay, thereby allowing for broader usage as a guide. Usually followed by unnumbered street locations, the large-type names of the attractions serve as the first words in the paragraph about them. Somewhat of an oversize paperback, the book has pages that are double-columned but the amount of information may be too restricted for some items, and maps are omitted. Other works in the series have dealt only with European countries. 245 p.

Europe's Monastery and Convent Guesthouses: A Pilgrim's Travel Guide / Kevin J. Wright (Liguori, 2000).

The first parts explain the history of separate orders, offer biographies of outstanding figures, define monastic terms, and suggest ways of arranging a stay. Next comes the bulk of this work, the annotated directory set up by place under country. It is gracefully presented with name, address, telephone and fax numbers, and any electronic contact centered on the page, and is followed by several sentences about the house's founding, its attractions for visitors, and its accommodations. Small photos accompany some sites. In a separate part, a few additional European monasteries and convents are likewise listed, but without the notes. Addresses for monastic and travel-related websites appear at the book's end. The title is useful as an introduction to these houses and as a directory, but several travel guides will have more on individual religious establishments, which may have to be directly contacted for omitted details such as driving directions and the costs that may be charged for a stay. 241 p.

Jewish Heritage Travel: A Guide to Eastern Europe / Ruth Ellen Gruber (National Geographic, 2007).

Well-written and interesting, much of this informative book can be read for its own sake rather than as a travel guide. There's a history of Judaism for fourteen countries and a history for many significant towns and cities, which are marked on a simple map at the front. Typical topics are the appearance and condition (often that of neglect) of remaining synagogues, neighborhoods, and cemeteries, and the effects of the Holocaust. Speaking in the first-person, the author quotes at times the observations of natives. Hotels, restaurants, and practical advice are omitted. 338 p.

Jewish Travel Guide. International ed. Annual (Valentine Mitchell in association with the Jewish Chronicle).

In the A to Z directory, each country begins with a short history of its Jewish inhabitants (Israel's is the most detailed), then under its towns and cities are categories for bakeries, booksellers, community organizations, contact information, Jewish centers, synagogues by denomination, etc. The fullest entries have name, address, telephone number, fax, e-mail, website, and occasionally an annotation. Front matter has names and addresses for tours, holidays, and cruises of interest to the Jewish traveler, and there are tips for those who want to keep kosher while traveling. Examined: 2007; 402 p.

The Jewish Travel Guide / Betsy Sheldon (Hunter, 2001)

Here are points of Jewish culture and religion as it exists in major cities of the United States plus two in Canada. Common sightseeing categories are museums and galleries; historic sites; monuments, markers, and memorials; neighborhoods; and general interest sites with a Jewish connection, the entries receiving a paragraph. Following these are addresses and telephone numbers of orthodox, conservative, and reform synagogues, though the ones with some historic importance may have background information. Kosher dining establishments are noted in terms of their cuisine, and Jewish community centers for what they offer. Shops may just be a listing, while events and heritage tours are described. Treatment of the city ends with a handful of services, groups, and titles. The states and Canada have listings for other Jewish attractions. A British annual publication shares the same title (see previous entry). 259 p.

The Jewish Traveler: Hadassah Magazine's Guide to the World's Jewish Communities and Sights / edited by Alan M. Tigay (Jason Aronson, 1994).

From the obvious (Vienna) to the exotic (Samarkand), there is an alphabetical arrangement of over one hundred cities on every continent except Antarctica. Each city receives a substantial amount about it within several two-column pages. An introduction is followed by sections on Jewish history, the current community, and important sights—this last establishing the work as a travel guide. There may be other segments on well-known personalities, culture, general attractions, side trips, recommended reading, and travel suggestions. The book has more of history than of sightseeing, which could have been increased by following a guide's lead, as in connecting individuals with a specific location. Perhaps due to its bulk it does not lend itself to be toted readily along on a journey, but does offer advice about where to go. 574 p.

The Liguori Guide to Catholic U.S.A.: A Treasury of Churches, Schools, Monuments, Shrines, and Monasteries / Jay Copp (Liguori, 1999).

This follows the typical geographic arrangement of region, state, and town or city, all of which are bolded, as is the name of the attraction which appears in the paragraph that discusses it. Next to the name is parenthesized its address and telephone number. The majority of sites are churches whose history and design or architecture may be summed in just a few words or, in special cases, fill as much as a page. A minority of entries come with small photographs that are generally of the structure's exterior. This is the resource for those who wish a gathering of both the important and little known, from Mother Seton House to the Monastic Heritage Museum. However, web addresses are lacking in a book that is certainly portable and probably could fit in a glove compartment. 326 p.

Oscar Israelowitz's United States & Canada Jewish Travel Guide / Oscar Israelowitz. 9th ed. (Israelowitz Publishing, 2007).

    The Jewish Travel Guide (above) is as selective as *Oscar Israelowitz's* is inclusive. Alphabetical by state and Canadian province, under them are categories with simple lists that have only name, address, and telephone number. These are for Jewish sites (museums, historic places, etc.), eating kosher, JCCs and YMHAs, synagogues, and mikvahs (ritual baths for women). This directory very occasionally has descriptive comments for its entries. Among other Jewish travel guides by this author are those treating New York, Israel, and Europe. 393 p.

Overnight or Short Stay at Religious Houses around the World / James J. Hughes, Victoria D. Hughes. 5th ed. (Hugen Press, 1995).

    This worldwide directory is arranged by continent and, in two instances, by area (Central America and the South Pacific). Countries are alphabetical and subdivided by region, district, or state, and grouped within them are the entries. They contain location, a numeric code, name of house, address, telephone number, and letter codes for types of houses (retreat, guest, ministries) and denomination, which are overwhelmingly Christian sects. There is no evaluation or narration, but the inclusion is worldwide, even though this is somewhat lopsided—Chile, for example, is the only country featured under South America. However, it is doubtful if all this information can be found gathered in any other source. Twenty photographs of houses are at the very beginning, while maps at the end show four European countries. 152 p.

Pilgrimages: A Guide to the Holy Places of Europe for Today's Traveler / Paul Lambourne Higgins (Prentice-Hall, 1984).

    This is a work for people interested in the topic rather than those expecting a specialized guidebook to a region. It recites history, legends, and stories associated with Christian and a few pagan locations, plus it gives architectural descriptions and comments on various mystical forces found at the sites. A short section after each discussion of a location is called "tips for travelers" and offers general advice on getting there and what else to see, but lacks addresses and other aids, which are also missing around the main topics; so a practical guidebook is needed as a supplement. Coverage is by regions of Western Europe and is selective rather than inclusive. However, the author's display of his psychic feelings may best be appreciated by those in tune with the other world. A companion volume is *Pilgrimages USA* (Prentice-Hall, 1985). 146 p.

A Place Apart: Houses of Christian Hospitality and Prayer in Europe (series) (Raphael Publishing).

The name of the city or town under a country arrangement is unfortunately not set apart to maximize visibility. Every entry is grouped in the same, plain way, with the first section made of the house's name, address, telephone and fax numbers, contact name, and religious order, which is usually a type belonging to the Roman Catholic Church. The other parts of the entry have for whom the house is open (e.g., pilgrims, men, women) and whether intended for retreats, renewals, etc.; a description of the accommodation that may note the number of rooms and the amenities; areas of the structure open to the guests; the history of the site; and how to get there by rail or by car. Examined: *A Place Apart: Houses of Christian Hospitality and Prayer in Europe. Belgium, France* (2000; 117 p.)

A Place for God: A Guide to Spiritual Retreats and Retreat Centers / Timothy Jones (Doubleday, 2000).

Preceded by chapters about spiritual retreats, the first part of each entry in the directory proper contains the name, address, telephone number, and Christian denomination, and it has up to three icons that represent the availability of spiritual guidance, accessibility, and whether a shelter affords solitude. Then comes a description of the place in one or more paragraphs, a comment on the accommodations and reservations, points of interests on the grounds and perhaps nearby, and automobile directions to it. The neat and oblong package could fit in a glove compartment and is very well formatted for browsability, except for some flaws. Though arrangement for the United States is by region and state, there is no running title at the top of a page to identify the state, and within a state the order is by the name of the retreat, which is probably less helpful than by locale. A small part at the end covers Canada by province. A simple outline map of a region shows major highways and a few cities, but not the location of the retreat. 464 p.

Sacred Places around the World: 108 Destinations / Brad Olsen. 2nd ed. (Consortium of Collective Consciousness, 2004).

This is on the outer limits of fitting into the travel guide category, since the book is chiefly a description and history of each site with very general observations given about the means of going there and nothing about accommodations, etc. Chapters cover continents—though Australia and the Pacific are lumped together—or parts of them while the maps, drawn by the author, are marked with the names of the entries and are useful chiefly for showing relative locations. A short introduction considers types of sacred places—caves, pyramids, lost cities, and the like. A believer who admits that some of his views do not accord with modern science, the author has also written works on this topic that center on Europe and North America. Photos and drawings are throughout. 280 p.

A Travel Guide to Jewish Europe / Ben G. Frank. 3rd ed. (Pelican Publishing, 2001).

Throughout this narrative of Jewish history in twenty countries locales are bolded as they appear in the text, though their addresses are not placed consistently after their names. Coverage is anywhere from the beginning of Jewish settlement to life in the present day. The most important cities show categories of subjects such as Jewish sites, kosher restaurants, synagogues, and organizations, examples of which often have one to several paragraphs describing them. Attractions in other cities and towns are duly observed, while there's a scattering of photographs of buildings and memorials. Six of the countries are Eastern European, and another is Turkey. 752 p.

Traveling Jewish in America: The Complete Guide for Business & Pleasure / edited by Ellen Chernofsky. 4th revised ed. (Wandering You Press, 1997).

This plain directory is alphabetically arranged by state, then by city and town. The largest category is that for synagogues, which in addition to name, address, and telephone number has the rabbi's name and the frequency of services. Next are kosher places to eat out or to buy food, with a few words on what is available. Categories that are most likely to appear under larger population centers are kosher accommodations within walking distance of synagogues, mikvahs, day schools, bookstores, and "other." Although a little over one inch thick, the book is of digest size and could probably fit in an average glove compartment. 525 p.

US and Worldwide Guide to Retreat Center Guest Houses / John and Mary Jensen (CTS Publications, 1995).

The authors define retreat center guest houses as monasteries, abbeys, priories, convents, and religious centers where individuals and groups can have room and board. The biggest section is for states of the U.S., while others are for Canadian provinces and the rest of the world, chiefly countries of Europe. Within state, province, or country the listings are in no order and their bolded labels have a crowded appearance, even though name, address, telephone number, and contact name are slightly set apart. Several labels have a checkmark next to them to indicate if a thing is present (e.g., "Twin Rooms"), but if there is no checkmark there is also no label. Such matters as smoking and quiet time are limited to a line or so under "Guest Rules," but a substantial paragraph covers attractions on the site or nearby points of interest. The guest rate and individual deposit are featured in denominations of the country unless otherwise indicated. There is the occasional outside photograph or illustration of a retreat. An appendix of additional houses gives only name, address, and telephone number. 165 p.

RELOCATING

America has been called a mobile society. People readily and frequently move to another state or country. Whether temporarily or permanently, the majority of transplants move because of employment (notably business and the military), studies, family, or because they are retirees or expatriates.

Books describe how to cope with a brave new home and the continuing demands of an old one left behind. They report on the transport of belongings, culture shock, language problems, safety, legal hassles at home, and other matters. Some works target types of transplants (retirees) or special problems (taxes). There are also periodicals about aspects of this subject, such as the monthly *International Living* (International Living).

When people consider a move, a major concern is the prospective locale's livability and how it compares with others. Works on place and city rankings clarify the issue.

Get information about a community through its chamber of commerce, whose address can be obtained through a website such as a link within the "U.S. Chamber of Commerce" (www.uschamber.com) or through a reference that can be as specific as the *World Chamber of Commerce Directory* (see title in **Major Travel References** in the **Introduction**) or more general, as with the directory *City Profiles USA*.

Businesses help people relocate. In the yellow pages look for them under "Movers."

Subject Headings: Americans—Foreign countries; Cities and towns—Ratings; Moving, Household; Quality of life; Social indicators

Titles

America's Top-Rated Cities: A Statistical Handbook. 7th ed. (Grey House Publishing, 1999).

Within each of the four regional volumes the names of the cities are in alphabetical order and have statistical information covering a lot of aspects: employment and earnings, population characteristics, taxes, cost of living, public safety, etc. There is a page of background commentary followed by another page or so that discusses rankings for the city according to various criteria. Although there is other text, the work is chiefly tables compiled from a variety of sources, the numbers understandable to the average person since there is enough descriptive headings to make the meanings clear. How important is, say, the male to female ratio or the size of a library system depends on the reader because with a few exceptions—e.g., the best businesses to work for—the qualitative significance of "top-rated" must be inferred. The publisher also has related titles dealing with smaller cities, and with health and environment. Updated editions of this title are available. 4 vols.

Buying a Home Abroad / David Hampshire. 3rd ed. (Survival Books 2002).

After a brief consideration of reasons to buy a home abroad and which country to choose, there are other matters addressed, such as driving and health. As in *The Daily Telegraph Guide to Living Abroad* (below), the context for the reader is British, although Americans can still glean useful facts about home buying in general, with additional details to think about should the home be abroad. For example, among utilities the price of bottled gas varies from country to country. Also like the *Daily Telegraph Guide* a chunk of space has country profiles with general background information complemented by that pertaining to finance and property. The same publisher has produced a group of titles that begin *Buying a Home in* [name of place] and *Living and Working in* [name of place]. 252 p.

*Cities Ranked & Rated: More Than 400 Metropolitan Areas Evaluated in the U.S. & Canada / Bert Sperling & Peter Sander. 2nd ed. (Wiley Publishing, 2007).

The heart of this big volume is the tables portraying in name order the 400 cities and towns, which also have paragraphs describing them, plus an overall score and rank. Categories are for population; economy and jobs; cost of living; climate; education; health and health care; crime; transportation; leisure; arts and culture; and quality of life, all of which are subdivided. Whether as percentages or scores, numbers here in each case are compared with the overall national average. Earlier chapters have tables with percentage of population change by place, the place by rank, and statistics by state; and they supplement a discussion of categories. In the earlier edition, the cities and towns were ranked against one another according to the categories, so that someone who valued leisure the most might pay closer attention to the highest ranks on that table. Canada metro areas are in a small chapter at the end of the work. 850 p.

The Comparative Guide to American Suburbs: Covers over 2,400 Suburban Communities in the 50 Largest Metro Areas—with Rankings. 3rd ed. (Grey House Publishing, 2005).

Under its metropolitan area, a suburb is characterized in terms of geography (as, the square miles it covers and its elevation) before blocks of facts concerning its history; population elements; economy; income; cost-of-living index; crime; home ownership and value; educational levels of the citizens; school district figures; local newspapers; and additional contacts via web and telephone numbers. Within these it is noted where things rank. At the end of the suburb group, subjects are split into lists to show how suburbs relate to one another, from highest to lowest, though the highest might refer to such negatives as unemployment rate. It would have been a bonus to have the rankings combined so as to show qualitatively a final list of best suburbs that are part of a metropolis. State maps identify counties, with grays designating metropolitan statistical regions. A later edition is available. 1295 p.

Craighead's International Business, Travel, and Relocation Guide to 84 Countries. Biennial (Gale).

This large, multi-volume reference work has for each country a simple map and several key facts before discussions of what a relocating person can bring along (vehicle, furnishings, etc.) and what the natives are like, as well as their attitudes and business customs. Among the issues about living abroad are advice on choosing a school, finding a home, and the quality of life to expect. One or more of a country's major cities get a capsule description in a few lines. The broadness of covering travel, business, and relocation, and compacting subjects, makes for generalizations, some bland, as the suggestion that one way to meet people is through joining a local civic organization. However, this work is good as an overview. Note that the number of countries may change according to the newest edition. 4 vol. Examined sample pages of 2000 edition at www.gale.com website: 2006

The Daily Telegraph Guide to Living Abroad / Michael Furnell & Philip Jones. 12th ed. (Kogan Page, 1999).

The target audience is British and not American, which means there are references to British laws, British money, and British conventions. Beyond looks at expected relocation situations there is material about less-covered possibilities, among them renting one's home while away or participating in a timeshare to get a flavor of a foreign place. There is information here specific to several countries that is not provided in any of the other relocation guides—for example, about death overseas. Well over one-half of the work is filled with profiles of islands around Britain and countries in Europe, those around the Mediterranean, and those that are first-world and English-speaking (among them Australia and the U.S. state of Florida). Sections within the profiles include the subjects of taxation; language; the expatriate community; residence qualifications; housing;

buying property; where to live; health services; and climate. Perhaps not the first choice for an American, as a supplement it may offer a perspective that the other works do not. 391 p.

The Expert Expatriate: Your Guide to Successful Relocation Abroad—Moving, Living, Thriving / Melissa Brayer Hess and Patricia Linderman (Nicholas Brealey in association with Intercultural Press, 2002).

Subjects that are substantially tackled include methods of learning the host country's language, the physical move and why and what to take, culture shock, moving children and pets, the mental transition to a foreign environment, special issues for yourself and your spouse, and keeping in touch with the home environment. For variety, first-person narratives are scattered in graphic boxes throughout the book, while paragraphs are occasionally interrupted by lists of things to consider. Besides the lucid understanding of what faces those who are going to live temporarily abroad, this is full of common sense and practical psychology about coping with foreign customs and the workings of other cultures. A later edition is available. 273 p.

Gap Years for Grown Ups / Susan Griffith (Vacation Work Publications, 2004).

If you have wanted to take a substantial gap of time from your daily life in order to travel, this is a work to consult. Besides giving reasons for doing this, the first third thoughtfully details steps involved in implementing the decision—getting time away from your employer, managing your financial affairs, renting your property or not, etc. The greatest portion of the book offers suggestions about how to spend the time off, with names, addresses, and descriptions of useful organizations. Opportunities run from volunteering for conservation and other causes to finding various types of work (e.g., teaching English) and forms of adventure travel. A closing discussion is on re-entering the life left behind. That the perspective is British may be an advantage for the American reader, in that the lists of many programs may be different from that in American books. A later edition is available. 334 p.

Getting into America: The Immigration Guide to Finding a New Life in the USA / Henry G. Liebman. 3rd ed. (How To Books, 2004).

This is an explanation of the red tape required for entering America, especially the function of visas, types of which cover traveling for pleasure, arriving as a fiancé(e), working, and studying. Employment receives attention in such ways as temporary working visas and sending staff to a new business or an old one. The single longest chapter deals with five methods for obtaining a green card, which is the federal government's recognition of an alien's right of permanent residence. A short chapter considers naturalization, while among the appendixes are lists of legal forms and typical citizenship questions. Going through the book might resemble reading law instructions, but it does supply the immigrant with explanatory information from a variety of U.S. documents that share the same issues. 162 p.

The Global Citizen: A Guide to Creating an International Life and Career / Elizabeth Kruempelmann (Ten Speed Press, 2002).

The book has such a broad travel overview that it fits uneasily in any single category, including **Relocating**. Containing a personality test, it first assesses if the reader has a strong desire to travel and live abroad, then offers suggestions for ways of accomplishing this—as through studying, volunteering, or working. There is also advice about finding ways of funding one's travel (e.g., scholarships and loans), adjusting to life overseas, and how to re-adjust to life upon returning home. Addresses and descriptions of various helpful organizations are scattered through the chapters. Throughout is the assumption that travel, with its great benefits, should be adopted as a way of life. 384 p.

The Grown-Up's Guide to Running Away from Home: Making a New Life Abroad / Rosanne Knorr. 2nd ed. (Ten Speed Press, 2008).

Over twenty chapters about moving overseas run the gamut in approximate order of realization, from reasons and conditions for going (supplemented by a self-inventory) to settling in before the eventual return. Between is advice for choosing a destination; saving money for the move and while living abroad (illustrated by sample accounts); finding a job, leisure activities, and a home; transplanting family and belongings; dealing with regulations; staying in touch once there; and safeguarding health and property abroad. Numerous headings parcel the information in the amiable narration, which occasionally draws upon the author's own experiences. 198 p.

International Relocation: A Practical Guide to Living and Working Overseas / Marc Bond with Rita Bond (AAPG Publications, 2000).

Each of its chapters begins with a summary of what is to be learned in it and its major points. Then for perhaps a page there is a first-person account of the authors' experiences or observations that add little to inform the reader. The rest of the chapter is a discussion that may be broken up into subheadings, and different typefaces as well as bullets relieve the blocks of texts or call attention to something important. This enabling of readability is offset by the parentheses in sentences used to footnote other authors, a scholarly apparatus that may deter some of its audience. A repeating theme is about adjustment to change and to other cultures. The final fourth of the book is a mixture of checklists, exercises (e.g., management of stress, net cash flow), and different resources. As for the "practical guide" part of the title, there are too few plain and nitty-gritty examples, while there is a lot of the textbook about the work. 457 p.

Moving: A Complete Checklist and Guide for Relocation / Karen G. Adams (Silvercat Publications, 1994).

The book is composed of checklists of instructions in sentences chiefly direct and declarative. Each instruction has a small checkbox next to it and is separated from the succeeding by a blank line, but there is no highlighting of important points. Chapters are subdivided into "A," "B," "C," etc. The household move itself is in countdown chapters of planning: six-to-eight weeks, four-to-five weeks, two-to-three weeks, one week, and one-to-two days. Lists follow—for professional packing, arriving at the destination, moving in, international moving, and what to do after settling in. Appendixes have a few more checklists and brief discussions on some specialties. The emphasis is on the physical and practical side of moving and not on relocation to another country, with few aspects of this treated. 140 p.

Moving and Living Abroad: A Complete Handbook for Families / Sandra Albright, Alice Chu, Lori Austin; revised by Sandra Albright, Chase de Kay Wilson (Hippocrene Books, 1993).

The expected practicalities are confronted: readying possessions for the move, considering whether to buy or rent accommodations over there, finding a mover, etc. Newcomers must learn about adaptation to a foreign culture, which involves ways to cope with culture shock, learning new etiquette, becoming familiar with the commercial customs of businesses, and possibly communicating in another language. There are also observations on what help to expect from one's company and how to re-adjust upon the return. This is written more from a woman's point of view than a man's, as evidenced by the parts about the effect of the move on the family and about women who pursue their careers abroad or are married to men who do. One subject that probably does not have pages devoted to it in other relocation books concerns dealing with servants. This is a chummier book than *International Relocation* (above). 258 p.

Moving & Relocation Sourcebook and Directory. 2nd ed. (Omnigraphics, Inc., 1998).

As *The Comparative Guide to American Suburbs* (above) deals with communities that are part of a metropolitan area, so this title profiles the metropolis itself. Alphabetically arranged by city name on the large, two-column pages, entries begin with facts related to the city's land area, latitude, time zone, etc., and then offer something about climate, with monthly breakdowns of temperature and precipitation. Other sections include a history narrative of the city, population figures broken down into various categories, economy and major employers, and quality of living indicators. Among the categories consisting chiefly of names and contact information are those related to government, higher education institutions, hospitals, transportation centers, utilities, banks, shopping, media, attractions, sports teams, and annual events. This work omits comparisons and qualitative evidence. Later editions are available under the altered title *Moving & Relocation Directory.* 898 p.

**Places Rated Almanac: The Classic Guide for Finding Your Best Places to Live in America* / David Savageau. 7th ed. (Places Rated Books, 2007).

The bulk of the large reference book is a variety of lists and tables with rankings of 379 metropolitan areas. Nine chapters view places in terms of ambience (as through arts and culture); housing; jobs; crime; transportation; education; health care; recreation; and climate. Each chapter begins and ends with a discussion of its subject and includes supplementary matter in shaded boxes, such as the top twenty cities or areas, which also have numeric scores. However, the substance of a chapter is the alphabetically arranged cities or areas—in three columns per page—with self-explaining statistics and with subject lists (e.g., schools and colleges by place under the education heading), the readability heightened through bolding and indenting. The end of the book brings in all the preceding scores for an overview of how a place qualifies in its nine categories (the order is alphabetical rather than by rank), with each of the top 40 scores highlighted—though there is no corresponding notice offered to the bottom 40. This is an imposing amount of data put in digestible shape, and its editions continue. 662 p.

Profiles of America: Facts, Figures & Statistics for Every Populated Place in the United States. 2nd ed. (Grey House Publishing, Inc., 2003).

With subject coverage similar to *Moving & Relocation Sourcebook and Directory* and *The Comparative Guide to American Suburbs* (both above), the set of geographically arranged volumes aims at describing *all* U.S. towns and cities. Under each state, a county is typified in such terms as its square miles, location of its administrative center, monthly weather highs and lows, and amount of precipitation and snow. Some characteristics come with percentages—for population elements, religion, economy, education, and elections. There are dollar amounts for income, taxes, and housing, and telephone numbers for additional information. A similar pattern is followed by the separate communities profiled within the county, with categories omitted and one added for transportation (about commuting and travel time to work). The result is to give at least a heads up for someone who might be thinking about a move to the area. 4 vol.

So You're Going Overseas: A Handbook for Personal and Professional Success / J. Stewart Black, Hal B. Gregersen (Global Business Publishers, 1998).

International assignments may take a worker over there, as opposed to retirement or enjoying a long vacation. This is the outlook of the authors as they give advice that is tinged with business-like attitudes and approaches. They look at the various financial pressures that drive international companies, and at the compensation as well as various payment allowances that might be expected. Likewise there is treatment of computer programs and training for "job toughness" in dealing with another culture, and there is a discussion of the troubles in finding another job upon returning. Short shrift is given to the moving and adjusting process, for this is a *study* of a businessperson going overseas, with little of it serving as a manual with how-to examples. The font size is largish, providing less wordage than a number of other titles in this section. 201 p.

Tax Highlights for U.S. Citizens and Residents Going Abroad (Internal Revenue Service, U.S. Department of the Treasury). www.irs.gov/pub/irs-pdf/p593.pdf

The document has facts about filing (who, when, and where), reporting on income earned abroad, tax withholding, foreign income taxes, and briefly how agreements with other countries affect taxes. Examined website: 2008

Tips for Americans Residing Abroad (Bureau of Consular Affairs, U.S. Department of State). travel.state.gov/travel/tips/tips_1232.html#residing

This older title, which is still available, has been submerged in *Tips for Traveling Abroad* (see **Law** for a review). Looking abroad, it briefly addresses marriage, birth, divorce and death, federal benefits services, driver's licenses, etc. Examined website: 2008

Organizations

American Citizens Abroad. www.aca.ch

In addition to helping citizens living outside the United States in such matters as taxes, health insurance, and citizenship, the nongovernmental association reviews pertinent book titles and has a list of websites. Examined website: 2008

Association of Americans Resident Overseas. www.aaro.org

Like American Citizens Abroad, it informs its audience about matters relevant to their needs and interests. Examined website: 2008

Internal Revenue Service, U.S. Department of the Treasury. www.irs.gov

Those living abroad can find at this site such documents as *Tax Guide for U.S. Citizens and Resident Aliens Abroad* and *Foreign Tax Credit for Individuals*, and receive specific answers under "Frequently Asked Questions." Examined website: 2008

Overseas Briefing Center, Foreign Service Institute, U.S. Department of State. www.state.gov/www/obc/prepare/checkl.html

The preparation checklist—organizing household effects, scheduling immunizations, shipment of pets and automobiles, etc.—is for the benefit of government employees assigned overseas, and for their accompanying families. However, the site may provide pointers to anyone relocating abroad. Examined website: 2008

SAFETY AND SECURITY

Protect yourself and your valuables from risk. Books in this section discuss precautions to take against thieves, terrorists, health hazards, and other threats; and then what to do in case the worst happens.

One way of gauging a country's safety is through the travel advisories and warnings from the Department of State, though they have their biases in interpreting danger. For the security situation affecting the United States, check with the Department of Homeland Security, especially in regard to air travel rules.

See also **Emergencies**.

Subject Heading: Travel—Safety measures.

Titles

The Caretaker Gazette. Bimonthly (Caretaker Gazette). www.caretaker. org

While under "House Sitting & Stewards" the yellow pages identify local businesses offering sitters who will stay in homes of vacationers, this subscription newsletter contains employment listings for taking care of properties around the world, and includes advice for caretakers and property owners. Examined website: 2007

The Complete SAS Guide to Safe Travel / Nick Cameron (Piatkus, 2002).

With the title referring to a rugged unit of the British military, the guide offers suggestions for either guarding against or adapting to the dangers and problems that might appear throughout the world. In general, there are one or more introductory paragraphs on a subject followed by plenty of typographical bullets that serve to package short and focused responses. The context may be practicing cultural sensitivity, buying the correct clothing, handling animals for riding, confronting terrorists, or fooling criminals. The scope of situations is wide. Those involving air or rail journeys may be familiar to conventional travelers, while others might happen to people who are either unlucky (e.g., caught in a riot) or too adventurous (e.g., wandering off in a desert). It is unknown whether worriers will feel more secure as a result of the survival advice or find more reason than ever to be concerned, since any place could be a target. 422 p.

Don't Go!: 51 Reasons Not to Travel Abroad: But If You Must—176 Tactics for Coping with Discomforts, Distress and Danger / Hannah Blank

(Prism Corp., 1996).

The 51 are numbered in the table of contents but not in the text, where they are separately discussed along with the (unnumbered) 176 ways to avoid or lessen their likelihood or, if they occur, to handle the problems. As the subtitle suggests, there's more here than safety and security. For example, unlike other works under this heading, the Blank book has a chapter about coping with culture shock (language, food, cleanliness, poverty, etc., of another culture); and along with a discussion of discomforts and nuisances, this takes up more text than the serious stuff on health and crime. A smaller second part applies a "be prepared" attitude to getting ready for a trip, packing, and en route travel. 140 p.

Robert Young Pelton's The World's Most Dangerous Places / Robert Young Pelton. 5th ed. (Harper Resource, 2003).

Qualifying tangentially as a travel guide, it spends little to no time with attractions, accommodations, and eateries. This thick volume is a personal view with a lot of irreverent and black humor describing places most tourists are likely to visit only from the comfort and safety of their armchair. About two-thirds of the book is devoted to a list of hazardous destinations that begins alphabetically with Afghanistan and includes, surprisingly to some, the United States. Lawlessness, extremist groups, and backgrounds of dictators are constant subjects, with early chapters focusing on dangerous jobs, diseases, drugs, guns, and the like. The author provides anecdotes of his experiences as well as bits of an encyclopedic knowledge about a country's history, customs, and current conditions. For supplemental information there are addresses, websites, and maps. Journalists and others who travel to such places will not be harmed by reading this. (Pelton has also written the entertaining *Come Back Alive: The Ultimate Guide to Surviving Disasters, Kidnapping, Animal Attacks, and Other Nasty Perils of Modern Travel* (Doubleday, 1999); this look at handling extreme and worst-scenario situations might apply more to survivalists than tourists.) A later edition is available. 1074 p.

The Safe Tourist: Hundreds of Proven Ways to Outsmart Trouble and Still Have a Wonderful Trip / Natalie Windsor; edited by Rich Lippman (CorkScrew Press, 1995).

The book is a collection of subject-divided tips that are from one to several short sentences and can make for a rather disjointed reading experience. A number of them are written in a verb-first, declarative manner ("Pay for big-ticket items on your credit card"), but all are "eye-marked" by having a small box next to them, and they have important phrases bolded. Beyond advice about protecting yourself, your home, your money, or your pet, there are discussions of scams, accommodations, traveling by different sorts of transportation, and smart actions for women, men, children, and businesspeople. At the end is a checklist of items to bring on a trip. The book is of a size that could fit it into a medium to large sports coat pocket or a lady's pocketbook. 215 p.

The Safe Travel Book / Peter Savage. Revised ed. (Lexington Books, 1998).

A traveler's well-being is contingent on his or her health, physical safety, monetary security, and conforming with the laws of any visited countries. These categories are emphasized throughout, but it is in the first half of the book where they are associated with planning a trip. The scope extends from terrorism prevention and airline crash landings to more mundane problems that are likely to be considered inconveniences. The author gives welcome advice for the average traveler who wishes to be prudent, and probably addresses the expectations of pessimists or those who fear that they might encounter extreme conditions. In the mixture of comments about passports, brands of credit cards, jet lag, and dealing with emergencies are names, addresses, telephone numbers, and titles of resources. The possible predicaments with which women might be obliged to deal receive some attention. Subjects within chapters are numbered, which allows for locating them with greater ease. 222 p.

Security Guidelines for American Families Living Abroad. Revised (Overseas Security Advisory Council, U.S. Department of State, 2005). www.osac.gov/ResourceLibrary/index.cfm

This online nuts and bolts self-help manual is a detailed and humorless compilation of advice from security professionals about protecting oneself and loved ones overseas from criminals and terrorists. Among the topics covered are risk assessment for the location and selection of residence; emergency preparations; locks; intrusion alarms; trusting domestic help; automobile travel; threats from mail; quality of foreign law enforcement; and evacuations. There is enough in here to make anyone paranoid. (A counterpart title available from the same site is *Security Guidelines for Children Living Abroad* and another, aimed at businesses, is *Security Guidelines for American Enterprises Abroad*.) Examined website: 2007

Travel Can Be Murder: The Business Traveler's Guide to Personal Safety / Terry Riley. 3rd ed. (Applied Psychology Press, 2001).

Each of the 707 numbered tips here has its own small heading and is under subdivisions related to a broader subject chapter. However, unlike other works in this section, this one is concerned almost exclusively with dangerous and life-threatening situations, much of them deliberately brought on by criminals and baddies. One need not be a business traveler to profit from the no-nonsense presentation, which addresses both prevention and minimization, and supposes some of the worst possible situations, such as being held captive; in which instance it suggests how to react (e.g., "Escape at the first opportunity"). The paperback is portable and small, but it has considerable wordage. 205 p.

Travel Safely: At Home and Abroad: Don't Be a Target! / R. W. Worring, W. S. Hibbard, S. Schroeder. 3rd ed. Revised (Uniquest Publications, 1996).

The advice doesn't limit itself to safety issues but it also flags situations that could prove inconvenient (abroad "be sure you understand military time or else you won't understand the train schedule"). The subdivided content is full of bulleted suggestions that are sometimes preceded by a short introductory paragraph. Safety areas principally deal with departure; self-protection for women and other categories of travelers; the means of moving from place to place; the common experiences of travel; and matters of the law and of security. *Travel Safely* is less detailed and with fewer pages than, for example, *Travel Can Be Murder* (above), but on the other hand, like *Don't Go!* (also above) its scope is broader. 136 p.

*Travel Security Sourcebook / edited by Chad T. Kimball (Omnigraphics, 2003).

Imagine a hazard and advice about avoiding it is probably here. The book consists of excerpts from publications offered by Centers for Disease Control and Prevention and other governmental agencies as well as some from the commercial side. Chapter topics under each part are wide-ranging, so in the case of air travel there is content on how airport security works, safeguarding personal baggage, shoulder harness protection in a small plane, discrimination on airlines, and more. Other travel parts tackle ways of self-protection during crises and emergencies (e.g., bomb threats or earthquakes); health dangers (diseases, altitude sickness, etc.); thieves after one's property; and what items not to bring into the United States. Also, there is an array of individual subjects, from security for women, the elderly, and students traveling abroad to international child abduction and safety in rental cars. Bullets and bolding contribute to readability. 578 p.

SHIPS, BOATS, FERRIES, ETC.

There is a lot of writing about cruises and water travel. Guidebooks dedicated to cruises combine advice (what to take, shipboard etiquette, etc.) with descriptions of individual cruise lines and their ships, plus what to see and buy at ports of call. Beyond these comprehensive views are books that deal with one aspect of cruising, whether it is children, discounts, or jobs.

Besides appearing in cruise magazines and newsletters, articles about the subject are occasionally in popular magazines and generously in a variety of travel magazines. The travel sections of newspapers report on the cruise scene, with a few going so far as to annually devote an issue just to it. For local information, the yellow pages contains such listings as "Boat-Charter."

An obvious if biased source of information about a cruise ship comes from its own brochures, selectively available at travel agencies. However, for more balanced evaluations of ships ask for help from a travel agent, and also pay attention to readers' comments in newspapers and magazines. If concerned about health or sanitation standards aboard, visit the "Vessel Sanitation Program" website (below) for government inspection summaries by ship line or by particular vessel.

It is possible to preview the physical arrangement of a cruise ship. Besides being on the internet, diagrams of decks show up in cruise company brochures, which also have when and where a ship sails.

Yet the determining fact in choosing a cruise is frequently its cost. Cost lists, as well as schedules and ports of call, are found in the substantial *Official Steamship Guide International* (below) and other titles. Cruise bargains for those who are willing to take cruises on short notice are merchandised by discount travel clubs. Like airline ticket bucket shops, they buy cheaply and resell at a rate cheaper than that offered by the cruise company or tour operator. Articles about them with addresses appear now and again in newspapers and magazines, and they maintain an online presence. (See also **Budget Travel**.)

Once aboard a cruise ship passengers can keep informed through various sources. Look for a centrally situated general information counter, often in association with the purser's office. Each day a sheet of events, restaurant menu items, and news may be delivered to the guest's room. A floating mall, a ship sells newspapers and magazines, and offers postal, internet, and telephone services.

Rather than cruise for pleasure, some people seek adventure or education, and there are ships that cater to this crowd. If coverage of them in cruise books and magazines is incomplete, search online or write to the cruise lines themselves. In addition, adventure operators or study abroad associations may be able to help. (See also **Adventure Travel** and **Study and Travel**.)

The great cruise ships have competitors. On the ocean some prefer traveling by freighter, while on canals and rivers there are barges and smaller boats that carry passengers. An abbreviated sense of cruising comes from ferries, the carriers of cars and passengers. Beyond these are houseboats, yachts, and sailboats. For every pleasure and recreational craft there are books, magazines, and businesses.

While the selection below emphasizes the passenger's perspective, sources for the do-it-yourself sailor have not been completely neglected.

Subject Headings: Cruise ships—Guidebooks; Ocean travel—Guidebooks; Sailing

Titles

Berlitz Complete Guide to Cruising & Cruise Ships / Douglas Ward. 17th ed. (Berlitz Publishing, 2008).

Absorbing one-fifth of this thorough work, the first part (with color photos) gives standard details on cruising: life aboard, choosing the right cruise, special requirements for passengers, different cruises (e.g., expedition), etc. The rest of the annually published book is an A to Z profile of cruise ships by name. Receiving at least one page, an entry begins with a three-column list that has dozens of facts, such as amount of tonnage; name of builder; country of registry; number of total crew; types of cabins; and presence of slot machines, self-service launderettes, and libraries. The ship, accommodations, food, service, entertainment, and cruise are rated in an overall ship score out of a possible 2,000 points, which are interpreted from * to *****+. In the description bolded headings have paragraphs devoted to an overview, accommodations, the cuisine and dining, entertainment, and spa/fitness. If knowing about a cruise ship rather than a port of call is of chief importance, consult this handy book. 708 p.

Cargo Ship Cruising: A Guide to the Joys of Sailing the World in Passenger-Carrying Cargo Ships / Robert B. Kane with Barbara W. Kane (Voyaging Press, 1997).

Since well over half of the book is a travelogue of the authors' experiences, the remainder has to serve for guiding the reader through discussions about what to expect from choosing this mode of transportation and preparing for a trip. Among the points is that flexibility must be assumed by the passenger, who should receive good food on board, but will have to be create his or her own amusements. Facilities are gone over, and there is a bit on understanding meteorological and nautical features. Several pages' worth of listings provide name of line, port stopovers, number of days at sea and number of possible passengers, cost, and the type of ship. But there are no accompanying addresses or (doubtless as a result of the book's age) websites and, as stated, a limited amount of text has been directed to the traveler. 106 p.

Caribbean Ports of Call: Western Region / Kay Showker. 6th ed. (Globe Pequot Press, 2002).

After a brief introduction to the Caribbean and to cruise life, there is up to a page of description of the lines that sail here. Most of the book is a traditional guide to the places visited by ship, collecting tourist interests into familiar categories whose ratings from one to five stars of attractions, restaurants, sports, shopping, etc., is in proportion to their presence at a locality. "Fast facts" for each of the island groups or destinations has a number of icons explained by the accompanying text. Thoughtfully designed with bolded stopping "places" for the eye, the double-columned pages have maps for countries, islands, and several of the port towns. Two other volumes about the rest of this expanse are subtitled *Northern and Northeastern Regions* and *Eastern and Southern Regions*. A later edition is available. 231 p.

Children Afloat / Pippa Driscoll (Fernhurst Books, 1989).

The specialty audience is parent-sailors who boat with their children. The safety portion looks at fitting life jackets for the young, the climbing of stairs, and other matters. There's also advice about the importance of a good attitude, making the boat child-proof, provisioning, planning a cruise, entertaining by age group, and teaching children how to sail. A number of candid photographs with captions support the text. For those interested in *ship*-cruising with tykes, consider *Cruise Vacations with Kids* (below). 95 p.

The Complete Cruise Handbook: Your Porthole Companion to the World of Cruises / Anne Vipond (Ocean Cruise Guides, 1996).

While the book is "complete" in that it touches on the tried and true—reasons for cruising, ports of call, preparation, etc.—the quantity of information supplied is much less than in many of the other titles that have been annotated here, as the word and page count testify. This also means there are such omissions as cruises for passengers with special needs. Numerous pages have photos or illustrations. This is more a glimpse than an examination of the subject. 176 p.

Cruise Ship Jobs: The Insiders Guide to Finding and Getting Jobs on Cruise Ships around the World / Richard B. Marin (Portofino Publications, 1998).

One-third of the space is allotted to a directory of cruise lines. Here are names of the lines and the ships, their destinations, short discussions about the companies, addresses for work applications, and rundowns on what personnel are wanted. It is a noteworthy omission that, except in one instance, neither e-mails nor websites are supplied for any line or business. Elsewhere are summaries of jobs aboard and of concessions that hire out to a ship, with succinct descriptions of their type and some addresses. Answers to frequently asked questions are provided, with a special look aimed at those who wish to work as entertainers. Skimpy in its content, this could have used the breadth and depth of *How to Get a Job with a Cruise Line* (below). 143 p.

Cruise Travel. Bimonthly (World Publishing Company). cruisetravelmag. com

Among the recurring columns are those dealing with ship of the month, cruise of the month, and port of the month. There are also profiles of destinations and cruise lines, various articles, and listings of ship schedules, itineraries, and fares. Examined website: 2007.

Cruise Vacations for Dummies / Heidi Sarna and Matt Hannafin (Wiley Publishing, Inc., 2007).

Why shouldn't the subject of cruising be a part of this extensive series aimed at beginners? The layout is typical for *Dummies*, with plenty of breaks in the text, large headings, and icons. This contributes to the fast flow of the writing, which allots the greatest amount of space to ports of call (with maps). The second largest section has the descriptions of cruise lines and their ships, along with small photographs. Categorized into mainstream, luxury, and small and sailing ships, each line is characterized through sections on dining, etc., and comes with a table showing separate ship prices and itineraries. The book also looks at picking a cruise, preparing for it, what experiences to expect aboard, keeping children engaged, and more. One of the best books to give a close view of the cruise experience, it is friendly and comes with useful and perhaps unfamiliar tips. It is updated every one to two years. 480 p.

Cruise Vacations with Kids / Candyce H. Stapen. Revised 2nd ed. (Prima Publishing, 1999).

There are three areas discussed. After mostly general cruise tips for adults, the focus moves to children, with a presentation of programs for them by line. Additional sections discuss teens, babysitting services, dining (e.g., the availability of children's menus), the adaptability of cabins for children, and discounts for the young. Non-traditional cruises are treated separately and by type: ecological and educational trips to spots known for their wildlife or scenery, travel by windjammer, and journeys on rivers. Finally, there are brief, general facts for tourists about destinations throughout the world. Much of this is broad and superficial, with attractions for children too often being identified by no more than a name. Consult *Cruise Vacations with Kids* before a trip as a way of deciding which cruise to book for the family, but whether it needs to be taken along is questionable. 485 p.

Cruising World. Monthly (Cruising World). www.cruisingworld.com
   This devotes itself to those who sail and yacht. There are descriptions of destinations, ports, and harbors, stories about sailing experiences and personalities, discussions of seamanship, news, recipes, etc. Examined website: 2008

The Essential Little Cruise Book: Secrets from a Cruise Director for a Perfect Cruise Vacation / Jim West. 3rd ed. (The Globe Pequot Press, 2003).
   At under six inches high, the portable book begins with choosing a cruise and ends with facts about disembarking. In-between are chapters on preparation, shipboard conventions and guidelines, shore excursions, health, families and special groups, and more. Chapters are solely composed of multitudinous collections of short observations and advice, each normally one to four sentences long, allowing for painless absorption, especially by those with limited attention spans. However, the style of so many simply worded sentences does take on repetitiveness. While the author gives advice that is useful to any traveler—e.g., don't overpack— much is specific to the cruising passenger. 203 p.

The European Waterways: A User's Guide / Marian Martin (Sheridan House, 2003).
   Omitting itineraries, this professional how-to manual for the serious boater begins with observations about the inland cruising experience and goes on to consider the qualities a buyer might want in a boat, the selection and readying of boat parts, usage fees, and the regulations that can vary by country. One chapter is just for U.S. visitors (importing your vessel, competence certificates, etc.), while three are devoted to inland locks. There is also advice about maneuvering on canals and small and great rivers as well as the water traffic that will be encountered. Choosing

a few popular ports, the author talks about arriving at them, their layout, places to moor, facilities, and provides maps for most. In addition to photo-graphs are a plentitude of illustrations, among them examples of signs and signals, and the shapes of boats by day and night along with their lights. 181 p.

Ferries of America: A Guide to Adventurous Travel / Sarah Bird Wright (Peachtree Publishers, 1987).
Headings on the left-hand of the page are detailed on the right. They are states whence the ferry departs; places served (from where-to-where); the body of water on which the vessel travels; the ferry service history; local points of interest; crossing time; whether the ferry type is passenger or vehicle and how much of either cargo it can carry; its operating season during the year and schedule during the day; restrictions that might apply; facilities on board; fare; reservations that might be required; directions to the ferry departure point; a location keyed to maps of the states; and pre-website contact address with telephone number. Though some of the facts—for example, schedule and fare—are outdated, the amount of information and its compilation in one spot makes this worth consulting. 547 p.

Ferryliner Vacations in North America: Ocean Travel and Inland Cruising / Michael and Laura Murphy (E.P. Dutton, 1988).
Moving port-to-port, ferries provide flexibility for vacationers and are different from cruise ships. In order to be qualified for this book, ships must adhere to such standards as having cabins and taking voyages of over seven hours in duration in open water, while their port cities or towns must have some draw. Most of the volume consists of chapters that encompass large areas of the coasts, notably those in Alaska, Canada, Maine, and Mexico. There are considerations of scenery, buying tickets, boarding procedures, individual ships and their facilities, and itineraries. A table of departure points and destinations summarizes important data (sailings per week, duration of trip, cabin costs, etc.). This is not the place to get ideas about what to see once on land, though there is a little—but there is often advice about making bus, rail, and other connections and where accommodations are to be had. Due to its 1988 date, be sure to verify time-sensitive information. 277 p.

Freighter Space Advisory. Bimonthly (Freighter World Cruises, Inc.) www.freighterworld.com
The newsletter published by the specialty travel agency, Freighter World Cruises, assumes its audience already is versed in travel by

freighter, so its purpose is to highlight several ships. Five of them take up three pages of the issue under examination. An itinerary of anticipated stops and overall days of voyage are provided along with a table of fares in dollars and euros keyed to the ports of leaving and arriving, and to the number of days gone. A short description of the ship gives the maximum number of passengers that can be accommodated, the location and furnishings of the accommodations themselves, and particularly whether the outside view is clear or obstructed. There are also good black-and-white photos of ships and their interiors, only some of which are featured in the text. There is an age limit supplied and a request to call the agency for booking. The website (examined 2008) highlights a variety of cruises. Examined: issue from 2002

How to Get a Job with a Cruise Line: How to Sail around the World on Luxury Cruise Ships and Get Paid for It / Mary Fallon Miller. 5th ed. revision 1 (Ticket to Adventure, 2004).

A frequently-asked-questions chapter precedes one that profiles available cruise positions, which are supplemented by first-person narratives about them; and a few later chapters look at specific groups of workers. There is a designation of the top ten entry level jobs and tips about applying for a job, plus the ten "best" ways to apply. Summary profiles of cruise lines provide such things as nationality of the crew and the type of passengers attracted, along with job contact addresses. There is also a directory of cruise lines and one for concessionaires. Among other matters the book discusses, however briefly, are the cruise line industry, where to find travel and training programs, and employee benefits. Unpaged.

Official Steamship Guide International. Quarterly (Official Steamship Guide International). www.officialsteamshipguide.com

Having much breadth but little depth, this valuable resource is for those who want an idea about the thousands of cruises taking place throughout the world. After one section on individual cruise lines and another of brief facts about each cruise ship, the bulk of the volume collects cruise schedules by areas of the globe, including the trans-Panama Canal and the transatlantic. With arrangement by month and dates of departure and return, the entry provides the number of nights on the voyage, the name of the ship, a number coded to the cruise operator along with its abbreviated name, and ports of call. There is separate coverage for world and extended cruises that take more than 30 days, plus a page apiece listing of companies that handle river cruises or passenger freighters. Examined: issue from 2007; 144 p.

River Rafting and Outdoor Recreation Guide / Alvin Fixler (Morris Publishing, 2004).

The book's main and perhaps single virtue is that it gathers between covers a large list of businesses that offer rafting. With plain typography and unjustified columns this work is alphabetically arranged by state, though only certain ones are represented (Idaho in particular). The selection of companies and outfitters comes with name, address, and telephone number. Some entries add the name of the contact person, plus types of watercraft available and places that they take their guests; but for important details such as the difficulty rating of rapids on a particular river, the searcher must look elsewhere. A separate section identifies rafting companies that offer free trips to reward those who organize groups. 93 p.

The Seagoing Hitchhiker's Handbook: Roaming the Earth on Other People's Yachts / Greg Becker (High Adventure Publishing, 1994).

This specialist guide is aimed at the person who has sailing skills and wants to work his or her way about the world by water. After introductory matter and advice about how to hitch, the bulk of the book describes routes and ports in several oceans and seas. It may consider places in terms of sailing conditions, harbors or wharves and their location, services for boats, availability of yachts, and the best time of year to sail. Mentions of attractions such as good beaches and diving are occasional and minimal. Where ports are numerous on the east and west coasts they appear simply as names, telephone numbers, and with a few facts. 214 p.

Stern's Guide to the Cruise Vacation / Steven B. Stern. 17th ed. (Pelican Publishing Company, 2006).

Well over half of this useful, thick work discusses ships according to their lines, beginning with capsule data (number of passenger that can be accommodated, destinations, rating, etc.) for each ship, followed by pages that might contain the vessel's history, critiques of its food and décor, the price, and a concluding section that summarizes the strong points. For those who are more visually attuned, following the discussions are photos of selected ships inside and out, and facsimiles of both menus and of newsletters announcing daily activities. Among the chapters, there's one on individual ports of call and their attractions, while others pay special attention to such passengers as children, joggers, and singles. At the beginning expect advice on how to pick a cruise and prepare for one, and at the end a table rates ships by broad features. Of very large scope, the continuously updated editions attest to this work's popularity. 832 p.

The Unofficial Guide to Cruises / Kay Showker with Bob Sehlinger. 10th ed. (Wiley, 2007).

The first of this thorough book's three parts offers typical planning advice such as what to expect on a cruise and how to go about shopping for and booking one. However, the heart of the volume is a close look at the cruise lines and their various ships. Facts about a line (strengths, shortcomings, fellow passengers, etc.) precede separate sections describing each of its ships in terms of an overview; itinerary; cabins; dining; service personnel; facilities and activities; sports, fitness, and beauty; and children's facilities. An accompanying graphic box summarizes a line's standard features. The small third part is about the cruising alternatives of river and barge, adventure and culture, coastal and ferry, sail, and freighter, with much less detail than that distinguishing the cruise ships. Maps highlight cruise areas of the world. Author Showker is also responsible for the *Caribbean Ports of Call* volumes (above). 690 p.

Organizations

Cruise Lines International Association. www.cruising.org

This trade organization comprises a large number of major cruise lines. It provides information about cruising, with its website able to search cruises by destination, cruise line, or special interests. Examined website: 2007

Semester at Sea. www.semesteratsea.com

Administered by the Institute for Shipboard Education and academically sponsored by the University of Virginia, the Semester at Sea program offers education courses aboard the passenger *MV Explorer* as it sails the world. Primary focus is on undergraduate study, but there are also continuing education programs. Examined website: 2008

Vessel Sanitation Program. Centers for Disease Control and Prevention. U.S. Department of Health and Human Services. www.cdc.gov/nceh/vsp

To attack the problem of gastrointestinal disease outbreaks, the program scores cruise ships with foreign itineraries that arrive in the United States. Ship inspections rate water supply; spas and pools; food protection; employee hygiene practices; general cleanliness and physical condition of the ship; and training programs about environmental and public health practices. The site has a searchable database by ship. Examined website: 2007

SHOPPING

One common activity of travel is buying gifts, mementos, and local crafts. However, for shopper-travelers the greener pastures of discovering something unique or cheap, acquiring merchandise surpasses other enjoyments. Veteran shoppers have their own ways of finding out about what is for sale. They consult websites, store mailing lists, news ads, collector's magazines, or fellow fans.

Related to this type are buyers for a business, who should know the niceties of importing (see *How to Be an Importer and Pay for Your World Travel* under **Work**). The non-professional may get involved in importing when the object is a car, where the aim is probably to save rather than make money.

A basic way of discovering a country's products is to turn to its free tourist literature, where articles and ads typically boast of specialties. More directly, a traveler who is new to any place and ignorant of its native craft can visit its shopping centers and markets for an on-the-spot education. Whether shoppers or not, travelers on guided tours may be insistently steered to stores that may have an understanding with the guide (it is one way of making a selection).

If single chapters on shopping in country guidebooks aren't enough, there are books just on shopping. Though short on lodging and food descriptions, these tourist guides concentrate on kinds of purchases—such as groceries or clothes—and give advice on what and where to buy, and they may discuss shopping history, bargains, shipping items home, and legal pitfalls; and hopefully they have maps showing shop locations. Of the variety of shopping guides, one type concentrates on places that are known to offer bargains, such as flea markets and outlets; and another provides a directory format.

Whatever is bought abroad must pass through U.S. Customs. Its publications alert citizens to products that may be legal abroad but are illegal in the United States, and instances when duties are exacted.

Subject Heading: Shopping—[Country Name or State Name]—Guidebooks

Titles

Antiques Hunter's Guide to Europe / Judith Miller (Marshall Publishing, 2001).

Color photos and illustrations of scenes and objects stud the pages of this attractive book. There is a healthy collection of places to shop for antiques in each locale—occasionally discussed separately—and asides about shops, markets, and auction houses. However the title is a bit inaccurate, since the greater theme is that of the past. Short sections about each European city or part of a city normally provide historical highlights, recommendations where to eat and stay, places to visit, shopping comments, and a view of an interesting spot that requires travel time to it. Don't expect to read much about any one thing, since a few words often suffice for descriptions, but the likelihood of finding the stores in other travel guides appears slight. Small, color maps of each city have a hand-drawn quality, and it is questionable if they are to scale. 288 p.

GSP and the Traveler: Bringing in Articles from Developing Countries (U.S. Customs and Border Protection, 2005).

For a description of this title, see Customs and Border Protection, U.S. Department of Homeland Security, under "Organizations," the **Law** section.

*Impact Guides (*series) (Impact Publications).

A country cum shopping guide, the *Bermuda* volume takes up over two-thirds of its space with remarks about travel, the country, attractions, restaurants, and hotels. The shopping section offers advice about smart shopping and where to buy, and there are subject-divided groups of merchandise under what to take home and the best quality shops, which come with name, address, hours open, telephone number, electronic contact, and a compact description. A few black-and-white maps show some shop locations, while small photographs feature select products. Books in this series begin with the title *The Treasures and Pleasures* and all appear to be authored by Ron and Caryl Krannich. Examined: *The Treasures and Pleasures of Bermuda: Best of the Best in Travel and Shopping* (2006; 206 p.)

Know Before You Go: U.S. Customs and Border Protection Regulations for U.S. Residents (U.S. Customs and Border Protection, 2005).

For a description of this title, see Customs and Border Protection, U.S. Department of Homeland Security, under "Organizations," the **Law** section.

Official Directory to U.S. Flea Markets / edited by Kitty Werner. 8th ed. (House of Collectibles, 2002).

State-by-state listing follows a format of bolded headings for featured markets. The date heading commonly has a Saturday and Sunday, followed by times of opening and closing, and whether there is an admission rate for entry and parking. Location is a matter of address and sometimes driving directions. The description is the largest part of an entry, contributing the year that the market opened, its number of dealers and their trade, and the various amenities, which are enhanced by relevant icons in the margin. The final headings concern dealer rates and contact information, which includes e-mail and URL. At the end of a state's section is a group of flea markets that have not been personally contacted and that are identified simply by name, address, and telephone number. This attractive book delivers on its subject and has wide, eye-friendly pages. 455 p.

Outletbound: Guide to the Nation's Best Outlets. 13th ed. (Outlet Marketing Group, 2003). www.outletbound.com

Most of this flat, wide paperback is a directory that has a number before each featured entry, which is in regimented format. Arrangement is by U.S. region, state, and city or town. There is usually the number of minutes or miles an outlet center is from a city, often unneeded comments about the outlet, simple directions, hours when open, telephone number, address (sometimes omitted), and a list of store names, which is the longest section. Also given are the names of on-site food services and dining establishments, lodging, and local attractions. A few entries are provided for Canada. Large colored state maps key the locations, and a manufacturer index identifies an entry by its number. No information is available about individual shops. Outlet Bound's online database is searchable by state, store, brand, or category. 128 p.

Suzy Gershman's Born to Shop Italy: The Ultimate Guide for Travelers Who Love to Shop / Suzy Gershman. 12th ed. (Wiley Publishing, 2008).

This is an example from a group of titles previously listed as belonging to the *Born to Shop* series, which look at shopping from the perspective of a variety of countries and cities. *Italy* begins with a chapter on the best when it comes to buying, and later there are observations on such matters as outlet malls. The majority of the volume is arranged by major city or by area. While there is travel advice—places to stay and eat—the subject of shopping naturally is the star. There is information about what specialties to purchase, shopping hours, shopping neighborhoods, and an A to Z of things to buy and types of shops. Although discovering bargains is an important tenet here, some of the shopping is for luxury items, so the book should not be taken for a budget guide. The compact, oblong size allows it to be slipped into a purse or a deep pocket. The author has been responsible for numerous books on this subject, and with her personal and at times humorous style she is happy to explain her likes and dislikes. 343 p.

Businesses

Unclaimed Baggage Center). www.unclaimedbaggage.com
    This is a store in Scottsboro, Alabama, that is the final destination of unclaimed airline luggage, whose contents are put on sale to the public. Examined website: 2008

SPECIAL INTERESTS AND HOBBIES

General guidebooks are likely to either overlook special interests or skimp on them. Specialty guides have come to the rescue. They are eclectic, and have degrees of specialization. So the country series *Blue Guide* (W.W. Norton) and *Michelin Green Guides* (below) explore many things associated with culture, while other guides may narrow their focus to art or history. Some guides take the format of directories, describing sites via address and locality.

Even with the presence of the internet, finding if a specialty travel guide exists can be tricky. As stated under **Recreation, Sports, and Ranch Vacations**, in a brick and mortar bookstore a guide may be in the travel section or with one's subject interest. Subject searches in a library's catalog—that hopefully will be online—can begin with the term describing the traveler's interest. Then consider narrowing the focus to such a Library of Congress subdivision term as "guidebooks" or "description and travel." The subdivision in a record may not immediately follow the subject as, for example, "Herb gardens – United States – Guidebooks," where "United States" interposes itself; and depending on whether the search has been by subject or keyword, the results may vary.

Fortunately, a work need not be a travel guide in order to give background information, which can supplement a true guide's prosaic contents. A hunt for specific information can be the stuff of research, with a consultation of Amazon.com, *Books in Print*, bibliographies, or librarians as a mere beginning. If the subject is obscure enough, the traveler may have to rely on his or her ingenuity for customizing a personal guide from general information sources. The knitting hobbyist may discover factories, shops, and museums involved with cloth, and the bird-watcher lists the world's important nature preserves.

Among titles *Directories in Print* periodically compile subject directories, whose record of addresses can be adapted to fit travel information requirements. And *Specialty Travel Index* (below) is a convenient and inevitable choice, made imperfect only by its necessarily limited number of specialties.

The following subject grouped reviews represent a sample of what is available, with most U.S. centered.

Titles (by Subject)

Arts

Intertwined with a country's culture, the arts are major tourist draws.

Famous architectural monuments (the Eifel Tower) and works of art may symbolize a country, while other arts that contribute to specific cultures include music, movies, and the written word. Guides have supported travelers' interests in these areas.

Architectural Guides for Travellers (series) (Penguin Books).

The order is alphabetical by name, and several pages of text are devoted as much to the history of a building as to its architectural features and how they have been altered through the ages. All the buildings have photographs, plus sometimes a close-up of a detail, and infrequently a map or illustration. There is none of the typical travel information, such as how to get to a place, address, telephone number, or near attractions. A simple map marks each location, and a single page contains a glossary of terms. Examined: *Chateaux of the Loire* / Marcus Binney (1993; 150 p.)

Atlas of European Architecture / Brian Sachar (Van Nostrand Reinhold, 1984).

The two columns per page in this narrow, tall book are filled with plenty of entries, which are limited to name, date of construction, location keyed to city and country map outlines, perhaps a brief descriptive note, and a few other tidbits along with the occasional small photograph. Towns and cities are arranged under country. This comes closer to a locator or directory rather than a guide. 369 p.

Da Capo Jazz and Blues Lover's Guide to the U.S.: With More Than 900 Hot Clubs, Cool Joints, Landmarks, and Legends, from Boogie-Woogie to Bop and Beyond / Christiane Bird. 3rd ed. (Da Capo Press, 2001).

Aimed at those with a love for this type of music, the book has a regional arrangement of cities whose introductions to their musical heritage is followed by such subdivisions as sources for finding what is playing where, locations associated with jazz and blues, detailed looks at individual clubs and other venues, relevant radio stations, and record stores. Throughout are personal choice lists of bests in customized categories. 486 p.

Great American Places (series) (Preservation Press).

Put out by the National Trust for Historic Preservation, the series gives the architecture and history of such structures as movie theaters, bridges, and lighthouses, providing information about them that nowhere else could be found so readily. A photograph commonly accompanies several sentences about each featured site. Arrangement is by region, then state, and the execution is accomplished and professional. Examined: *Great American Movie Theaters* (1987; 272 p.)

Hollywood, The Movie Lover's Guide: The Ultimate Insider Tour of Movie L.A. / Richard Alleman (Broadway Books, 2005).

The public and private sites featured have appeared in movies or have been associated with a celebrity or with show business. After the name and street address for the property comes the heart of the work, text that may be made up of history, anecdotes, or gossip. Learn details about the varying fortunes of a place or those celebrities who made it notable. The arrangement is by areas that are part of greater Los Angeles, and the single finding aid is the simple street maps marked with numbers representing the locations discussed in the text. The general index only has those place and street names, stars, and movie and television show titles that are prominently part of the entry. A companion volume deals with New York. 495 p.

*Michelin Green Guides (series) (Michelin).

This is a major series of cultural guidebooks to countries, regions, and cities chiefly of Europe (the United States is next in receiving the most attention). Sights are ranked on a one to three star basis along with explanatory text. Instantly distinguishable by its green covers, height, and narrowness, a book of the series would fit only in a very deep pocket. Besides offering suggestions for driving and walking tours, it has especially clear maps, plus illustrations. A front section has chapters on aspects of its subject's history and culture, plus glossaries. The series title varies. (Similar in emphasis, the **Blue Guide* series is more cerebral and detailed.) Examined: *Sicily* (2003; 399 p.)

The National Trust Handbook for Members and Visitors. Annual (National Trust).

Arranged by region, descriptions on the two-column pages are of historic properties and wilderness areas owned by Britain's National Trust. Color photos enliven the text throughout, while seven road maps clearly mark the locations of the attractions. Though website addresses are lacking, a lot is crammed into an entry, with name, address, map location reference, an overview paragraph, telephone numbers, a chart of times when open, prices, and one set of symbols for property features and another for facilities. (America's own organization, the National Trust for Historic Preservation, has produced *Travel Guide* [2006] and has cooperated in the publication of books chronicling the architecture and history of various communities [see this section for *Great American Places*]). Examined: 2004; 400 p.

Pop Culture Landmarks: A Traveler's Guide/ George Cantor (Visible Ink, 1995).

The majority of the attractions are from the twentieth century and they cover a host of subjects, from famous people such as Joe Louis and Rod Serling to food (Popcorn Museum), monuments (Vietnam Veterans Memorial), shops (Nike Town), and automobiles (Corvette plant tour). As these examples show, both the traditional and odd are included. Considering the vagueness of what is pop culture, the entries are selective rather than exhaustive, but for those that are here, several paragraphs of thoughtful history are supplied. A concluding section has the address and, sometimes, locating advice, hours, admission, and telephone number. Maps outlining the states are marked with the positions of the landmarks. A newer title in the same vein is *James Dean Died Here: The Locations of America's Pop Culture Landmarks* (by Chris Epting; Santa Monica Press, 2003) and its sequels. 401 p.

Cemeteries

Availing themselves of the opportunity to discover the last resting places of the noted dead, some travelers use graveyard guides. Each cemetery may come in for a description.

American Military Cemeteries: A Comprehensive Illustrated Guide to the Hallowed Grounds of the United States, Including Cemeteries Overseas / Dean W. Holt (McFarland, 1992).

An invaluable and detailed resource about military cemeteries and the soldiers interred there, it is only secondarily a guide for visitors. Location information is thin. There is only name and address, and no driving instructions. Entries are arranged by cemetery name, though there is a geographical cross-reference in the back. Some of the sites have maps with sections drawn in, but they do not mark out the monuments and graves noted in the text. Following a history and description of each national cemetery are the locations of graves of individual Medal of Honor winners and their citations. 512 p.

Dead Ends: An Irreverent Field Guide to the Graves of the Famous / David Cross and Robert Bent (Plume, 1991).

Entries are alphabetical by name of the celebrity, followed by birth and death dates, then icons representing the occupation in which fame or notoriety was achieved. There's a brief biography followed by a note on where the body was buried or cremated, with the name of the cemetery, its town or city, and state or country. But there is neither street address nor directions about how to get to the cemetery and where in it the deceased is found, nor if cemetery maps are available, as they sometimes are. While personalities from the entire world are included, the United States is by far the leader, with California the most mentioned state. The majority of deaths are in the twentieth century, and some animals are here, such as Morris the Cat. Names are displayed geographically in the back by state, then by country. 304 p.

Resting Places: The Burial Sites of over 10,000 Famous Persons / Scott Wilson. 2nd ed. (McFarland & Company, 2007).

This very interesting multi-volume reference was not made with travelers in mind. The two-column pages have alphabetically ordered last names, accompanied by identifying numbers. A capsule comment about the deceased sometimes adds the cause of death or details of the funeral, and usually there is either the place of burial, which may have the lot or section number of the cemetery, or where the ashes were scattered. An index in the back by town—but inconveniently not by country or state—gives the number that is referenced to the person. Would-be visitors must flip between the index and the text in order to see who is where. There are neither directions nor maps to the sites, most of which are in the United States. 2 vol. (916 p.)

History

It is difficult to travel without recognizing the overwhelming impact of history. If the sights don't remind you, the guidebooks will. Those that write about history may do it through an associative subject—museums, for example—or more directly, like the items below, where the American bias is less a matter of premeditated selection than it represents what is published. One series omitted is *Traveller's History* (Interlink Books), which are general histories with brief gazetteers, so the title word "Traveller's" could be minimized.

Directory of Historical Organizations in the United States and Canada / American Association for State and Local History. Biennial (AltaMira Press).

The size of a city telephone directory, with three columns per page, it has an arrangement by state and province, then town and city. Museums are here, as are addresses for state parks, living history groups, historic building associations, and genealogical societies. A large index in back is by "themes of interpretation," beginning with "African American" and ending with "Women's Studies," and in-between having such areas as "Decorative Arts," "Lighthouses," and "Sports"; since the entry itself may omit allusion to the subjects, the index is indispensable for getting full value from the reference. The history-oriented traveler will use this resource for planning ahead and will find the most useful parts of an entry are those that supply contact information (including telephone number, e-mail, and the website), purpose of the organization, a compact rundown of what is in its collection, hours of availability, and admission price. Note that coverage is limited to *state* and *local* historical organizations, so there are purposeful omissions. Examined: 15th ed. (2002; 1358 p.)

Discovering Historic America (E. P. Dutton, 1982-1983).

Each volume encompasses a collection of states, which are divided into their own regions (reflected in a black-and-white map for the state), the regions into towns or vicinities; and under them are separate descriptions of museums, churches, residences, historic districts, parks, etc. Opening times, costs, and telephone numbers are given, as appropriate, but it would have helped to have had them bolded or made to stand out. There are symbols for sites of family or military interests. A state also has a separate list describing in a few lines the historic accommodations that are available. The book's eight-inch height means that the two columns per page make for both small print and photographs, which are frequent. Still, this is a good collection of places for the history-minded. Examined: *Discovering Historic America: Mid-Atlantic States* (1983; 336 p.)

National Landmarks, America's Treasures: The National Park Foundation's Complete Guide to National Historic Landmarks / S. Allen Chambers, Jr. (John Wiley and Sons, 2000).

Along with a paragraph on background, the two-columned pages of this substantial and attractive book give the name, street address, and town or city of properties that are outside of the National Parks system, yet are considered candidates. There are many different ones, including historic districts; public buildings and public spaces; places associated with notable personalities; forts; ships; archaeological remains; significant architectural constructions; business enterprises; and battlefields. Arrangement is by state, then rather inconveniently by county. Three pages recognize jurisdictions outside of the U.S. The many photos and the scattering of blueprints are in black-and-white. 548 p.

The Smithsonian Guides to Historic America (series). Revised ed. (Stewart, Tabori & Chang, 1998).

Combining some travel guide aspects with plenty of commentary about the past, each of the twelve volumes covers a part of the continental

United States. There are noteworthy color photos of scenery, architecture, paintings, and things of historic significance, plus maps. Details of sites include addresses, hours of operation, and whether there is a fee. In the encompassing narrative, sites of interest are brought out by bolding. Examined: *The Plains States* (1998; 461 p.)

Industry

Factory visits can be educational and enjoyable, and the individual may even come away with free samples. Mention of such a site may easily escape a general guidebook.

Company Museums, Industry Museums, and Industrial Tours: A Guidebook of Sites in the United States That Are Open to the Public / Doug Gelbert (McFarland, 1994).

After name, address, and telephone number, an insert provides the hours, admission costs, length of tour, driving directions, and a list of nearby industrial sites of interest. Several paragraphs provide background and tour details. 314 p.

Inside America: The Great American Industrial Tour Guide / Jack & Eunice Berger (Heritage Publishing, 1997).

Spiral-bound, this is arranged by state, then by town, with each entry having the same format. The business name is followed by one or two parenthesized words denoting what line it represents, and then comes address and telephone number, across from which is the SIC code (for the type of industry), and the name of the contact person. A second section offers a few sentences about the tour and has driving directions, and a third has spaces for hours and days open, while a yes or no choice exists for "advance notice," "fee," and "HP access" (although not defined the initials refer to people with disabilities). There's a general subject index and one for SIC code numbers and the type of business. The contact name may very well be out of date, and there is less information provided about a tour then some of the other titles, but it may cover a portion that they don't. 352 p.

Watch It Made in the U.S.A.: A Visitor's Guide to the Best Factory Tours and Company Museums / Karen Axelrod & Bruce Brumberg. 4th ed. (Avalon Travel, 2006).

A two-column page is allotted to each entry, starting with a company's (or museum's) name, address, telephone number, and website. About half of the text provides background along with a description of the manufactory process or business operation. The remainder has bolded headings for cost; freebies; videos or DVDs shown; reservations needed;

days and hours open; length of tour; minimum age; presence of disabled access; group requirements; special information; gift shop; directions; and nearby attractions. The arrangement is by region, then state, while in back one index is for company and a second groups together types of products. Photos are in color for a collection of over twenty "featured tours," but only a few black-and-whites show up in the remainder of this polished and attractive work. Despite the driving directions to each locale, the volume is unlikely to fit in the glove compartment of a car. 421 p.

Nature

The natural world is a big draw for travelers who may seek something different from city attractions or are just interested in nature.

Dinosaur Safari Guide: Tracking North America's Prehistoric Past: Complete Descriptions and Directions for over 170 Dinosaur (and Other Prehistoric Creature) Sites, Museums, Fossil Exhibits, Tracksites, and Parks in the United States and Canada / Vincenzo Costa (Voyageur Press, 1994).

The 1990s saw a flurry of dinosaur guides. With typical location and entrance information this one frequently pairs a road map to each entry, where succinct sections include an introduction and a listing of the articulated skeletons and exhibit features. 259 p.

Exploring Rural Series (series) (Passport Books).

Each guidebook tackles a single European country, avoiding really big cities and presenting descriptive itineraries by region. Illustrations are in black-and-white, as are the maps which supplement the driving directions. Even though the coverage of so many towns and villages makes for a sense of hurry, there is still time for many value judgments ("scenic," "unspoilt," etc.). Examined: *Exploring Rural Germany* (1990; 164 p.)

National Geographic Guide to America's Public Gardens: 300 of the Best Gardens to Visit in the U.S. and Canada / Mary Zuazua Jenkins (National Geographic Society, 1998).

Vivid and frequent color photographs highlight the text which offers one or more paragraphs about the establishment and present holdings of gardens by state or province, though the Canadian section is short. Practical facts appear at the end of each entry, with name, address, telephone number, hours open, number of total acres, and the names of any special collections. A baker's dozen of colored letters determine if pets are allowed, if a greenhouse or conservatory is present, if fees are charged, etc. 384 p.

Roadside Geology (series) (Mountain Press).

Covering U.S. states and regions (Montana, Yellowstone country), the series follows where highways, roads, and road cuts go through the state, and any interested layman will learn about the formation of the landscape and about mines, quarries, and other historic features involving geology. Fossils, caves, and glaciers all receive attention. There are many photographs of scenery, and surface and cross-section maps of geology are shaded in red and black with clear labels. Highway signs at the top of pages help orient the reader, while a glossary for the geologic terms used is in back. Examined: *Roadside Geology of Indiana* (1999; 315 p.)

The Whale Watcher's Guide: Whale-Watching Trips in North America / Patricia Corrigan. Updated ed. (NorthWord Press, 1999).

A cleanly-designed directory of tours offered in the United States, Canada, and Mexico has for each listing sections giving the operator's address, species of whales that could be seen, season of operation, size of boat, duration of trips, costs, port of departure, and availability of a naturalist. Icons identify which excursions have food, beverages, binoculars, etc. There's also some discussion about whales themselves. 303 p.

Off the Beaten Path

Although some guides include overlooked or alternative attractions among the more kosher, there are those that take pride in exclusively trumpeting the unusual or obscure.

Europe off the Wall: A Guide to Unusual Sights / Anneli S. Rufus and Kristan Lawson (John Wiley & Sons, 1988).

This country-by-country collection of anatomy museums, eccentric architecture, atypical churches, and unique festivals also has more serious or educational themes, such as a museum dedicated to emigration and another that displays musical instruments. Able to fit in a glove compartment or some three-quarters down into a standard hip-pocket, the oblong book provides name, address, opening hours, and sometimes fee information, followed by around two or three sentences describing some curiosity that otherwise might not be discovered by a tourist. The style is familiar and here and there jokey, as might be expected. Except for what was then known as Yugoslavia, all the places are western European. Outlines of countries mark where key cities and towns are. The authors have done other books on this topic. 314 p.

Going off the Beaten Path: An Untraditional Travel Guide to the U.S. / Mary Dymond Davis (The Noble Press, 1991).

This environment-oriented guide is also designed to appeal to the socially committed and those interested in an alternative lifestyle. Places to investigate are buildings that conserve resources, energy sites (solar, wind, etc.), cooperatives, intentional communities, wilderness areas, vegetarian restaurants, and the like. Since this bills itself as a travel guide, it would have made more sense to have arranged the numerous chapters geographically rather than by broad parts (e.g., "hiking trails" is one of several chapters under "outdoor recreation"), although in back there is a state geographic index that is subdivided by city or by region within the state. Name and, when appropriate, the address and telephone number are followed by a description that is anywhere from a paragraph to beyond a page. 466 p.

Haunted Places: The National Directory: Ghostly Abodes, Sacred Sites, UFO Landings, and Other Supernatural Locations / Dennis William Hauck. 2nd updated and revised ed. (Penguin Books, 2002).

Ghosts are the most populous stars in this large, two-column listing by U.S. state, then town or city. The name of the mysterious scene is followed by an account of supernatural or odd incidents that took place there. For both public place and private residence, location or address is given. Besides human specters, there are stories about poltergeists, unearthly sounds, ghostly appearances of ships, lights, and similar objects, plus other unexplained phenomena or sacred traditions from the long past to the late twentieth century. 486 p.

The Palace under the Alps: And over 200 Other Unusual, Unspoiled, and Infrequently Visited Spots in 16 European Countries / William Bryson (Congdon & Weed, 1985).

Arranged by country, the spots have headings that are either their names or are designed to catch the eye: "World's Most Challenging Maze," "The Garden of Monsters," "Golfing at Midnight," etc. A description with history of the intriguing attraction may run to about a page, and a brief ending section called "details" explains where it is, how to get there, and its opening hours. With its hardcover *Palace* is less portable than *Europe off the Wall* (above), and it has fewer entries, though more about each of them; also it has a shaded map of each country marked with the locations featured in the text. As with similar books in this section it ignores conventional sights, so it could serve either alone or as a good supplement to a mainstream guide for a traveler who is after something less familiar but equally worthwhile. Bryson has written a number of popular travel books. 256 p.

People

Of guides that target population groups in the United States, the most numerous—for Jewish and African American—have been noted under the sections of **Religion** and **Travelers**, but there are also others, as this sample shows.

Hippocrene U.S.A. Guide to Historic Hispanic America / Oscar and Joy Jones (Hippocrene Books, 1993).

Close to one-half of the work narrates several events chiefly concerned with the Spanish exploration by Coronado and others of territory that was to become American states. The remainder devotes chapters to the Mexican-American border, California, Arizona, New Mexico, Texas, and a few more states. Although museums, parks, and even restaurants are here, featured sites are more likely to be missions and Indian reservations, whose Spanish link is frequently ambiguous. Many entries are rather short, and they vary in what they describe. A few simple maps show locations within a state. All in all, this is an unfocused and unsatisfactory work that avoids going into depth about its subject. 168 p.

Indian America: A Traveler's Companion / Eagle Walking Turtle. 3rd ed. (John Muir, 1993).

The listing of name, address, telephone and fax numbers are for tribal offices, reservations, museums, and important sites, which are arranged first under regions, then selected states of the contiguous United States. Within a state the order is inefficiently arranged alphabetically by name rather than geographically, which makes planning a trip to an area more difficult. Details of the entries vary, but sections may designate relative location, public ceremony or powwow dates, art forms and crafts, and miscellaneous visitor information. Also, history and other features about a tribe appear in due course. Supplementary chapters list Alaska bands and offer a lengthy calendar of Native American events. A later edition is available. 460 p.

*Specialty Travel Index: The Directory to Special Interest Travel. Biannual (Alpine Hansen Ltd.). specialtytravel.com

This basic print resource for types of travelers as well as for special interest tours is arranged alphabetically by tour operator, whose offerings and destinations are briefly presented. The contents are also referenced through topical and destination indexes, so someone may use either of these approaches. The website is searchable in these three areas, and it has feature stories. Examined website: 2007

STUDY AND TRAVEL

Learning is a natural consequence of travel, which educates us through new experiences. When foreign history, culture, customs, and society are constantly confronted, lifelong conventions are challenged. For example, in some countries haggling is expected between buyers and sellers, and the efficient use of time varies according to a people.

Some pursue travel as an intentional learning experience, doing it for fun or for academic credit. If they are independent they may arm themselves with a *Blue Guide* or *Michelin Green Guide* (see **Special Interests and Hobbies**) and visit every museum, literary landmark, and art gallery they can manage. Alternatively they can join that type of tour whose avowed purpose is to teach. These educational or study tours combine learning with travel's adventurous expectancy.

Educational tours visit the canonical spots of historic associations, with experts in history, literature, art or other academic areas serving as guides and lecturers. Readings may be suggested, and discussions may be held after each day's touring and talks. Sometimes college credit is provided for participants, who can range from students to adult learners. Age may be a determining factor for an entry in some programs, such as Elderhostel (below), which is for learners in their fifties and older. Among sponsors of educational tours are academic institutions, museums, and student-oriented organizations.

Touring is by water as well as by land. Especially in the Mediterranean educational touring by ship is popular. The most ambitious learning cruise is probably done by the Semester at Sea program (see under **Ships, Boats, Ferries, etc.**), which blends together classroom and touring activities on a vessel sailing around the world.

Educational tours are comparable to school field trips. As for study abroad programs, they are typically classroom-based, though field trips may be occasionally incorporated. Moreover, for a learner abroad the world is the classroom, where he or she is exposed to daily interaction with the host country's people, customs, activities, etc. An obvious instance is the student of a foreign language who is in a country where the language is spoken.

Students who attend a college or school in another country may find courses and homework not unlike that in the United States. Some courses can highlight cultural and other aspects of the country in which they are taught; for example, the study of Shakespeare in England adds a local meaningfulness that cannot be manufactured in other countries.

There are numerous works that give information on study abroad. One of the giants in the field is the Institute of International Education. It is responsible for several key publications, including *IIEpassport, Short-Term Study Abroad* and *IIEPassport, Academic Year Abroad*, catalogs of course offerings (below).

Students who go abroad may do so through an exchange. The exchange programs of schools and colleges ease and encourage the transfer.

Different from tours and study abroad programs are experiential educational opportunities provided by volunteer organizations. The non-profit Earthwatch, for example, allows amateurs to assist professional scientists in their researches (see the subsection **Volunteer Work** under **Work** for a review of this and other organizations).

Several titles encompass both study abroad and work abroad, partly because work in another country can be very educational.

See also **Work**.

Subject Heading: Foreign study—Directories

Titles

Advisory List of International Educational Travel and Exchange Programs. Annual (Council on Standards for International Educational Travel). www.csiet.org

For those that meet its standards, the Council reports on travel and exchange organizations designed for U.S. high school students going abroad and students from abroad coming to the U.S. The online version has name, address, contact information, and listing status. Examined website: 2007

Alternative Travel Directory: The Complete Guide to Traveling, Studying & Living Overseas / editor Clayton A. Hubbs. 7th ed. (Transitions Abroad Publishing, 2002).

A good starting place to search for information, it contains a broad range similar to the periodical *Transitions Abroad*. Of the three areas mentioned in the title, only one chapter deals with living abroad, but others highlight certain aspects of independent travel and study abroad (e.g., the older traveler, best programs and resources for language schools), and are composed of resources, chiefly lists of publications, organizations, and programs, all of which come with short descriptions. The two-column per page directory has interspersed throughout short articles on special aspects of a topic. For those interested in specific countries, many of the subjects are subdivided geographically. 260 p.

Elderhosteling, USA!: An Elderhostel How-to Guide / Larry Dada (Eldertime Publishing, 1994).

For those in their fifties and over, Elderhostel offers many study programs, which the book has characterized as typical and typical non-typical (intensive, short week, etc.), and describes in detail. *Elderhosteling, USA!* tells what the organization is and does and what the experience is like and how to get the most out of it. Anecdotes and quotes from participants enliven the text. There are looks at those who participate and the expectations about fellow students, accommodations, and the kinds of food; and why certain choices should be avoided, as when a smoker is alerted that a program is non-smoking. Since singles make up the largest group, they are separately treated. In a way the book is a commercial for this organization, but it does form an introduction for the non-initiated who may be interested in participating. 154 p.

The Europa World of Learning. Annual (Routledge, Taylor & Francis Group).

Like UNESCO's *Study Abroad* (below), this major multivolume reference resource found in libraries encompasses the world. Arranged by country, it can be used to locate basic facts about various educational bodies, universities, libraries, museums, art galleries, learned societies, and research institutes. In addition to physical and electronic addresses (and depending on the category), the entry may contain names of disciplines, collections, people and their positions, etc. At a pinch, consult this formidable directory to discover a country's academic attractions. Examined: 58th ed. (2007; 2914 p.)

Fodor's Great American Learning Vacations. 2nd ed. (Fodor's Travel Publications, 1997).

Although separate authors are responsible for each of the nineteen subject chapters, the same pattern is repeated throughout. An overview precedes a list of frequently asked questions that are designed to help the interested learner choose the right mind or body activity, from archaeological digs to holistic centers and writers' workshops. Favorite examples (of cooking programs, crafts, specialty tours, music camps, etc.) are arranged by state under regions of the nation and described in as much as a column's length on the two-column pages. Inclusion implies worthiness, so judgments are usually upbeat. The accompanying prices are out-of-date. At the end is a brief roundup of organizations, periodicals, and books, after which are pointers to related chapters. Bolding and typography break up the text and enable the reader to find new sections quickly. 323 p.

Guide to ACA-Accredited Camps. Annual (American Camping Association [now, American Camp Association]). www.acacamps.org

Arranged by state, capsule entries on the three-column pages begin with name of the camp and date of its establishment, its address, telephone number, and name of the director, along with several possible icons (representing "day camp," "financial aid available," etc.). There are bolded labels for a brief overview; a list of activities; the length of the sessions (as in number of weeks or which months); the number of campers that can be accommodated; the age range of the clientele; a range of fees; contact information (by mail, telephone, and online); and the operator of the camp. Most of the camps are for children and teens, with the second largest category that for special populations, such as those with disabilities. Indexes sort the camps by subject areas. An ACA imprimatur should give confidence about an entry's reliability. The contents of this title appear to have migrated to online only. Examined: 2002; 362 p.

*IIEPassport, Academic Year Abroad: The Most Complete Guide to Planning Academic Year Abroad. Annual (Institute of International Education and Educational Directories Unlimited, Inc.). www.iiepass port.org

The size of a city telephone directory, with three columns per page, it has programs arranged within geographical regions by the countries and cities in which they are taught. This companion to *IIEPassport Short-Term Study Abroad* (below) comes with the same format and arrangement for entries throughout the world, and most of the same index groups. Especially for college undergraduates this is the place to start a search about where to study abroad. Its major competition is *Peterson's Study Abroad.* Examined: 34th ed. (2005; 746 p.)

*IIEpassport, Short-Term Study Abroad: The Most Complete Guide to Summer and Short-Term Study Abroad. Annual (IIEPassport Study Abroad Print Directories).

The large directory is first arranged worldwide, then by parts of the world, down to the level of town or city in a country. Entries are compact, with the sponsor and program's name, then bolded headings before site of study; dates; subjects taught; eligibility requirements; credit given; language of program instruction and if the format is by lecture or otherwise; costs; kind of housing; deadline for registering; other information; and who to contact. Indexes are by sponsoring institution (weighed toward U.S. colleges and universities); consortia; field of study; options for the non upper-level undergraduates or for those wanting alternative learning opportunities, such as internships; cost range; and duration. Divisions of this last are by season—summer having the largest share—and are further subdivided beginning with "under 2 weeks," and continuing through two-week intervals up to "more than 16 weeks" and "multiple program lengths"; while a final time division covers the entire year. Examined: 54th ed. (2004; 589 p.)

International Exchange Locator: A Resource Directory for Educational and Cultural Exchange (Alliance for International Educational and Cultural Exchange, 2005).

This serial publication identifies private and public exchange programs originating in the United States. The largest section is an alphabetical list of exchange organizations, one to each large page, with location information, a description of it and its activities, its publications, names of individual programs, and more. Smaller sections provide location and description for organizations with an interest in exchanges, for international organizations, for federal government exchanges, and for pertinent congressional committees. The list for foreign affairs agencies chiefly has physical and electronic addresses, contact names, and telephone numbers. Among several end tables are collections of organizations as related to academic level (such as undergraduate students), exchange categories (arts/cultural, homestays, senior citizens, etc.), and geographic focus by region. 371 p.

The ISS Directory of International Schools. Annual (International Schools Services). www.iss.edu

Listed by country, this is a major place to find a roundup of particulars about K-12 American or international schools, with one or two pages devoted to each. The first of five sections for an entry has contact information, and is followed by a second for staff, with positions and names of some, plus how many and what nationalities. In the space devoted to general information there are numerous snippets, from the range of grade levels and the enrollment numbers to the amount of tuition and other fees. The educational program section identifies the type of curriculum, average class size, language of instruction, staff specialist positions, special and extracurricular programs, sports, etc. A concluding part about the campus tells if it is either suburban or urban and describes it by its size in hectares, its number and type of facilities, and its number of instructional computers and the volumes in the library. For each country there's a sketchy map and a few facts. Examined: 2002; 804 p.

The 100 Best Vacations to Enrich Your Life / Pam Grout (National Geographic, 2007).

The best are presented in categorical orders labeled "arts & crafts getaways," "volunteer vacations," "brain retreats," and "wellness escapes." In descriptive paragraphs covering two or three pages, the choices make for a stimulating read. Many are hardly commonplace activities, since they include learning to sculpt, taking care of the homeless, training to be an astronaut, and discovering how to surf. For every entry there is a separate section that may contain an interesting bit of related history, mention of other opportunities, or added sidelights, and completing it all is name, address, telephone number, and URL. The type appears blue on a creamy background. 288 p.

Peterson's Short-Term Study Abroad. Annual (Peterson's).

With coverage of the summer, spring break, and the winter interim, this takes up the slack where its companion publication *Peterson's Study Abroad* leaves off. Its competitors are the two Institute of International Education directories, *IIEPassport, Short-Term Study Abroad* and *IIE-Passport, Academic Year Abroad* (both above), and the two pairs closely resemble one another in range and layout. Except for the country-to-country programs chapter, directory arrangement is alphabetical by country, and then by city. Entries consist of the name of the sponsoring university or organization and its program followed by the identity of the host and a number of bolded headings preceding academic focus, program information, session dates, eligibility requirements, living arrangements, costs, and where to find more information. Indexes in back are by field of study, program sponsors, and host institutions. Examined: 2007; 524 p.

Smart Vacations: The Traveler's Guide to Learning Adventures Abroad / edited by Priscilla Tovey (St. Martin's, 1993).

Vacations that stimulate the mind may appeal to people with special interests as well as those hunting for something different or those who simply enjoy learning. The first section is about how to choose and join a learning trip, and it mixes observations on this type of learning with the basics of travel. This is familiar advice; for example, that reading about a destination enhances experience. However, most of the book is a directory. First come categories of programs by subject (arts, voluntary service, etc.), by group (for educators, etc.), and by continent and region. The entry format has name, address, and telephone and fax number preceding information sections about the host organization, its programs, eligibility for joining, locale, when the programs operate and how long they run, type of accommodations, costs, and age of the participants. The absence of e-mail and web addresses can be explained by the date of publication.

Behind this venture is the Council on International Educational Exchange (www.ciee.org), which offers study abroad programs. 318 p.

Study Abroad. Biannual (UNESCO).

In English, French, and Spanish, this imposing collection by country of post-secondary educational institutions has university courses that may be of interest to international students. The more complete entries start with a block for name, address, telephone number, fax, URL, and e-mail. They proceed to a summary of offerings, with subheadings for fields of study; degrees; eligibility requirements; duration of studies; fees; kinds of financial assistance; language of instruction; application deadlines; and scholarships. Though not comprehensive, the strength of the UNESCO work nonetheless is in its scope rather than the amount provided on each school. Where else would someone conveniently find the price for a year's study in Uzbekistan? Examined: 2005; 688 p.

Study Abroad Survival Guide, 2006 / Dina Taylor West (Magic Valley Publishers, 2005).

Written by a college student, this is addressed solely and directly to an audience of college students, who (the book appears to assume) are thoroughly unfamiliar with the concept of traveling abroad. With every other line a blank, the brief work is written in repetitively short sentences that contain bite-sized chunks of simple information. Reporting is of the fundamentals, from preparing for a trip to the return home and a new perspective on life. In-between the student learns about what to take, keeping safe and healthy, travel etiquette, culture shock, and popular living arrangements abroad. There is little about studying in another country. 116 p.

Summer Opportunities for Kids & Teenagers. Annual (Thomson Peterson's).

This major reference work has a great many summer programs, which are arranged by state for the United States, followed by a second section arranged by country. Travel programs are classed separately. Directory entries show program name and sponsor, general information, program focus, arts and sports offered, types of trips, application deadline, jobs available, etc. On the wide two-column pages selected programs receive in-depth (two page) descriptions. For convenience, features of each entry are put in a table at the front. Among seven indexes one has an alphabetical arrangement by program name and another has primary activities, which are placed under two hundred headings (e.g., community service, homestays). Later editions have been titled *Summer Programs for Kids & Teenagers*. Examined: 23rd ed. (2005; 987 p.)

*Transitions Abroad. Bimonthly (Transitions Abroad). www.transitions abroad.com
Each issue provides facts, articles, first-person accounts, and ads that reflect study, travel, work, or living abroad. Listing helpful titles, organizations, and websites, this important magazine is written especially with students in mind. The website has reprints of articles selected from past and current issues. Examined website: 2008; and back issues

Travel and Learn: 1001 Vacations around the World / Evelyn Kaye. 4th ed. (Blue Penguin Publications, 2001).
For those seeking educational travel choices, the work opens with a short introductory section that suggests a range of interests (outdoor adventures, crafts, and a handful of others) along with organizations that offer programs related to them. Save for a few concluding pages of resources, the rest of the book is an alphabetical list of eighty-some organizations, and not 1001. For each a block of contact information precedes several paragraphs of description on what it offers, followed by a short collection of the things included and a breakdown of costs based on various conditions. While there are no subject categories with an entry, the earlier section or the index can be used to locate any. The selection has an arbitrary feel. 236 p.

Your Gap Year: Everything You Need to Know to Make Your Year out the Adventure of a Lifetime / Susan Griffith (Crimson Publishing, 2008).
In Britain, a "gap year" traditionally means time taken off after graduating school and before entering a university. What to do with this time? Work, volunteer, travel. Principally intended for a school graduate from Britain, the book has an introduction that offers reasons for students to take a year off before entering college and suggests how they can prepare. In a second part are short profiles of destinations throughout the world, and in a third bolded headings and their text compose a detailed directory of specialist gap year programs that are further grouped according to their status as expeditions, work, volunteering, paid seasonal jobs, au pairing, or courses; opportunities for North Americans also receive treatment. Some of the same groupings are later treated in the last part that is arranged geographically. One of several titles about gap years, it is worth consulting for those who wish to hear a British point of view and see British directory choices. 460 p.

Organizations

Council on International Education Exchange. www.ciee.org
Through its programs this large organization gives opportunities for students as well as educators to go abroad. Examined website: 2008

*Elderhostel. www.elderhostel.org
Elderhostel is the major purveyor of travel learning programs for older adults. The offerings in its paper catalog of programs are also available online. Examined website and catalogs: 2008

International Student Travel Confederation. www.istc.org
According to its website, the purpose of this confederation of not-for-profit associations is to make travel affordable to students. It accomplishes this through its many student travel companies. Among ISTC's offerings are the International Student Identity Card, the International Youth Travel Card (for those under 26), and the International Teacher Identity Card, all of which are good for certain travel discounts. Work exchanges are also available. Examined website: 2008

TELEPHONING

Even with the existence of the internet and smartphones capable of downloading programs useful to travelers, the familiar telephone directory is a central information source. In the print or online yellow pages conveniently find telephone numbers and addresses for a tremendous variety of travel subjects, whether accommodations and passport photo services or museums and amusement parks. For a physical collection of telephone directories from other cities or countries a library is the best bet.

There are toll-free directories which contain numbers for airlines, hotels, and car rentals among their subjects. General titles focused on the United States include the semiannual *National Tollfree Directory* (STR Business Media) and the annual *Toll-Free Phone Book USA: A Directory of Toll-Free Telephone Numbers for Businesses and Organizations Nationwide* (Omnigraphics).

Some information is telephone-specific, such as tourist attractions that may have recorded messages about events of interest to visitors. To answer questions from the public by telephone the United States government has toll-free lines, including one to Overseas Citizens Services (see contact information under the Bureau of Consular Affairs at travel.state.gov/law/info/info_615.html).

To call long distance in the states or overseas read instructions in a telephone directory or dial directory assistance. A listing of country and city codes needed to dial overseas appears in telephone directories and can be found in some general reference works, as *The New York Public Library Desk Reference* (Hyperion, 2002). International calling plans and direct services that allow the caller cheaper rates are among the offerings available from various long-distance carriers.

Should there be a need to speak on the telephone to someone who does not know English, businesses exist to solve this issue. Locate them through an online search with words such as "telephone" and "interpreters," or in the yellow pages check the heading "Translators & Interpreters."

Subject Headings: Toll-free telephone calls; United States— Commerce—Telephone directories—Yellow pages; Business enterprises —United States—Telephone directories—Yellow pages.

Books

The Toll-Free Traveler: The Complete (800) and (888) Directory for Pleasure and Business Travel in the U.S. and Canada / compiled by Don

W. Martin & Betty Woo Martin (Pine Cone Press, 1997).

Content that is designed to either point elsewhere or be an end in itself is together here. The U.S. centered directory has several categories of transportation types as well as general subject groups, among which are adventure travel, lodgings, and state and foreign tourism offices. There is variation in the amount of information in the categories. Airline names are followed by toll-free numbers and, infrequently, the names of their locations, while "water travel" has the cruise line, its toll-free number, and a sentence describing it and where it goes. The concluding chapters with tips about traveling and touring are intelligent and perceptive, but they compose only around thirty smallish pages. The oblong-sized work has a random feel about its inclusiveness and its completeness, so its usefulness is questionable. 162 p.

Traveler's Hotline Directory / Dorothy DuBois (Visions Resources Publishing, 1991).

This telephone book has lots of 800 numbers, some of which are called by the author "hotlines." Filling up many pages are long, simple columns of the numbers accompanied by the name of the organization or business and its state. However, the format varies, with some places presented in paragraphs of names, addresses, and numbers that may have a brief description. The chapters are by subject, which in turn is subcategorized. So, "preplanning" has hotlines for credit cards, passport and visa services, travel insurance, and others. A gamut of typical travel aspects is here, with the biggest chapters providing numbers and addresses for accommodations and for travel agencies. The shift from lists to directory paragraphs makes for some difficulty in usage, while the fullness of entries is never certain; plus, there are omissions (e.g., country code dialing omits Sweden). 284 p.

Traveler's Yellow Pages / Seth Godin, editor (Houghton, Mifflin, 1996).

From "airline paging numbers" to "weather" there are dozens of categories that take up an average of five yellow-colored pages for fifty U.S. cities. The categories favor business travelers, but there are some (e.g., "chiropractors") that could be of use to any weary vacationer. An entry consists of the name of the business, without an address, and its local (or sometimes 800) telephone number. Some names are followed by a digit which corresponds to the same marked on a crude highway map that precedes each city section. An oblong volume that is compact enough to fit in a pocket book or sports coat pocket, its design allows it to be consulted on the road or as necessity requires. 274 p.

TICKETS

One travel pleasure is attending cultural and entertainment events. Tickets may be bought from Ticketmaster and other ticket agencies which may be found on the internet or are listed under "Tickets" in the yellow pages. They are also sold at ticket box offices, hotels, and some department stores.

Cities with active theater programs—New York and London are two major ones—may have discount ticket booths, whose locations can readily be discovered online and in guides.

The organization responsible for an event may be a source for tickets or will refer the buyer to one that is. A print alternative to looking up organization addresses online is to check the *Encyclopedia of Associations*, while for a roundup of events seek publications that are or contain calendars (see **Calendar Information**).

TIME

Travel is time-driven. Travelers who enter unknowingly into new time zones may miss appointments or find businesses are closed, while those who make telephone calls abroad to home should take into account time differences to avoid interrupting someone's sleep.

To figure any time in the world, do a search for "time zones" online; or locate the twenty-four divisions on either globes or the chart of time zones found in selective atlases and travel guides. For greater detail *International Time Tables* has time in tabular form arranged by country.

Subject Heading: Time measurements—Tables

Titles

The International Atlas: World Longitudes & Latitudes, Time Changes and Time Zones / compiled and programmed by Thomas G. Shanks. Revised 3rd ed. (ACS Publications, 1991).

Consultations here are not for the faint-hearted, perhaps in part because the rather crowded small print was designed for those with an interest in astrology. At the beginning of each country heading—except for the United States, which is in a separate volume—one or more timetables gives, under past and future years, hours of deviation from Greenwich time. For more detail, a table of towns and cities in three columns per page are listed by longitude and latitude, and this is accompanied by the difference of time, to the second, from Greenwich. Most people will not want this level of focus. Newer editions have since been published. 426 p.

International Time Tables / Gary L. Fitzpatrick (Scarecrow, 1990).

The arrangement is alphabetical by place, which can be as obscure as Diego Garcia Island. After the entry's name is the number of time zones within its borders, whether the time remains the same for the entire year or there is an equivalent for daylight savings time, and how many hours different is its time zone from Greenwich Mean Time aka UTC. The small tables are four rows down and twenty-four columns across, which represents the hours of the day, beginning on a Sunday and whatever the local time would be at 12:01 UTC. The twenty-four hours are given both in terms of military time and the a.m. and p.m. equivalent (e.g., 20:01 equals 8:01 p.m.). When a country or possession has daylight savings time, a similar table appears. Days and months are given when the time change begins and ends. A color fold-out map has on one side standard time zones of the world and on the other those of the (former) USSR. For its specialty this wide volume is very interesting and useful. 106 p.

Standard Time Zones of the World (Central Intelligence Agency, 2004?). https://www.cia.gov/library/publications/the-world-factbook/reference_ maps/time_zones.html

This color map comes with grids marking longitude and latitude as well as twenty-four-hour time zones. Unless it is magnified, the online version is harder to read than the paper. Examined website: 2009

TOURS

Following a planned itinerary, prepaid multi-day package trips may encompass lodgings, transportation, a leader, entrance fees, and meals. The leader can double as a guide, providing commentary at intervals as well as arranging rest stops, smoothing the way to the nightly ritual of checking into a hotel, and handling the many sundry problems that consistently arise.

There are numerous specialty tours. Some focus on one type of interest, as wineries or art museums. Others sell themselves according to their means of locomotion, as with bicycle and walking tours. Two of the largest groups are adventure and study tours. Another variation, the fly/drive package, dispenses with guide, bus, and fellow tourists and instead has a rental car, a suggested itinerary, and vouchers for meals and rooms. Besides commercial companies, some non-profit organizations offer tours.

Many day tours—city sightseeing or an excursion—can be conveniently booked through a guest's hotel or a tourist office. The tours typically provide transportation and a guide.

Tours and tour operators may be discovered online and through their brochures at travel agencies. Brochures promote a trip, and advice on critically reading them is supplied by the United States Tour Operators Association (www.ustoa.com) under the link "Shopping Tips." It and other trade organizations may have additional useful information.

Tours are also advertised, as well as discussed, in travel magazines and newspaper travel sections. Other places for locating operators are through a country's tourist office and the yellow pages. Lists of tour operators or tours are available to travel agents from professional publications and may be in country guidebooks and some books mentioned within *Travel Resources*.

Treatment of the rewards and limitations of group touring is more likely to be dealt with in books of travel advice and in articles, but it may pop up as an aside in a variety of titles.

Complaints against a tour company should first be taken to the company. If the response is unsatisfactory, write the United States Tour Operators Association or the consumer affairs division of the state or federal government.

Subject Heading: Package tours

TRAVEL ADVICE

The word "travel" is a derivative of the word "travail," which suggests how demanding the experience can be. Some country guidebooks offer no advice about how to travel, while others bring it in. Then there are books whose sole concern is travel advice. The books are about the craft of traveling, and they describe what to expect and the means to cope with it as well as getting the most from a trip. Such works are particularly valuable for the novice traveler.

They give answers to the usual questions: What should I pack for my trip, and how should I pack it? How do I keep my money secure? What is the best way to remain comfortable while flying? How do I keep healthy? What and how . . . ?

A few works are tied to Europe or other regions, but their advice can be generalized to any travel situation. Others are concerned with a single aspect of traveling, such as the Manston book on protecting one's home.

Subject Headings: Travel; Travel—Handbooks, manuals, etc.

Titles

Adventure Travel in the Third World: Everything You Need to Know to Survive in Remote and Hostile Destinations / Jeff Randall and Mike Perrin (Paladin Press, 2003).

This is not a guide for the conventional traveler, but for those who are willing and perhaps eager to encounter marginal situations in order to visit the most out-of-the-way locations. The book provides unvarnished and perhaps uncomfortable advice based in part on the firsthand experiences of the authors. It is built on the problems and certainly the dangers to be faced and ways to minimize them both in the city and the bush. Part of the contents is a wilderness survival guide, especially for tropical environments, plus the ways to handle various medical problems and emergencies. 261 p.

The Creative Traveler: A Guidebook for All Places and All Seasons / Gini Graham Scott (Tudor Publishers, 1989).

In a unique and fascinating approach, this work looks closely at common travel experiences and brings out both their obvious and not so obvious values, asking the reader to think about them in various lights. Discover what dress says about how people live and what they hold important. Improve contemplation of a painting by projecting inside of it and making observations with all of the senses. Several chapters consider the means of making better mental use of time spent riding in a car or airplane, or just waiting, and others are about meeting people. Put to work the imagination, the senses, and the surroundings to enhance travel enjoyment, part of which is training the mind how to relax. 140 p.

Don't Let the World Pass You by!: 52 Reasons to Have a Passport / Sara Benson, coordinating author (Lonely Planet Publications, 2005).

Each reason to travel makes for a compact chapter in this compact book. The focus is away from the practical and on the reflective—such as, the passport as a memory record of journeys, travel as a means of testing the truth of personal preconceptions about other cultures, and the various motives that might induce people to get away. The type varies in size, color, and bolding, and there are numerous insets that introduce miscellaneous lists or facts or anecdotes. Consistently encouraging, and inciting the reader ("you") to see the world, the text nonetheless often employs a flippant tone. 184 p.

Fodor's How to Pack. 2nd ed. (Fodor's Travel Publications, 2003).

What some guides limit to several paragraphs this builds into a short book. The subject begins with the different choices in luggage (pullmans, duffels, etc.) and consideration of their durability and usefulness. Clothing and other things to take along are suggested according to destination or the activity. The largest amount of space is allotted to reasons for types of toiletries, clothes, and more (e.g., travel aids) to take and several ways to arrange them and make them fit in the luggage. There are useful illustrations, of greatest service when they demonstrate the different types of "how to's" for folding clothes in order to pack them. Additional matters are the items the passenger can carry on a flight, packing for a return trip, and dealing with delayed or lost baggage. Full of checklists, this is knowledgeable, easy-to-read, and well laid-out. 184 p.

Great Traveling After 55: A Step-by-Step Travel Guide for Inexperienced as Well as Veteran Travelers with Specific Suggestions for Those over 55 / Ruth J. Colvin (Nivloc Press, 1989).

Omitting chapters on what to see and do in specific countries, this book is one of pure and basic advice reflected through personal travel experiences and written in a casual style from an enthusiastic traveler. Though there is the familiar guidance on what to plan for and bring, the negotiating of airports, and travel in foreign countries and the United States, the author's various stories bring helpful insight to her proactive approaches. Despite the title, the traveler over 55 is seldom the subject. 162 p.

Manston's Before You Leave on Your Vacation: How to Protect Your Home, Valuables, Pets, and Plants from Theft and Neglect / Robert C. Bynum and Paula R. Mazuski (Travel Keys, 1988).

Like the titles on packing, *Manston's* makes a book out of an aspect of travel that at most would get a chapter in the works of general travel advice. Travelers who are uneasy about being away because of what might happen to their home should feel more prepared after absorbing these discussions. There is a rundown about property owned and how to protect it from criminals through electronic security systems, strengthening ways of entrance, and projecting the impression that someone is at home. Or a house sitter may be the thing needed. Unforeseen problems can be planned for, while vehicles that sit idle and lawns that grow have means of being maintained. Augmenting the subjects discussed, separate forms in back (that make up one-quarter of the contents) have blank spaces to be filled in about the people left in charge, the utilities, telephones, appliances, plants, pets, valuables, etc. 126 p.

The New York Times Practical Traveler Handbook: An A-Z Guide to Getting There and Back / Betsy Wade (Times Books, 1994).

Since the subjects are arranged in strictly alphabetical order, the selection of the headword is pivotal to findability, and unfortunately there are instances where the entry may be a "stuck at the airport," with no cross-reference from "airport." Since this is aggravated by a lack of any table of contents or index, there is no way of being sure what is included nor how it is described; so those interested in the topic of exchanging money will look for "exchanging" or "money" without success. Despite the dictionary arrangement, this catchall of suggestions by a *New York Times* travel columnist would be better read in normal beginning-to-end order, or perhaps chosen according to the entry. If there had been more thought about these pitfalls, the essays on specific aspects of travel would have been of greater value. 286 p.

1,001 Smart Travel Tips. 2nd ed. (Fodor's Travel Publications, 2008).

There are probably more than 1,001 tips, and a separate paragraph is dedicated to each one. They are placed under fourteen chapters, from planning and packing to forms of transportation, hotel stays, and individual destinations throughout the world. Within the chapters are subgroups providing focus; for example, a car travel chapter has parts on what to carry in the vehicle, renting one, fueling up, etc. The tips are practical, readable, to the point, and may provide something a traveler had not considered. A collection of addresses and a few checklists close the volume, which is about the size of a thick paperback. 320 p.

Pack It Up: Traveling Smart & Safe in Today's World / Anne McAlpin. Revised 3rd ed. (Flying Cloud Publishing, 2004).

Partly a collection of what to take on a trip and how to take it, the format is made up of a few checklists and numerous bulleted paragraphs, which allow for easy reading and locating, abetted by illustrations for packing clothes and for tying several forms of scarves. Gifts to take and packing toiletries receive separate considerations. Despite the announced scope of the title, space is also devoted to general travel concerns, as with the chapters on security, money, and plane trips. One of the longest chapters is about cruising, where in addition to luggage and wardrobe tips there is advice about general matters, selecting a cabin, dining, and the like. A later edition comes with a DVD. 150 p.

The Packing Book: Secrets of the Carry-on Traveler / Judith Gilford. 4th ed. (Ten Speed Press, 2006).

Physically larger and over eighty pages longer than *Fodor's How to Pack*, the Gilford work covers about the same territory, but expands the details. For example, several paragraphs about children in *Fodor's* evolves here into two individual chapters, one for children and one for teens, with subheadings. However, there is less accent on a posh wardrobe and making room for the purchase of goods. As with the other work, it is supposed that travel will be by air, so *The Packing Book* devotes a chapter to what should be worn and carried aboard the plane. Illustrations show types of luggage and ways to pack a suitcase or garment bag, while graphic tables include a "luggage buyer's checklist" and an "itinerary wardrobe planner." Checklists and bulleted lists are common, and among them are those for non-clothes travel gear, though advice on the method of packing these is omitted. The work is for those who want a lot of information about this important aspect of travel. 269 p.

Planning Your Gap Year: Hundreds of Opportunities for Employment, Study, Volunteer Work and Independent Travel / Nick Vandome. 6th ed. (How To Books, 2003).

Previously titled *Spending a Year Abroad*, its most likely audience is the teenage school graduate or young traveler who is willing to live on a spartan budget and if need be earn money at teaching, manual labor, and other types of jobs. To get an idea of the standard of living envisioned, the chapter entitled "selecting equipment" has as the first few headings "camping," "backpacks," and "sleeping bag." There is general advice on such matters as buying tickets, staying healthy, the pitfalls of travel, and returning home. Since this is a British perspective, addresses given are in

Britain. A newer edition is available. (For more about the "gap year" see *Your Gap Year* under **Study and Travel**.) 187 p.

The Practical Nomad: How to Travel around the World / Edward Hasbrouck. 4th ed. (Avalon Travel Publishing, 2007).

Particularly suitable for the independent backpacker and the adventurous on a budget, the thick, text-heavy book goes into nitty-gritty depth about the practice of travel to places both touristed and not. As a travel agent, the author borrows from his experience to give some behind the scenes advice. He devotes almost one-quarter of the book to the subject of air transportation, which pays attention to finding cheap tickets, choosing a travel agent, timing when to buy a ticket, getting a price estimate, and so on (there's also a table that evaluates types of fares and tickets). All the other usual aspects of travel are treated in detail, from determining where to go and the types of transportation (rail, bicycles, walking, ships, etc.) to visas, border formalities, packing, and budgeting. Along with some candid opinions there are also touches of political commentary, and reflections on American and other cultures. A substantial resource section arranged by broad topics has annotations for books, businesses, organizations, and websites. 601 p.

The Savvy Adventure Traveler: What to Know Before You Go / Ellen Dudley (McGraw-Hill, 1999).

While adventure can mean whitewater rafting and other daredevil activities, here it is journeys into the back paths of exotic locations. This specialized work on travel has facts and viewpoints not replicated by other titles in this section, as in its explanation of how an adventure company labels trips by difficulty. Interspersed in the text are separate boxes that contain tips about what to do or what to look out for, true horror stories about an adventure that went catastrophically wrong, and something "for women only." A consistency of warnings about extreme instances or the possibility of such an occurrence evokes an air of sensationalism, which may discourage beginners from trying this kind of trip. The many bulleted lists throughout enhance readability and compact the facts. 166 p.

Smart Packing for Today's Traveler / Susan Foster. 3rd ed. (Smart Travel Press, 2008).

The reader who likes to visualize what to take will be well-served. There are numerous illustrations, of which a few are luggage or gadgets, but most are clothes, with examples of styles for various occasions, whether for transit between points or appearing at a business conference. Suggestions are given about dressing for the climate and the individual culture. Fabric types are also discussed, and packing for airport security. In addition the author examines kinds of luggage, the ways to pack items, and what to pack based on the situation—a cruise, adventure travel, children who are brought along, etc. While this thorough and informed treatment is chiefly concerned with packing and its associations, the book's later part enlarges to offer some useful, general tips about travel. Bolded subheadings throughout distinguish the content and make it more locatable. 246 p.

The Smart Traveler's Passport: 399 Tips from Seasoned Travelers / Erik Torkells and the readers of *Budget Travel Magazine* (Quirk Books, 2007).

The small, thick book averages per page two short tips, each followed by its contributor's name and place of residence. While this means there is a variety of advice, some of it seems more anecdotal or curious than particularly useful; though an individual searching for ideas might find this an interesting read. The tips are arranged into nine categories, from developing an itinerary to keeping in touch and making friends. 224 p.

Tips for the Savvy Traveler / Deborah Burns (Storey Communications, 1997).

A format that is a combination of short paragraphs with bolded beginnings, checklists, and several boxes expedites absorption of information into digestible amounts. The range of subjects is conventional, with chapters on what to know before a trip; traveling by plane or ship; finding accommodations and food; shopping; photography; safety; and types of travelers, as in those traveling with children. One of the less familiar discussions is ways of making the most of a visit to another country by participating in the culture. Beyond the multitude of commonsense ideas are some imaginative enough to be new even to experienced travelers, who are not the target audience. 244 p.

*The Travel Detective: How to Get the Best Service and the Best Deals from Airlines, Hotels, Cruise Ships, and Car Rental Agencies / Peter Greenberg. Revised and updated (Villard, 2005).

With a skeptical and investigative mind aimed at the travel industry, this travel journalist conveys his noteworthy facts and advice in a comfortable and sometimes humorous style that includes a number of anecdotes featuring both his unfortunate experiences and those of others. The first three-quarters of the volume are dedicated to air travel, wherein passengers are acquainted with security issues plus their rights and options when it comes to budget and convenience. The lowdown on the airline as a business shows an enviable expertise. Some solutions or remedies appear geared to very specific situations or are overly concerned with saving time or money, while others may be the sort that are of interest to many people, such as maximizing frequent flyer opportunities. Several travel matters are likewise put under the microscope. The author shows himself an aggressive battler for the consumer, who may become pessimistic, since the book suggests consistently negative scenarios, though ways are offered to alleviate them. Greenberg has also written the more comprehensive as well as thicker and newer *The Complete Travel Detective Bible* (Rodale, 2007). 467 p.

Travel Tips International: A Guide for the Practical Traveler / Deborah J. Hill (Renaissance Publications, 1990).

Exceptionally detailed coverage is subsectioned by chapter and part number (e.g., 1.1, 1.2, etc.), which mark headings and introductory matter in the twenty-four chapters. Both the numbering and bullets for tips enable quick scanning, as do the gray boxes. Similarly displayed throughout are references to relevant book titles and organization addresses. The range is wide enough to touch on some unusual topics, such as the problems of being out beyond a country's curfew. Social customs receive their due: "In many parts of the world, *lunch*, rather than dinner, is the biggest meal of the day" (p. 107). Among the appendixes is a directory of foreign embassies and consulates in the United States and a list for international direct dial telephone numbers. A slightly newer edition is available. 290 p.

**The Traveler's Handbook* / editors Jonathan Lorie and Amy Sohanpaul. 9th ed. (Globe Pequot Press, 2006).

With a British viewpoint, it dedicates 40 percent of its contents to countries, whose two-page-apiece profiles consist of minimum facts about when to go; transportation; red tape; degree of safety; etiquette; voltage; food and drink; tourist highlights; country websites; English-language newspapers; and so forth. The remainder of the work is chiefly made up of individually authored articles, each of a few pages, which explore an encyclopedic array of specialties. For example, under the grouping of kinds of travelers separate attentions are paid to the first-timer, the extreme sports traveler, the cyclist, the polar traveler, and many others. There are also collections of articles under such headings as "culture shock," "healthy travel," "safe travel," "what to take," and "working abroad." Lists of organizations, businesses, websites, and book and magazine titles appear in the appropriate sections. For those who are seriously interested about finding the maximum range of information about traveling, this is the best resource, which is bulky but of almost digest-size. Its generic name fits. 960 p.

Traveler's Tool Kit: How to Travel Absolutely Anywhere / Robert Powell Sangster. 3rd ed. (Menasha Ridge Press, 2000).

Here are in-depth details for the person seeking to maximize his or her knowledge about travel, including subjects that are slighted or omitted from other advice books. Some examples: in a discussion of how and where to make hotel reservations there is one list of sensible reasons why to make them, and another equally sensible why not to make them; there is a countdown of how and when to prepare for a trip; and there is a review of what the black market is and why it exists. Besides giving useful addresses and numbers, this author and committed world traveler offers, in a casual style, personal anecdotes that may inform or entertain and perhaps cause the reader to think about the subject. There is shrewd advice about handling various people to people interactions—which occurs frequently in traveling—and about one's own outlook and behavior. While a beginner could profit from this work, the underlying concept is that of traveling independently or confidently anywhere in the world. 516 p.

Businesses

American Society of Travel Agents. www.travelsense.org/consumer/index.cfm
See **Complaints** for a description.

WEXAS. www.wexas.com
Membership in this British-centered travel club includes the general purpose quarterly magazine, *Traveller*. Examined website: 2008

TRAVEL AIDS

Money belts, wall-plug adapters, immersion heaters, portable alarm clocks, electronic translators, foreign exchange converters, and waist packs are items that have been made for the traveler. Others may be adapted from camping equipment. Some aids are familiar items that appeal to travelers because they are designed to be portable or have been miniaturized. More recently, the appearance of many new electronic devices has opened up a variety of opportunities.

Aside from online stores and travel book or specialty shops, major outlets for travel aids are outdoor and department stores. Moreover, such student-oriented groups as Harvard Student Agencies and American Youth Hostels sell equipment as part of their services.

Use the yellow pages or internet directories to locate any type of store. Through promotion literature and other publications, manufacturers may provide information about their brand as well as give valuable advice about the type of product. For example, a manufacturer of plug adapters might put out voltage and adapter requirements for various countries.

Titles

Electric Current Abroad (International Trade Administration, U.S. Department of Commerce, 1998). www.ita.doc.gov/media/publications/pdf/current2002final.pdf

Written for U.S. manufacturers, exporters, and travelers, the booklet has illustrations of plugs and their receptacles in commercial use keyed to a table of plug types by country. A second, more detailed table of countries—some of which are broken down into cities—provides technical figures on electric current characteristics, with one column answering if electric outages or interruptions are rare. 30 p.

Thomas Register. Annual (Thomas Publishing Company). www.thomas net.com

This brawny multi-volume library standard is arranged by product, under which is the companies that manufacture it. This work is useful for verifying the existence of a product or locating its producer, which in turn may lead toward where it can be purchased. After 2006 the publisher states the print will give way to the electronic version. The title is also known as *The Thomas Register of American Manufacturers*. Examined: 2006

"World Electric Guide." kropla.com/electric.htm

This site's links include those to a table that describes electrical systems world-wide, illustrations of electric plugs, general advice, and a list of sources for telephone and electrical travel accessories. Examined website: 2008

TRAVEL WRITING

Combine the twin aspirations of traveling with writing, and get paid for it. Since travelers enjoy relating their experiences, travel writing sounds like a perfect way to earn money.

For beginners what to write about, how to sell, and where to sell are vocational survival questions. The books below offer answers. (Going by this section, it would seem that most titles about travel writing start with the letter "t" or "w.")

Also of assistance are general guides on writing and selling articles.

Subject Heading: Travel writing—Vocational guidance

Titles

How to Make a Living as a Travel Writer / Susan Farewell (Marlowe & Co., 1997).

This book shows that travel writing concerns both the business of writing and an interest in traveling, and advice meted out deals with one or a combination of these. The business part looks at the game from start to finish—preparation, selling, making the right connections, knowing how to self-promote, and record-keeping. This material can also be picked up from general books on writing. The subject of travel has strategies about wangling a free trip and brief treatment on writing or editing a guidebook. A number of travel articles are used as examples of destination categories in terms of being single, multiple, or paired with a theme. 205 p.

The Travel Writer's Guide: Earn Three Times Your Travel Costs by Becoming a Published Travel Writer! / Gordon Burgett. Revised 3rd ed. (Communication Unlimited, 2002).

Offering methods along with advice and facts, the work begins with a discussion of getting results as a professional and concludes with a list of 365 questions as the take-off point for writing travel articles. In-between are sound observations from Burgett, a working travel writer, who shares such ideas as reckoning a budget of expenses for a trip against the estimated earnings from the planned-for sale of articles to magazines and newspapers; and making an itinerary for each day of a trip. Among the chapters is one that concerns techniques for getting organized before a trip, while another tackles taxes and looks for the best way to save on expenses. Unlike the two books titled *Travel Writing* (below) there are no examples of travel articles to speak of, but this one does have practical details not found in them. 264 p.

The Travel Writer's Handbook: How to Write—and Sell—Your Own Travel Experiences / Louise Purwin Zobel and Jacqueline Harmon Butler. 6th ed. (Surrey Books, 2007).

There are many details and a big range of marketing angles, as in the longest chapter called "Twelve Sure-Fire Patterns for Travel Articles." Other chapters dissect the ways of interviewing, offer techniques for employing photographs, and discuss doing research, which involves taking advantage of a library or online resources, with the authors also dropping in the titles of books and periodicals that can be of help. Since writing is looked upon as a business, there is commentary about selling a story, writing a query, and taking advantage of freebies and tax deductions. Throughout substantial groups of paragraphs separated by bolded subheadings make *The Travel Writer's Handbook* seem to have a greater expanse of words than any other entry in this section. For its practicality and instructiveness it is another good work to consult. 290 p.

Travel Writing / Cynthia Dial (Teach Yourself Books, 2001).

Among the chapters are those devoted to preparing for a trip that will be written about, marketing to newspapers or to magazines, putting together an article and selling it, authoring a book, making a place for photography in submissions, and keeping records. There is also advice on what to put in a piece and how to prepare a query letter. Contributing to scanability, chapters are frequently broken into sections with bolded headings (e.g., "Put on your travel agent hat"), and the familiar style has an abundance of short, clear sentences. Samples from other travel writers are featured in boxes. Both this and the O'Neil title (below) are very useful. A newer edition is available. 184 p.

Travel Writing / Don George with Charlotte Hindle (Lonely Planet Publications, 2005).

Distinctive features of this solid work include around forty pages devoted to examples of good travel writing and the over two dozen interviews with travel editors and travel writers of articles and books; typical questions deal with how they started their careers, what tips they would give to beginners, and what are the characteristics of good and bad travel writing. Under the chapter about getting published, newspapers and magazines are analyzed from the differing prospects of the United States and the United Kingdom, plus there is consideration of the book market (with the demands of guidebooks getting a separate chapter), the internet, and other opportunities. Also receiving their due is what it takes to be a travel writer, advice about writing, and tools (e.g., journal, camera). Find publisher addresses, writer-related websites, and similar matter in an appendix that has been divided into the U.S., U.K., and Australia. 272 p.

Travel Writing: See the World, Sell the Story / L. Peat O'Neil. 2nd ed. (Writer's Digest Books, 2006).

When walking in a city intentionally become lost in order to write from a new angle. This is one of many interesting pieces of advice from the author, a travel newspaper journalist and editor, whose accounts of her experiences back up her useful ideas. She explains the importance of keeping a travel journal and demonstrates how her jottings were re-written into a salable article, giving a before and after. Topics broad and narrow are explored, as traveling incognito, paying attention to prose style and other fine points of composition, checking facts, using photographs, handling rejection of an article, and working as a professional. Throughout are graphic boxes that offer exercises for the would-be travel writer. The strong emphasis on travel *writing* comes with a presentation of knowledge that is both accomplished and perceptive. 310 p.

Writer's Market. Annual (Writer's Digest Books).

Besides its several thousand listings of publishers, magazines, and other markets, the bible for writers has information on submission, royalties and payments, types of material and subjects wanted, editorial response time, etc. The areas of consumer magazines and trade journals each have a heading for travel, as does a book publishers' subject index in the back. Examined: 2007; 1170 p.

Writing about Travel / Morag Campbell. 2nd ed. (A&C Black, 1995).

The very British perspective means that a word like "nappies" will be used instead of "diapers" and the magazines and other publications mentioned in the text are almost always from Britain. This probably is also reflected in an attitude that renders its subject more theoretically than many American approaches, so readers expecting lists of plain, concise steps or numerous examples may be disappointed. Yet that this title offers another country's point of view on travel writing can be a refreshing contrast to the American books. Of somewhat abbreviated length, the treatment has omissions, though there are nuggets of interest to be found here. 107 p.

Writing about Travel: How to Research, Write and Sell Travel Guides and Articles / Brian & Eileen Anderson (How To Books, 1998).

Somewhat mechanical and meager in its coverage, it talks about what writers' tools to buy or use, the taking of pictures, how to research the market, finding a publisher, securing a contract, and other important points. To dramatize the experiences of new writers, hypothetical case studies with recurring characters are laid out at the end of each chapter. Like *How to Make a Living as a Travel Writer* (above), the focus detours at times into advice on writing *per se*, without the qualification of travel. Its British origin sometimes shows, and the book is comparable neither in breadth of details nor understanding with several of the titles surveyed here. 128 p.

TRAVELERS

Standard country travel guides are usually written for a make-believe, generic traveler. Sex, age, race, marital status and other conditions are immaterial to their outlook.

However, there are guides that recognize that the single person has needs different from the family; that gays and women have unique concerns; and that pets are travelers too. Typical advice is customized for these and other types of travelers. The works in turn may be combined with another travel topic, so the result can be as particularized as *The Discount Guide for Travelers over 55* (E.P. Dutton, 1988).

Information aimed at types of travelers may appear in general travel magazines and newspaper travel sections. Likewise, entire publications exist for these travelers. An organization that represents a type's interests may be able to answer its travel concerns, and if it cannot it should know an authority that can.

What follows are sources arranged by categories of travelers.

African American
The titles in this section concentrate on the interests of African Americans, though they will appeal to anyone interested in black culture, especially from an American perspective.
Subject Heading: African Americans—Travel

Titles

The African-American Travel Guide / Wayne C. Robinson (Hunter, 1998).
Each selected U.S. city and the area outside it—and two Canadian provinces—have their most thoroughly described entries under "Historic Sites & Landmarks" and "Museums/Exhibits." Besides the name, address and, as appropriate, telephone number and hours of operation, there is an explanation about a site's significance or a museum's holdings. Lesser amounts of annotations usually accompany the collections of shopping places (galleries, bookstores, fashion), restaurants, entertainment, and lodgings. There are also listings for travel agents, "heritage tours," media representing the interests of its audience, addresses of African American churches, and a calendar of events. City and province maps have numbered locations corresponding to a short list on them, but there is no link established with the formal entries. The handy layout makes scanning for a place easy. 308 p.

The African-American Travel Guide: To Hot, Exotic, and Fun-Filled Places / Jon Haggins (Amber Books, 2002).

The basics about preparing for a trip overseas comes with occasionally unconventional advice, such as flushing out one's system with a laxative before departure so as to reduce the chances of a conflict with foreign bacteria. The most frequently asked travel questions chapter contains both the general and the specific (e.g., "will I see animals in Africa?"). Two-thirds of the book deals with a selection of destinations that it is implied has an important connection with black history, but for those lands outside of Africa, this is not necessarily made plain. Some of the places are off the beaten tourist path—the Ivory Coast, Dakar, Senegal, Uruguay, etc.—while Egypt, the Virgin Islands, and Jamaica are among those that are more familiar. Much of the text is a first-person travelogue of what the author did and saw, and while there is a short hotel list in an appendix, those who expect something more substantial, as well as a rundown of country sights, should look elsewhere. 226 p.

Black Heritage Sites: An African American Odyssey and Finder's Guide / Nancy C. Curtis. (American Library Association, 1996).

The large geographically arranged volume has a historical introduction before each of the regions, whose states are subdivided by city and town. The pages allotted to states vary, with New York claiming thirty-five and Idaho squeaking through on two. Save for the major cities, most spots have a single entry, which may be a museum, library, house, monument, church, historic site, etc. The author can spend several paragraphs explaining the significance of her choice as it relates to black interests, and she ends it with a format of separate lines on date of founding, address, telephone number, visiting hours, fees, and sources for her information, which is often the results of a telephone conversation with someone responsible, perhaps supplemented by a book or article title. At intervals the double column pages display photographs of buildings as they now look. A two volume set that has maps is also available. 677 p.

Hippocrene U.S.A. Guide to Black America: A Directory of Historic and Cultural Sites Relating to Black America / Marcella Thum (Hippocrene Books, 1991).

Arranged by state, then by town or city, entries are for museums, cemeteries, churches, plantations, colleges, monuments, statues, forts, halls of fame, houses, and other associations with African Americans or Africa, though there is an inclusion of white American sites when the subject warrants it, as with abolition. Well-known and obscure facts are narrated within a historical framework, which forms the backbone of this work; a lot is to be learned here about the past, with the nineteenth century probably receiving the most attention. The directory portion is inadequate, since each item has a street address but no telephone number or zip code, and the sense of this being a "guide" would have been strengthened through route maps or driving instructions. However, hours of operation and admission costs are added to sites when appropriate. The book can be enjoyed for its discoveries of what is frequently not in history texts. 384 p.

Pathfinders Travel: The Travel Magazine for People of Color. Bimonthly (Pathfinders Inc.). www.pathfinderstravel.com
   The print magazine's features emphasize United States destinations, and there are vacation tips, plus more. Examined website: 2008

Age (Over 55) and Retirees
   A significant proportion of people who travel are older. Logical reasons for this are that at this time of life these travelers can afford it, have retired, regard it as a long-deferred treat, or are now free from family obligations. Therefore, this group is well-represented in published material. A subset of this area is the numerous titles that deal with retiring and the change in location that can accompany this. Also note that travel organizations for singles frequently have a high concentration in this age group. General interest magazines aimed at older people (e.g., *Modern Maturity* [American Association of Retired Persons]) may include articles on travel.
   See also **Relocating**.
   Subject Headings: Retirement, Places of; Aged—Travel

Titles

America's 100 Best Places to Retire / edited by Elizabeth Armstrong. 4th ed. (Vacation Publications, 2007).
   Information on an alphabetically arranged town or city typically takes up three, three-column pages in this large book. After a symbol next to towns representing "low-cost edens" or "undiscovered havens," an upbeat description of a location and its attractions incorporates positive observations on living there by current retirees. An associated boxed space profiles a community through numbers (population, amount of rain, etc.), various tax facts, housing and visitor accommodation costs, and summaries of religion, education, public transportation, and health. A good quarter of the places are in Florida. At the volume's front each entry is fit into one of ten lists whose categories range from best art towns to best four-season towns. 349 p.

The Mature Traveler's Book of Deals: The Very Best Discounts around the World for Travelers over 50 / Gene & Adele Malott. Revised ed. (GEM Publishing Group, 1998).

The first chapters have names and views about how to save on accommodations, airlines, and the other customary categories, plus skiing. Some of the advice applies to any adult traveler, regardless of age—becoming an air courier, for example. However, when it comes to some discounts many entries show that age limits may start at 50, 55, 62, etc. A chapter on singles offers ways of avoiding a singles supplement, and another has strategies for low and no cost traveling, though often the trade-off is the requirement to work at it, as in going for free on a tour provided one acts as the leader. Following this are final chapters arranged by countries, states (for the U.S.), and cities where a mélange of services, companies, hotels, and attractions each receives a line about its discounts, which are presented in either percentage or dollar amount; telephone numbers are the principal contact information. Though haphazard in design and selection of entries, contents of this small book are nonetheless relevant to its audience. 138 p.

Retirement Places Rated: What You Need to Know to Plan the Retirement You Deserve / David Savageau. 7th ed. (Wiley Publishing, 2007).

For 200 U.S. towns and smaller cities there are ranking and score numbers, and in the longest chapter—on climate—tables cover by month the highs, lows, humidity, wind, precipitation, and snow. Other chapters have rankings for the economy (including jobs and their impact); services, such as hospitals, physicians, libraries, and continuing education; ambience (good restaurants, culture, waterways, nationally protected lands, etc.); cost of living factors; housing; and personal safety (which contains scores for violent and property crime rates). Near the book's end, the scores of places are added together to give overall rankings. A summary of rankings appears in each chapter's introductory matter, where topics are also elaborated upon and an occasional box with extra information appears. This large volume, usually with two columns per page, is impressive in the amount and the clear detail of what it supplies. The author has also produced the similarly realized *Places Rated Almanac* (reviewed in **Relocating**) and *World Retirement Places Rated* (Places Rated, 2008). 302 p.

Travel and Older Adults / Allison St. Claire (ABC-CLIO, 1991).

The first third deals with travel basics along with those aspects that would be of interest to its audience, and the remainder is an annotated list of organizations, businesses, and reference resources which reflect subjects in the earlier part—though it would have been more useful if suitable discussions and lists had been paired. A chapter on planning considers traveling alone or with a group, choosing a travel agent, finding information, foreign travel, and other matters. And those that follow examine health and safety, the disabled, driving, ship cruising, and adventure and special interest trips. Throughout, a lot of territory is thoughtfully covered in print type one suspects is designed for older eyes, and there's a concern with areas a general travel advice book might overlook, such as that about RVs. 255 p.

Travel 50 & Beyond. Quarterly (Vacation Publications, Inc.).
    Articles are concerned with destinations, especially those in the United States. The idea that the magazine is for those fifty and over is not apparent. There are the expected color photographs, and ads abound. Examined: issue from 2006

*Travel Unlimited: Uncommon Adventures for the Mature Traveler / Alison Gardner (Avalon Travel Publishing, 2000).
    Vacations and tours are grouped under the subjects of nature, ship-based touring, education, culture, and volunteering. An entry has a name, address, telephone number, e-mail, and website followed by perhaps half-of-a-page review that appears to have been influenced by an advertising flyer. Then comes the entry's subheadings: "fellow travelers" supplies approximations in percentages of participants over fifty, ratio of men to women, and number of singles; "destinations" lists countries and areas involved; "comfort zone" concerns accommodations, food and, where warranted, activities; and "costs" discloses dollar amounts and what is included, or not, in the price. Other parts of the book observe selected countries, and various insets include "field reports" from travelers, plus informative asides. The index orders countries into types of tours and recreations. The author notes that the work is aimed at the fifty-and-over crowd, but adds that few entries are exclusive to it. Those looking for trip ideas should find this compilation of exceptional use. 566 p.

Unbelievably Good Deals and Great Adventures That You Absolutely Can't Get unless You're over 50 / Joan Rattner Heilman (McGraw-Hill, 2007).
    For people who have reached a certain age there are companies and countries that present bargains, and their names are collected in a directory that has gone through many editions. The over fifty can use the companies for discounts in accommodations, air, car rentals, various forms of public

transportation, and tours. Also one chapter explains country-by-country the savings exclusively available for the older person. Other subjects concern intergenerational trips and rundowns of programs that are for singles, learning, sports, or volunteering. Descriptions average multiple lines and are followed in part or in whole by address, telephone number, and URL. The type is large and in the category subsections the names of companies, programs, countries, and states are bolded. The writing is less exuberant than the title suggests. 297 p.

Where to Retire. Bimonthly (Vacation Publications).

Find departments and features with photos intent on promoting retirement places and dealing with activities for retirees, financial planning, lifestyle, semiretirement, etc. Advertisements follow the same concerns. Examined: issue from 2002

Where to Retire: America's Best and Most Affordable Places / John Howells. 6th ed. (Insiders' Guide, 2006).

The author provides introductions to twenty-seven states and selects towns and cities in them for treatment, going over in several expansive paragraphs subjects on the order of recreation, cultural attractions, shopping conveniences, ambiance and weather, affordability of living, scenery, number of population, or quality of life. Brief accompanying tables are of state tax profiles, temperatures and precipitation in the area, and cost of living expenses, which are divided into several categories. Chambers of commerce addresses, telephone numbers, and websites are also supplied throughout. As usual with these works, assessment of a place will be chiefly positive, if only because otherwise there would be no reason to feature it. 394 p.

The World's Top Retirement Havens: How to Relocate, Retire, and Increase Your Standard of Living / edited by Margaret J. Goldstein (John Muir Publications, 1999).

Nearly half of the fifteen countries featured are European, with the remainder North and South American, and one from Asia (Thailand). Under each country are the same sections composed of facts and advice: an introduction to the region, its culture, and its history; a description of recommended living areas; renting; buying real estate; a sample for cost of living; day to day living concerns; taxes; making the move (which involves acquiring the right documentation and following the rules); medical care expenses; financial matters; costs and types of transportation; and leisure time alternatives. Since affordability may be a person's determiner for moving abroad, there are estimated figures on buying, renting, etc.

included in many of these sections. It may be overly hopeful to say that following this book will "increase your standard of living." 303 p.

Organizations

American Association of Retired Persons. www.aarp.org/travel
    In addition to serving as a source of information, this organization offers travel discounts for members. Examined website: 2008

*Elderhostel. www.elderhostel.org
    For the annotation to this organization as well as to the book *Elderhosteling USA!* see under the section **Study and Travel**.

Business
    Since business and non-business travel guide information overlaps, the difference is in emphasis. The former slights sightseeing, etc., in favor of describing important cities and giving advice about such matters as airports and their amenities, rental cars, tipping, hotels, etiquette, fashion, and costs. The latter may have a separate chapter on business concerns, or with a little imagination a traveler may adapt its general contents to business needs. A popular area that continues to grow, business travel works may target a region of the world or a special subject such as health.
    For other business titles see **Accommodations**, **Air Travel**, **Manners and Customs**, and **Money**.
    Subject Heading: Business travel

Titles

The Business Traveler's Survival Guide: How to Get Work Done While on the Road / June Langhoff (Aegis Publishing Group, 1997).
    There is no travel advice *per se*, for the subject is usage of the computer and other technology while the employee is away from the office. Non-technical advice on notebooks, faxes, pagers, voice mail and e-mail, and even the telephone deals with choosing the right ones, maintaining and protecting them, and effective strategies for using them at temporary worksites. The print is easy to scan thanks to abundance of white spaces, bolded headings, and bulleted lists. What effect the intervening years of technology change has done to the advice is open to question. 128 p.

The Business Traveler's World Guide / Philip Seldon (McGraw-Hill, 1998).

This ready reference to eighty-seven countries is arranged by continent and region, except for separate entries on the United States and Canada. Its format is a digest of disparate country information after bolded headings (official name, population, business hours, etc.) except for a page of discussion about "local customs, business protocol and courtesies." A subsection on a country's city or cities includes airport information (distance from the city, minimum connection time, etc.) and limited lists of names, addresses, and telephone numbers of hotels, restaurants, entertainment places, and shops, plus only the names of several attractions. Providing an array of basic facts in a tote-able size, the work has more scope but less depth found in more focused titles (as those on business manners and customs). *Global Road Warrior* (below) is similar in coverage but usually more detailed. 668 p.

Do's and Taboos around the World for Women in Business / Roger E. Axtell and others (John Wiley & Sons, 1997).

In this general guide to conducting business abroad, the introductory material on behavior and travel includes advice on dating, protocol, safety, and health. Next, the status of women is described along with concrete examples of etiquette or protocol guidelines in each of the chapter reviews of select countries and regions, Europe especially. In a third section there are anecdotes of how some women got their jobs, and profiles of successful women. Finally, the book investigates such matters as the pros and cons of working abroad, preparing for the move, the effect on the family, and culture shock. As can be seen, a lot of ground is covered that is beyond the suggested scope of the title. Some of the information is summarized in Axtell's *Essential Do's and Taboos* (see under **Manners and Customs**). 252 p.

*Doing Business in Asia: A Cultural Perspective / Robert Burns (Longman, 1998).

The cultures of several Asia countries are examined from the view of those who would like to do business there while remaining sensitive to local customs and values. Chapters on countries, from China to Vietnam, give insight into the influence of ethnicity, religion, and local behavior. There are sections about the etiquette of meeting people (including non-verbal communication and forms of address), the corporate culture and how to perform negotiations, and socializing after official business, which carries such nuggets as "It is an expectation that the host will try to get their guests drunk" (p. 75); other useful information encompasses what to wear. A separate chapter explores overseas assignments. The content holds an interest beyond the book's business *raison d'être*. 308 p.

The Financial Times Guide to Business Travel / edited by Stuart Crainer & Des Dearlove (Financial Times/Prentice Hall, 2001).

Taking up a bit more than one-half the volume, advice on business travel looks at areas such as packing, working from a hotel room, health, and other cultures. The penetrating coverage brings to light little-considered details (for example, power napping). Well written and with a stream of humor running throughout ("she who travels light, travels fastest—and loses her baggage less frequently"), the book has chapters that typically have insertions within every two pages of text—which may be a box on some related subject, bolded headings, or a profile of a business traveler with his or her choice of a favorite hotel, airport, and things to take. Most of the book's remainder profiles various cities of the world, with each having the same pattern of headings that address the usual concerns of getting about, manners ("Behaving yourself"), major attractions from the perspectives of both a businessperson and a tourist, weather, public holidays, online information, and the like. 308 p.

*Global Road Warrior: 175-Country Resource for International Business Travel, Business Communications, Business Culture / Sibylla M. Putzi and others. 4th ed. (World Trade Press, 2007).

On the two-column pages an overview of each country— alphabetically arranged and with a map—is followed by a digest of ready information, with such categories as economy and trade (including percentages and dollar figures), and money and banking. Among headings specific to travel are those about visas and passports, immunization, departure formalities, tipping, travel warnings, and travel assistance (a list of addresses). A few paragraphs on a country's business capitals precede a selection of their hotels. On the communications side, there is a guide to using landlines and cell phones, plus illustrations of public phones and phone/modem plugs; and about the internet there are contact lists for service providers, internet cafes, and technical support. Features of business culture include something on courtesies, decision making, and meetings. A separate section is devoted to the businesswoman. Many entries are around twenty pages, and they end with a table of essential terms in the home language, unless it is English. A big set that packs a lot of material, it has an online version. 3 vol. (3634 p.)

The Survivor's Guide to Business Travel: How to Get the Best Deals, Travel in Style, Mix Business with Pleasure, Keep Healthy and Much

More! / Roger Collis (Kogan Paul, 2000).

The numerous chapters were originally newspaper travel columns, hence the occasional dialogs with authorities in the travel industry and the concern for current specialties, from hotel loyalty programs to global calling cards. The journalistic approach is also seen in citations of numeric facts (e.g., of company employees in hotels "56 per cent are not reimbursed for mini-bar rip-offs") and costs, which may be in pounds since the viewpoint is British. Subjects beyond business travel also receive inclusion, as six pages on malaria. Ends of several chapters consist of checklists of "do's" and "don't's," and humor is at work throughout the text. A later edition is available. 301 p.

The Unofficial Business Traveler's Pocket Guide: 165 Tips Even the Best Business Travelers May Not Know / Christopher J. McGinnis (McGraw-Hill, 1998).

Their headings in large, bold type, the consecutively numbered tips are divided into traditional chapters that concern preparation, what to bring, getting to and from the airport, the airport itself, using the telephone, and other travel issues that, though familiar in general, offer new thoughts (e.g., surviving a hotel fire or the dietary merits of certain food); one chapter on a less familiar subject concerns frequency traveler programs. There are a few names, addresses, telephone numbers, and websites. To enhance the text's browsability tips may be further broken down by bullets. Interspersed are a series of short chapters called "Confessions of a Frequent Traveler" in which the author describes his experiences of flying into various cities and making his way to his hotel. Since the rectangular book can crowd into the pocket of a sports jacket, it could be brought on a journey, though it is better to have absorbed some of its lessons already. An electronic version from the same year has upped the number of tips. 247 p.

When in Rome or Rio or Riyadh . . . : Cultural Q&As for Successful Business Behavior around the World / Gwyneth Olofsson (Intercultural Press, 2004).

There are eight chapters (getting acquainted, making a good impression, eating and drinking together, etc.), which are further categorized into sections that have introductory discussions, and then are aided by concrete examples in two ways. First, answers to posed, practical questions direct light on aspects of a culture—e.g., whether in Japan foreigners also have to remove their shoes indoors. In addition, throughout the volume re-occurs a list of over thirty countries that have a sentence or more apiece about the situation under focus as it relates to them. For those who are interested in how to behave in a particular part of the world, at the front of the volume a country-by-country index is broken down into subjects that appear in the text. The advice is knowledgeable and a lot of information can be readily gleaned by the reader. 326 p.

The Woman Road Warrior: A Woman's Guide to Business Travel / Kathleen Ameche (Agate, 2005).

In contrast to a conventional business travel guide, this one has more advice on handling one's own security, paying attention to documentation, and keeping in contact with relationships. The longest chapter discusses air travel, and within it the longest section concerns canceled or missed flights and similar unexpected annoyances. The next longest chapter is about choosing a hotel and staying there (perhaps for a long term), and the unexpected may take the form of a lost reservation or noise. Among other subjects in the guide are renting a car, packing, and ensuring personal well-being when on the road. Each chapter conveniently ends with a checklist of points drawn from it. Throughout the work short travel tips pop up within separate graphic boxes. A later edition is available. 180 p.

Disabilities

For people with a limiting physical condition—from those in a wheelchair to the diabetic—a wealth of travel information is available. The best place to start is with one of several specialized resource guides. They list within them publications, organizations, and businesses (such as tours and travel agencies). Some concentrate on accessibility of airports, cars, and parks.

There are organizations solely designed to aid the traveler with disabilities. Besides them, there are many organizations dedicated to individual disabilities, and they should have advice on traveling or should give referrals to wherever the information is obtainable. Also, hospitals and other health groups may be able to either advise or refer.

Concerns about the accessibility of a hotel room, airline, or cruise ship may be directed to the business itself. Departments of the United States government may also be able to answer questions.

Subject Heading: People with disabilities—Travel

Titles

Access America: An Atlas and Guide to the National Parks for Visitors with Disabilities (Northern Cartographic, 1988).

Accompanying the large text in this oversize volume of select parks are color maps of an area and its park, a color diagram of the visitor's center, and color charts for temperature and precipitation and for available handicapped facilities. Subheadings amid the general information about a park are for the benefit of those who have disabilities: "elevation" is provided for people with respiratory or heart conditions; "medical and support services" give the nearest hospital; "publications" are those that are specific to the park; "transportation" speaks of vehicle restrictions; and other headings are for "sign language interpreter," "TDD," and "dog guides." The section on "programs," which includes "trails" and "exhibits," designates if they are for a visual, hearing, or developmental disability. Supplementary information is given about accommodations and services that are accessible. Lists at the end supply independent living centers as well as dialysis centers and hospitals. This title is thorough and useful. 444 p.

Access for Disabled Americans: A Guide for the Wheelchair Traveler / Patricia Smither (Access for Disabled Americans Publishing, 1996).

A selection of popular tourist destinations in the United States and Mexico offers a limited list of places to stay and see; since their brief descriptions may or may not refer to accessibility, the assumption for the reader is that in the latter instance accessibility is present. Precise addresses for sights are problematical, while consideration of wheelchair travel by air, ground, and water in the introductory part is of the basic variety. A later edition is available. 145 p.

Air Travel Guide for Seniors and Disabled Passengers / Robert B. Ronald, Anthony Philbin, Adrianus D. Groenewege (The International Aviation Development Corporation, 2001).

A book that doesn't waste words, it starts with such elementary matters as wheelchairs and aircraft seating requirements; and proceeds to examine the accessibility of vehicular transport to and from the airport. Having arrived there, the passenger learns about negotiating stairs, the presence of pharmacies, trained staff, etc. The subject of boarding the plane and being in flight leads to a look at issues and special requirements, which may include situations where permission from a physician is needed. A closing chapter on rights of seniors or disabled passengers summarizes protective acts that have been passed. Appendixes, a twenty-page glossary, and an index take up nearly half the volume. 126 p.

Anyone Can Travel: The Essential Guide for Seniors, People with Disabilities, Health Problems and All Travellers / Melba M. Rous, Eileen B. Ward (Health Ideas, 2000).

Written for Canadians, this spiral bound book opens with general remarks about planning a trip, but then comes a glance at special needs from a host of travel aspects—services, care, varieties of travelers, etc. Wheelchairs are assigned their own section, and so are types of health problems (Alzheimer's, arthritis, asthma, and so forth). Among the modes of transportation, flying receives the most coverage, though much of the discussion can be of use to any traveler, as it can be for the points about health dangers and how to avoid or handle them; and for assorted issues that may arise. Unlike the other groups mentioned in the title, seniors are given only a few exclusive pages. 286 p.

Around the World Resource Guide: All to Help Make Life a Little Easier for People with Disabilities / Patricia Smither, editor. 5th ed. (Access for Disabled Americans, 2003).

The large, spiral-bound work provides bare-bones lists of publications (broken down into "travel," "hotel discounts," "magazines," etc.), helpful organizations, businesses, and services. To name, address, telephone number, and website is occasionally added a little explanatory annotation. Atypically on the outside back cover and *without* page numbers, the table of contents shows 19 sections—from "publications—ADA laws" to "companion dogs" and "accessible home renovations." Some of the headings relate more to disabilities than travel, such as "true life stories" and "websites—all subjects." A "world resources" section offers addresses in countries other than the United States, notably Europe. Averaging between four to six entries per page, the resource is for referral only and offers no advice. A later edition is available. 323 p.

Barrier-Free Travel: A Nuts and Bolts Guide for Wheelers and Slow-Walkers / Candy Harrington. 2nd ed. (Demos Medical Publishing, 2005).

In a book designed to inform those who are in wheelchairs or have other mobility issues, travel by air receives the most detailed attention. Discussions range from boarding procedures and storing or protecting personal equipment to situations that involve stretchers or service animals. Negotiating with forms of land and sea transportation likewise gets its due, and there is an exploration of what to look for in an accessible hotel room. The challenges with traveling to Europe and other destinations could have been treated at greater length, but those who might like certain activities afforded by national parks, beaches, and water and snow sports can find a chapter about it. Another is dedicated to children who have accessibility needs. The facts about dealing with a travel agent, shopping on the internet, and traveling on a budget are covered in a way that relates to their target audience. The same publisher has produced *There Is Room at the*

Inn: Inns and B&Bs for Wheelers and Slow Walkers by Candy B. Harrington (2006). 292 p.

Breathin' Easy: A Guide for Travelers with Pulmonary Disabilities (Breathin' Easy Publications, 1999).

In this specialty work an arrangement-by-state of names, addresses, and telephone numbers for suppliers of oxygen equipment take up most of the space. The remainder consists of short sections for Canada and the rest of the world. There are some ads. 126 p.

Directory of Travel Agencies for the Disabled / Helen Hecker. 3rd ed. (Twin Peaks Press, 1993).

Dealing chiefly with the United States and arranged by state (with some not represented and usually more than one listed per page), the volume also has a little space devoted to Canada, followed by a score of countries from the rest of the world. Entries have name, address, telephone number, and contact person and, as with *The Disabled Driver's Mobility Guide* (below), there are accompanying codes ("DIAL" for dialysis, "V" for vans, etc.). The author is an RN and has brought out newer editions since this one. 45 p.

Disability Express: Travel and Disability Resource Library / compiled by Steve Illum, Brigitte Lillard, M. Gary Thompson. 6th ed. (Office of Leisure Research, Southwest Missouri State University, 1998?).

One-half of the directory devotes itself to accessible accommodations which are composed mainly of chains (e.g., "Travelodge Hotel"), though there is no order to the individual entries within the brand. Other chapters list tour operators and travel agencies, accessible attractions and accessible transportation, medical services, associations resources, plus references to articles on travel and disabilities. Stacked in two columns per page, each name and address comes with a telephone number and perhaps a few words of details, but nothing more. Travelers who seek advice need to look elsewhere. A newer edition is available. 397 p.

The Disabled Driver's Mobility Guide (American Automobile Association, 1995).

Sharing space with a sprinkling of ads, this directory of agencies by state and province offers disparate services and equipment for drivers with disabilities. The address and telephone numbers, sometimes followed by the name of the person in charge, comes with codes for each agency's offerings: arthritis/muscle fatigue evaluation, driver training, foot controls, vision testing, etc. The front part of the book has a little advice and various address lists by subject, such as that under manufacturers or insurers. A newer edition is available. 208 p.

Fodor's Great American Vacations for Travelers with Disabilities. 2nd ed. (Fodor's Travel Publications, 1996).

The vacations are at select, alphabetically arranged cities and natural areas, with maps accompanying both. The accessibility categories of mobility, hearing, and vision (symbols of "m," "h," and "v") are discussed as appropriate under various attractions, entertainments, and public transportation, with mobility being the most common. The two columns per page are divided into categories by headings with white letters on a black background, making for ease of visually locating separate topics. A particular spot to vacation might be divided into "What to Pack"; "Precautions" (as in lack of accessible restrooms); "Tourist Offices" addresses; "Important Contacts"; "Local Access Guides"; numbers and addresses for "Emergencies"; "Arriving and Departing" ("By Plane," etc.); "Dining"; and much else. General profiles of places and getting around are supplemented by disability information. This is a good and polished work. 605 p.

How to Travel: A Guidebook for Persons with a Disability / Fred Rosen. Large print ed. (Science & Humanities Press, 1998).

The disability can be a matter of mobility (a wheelchair, for example), hearing, seeing, breathing, or diabetes. Spare, no-nonsense statements fill chapters on getting around by air, rail, bus, and rental vehicle, plus the areas of touring, accommodations, dining out, river cruising, and ocean travel, all but the last limited to the United States. The large print in the sheet-sized book is chiefly a collection of specific tips and advice, but it also looks at the rights of those with handicaps. Short lists of resources at the end present books, periodicals, organizations with telephone numbers, and URLs. 110 p.

Information for Travelers with Physical or Visual Disabilities / compiled by Ruth Nussbaum (National Library Service for the Blind and Physically Handicapped, The Library of Congress, 2002). www.loc.gov/nls/refer ence/circulars/travel.html

In print and online, this collection of resources shows contact information along with descriptions for organizations, selected federal and travel agencies, and a few internet sites. Also, there is a brief section on transportation services in the United States; a short bibliography of titles in print, in Braille, and recorded; and a list of U.S. tourism offices. 20 p.

New Horizons: Information for the Air Traveler with a Disability (Aviation Consumer Protection Division, U.S. Department of Transportation). airconsumer.ost.dot.gov/publications/horizons.htm

The rights and services for these passengers are presented by the government in terms of the Air Carrier Access rules. Among the many matters addressed are getting advance information about an aircraft, situations when an attendant may be required, handling of mobility aids, accessibility concerns, seat assignments, and cabin service. Examined website: 2008

Rick Steves' Easy Access Europe / Rick Steves & Ken Plattner (Avalon Travel Publishing, 2004).

This polished effort has the features of the usual geographic guidebook from the prospect of those with disability concerns. Its "Europe" is limited to London, Paris, Bruges, Amsterdam, Haarlem, and the Rhine Valley, where various named hotels, restaurants, and rated attractions are described and accompanied by accessibility details. There are thirteen codes, for entryways, entries requiring assistance, toilets, hotel rooms, and so on, while buildings get ratings from level 1 (fully accessible) to level 4 (not accessible). Riding the subway, buses, boats, and other forms of transportation receive attention. The larger cities are treated in sections, and attendant hand-drawn, black-and-white maps may be themed to attractions, eateries, or accommodations, while others are of building plans. A later edition is available. 498 p.

Survival Strategies for Going Abroad: A Guide for People with Disabilities / Laura Hershey (Mobility International USA, National Clearinghouse on Disability and Exchange, 2005).

Encouraging its target audience to travel, the work is full of accounts of successful experiences along with quotes from more than twenty travelers to illustrate the statements and advice of the author. There are suggestions for different types of programs in which people with disabilities can participate, and this is dependent on where they want to go and their own interests. Unlike most guides, this presents ideas about raising money to fund a trip. Planning for a journey overseas may vary from arranging a support network to determining whether a wheelchair should be manual or motorized. Once arrived, a person must deal with the new world, as in terms of transportation, safety, and human interaction (where different cultures have their own views about disabilities). After returning home, he or she may discover a new self-knowledge and self-worth. Appendixes contain annotated resources. 225 p.

A World of Options: A Guide to International Exchange, Community Service and Travel for Persons with Disabilities / Christa Bucks, editor. 3rd ed. (Mobility International USA [MIUSA], 1997).
The thickness and size of a city telephone book, this is a heavyweight in more ways than one. Directory facts for an organization, group, or business are followed by a description that may be extensive. There are separate explanatory essays related to special aspects of travel, such as the American Disabilities Act (ADA) or financial aid, and there are firsthand accounts. A chapter on "international educational exchange programs" describes the goal, scope, and offerings of each program, followed by a discussion of what that means for persons with disabilities. Two travel chapters fill half of the contents: the first a continuation of the directory format and its information, with a number of subsections (airlines, hostels, sports organizations, etc.); the next an annotated collection of publications. A few addresses are outside the United States. 658 p.

Organizations

Mobility International USA. www.miusa.org
One of its missions is to empower those with disabilities through international exchange and through information. A manager of the National Clearinghouse on Disability and Exchange, among its titles is the journal *A World Awaits You* (www.miusa.org/ncde/away), which has personal-success stories and articles on aspects of travel, and *Survival Strategies for Going Abroad* and *A World of Options* (both above). Examined website: 2008

Society for Accessible Travel & Hospitality. www.sath.org
It promotes accessibility for travelers with disabilities. Examined website: 2008

Families
Parents, children, and travel are treated in several books. A few titles deal just with babies, and at least one series is written for the child traveler rather than the parent. Other books discuss children in relation to subjects such as summer camps and driving. To amuse children during a long car or plane ride there are numerous books with games and other activities (search for them by the subject heading "Games for travelers").
Of the infinite variety of travel guides, many frequently overlook the concerns of children. However, a good bet is to use an advice book on traveling with children together with whatever general guide book that is wanted, and the two in combination should give satisfactory coverage.

For books concerned about the health of children who travel, see under **Health**.

In addition to the titles on parents and children, travel is also a topic that can be found in books and magazines that deal with family reunions.

Subject Headings: Family recreation; Children—Travel; Games for travelers.

Titles

Family Adventure Guide Series (series) (Globe Pequot).

Each book in the series describes a state or, occasionally, an area. Based on their appeal to children, here are museums, parks, monuments, recreation areas, company tours, scenic landscape, and a few spots to eat or stay, along with seasonal events. Some merit a paragraph, others a line. Chapters are by broad regions, with towns and cities within them arranged approximately in the order that they are encountered on the road, and are shown on a simple map. While there are a lot of places to see, the names bolded, this is a *selective* grouping, so some towns are omitted. The book is best used for those who are willing to drive from place to place. Examined: *Missouri Family Adventure Guide* / Jane Cosby (1997; 162 p.)

Family Reunion: Everything You Need to Know to Plan Unforgettable Get-Togethers for Every Kind of Family / Jennifer Crichton (Workman Publishing, 1998).

While the travel sections of newspapers refer now and again to family reunions, books about them do not devote a lot of space about travel. This work has a single chapter on possible reunion sites and what to look for in them. Brief considerations range from the backyard to camps, college dorms, and houseboats, with descriptions of a few individual hotels and resorts thrown in. Some addresses are in an appendix. 280 p.

The Family Reunion Handbook: A Complete Guide for Reunion Planners / Thomas Ninkovich. 2nd ed. (Reunion Research, 1998).

Most of the information about travel is confined to one chapter describing styles of reunions—cowboy adventures, luxury resorts, etc.—and specific localities where they could be held in the United States (as well as one in Canada). An appendix offers a yellow-paged directory of accommodations and other sites, with a compact account of each. 253 p.

Family Travel & Resorts: The Complete Guide / Pamela Lanier. 4th ed. (Lanier Publishing International, 2001).

After a chapter of tips, safety, and health, a second one looks at age groups composed of babies, children, teens, and seniors (when they travel with their grandchildren). The chapter on food comes with several recipes, and a discussion of travel's educational benefits ends with a directory of living history, children's, and (most numerous) science museums. A brief look at U.S. regions is followed by a long chapter on outdoor activities, much of it names and addresses. Over a third of the book deals with resorts, some allotted a page of description that reads like a publicity brochure, though the majority have only their address and telephone number, which is arranged by state. Depth could be better and some inclusions are questionable. A later edition is available. 428 p.

The Family Travel Guide: An Inspiring Collection of Family-Friendly Vacations / edited by Carole Terwilliger Meyers (Carousel Press, 1995).

The greatest part of this anthology is composed of numerous firsthand accounts of family vacations in the United States and throughout the world. The chapters are written by the editor or one of a number of different contributors, which allows a variety of viewpoints, though the anecdotal approach can be like watching some stranger's vacation pictures. The narrative describes where the family stayed and ate and, chiefly, what they did. The early section has advice on traveling with children and ideas for kinds of travel (as home exchanging or RV-ing). At the end is a bibliography, and one of the indexes contains titles of movies and other entertainments mentioned in the text. 422 p.

Fun with the Family Series (series) (Insiders' Guide).

Polished, capably written, and well-designed, this example from the state guide series is arranged by county and the town within it. Each attraction has its name followed by the age range for which it is appropriate and one or more icons from a potential of almost two dozen that signify the presence of swimming, food, etc. An entry also comes with driving directions or address, telephone number, sometimes a website, seasons and times open, and whether free or not. Several paragraphs describe the museum, garden, historic property, park, boat ride, or whatever, while there are added recommendations about where to eat and stay, and throughout boxes highlight various facts. A highway map for every county shows the locations of the towns mentioned. Examined: *Fun with the Family, Connecticut: Hundreds of Ideas for Day Trips with the Kids* / Doe Boyle. 6th ed. (2006; 308 p.)

Great Family Vacations Series (series) (Globe-Pequot Press).

Under select cities and regions are the fundamentals about getting there and getting around, what to see and do (with subheadings), side trips, special events, where to stay and eat, and where to find more information. Addresses come with telephone numbers and at times websites in addition to other details that give a sufficient idea about the nature of the attraction or activity, some of which, like shopping, are aimed at the parents. In order that the names under discussion not be lost in the author's chatty paragraphs, they are bolded, while gray boxes single out certain attractions; and there are a few photographs. While in this instance the geographic scope is the "South," states are not treated equally—for example, five destinations are included for Florida in contrast with none for Mississippi. The series is United States only. Examined: *Great Family Vacations: South* / Candyce H. Stapen. 3rd ed. (2001; 303 p.)

Have Kid, Will Travel: 101 Survival Strategies for Vacationing with Babies and Young Children / Claire Tristram (Andrews McMeel Publishing, 1997).

Much more detailed than *Take Your Baby and Go!* (below) while covering the same territory (and some of the same advice), the book has, in addition to the conventional travel topics, those about first trips and travel with newborns, choosing carriers and strollers, pregnancy, the special needs child, and what to do in various kinds of emergencies. The table of contents handily lists the numerous descriptive subheadings (as "how to evaluate child care at all-inclusive resorts (before they take your money)" or "backpacking with kids"). Family vacation destinations themselves are not discussed. 189 p.

Kidding around (series) (John Muir).

This square book is written not for parents traveling with children but for the children themselves, as evidenced by the simple descriptions, large print, and drawings. Chapters in the *Chicago* example introduce such features as the city's history, parks, animals, sports, museums, and entertainment and eating. For every attraction on the left page, the right has a travel journal, a street map marked with the chapter's sights, a puzzle, or a game. At the end is a calendar of events and a directory of helpful addresses and attractions, with opening hours but no admission fees. The series looks at cities chiefly in the U.S., plus a few abroad. Examined: *Kidding around Chicago: What to Do, Where to Go, and How to Have Fun in Chicago* / Carolyn Crimi. 2nd ed. (2000; 133 p.)

Kids Love (series) (Kids Love Publications).

This book is a collection of hundreds of attractions for children according to regions in its state. Name, address, brief directions, URL, telephone number, hours of operation, and admission costs are typically provided. A paragraph describes the background or features of the park, historic site, museum, factory (e.g., for chocolate) and similar destinations. Seasonal and special events are organized by month and separately described. An activity index in back fills nine categories, beginning with "Amusements" and ending with "Tours." The graphic design of an entry could be more consistent, and since the name of a town or city is a little difficult for the eye to distinguish, it is not obvious that their arrangement in a region is by alphabetical order. A few lodging and dining places are thrown in. Examined: *Kids Love Illinois: A Family Travel Guide to Exploring "Kid-Tested" Places in Illinois . . . Year Round!* / George & Michele Zavatsky (2006; 258 p.)

Kids on Board: Fun Things to Do While Commuting or Road Tripping with Children / Robyn Freedman Spizman (Fairview Press, 1997).
   This has short but complete descriptions of simple games and other recreations that children might enjoy while traveling. With about two per page, they are grouped within eight areas: alphabet games, imagination games, musical activities, etc. An occasional icon signifies that some object must be brought along in order to play a game. There's an occasional bit of practical advice on handling children. 173 p.

Reunions. Bimonthly (Reunions, the Magazine, Inc.) www.reunionsmag. com
   The informative website for this title has numerous articles on throwing reunions and related details, such as choosing a date, paying for the reunion, types of reunions, resources, and lists of upcoming reunions. Examined website: 2008

The Single Parent Travel Handbook / by Brenda Elwell (GlobalBrenda Publishing, LLC, 2002).
   Is there a difference when children travel with one adult versus two? The author believes there is, with both parent and children having to become more self-reliant. Alternating intelligent advice with enlightening and numerous—maybe too numerous—personal experiences in a variety of countries where she traveled with her children, she holds paramount the interest and needs of the child. The book delves into trip preparations, among them getting U.S. documents that allow the child to go with the parent out of the country; and the section on the trip itself considers modes of transportation, interacting with the locals, and more. In one chapter dads tell their stories of single travel. The largest space is devoted to describing destinations and accompanying activities, which range from the U.S. to Egypt and the Galapagos Islands. 298 p.

Summer Fun: The Parents' Complete Guide to Day Camps, Overnight Camps, Specialty Camps, Teen Tours / Marian Edelman Borden (Facts on File, 1999).

There are explanations about how to evaluate the quality of different kinds of camps and what they offer the child, with evaluation forms in appendixes. Camp accreditation, safety, and staff are examples of the issues examined, and those that center on children include introducing the child to camp, anticipating various problems the child may face, and keeping contact with him or her. There is a separate look at specialty camps that are for children who have an interest in sports or other areas, and for those children who have disabilities. The final chapter about dealing with teens delves into working for pay, volunteering, and touring. The table of contents provides a summary of what each of the seven chapters is about. Though a short resources list has a few camp directory titles, no individual camps are treated in this well-done book of detailed advice to parents,. 190 p.

Super Family Vacations / Martha Shirk and Nancy Klepper. 3rd ed. (HarperPerennial, 1995).

The vacations are resorts, guest ranches, ski areas, history spots (e.g., Plimoth Plantation), cruises, adventure trips, and nature sites, all being subdivided by regions of the United States, save for some forays outside the country. Always keeping children in mind, a discussion for each vacation devotes a few pages that encompass sections on accommodations (with the sign of "$" to indicate price range), dining, activities (with icons for golf, fishing, etc.), programs and interests for children, "niceties" that may be special touches or amenities, nearby interests for families, and an address for more information. Descriptions can be generic, as housing that is "cozy" or a restaurant with a "unique atmosphere and cuisine," and they are almost always laudatory. 440 p.

Take Your Baby and Go!: A Guide for Traveling with Babies, Toddlers and Young Children / Sheri Andrews, Judy Bordeaux, and Vivian Vasquez. 2nd ed. (Bear Creek Publications, 1990).

The well-being of a child who travels is the pivot for this advice book. After briefly discussing the reasons for not deferring family travel, the book begins with a chapter about planning through the acquisition of equipment (such as a car seat or stroller) and clothing, and anticipating the child's needs. There are other short chapters on accommodations, restaurants, and car, air, and train travel, as well as on finding a baby sitter and dealing with health issues. Chapters end with a bulleted checklist that summarizes important points. This is basic coverage for a specialized audience. 80 p.

Take Your Kids to Europe: How to Travel Safely (and Sanely) in Europe with Your Children / Cynthia W. Harriman. 8th ed. (The Globe Pequot Press, 2008).

Showing a sympathy with the perspective of children and teenagers, Harriman also offers a lot of common sense and thoughtful observations about travel in Europe and the European lifestyle. The sections consider preparation (as, how to get off from school and work in order to travel), being on the road (what to eat and where, family accommodations, etc.), living abroad (finding a house, grocery shopping in other countries, coping with culture shock, etc.), and a "totally biased guide" of what to see and do with children in Britain, France, and other Western European countries, plus (briefly) Morocco and Greece. A final chapter has resources along the lines of book titles and websites. The author makes many of her points through recalling experiences of herself and her family, and on occasion quotes other families. In keeping with the stated and tacit insistence that travel is an educational opportunity for the young, this is a book to use and learn from. 334 p.

The Travel Mom's Ultimate Book of Family Travel: Planning, Surviving, and Enjoying Your Vacation Together / Emily Kaufman (Broadway Books, 2006).

The first part naturally begins with planning a trip, then offers advice about keeping children engaged and comfortable in types of transportation, plus it reports on multigenerational travel and lists specific museums and other spots where children can learn. In part two, destinations are discussed according to type (resorts, cruises, camping, etc.), from which individual resorts, cruise lines, campgrounds, etc. are chosen for descriptions. They are okay, from one to several paragraphs, and their inclusion should mean that the vacations will appeal to the entire family. Throughout the work the occasional checklist, box, and bullets help arrange contents. 261 p.

Travel with Children / Cathy Lanigan. 4th ed. (Lonely Planet, 2002).

About a fourth of the book has travel advice concerning children (categorized by age), trip plans and what to take, forms of transportation, children's needs and health, and travel during pregnancy. The rest of the book highlights countries of the world, some of which are off the family tourist track (e.g., the Balkans, Bangladesh). Most of the destinations bear a division on "things to see and do," with other popular ones designated "activities," "parks and playgrounds," and "festivals." While the information under these and other headings are relevant to children or taking care of them, its amount is sparse, both in number of offerings and what is said about them; so even when an attraction is presented, there is no address. Accounts of experiences from various families are found throughout the work, which finishes with a few pages of websites. 275 p.

Trouble-Free Travel with Children: Over 700 Helpful Hints for Parents on the Go / Vicki Lansky. 3rd ed. (Book Peddlers, 2004).

From babies to seven-year-olds or so, young children that travel make demands on their parents, a situation that is explored in this book of advice, from planning and packing to going by car, plane, train, or bus, and outings abroad. In each chapter the author offers a wide selection of short, bulleted tips that review what can be done for a child's safety, health, or enjoyment, while extra suggestions from readers are scattered through the text. This manual of practical hints should ensure a positive travel experience for both parents and their offspring. 136 p.

U.S. Family Travel Guide / editors, Donna Marino, Betsy Andrews & Caren Weiner Campbell (Zagat Survey, 2004).

Under the close to two dozen cities alphabetically arranged are the categories of attractions, hotels, restaurants, and restaurant chains. Name, address, telephone number, website, and an opinion-slanted paragraph compose an entry. Each is rated with four numbers—on a scale between zero to thirty—and assigned a cost range. For example, the four ratings for an attraction relate to its quality of child appeal, adult appeal, consumer amenities, and the friendliness and availability of the personnel; for a hotel and restaurant the rating types are somewhat different. Conveniently, the front offers lists of the most popular and top-rated attractions. Among the indexes in back is one that sorts attractions into types, while others group attractions, hotels, and restaurants by special features. Guided by reader response, this oblong, portable volume carries on the conceptual tradition of a publisher known for its restaurant evaluations, Zagat Survey. 364 p.

Gays and Lesbians

Sources include both guides and directories of businesses and services that cultivate gays and lesbians; and publishers (Damron, Ferrari) that concentrate on this audience. Of mainstream titles, *Specialty Travel Index* can be searched for tours designed with them in mind.

Subject Headings: Gays—Travel; Lesbians—Travel

Titles

Are You Two . . . Together?: A Gay and Lesbian Travel Guide to Europe /
Lindsy Van Gelder and Pamela Robin Brandt (Random House, 1991).

As the authors travel through Western Europe they observe the
treatment of gays and lesbians and report on their lifestyle. Written in an
informal and at times wise-cracking manner, and offering anecdotes both
current and historical, the book ends each chapter with practical advice on
where to stay and eat, what to see and do, what information to consult, and
what books to read about London or Amsterdam or any of the other
destinations. A general travel guide should be used to supplement this title,
which doesn't have enough practical facts for the basic traveler. 345 p.

Damron Women's Traveller. Annual (Damron Company).

Although the directory for lesbians is the approximate size of a
paperback, its thickness and two-column pages crowds in a lot of names
and addresses, with three-quarters of the work covering the United States,
where arrangement is by state and town. The remaining geographical areas
are Canada, Mexico, the Caribbean region, and a few countries in Central
and South America and in Western Europe. Subject categories may
include info lines and services, accommodations, bars, nightclubs, cafes,
restaurants, entertainment, bookstores, retail shops, publications, and
erotica. Entry remarks are terse and, in accordance with the category, may
cover hours, activities, clientele served, lesbian or gay-owned, etc. Ads are
scattered throughout, as are insets describing places and singling out
aspects of particular interest to lesbians. A final section has lists of
camping and RV spots, tours and tour operators, and a calendar of various
events. The publisher also issues *Damron Men's Travel Guide.* Examined:
2005; 635 p.

*Ferrari Guides' Gay Travel A to Z: The World of Gay & Lesbian Travel
Options at Your Fingertips.* 20th ed. (Ferrari International Publishing,
2001).

By far the largest portion of the book is the directory with its three
columns per page. Divided by continent or region (Canada and the United
States have their own sections), then country, then town or city, the
categories include "information," "accommodations," "bars," "dance
bars," "restaurants," "baths and saunas," "retail and bookstores," and
"erotica." The accommodations section bears more than just name,
address, and URL, since a description may be supplied by the owner,
while the entries in other sections have the occasional brief notes, such as
"gay-friendly" or a list of amenities, and any entry may be embellished

with several of some 32 symbols (representing "men," "Asian clientele," "leather," "frequented by hustlers," "beer and wine only," etc.). The book also contain descriptions of tour packages that are indexed by place and activity, and an events calendar divided into "art & films," "pride events," "women's retreats & festivals," and several others. This frequent revision keeps the interest of its audience foremost. 461 p.

Ferrari Guides' Women's Travel in Your Pocket. 19th ed. (Ferrari International Publishing, 2001).

Crammed into this thick, two-column paperback are addresses of particular relevance to lesbians who travel. Accommodations, information sources, bars, restaurants, and bookshops are geographically arranged, and a majority of entries have brief annotations, though the ones for U.S. accommodations are often the fullest. Front sections have descriptions of over eighty tour operators for gays and lesbians, and this is followed by a calendar of events. Ads appear throughout. In conception and look the book is a twin to the publisher's *Ferrari Guides' Gay Travel A to Z* (above). The publisher now appears to be defunct. 512 p.

Fodor's Gay Guide to the USA / Andrew Collins. 3rd ed. (Fodor's Travel Publications, 2001).

"Where to stay, eat, and play in the USA and Canada," proclaims the title page. Combining reader friendliness with practicality, though too large for a pocket, this well-planned and professional work uses a few icons, italics, bolding, and spacing so that the eye can quickly scan a page. Introductory paragraphs to a city and a discussion of attractions make reference to gay interests as needed. The section on "sleeps" (accommodations) describes the entries as if aimed at any general reader, usually paying attention to its intended audience in just a final note about the clientele being gay, lesbian, or straight; and along with the section on "eats" comes with a range of dollar signs. More relevant categories are socializing places ("scenes"), such as clubs and bars, and "the little black book" miscellanea of gay and lesbian community centers, bookstores, gyms, etc. Arrangement is by region, then city or town, with a group of popular cities having easy-to-follow street maps. 676 p.

Frommer's Gay & Lesbian Europe: The Top Cities & Resorts / David Andrusia and others. 3rd ed. (Wiley Publishing, 2003).

This is a polished, thick travel guide to selected cities that are chiefly in Western Europe. Besides generalities on transportation and tourist information, substantial paragraphs describe named accommodations (arranged by location in a city), eateries (including café culture), and sights and attractions, among which are parks, gardens, beaches, gyms, and swimming spots. Also there are sections on shopping, culture, and side trips to nearby locations; and there is a collection of spots related to night life, with remarks about sex and sexual opportunities. In a list of fast facts are addresses for AIDS organizations and the names of gay publications. In addition, references to the gay historical background of a place may be discovered. City maps, typically on two pages, carry numbered marks for dining, accommodations, and things to see. 621 p.

The Gay Vacation Guide: The Best Trips and How to Plan Them / Mark Chesnut (Carol Publishing Group, 1997).

A majority of chapters deal with types of vacations: active (cycling, hiking, etc.), cruises, special interest tours, resorts, and independent. Remaining chapters cover destinations abroad and those in the United States. Mention of numerous tour companies, travel businesses, and accommodations appear throughout the text, which goes into various travel opportunities that gays and lesbians are supposed to find particularly appealing. Opinions of travelers are also quoted. 214 p.

Inn Places: Gay & Lesbian Accommodations Worldwide. 12th ed. (Ferrari International Publishing, 1999).

The nicely designed book devotes as much as a full page of information to each lodging, sometimes adding its photograph. Across from its name is a note answering "how gay is it?" and whether gay or lesbian in orientation, and perhaps if gay-owned or gay-friendly. A favorable description is followed by a factual breakdown of up to over two dozen areas: clientele (e.g., "50% gay & lesbian"), distance or time to gay bars, vegetarian availability, rates, discounts, parking, exercise/health, nudity, pets, children, etc. The United States receives more space than any other region—a bit over one-half of the book. A later edition is available. 592 p.

Odysseus: The International Gay Travel Planner / Eli Angelo, Joseph H. Bain, editors. 16th ed. (Odysseus Enteprises Ltd., 2001).

The two-column work has breadth rather than depth, and distinct from some other world directories, it gives more space for countries outside the United States, which still takes up almost a quarter of the work. Under each country, brief facts about it are followed by a section on its law concerning homosexuality, and then more brief facts (airport, location, description) about towns and cities. Directory entries may receive just a line of commentary, or nothing, about gay and lesbian information, bars and clubs, restaurants, services (e.g., bookstores, health clubs), and accommodations which, unlike the previous categories, gives the type of clientele and a number of other details; additional sections may be on such interests as beaches. Inclusion of a business does not mean that it is gay-related. There are some ads and suggestive male photos, as the content seems to be more for gay men than women. A later edition is available. 693 p.

Spartacus: International Gay Guide. Annual (Bruno Gmünder).

The information at the front about using the book and about health is in English, German, French, Spanish, and Italian, as is the matter about the legal situation of homosexuals that precedes each country—from Albania to Zimbabwe—by which the directory is arranged, though it is acknowledged that some political entities are left out. Under a country only a few of the many towns, cities or islands receive individual discussion before the categories of bars, dance clubs, saunas/baths, fitness studios, swimming, hotels, etc., where there is name, address, telephone number, and perhaps a short note. The two-column pages contain a lot, and while color ads abound throughout, the infrequent city maps must be searched for. Examined: 35th ed. (2006; 1240 p.)

Honeymooners

Books about honeymoons have an excellent chance of also discussing travel, and there is a small segment of travel books that profiles places of appeal to romantic-minded couples. Since romance is in the eye of the beholder, any general destination guide may be mined for relevant information or at least supply supplementary facts. In each title below the balance of space allotted between the romantic and practical travel suggestions varies.

Subject Headings: Married people—Travel—Guidebooks; Couples—Travel—Guidebooks.

Titles

Checklist for a Perfect Honeymoon / Suzanne Rodriguez-Hunter (Doubleday, 1996).

The first third of this paperback's elementary advice about traveling ("check in early at the gate," etc.) covers a lot of ground but skips a lot of details. The second part profiles getaways as either pampered, "for just the two of you," city, beach, recreational, cultural, or adventure. The broad, capsule descriptions of select destinations omit virtually all addresses, though telephone numbers are given. There are brief looks at some resorts, cruises, destinations, and activities. An appendix has a list of U.S.,

Canadian, and international tourist bureaus. With its shallow depth and contents, this book is too flawed for a perfect honeymoon. 285 p.

The Good Honeymoon Guide / Lucy Hone. 2nd ed. updated by Nicki Grihault (Trailblazer Publications, 2002).

Aside from a few pages about honeymoon planning, the work is a geographical arrangement of destinations that begins with "islands of the world" and continues by continent or region, with countries compactly introduced and accompanied by a summary of facts about them. The value of the work lies in the information about the chosen hotels, resorts, and similar accommodations, which are described in such a way to suggest a comfortable familiarity with them. In addition, a shaded box sets off their name, address, and telephone number; reservations; getting there from the airport; a description of the amenities; dress code; weddings; minimum stay; rates; etc. Other recommended hotels receive less wordage, and perhaps because the viewpoint is British, the United States is given fewer pages than, for example, Europe. While there are suggestions about things to see and do in or around a city or other place, they are skimpy. Hotels that specialize in complete weddings are listed in back. 319 p.

*Honeymoon Vacations for Dummies / Reid Bramblett and others (Hungry Minds, 2001).

Chockablock with suggestions and facts, this reader-friendly "Dummies" book begins with a summary of significant points in its chapters-to-come, then goes on to discuss planning—choice of a destination, arrangement of a wedding there, etc. Its largest section has generous chapters about individual places to go, whether tropical islands, Disney World, or Paris, and concentrates on their accommodations and attractions, ending with bits of practical advice (driving, safety, tipping, etc.). Cruises are given their own bundle of chapters. To the usual "Dummies" icons (e.g., "Tips") are those that offer "Romance" and "Wedding Bells," which are for spots that arrange weddings. The book is useful for any visitor to the getaways covered, as is the advice on traveling, and the wit keeps the advice sprightly. 574 p.

Honeymoons: A Romantic Travel Guide / Elizabeth Harryman and Paul Lasley (E. P. Dutton, 1990).

On one wide page there are several color photos of the outside and inside of the hotel, inn, or other featured lodging that is judged to be honeymoon worthy, with a description of it on the facing page sometimes written in the first-person plural. Text may discuss background of the place, activities, ambiance, food, and any pampering aspects that contribute to the enjoyment of the couple. Separate, small paragraphs provide general information along with the price characterizations of "inexpensive," "moderate," or "expensive," plus what attraction may be nearby. Escapes in the United States receive the most attention, but there are some international destinations. 127 p.

100 Best Romantic Resorts of the World / Katharine D. Dyson. 5th ed. (The Globe Pequot Press, 2006).

To be listed, a resort had to score high within ten categories, such as a romantic setting, overall quality, and safety. For every property the enthusiastic description may take over a page, and then comes a breakdown into the short facts of name; contact points; romantic highlights; transportation means for arriving and leaving; distance from airport and cities or towns; the most romantic room or suite; amenities; dress code; wedding possibilities; rates and package costs; etc. The most attention is paid to resorts in the United States, followed by the Caribbean (along with Bahamas and Bermuda), a group of countries in Western Europe, and a scattering of spots throughout the world. Aside from a few color photos in front, the resorts are not pictured, so to view them prospective clients will have to visit the websites listed. 243 p.

Plan Your Honeymoon (Fodor's Travel Publications, 2001).

The subject of this paperback by a well-known travel publisher is not about destinations but about traveling to them through planning, managing, and enjoying. The first chapter has advice about the type of honeymoon the couple might like—urban or country, group tour or solo travel, active or relaxed, etc.—and the second considers how much they might wish to spend. Other chapters look at travel by plane, car, or train, and at special requirements for going to foreign places. Besides the inevitable observations that apply to travel in general, there are also such interests as have to do with finding privacy. Some first-person experiences appear throughout. 188 p.

Romantic Days and Nights Series (series) (Globe Pequot Press).

In the *Chicago* title, each of the thirty-one itineraries covers a day or more in the city and is based on various themes: African American history, gardens, dance, football, a western weekend, and others. Days are partitioned into mornings (less emphasis on these), afternoons, and evenings, with suggestions to couples of what to do and see, and especially where to eat lunch and dinner, with the food, ambiance, and a price range mentioned. Written in an upbeat and conversational style ("Are we awake yet?"), the book spends a few lines or so in describing attractions as they fit into each theme. Those who like a structured approach to sightseeing should have enough to fill their time, whether or not they choose to follow the author's schedule. There is very little how-to travel advice, for the book is about enjoying the city. Examined: *Romantic Days and Nights in Chicago: Romantic Diversions in and around the City* / Susan Figliulo (3rd ed., 2001; 269 p.)

Romantic Wedding Destinations: Guide to Wedding & Honeymoon Getaways around the World / Jackie Carrington. 3rd ed. revised and expanded (Innovanna Pubishing Co., 1997).

An upbeat description of the getaway and its attractions is followed by brief sections on local food, crafts, the weather (a chart), airline flights and car rentals available, and where to write for more information. Documentation and money are additionally covered in the discussion on international locales. For each destination the sections on wedding services—some of which provide sales pitches along with their name and address—and on marriage licenses are the most valuable, since they are overlooked by general guide books, which may be more detailed as well as more objective in other topics that appear in *Romantic Wedding Destinations*. Here and there are romantic illustrations and quotes. 202 p.

Ultimate Guide to the World's Best Wedding & Honeymoon Destinations: A Comprehensive Guide Designed to Assist You in Choosing the Perfect Destination, Whether It Be for the Most Romantic Wedding Ceremony, or for an Unforgettable Honeymoon / Elizabeth and Alex Lluch (Wedding Solutions Publishing, 2004).

The large book with attractive color photos on every page is a publicity plug for the featured places. The first one-hundred-and-thirty-some pages have generalities about the sights, activities, and practical facts related to a pick of destinations, which includes a mere three countries in Europe and for the United States only California, Florida, Las Vegas, and Hawaii. Within a country's description a special part that deals with weddings notes the laws that govern them and the types of documents required for this ceremony. The remainder of the book has resorts that were selected for their service, location, facilities, and surroundings, with information apparently supplied by the resort itself. In the page that is dedicated to each, there is one column with basic facts (contact information, size of property, rates, etc.), the nearby attractions, onsite facilities, wedding services, and a paragraph about "romantic features." 300 p.

Military

Titles aimed at military personnel cover features at military installations (especially lodging), prerogatives for traveling on planes, and the military life. The lion's share of works in this area has been produced by Military Living Publications (www.militaryliving.com).
Subject Heading: Military bases, American—Directories.

Titles

Guide to Military Installations Worldwide / Dan Craig. 6th ed. (Stackpole Books, 2000).

For every entry there are short introductory remarks, and paragraphs after bolded headings describe the base's origin and history, the availability of housing and schools, personal services (e.g., hospital, banking), recreational opportunities, and local area attractions, which include the distance to major cities; an address and URL assist those who seek more information. Entry arrangement for the United States is under state, and for the rest of the world usually under country, with sub-arrangement by branch of the armed services. Black-and-white maps with the outlines of U.S. states and of countries show the locations of the installations. 411 p.

Military Living's European Military Travel Guide, Plus Near East Areas / William "Roy" Crawford, Sr., L. Ann Crawford, and R. J. Crawford (Military Living Publications, 2003).

Information about individual U.S. military communities is grouped into several areas by country, each one summarized in about half of a column. Telephone numbers are given for main buildings, while driving directions involve routes to take to the base or other military destination, and the subjects of temporary military lodgings and Space-A travel come with a collection of alpha-numeric figures. Also various types of retail shops, places to dine, family services, and recreations are identified. Full-page, black-and-white highway maps show the country and smaller ones offer a general outline of the installation where personnel and their dependents live. The host of special abbreviations used throughout is defined in one among a number of unique appendixes. By the same team and publisher is a parallel volume for America, *Military Living's Military Travel Guide U.S.A.* (below). 178 p.

Military Living's Military Space-A Air Opportunities: Around the World / L. Ann Crawford, William Roy Crawford (Military Living Publications, 2001).

For those in the military and others who may travel by air on a space-available basis, this directory of arrival and departure locations has sections on driving directions to these places (if they are in the United States), registration, PAX (passenger) lounges, transportation (by air, on and off base grounds, parking), TML (temporary military lodging), travelers aid, amenities (barbering, laundry, USO, etc.), and local attractions. It follows the same design as its companion *Military Living's Temporary Military Lodging around the World* (below). As well as having maps for some bases the work contains appendixes lettered from A to Z, which includes passenger regulations and personnel entrance requirements for visitors to other countries. 208 p.

Military Living's Military Travel Guide U.S.A. / William "Roy" Crawford, L. Ann Crawford, and R. J. Crawford (Military Living Publications, 2006).

The wide three-column pages provide much of the same directory information as the other Military Living Publications (above and below). An entry's terse subdivisions consist of military installation name and address, its main telephone number, directions to it, temporary military lodging facts, presence of RV and camping spots, Space-A opportunities, retail and dining places, support and family services, types of recreation, and general information (e.g., the military units assigned). Throughout phone numbers accompany the listings, which are by state, with a few pages at the book's end for U.S. possessions. A map for each state gives an idea where to find the installations. 176 p.

Military Living's Temporary Military Lodging around the World / William "Roy" Crawford, Sr. and L. Ann Crawford and R. J. Crawford (Military Living Publications, 2005).

These accommodations in the U.S., U.S. possessions, and foreign countries are arranged geographically, then by name and address of the military site (air base, fort, recreation area, etc.). Bolded headings are for the main installation's telephone numbers; its location; references to maps (which are in another title); reservation facts; amenities; likelihood and time of lodging's availability; the credit cards accepted; on and off base transportation; location of dining places; and nearby attractions. Additionally, lodgings are briefly described, with rates, after a variety of symbols and abbreviations (such as TML, VAQ, VOQ, DV/VIP, and BEQ/BOQ), the explanations for which are in a large icon guide at the front. The full-sized, three-column pages of this frequently revised directory are designed for easy scanning and ready discovery. 208 p.

Worldwide Space-A Travel Handbook and RV, Camping Guide: CONUS and Abroad. 14th ed. (Spaceatravel.com, 2004).

For travelers who use military aircraft and facilities, the directory squeezes in almost too much for its relatively compact physical size. By far the directory's largest section, "CONUS" (the continental U.S.) is broken down into the Air Force group, the Navy, and the remaining service branches that offer Space-A flights; and after that are other geographical divisions, plus a list of flight destinations and a number of appendixes. Of the several entries that crowd a page, each contains a line route map and a meal diagram along with a flurry of notes covering such matters as name and address of the installation, quarters on and off base, the available ground transportation, the flights from, costs, and telephone numbers, all of which are placed in a design that presents a challenge for the reader to decipher. 284 p.

Pets

In pet travel books dogs receive the greatest attention since they are far more likely to be taken on a trip. When traveling with a pet dog (or cat), the owner is well-advised to know the accommodations that will accept it, and most of the titles below deliver on this matter. Others discuss the shipping of pets and how laws apply. For specific advice, consider contacting one of those groups concerned with the welfare of animals or someone who works with animals, such as a veterinarian.

Bringing animals into another country may require a rabies or health certificate, import permit, and a quarantine. Inquire about this from the tourist office, embassy, or consulate of the destination country, from one of the animal organizations below, or from the airline or other shipper. In the United States the transporting of animals is guided by the Animal Welfare Act.

Should a traveler leave his or her pet at home, someone could be hired to take care of it. To find a professional try a telephone directory's yellow pages and look for the heading "Pet Sitting Services."

Subject Heading: Pets and travel

Titles and Websites

Air Travel for Your Pet (Air Transport Association). www.airlines.org

Referring to regulations from the Animal and Plant Health Inspection Service of the U.S. Department of Agriculture, this trade organization of U.S. airlines reviews shipping animals by air, preparation for a trip, interline transfers, etc. Examined website: 2008

On the Road Again with Man's Best Friend: United States / Dawn and Robert Habgood. 2nd ed. (Dawbert Press, 2000).

"Man's best friend" may also be a cat, here. Along with name and address, the lodging listings, in three columns per page, have both 800 and direct dialing, URLs, number of rooms, range of cost, brief notes on pets ("under 30 lbs. welcome," etc.) and, for owners, details of such "creature comforts" as air-conditioning, pool, and continental breakfast. With a scattering of small cartoons, practical spacing between listings, and the bolding of accommodation name and its town or city, this is a more eye-friendly book than *Travel with or without Pets* (below), as well as being physically larger and having more in each entry; though the total number are fewer. Motels, resorts, inns, lodges, and bed and breakfasts are arranged under the alphabetized state, then town or city, and there's a logo marking those that are judged best. A separate section gives lists of national and state parks that are divided between those that do and do not permit pets. Later editions limit themselves to regions of the U.S. 888 p.

Pet Travel & Fun Authority of "Best-of-State" Places to Play, Stay & Have Fun along the Way / M. E. Nelson, editor. 12th ed. (Annenberg Communications Institute, 2003).

The biggest listing is for several thousand accommodations, which take up four-fifths of the volume. Arranged by state (including the District of Columbia but excluding Hawaii, which does appear in other parts) then town or city, an entry of lodging name, street address, and telephone number is typically all there is, though price receives an occasional nod. At the beginning of each state section are several brief tourist recommendations as well as short directory categories, such as places to eat where pets are welcome, dog parks and camps, festivals, beaches, skiing, boating, best places to stay, ranches, and resorts. In back an expanded "resorts" has its own separate listing by state, as does "kennels," "petsitters," and "emergency vets." The pages are yellow and broken into four columns, with whimsical drawings throughout. Dogs are the overwhelming focus. *Traveling with Your Pet* (below) has fewer entries, but provides details. 512 p.

Pets and Wildlife: Licensing and Health Requirements. Revised (U.S. Customs Service, 2002). www.cbp.gov/ImageCache/cgov/content/ publications/pets_2epdf/v1/pets.pdf

The ten-page pamphlet discusses prohibitions, restrictions, permits, and quarantine requirements related to the importation of animals into the U.S., with sections on birds, cats, dogs, monkeys, turtles, pet rodents, game, and endangered species. Examined website: 2009

Pets Welcome: The Best and Most Informative Guide to Hotels, Motels, Inns, & Resorts That Welcome You and Your Pet: National / Nadine Guarrera and Hugo N. Gerstl. 2nd ed. (Four Paws Press, 2001).

Arranged by state, then city or town, most entries share a page together. Directory information is in three blocks, beginning with accommodation name, address, and contact details. Bolded headings lead type of lodging; room rate prices (with an occasional note of discounts for AAA, AARP, AKC, etc.); pet charges and deposits; the pet policy (e.g., "no cats"); amenities for people and for pets; and a qualitative rating that varies from two to five paws and comes with the number of rooms and suites. A paragraph might enlarge about the lodging and mention nearby attractions that are of interest to humans. The inclusion of state highway maps and a single list for the best (five paw) places to stay would have been a useful addition. Newer regional editions are available. 605 p.

The Portable Petswelcome.com: The Complete Guide to Traveling with Your Pet / Fred N. Grayson & Chris Kingsley (Howell Book House, 2001).

In addition to name, address, and telephone number in each chapter, the lodging entries for the United States and Canada have a "pet policy" statement and sometimes notes on room rates and amenities; and there may be a pet friendly icon, a "seal of approval." Nothing beyond address and telephone number exists for the chapters listing U.S. campgrounds, pet sitters (there is also a short Canadian list), kennels, and emergency vets. The work is arranged by state or province, then town, though this is hidden in the entry itself. Brief front matter has remarks on preparing the pet for travel and about different modes of travel. 428 p.

Take Your Pet Too!: Fun Things to Do! / Heather MacLean Walters (M.C.E., 2001).

Most of the book is arranged by state, beginning with a short description of a few arbitrary sights, towns, and festivals or happenings where a dog is welcome; and occasionally there are addresses of accommodations. This is followed by a list of year-round events that has name, telephone number, location, and month, but lacks any description. Several additional lists, equally spare, show parks, campgrounds, beaches, and other out-of-doors spots. The short introductory matter concerns activities (dog camps, pet fairs, etc.), tips on travel and health, and more. 499 p.

Take Your Pet USA: A Guide of Accommodations for Pets and Their Owners. Updated (Artco Publishing).

Originally published in 1990, this book has been through a number of updated reprints. This is a straightforward directory for the U.S. by state, then town, with lodging addresses followed by that of veterinarians in the area. After addresses and telephone numbers may be notes describing "pet restrictions," a yes or no answer to "pet left unattended in room" and "exercise area for pets," and "rates," the most dated part of this and other directories. Here are the chains as well as the individually owned motels and hotels. The volume should be narrow enough to fit readily in a car's glove compartment. Examined: 1992; 446 p.

Travel with or without Pets: 25,000 Pets-R-Permitted Accommodations, Petsitters, Kennels & More. 8th ed. (Annenberg Communications Institute, 1998).

The yellow color of the pages and brevity of a listing, if not the abbreviated height of the book, is reminiscent of a telephone business directory. There are four columns per page, and per column about a dozen small-type entries, which consist of name of accommodation, one or more "$" to suggest cost, address, telephone number, and an occasional laconic note—but no web address, probably due to the date of publication. Geographically arranged by state, then city or town, the directory also covers Canada and, briefly, Mexico. Besides the list of pet sitters and ABKA kennels, there is a substantial number of veterinarian addresses, plus pet travel tips, and related subjects. The "without pets" part of the title is an odd qualification, considering the text of this resource. 510 p.

Traveling by Air with Your Pet (Animal and Plant Health Inspection Service, U.S. Department of Agriculture, 1999). www.aphis.usda.gov/lpa/pubs/travel.html

This is a briefly worded rundown of APHIS shipping regulations which are designed to make sure that most warm-blooded animals are treated humanely. It reviews the age of the animal, kennel requirements, feeding and watering, health certification, and trips outside the continental United States. Examined website: 2008

"Traveling with Pets, Importation of Animals and Animal Products into the United States" (Centers for Disease Control and Prevention, U.S. Department of Health and Human Services). www.cdc.gov/ncidod/dq/animal/index.htm

The site has authoritative information about the importation of dogs, cats, and other animals into the United States and about traveling with a pet. Examined website: 2009

Traveling with Your Pet: The AAA PetBook. 10th ed. (AAA Publishing, 2008).

The American Automobile Association rates over 13,000 lodgings and campgrounds that accept dogs and cats in the U.S. and Canada. Arranged by state and province, all communities are not in strict alphabetical order, for those that fall within metropolitan areas are gathered there, but accompanying alphabetical city indexes compensate for this. Into every entry a lot is attractively packed in a small space on the two columns per page. There is a pool of around twenty symbols and abbreviations, from the *de rigueur* standards ranking of one to five diamonds (two and three are easily the most numerous) to designations for the types of lodgings, discounts, and amenities. In addition, terse directions appear, starting from a highway and to the lodging's address (with telephone listing and rates, but omitting website), while a bolded heading of "Pets" contains notes (e.g., "accepted"). Front matter has advice on traveling with pets, plus listings for dog parks, national public lands, and emergency animal clinics. Campgrounds are left in a seventeen-page section at the end of the thick volume. 736 p.

Vacationing with Your Pet: Eileen's Directory of Pet-Friendly Lodging in the United States & Canada / Eileen Barish. 6th ed. (Pet-Friendly Publications, 2007).

The title page mentions "over 25,000 listings of hotels, motels, inns, ranches and B&Bs that welcome guests with pets," which will probably be dogs, the focus of the book. Absorbing about 90 percent of the volume, the small-print entries, arranged in towns by state or province, are crammed into five columns per page with simply name, address, rates, and telephone number(s). There are neither maps nor directions to the accommodations. The front chapters talk about pet travel training, travel by car or plane, the pet's health, and other matters, plus offer some tips for human traveling. The author has written several works on traveling with one's pooch. 704 p.

Businesses and Organizations

Animal and Plant Health Inspection Service. U.S. Department of Agriculture. www.aphis.usda.gov/animal_welfare/pet_travel/pet_travel.shtml

The "Animal Welfare" page has links to information about pets. The Service is also the source for "International Animal Export Regulations" (www.aphis.usda.gov/regulations/vs/iregs/animals). Examined website: 2008

The Independent Pet and Animal Transportation Association International, Inc. www.ipata.com

Trade association members relocate animals here and abroad for both pet owners and businesses. Among other services it provides the addresses of pet shippers for which the organization vouches. Examined website: 2008

Singles

There are books which look at the advantages and pitfalls of traveling by oneself, whether by circumstance or design.

Of those companies that specialize in singles, some will have the added service of paring singles, who may wish to travel with someone out of a desire for companionship, economizing, or safety. With exceptions, the companies seem to concentrate on the older traveler, though businesses that cater to another group, the young, indirectly attract a high proportion of single travelers.

Titles about the woman who travels solo have been placed below in **Women**.

For information not directed at the solo traveler, see **Travel Advice**.

Subject Heading: Single people—Travel

Titles

Travel Alone & Love It: A Flight Attendant's Guide to Solo Travel / Sharon B. Wingler (Chicago Spectrum Press, 1996).

Personal and chatty, the compact and basic advice comes in two parts. The first covers things to think about before going away—reasons to travel alone, how to overcome fear of being self-reliant, personal safety and protection of belongings, travel insurance, what to pack and how, etc. The act of traveling itself involves short chapters on flying, jet lag, accommodations, meeting people, and a few more subjects. There is little in the book that would not also apply to any average traveler. 160 p.

Travel on Your Own: Go Now, Here's How / Marilyn Nelson Clark (Primrose Press, 1994).

Applicable to any traveler, whether or not single, this elementary guide to travel has such standard ideas as arrive early at the airport and consider public transportation. The book's main sections are "Things to Do before You Leave," "Things to Do While Traveling," and "Things to Do upon Your Return." 202 p.

Traveling Solo / Jennifer Cecil (HarperPerennial, 1992). Each of the twenty-four activity chapters has several first-person narratives from contributors about their experiences with spas, cruising, cooking, volunteering, dude ranches, skiing, etc., and about the places where they had it. The observers' informal opinions and descriptions of their adventures average a page, while at the end of each chapter additional vacation spots are briefly mentioned. 325 p.

*Traveling Solo: Advice and Ideas for More Than 250 Great Vacations / Eleanor Berman. 5th ed. (Insiders' Guide, 2005). The first two-thirds of this work is an interesting collection of group vacations, with seven chapters on types of activities (learning a sport, stretching the mind, adventure travel, etc.) and three related to types of solo travelers—the single, women, and those fifty and over. Name, address, and contact information for an entry is followed by a paragraph describing it, and some have a graphic box showing how many years the company or organization has been around, the age range attracted, the most common age group, the percent by themselves, the number of participants, the male to female ratio, and perhaps the season of operation and the opportunity for room sharing. Sometimes a follow-up comment appears from a participant, who is identified only by gender and decade of age. The second part has chapters that concern general travel advice as well as favorite cities and their eateries, and bringing kids. One index in back separates the vacations into narrower categories. This title is the most substantial of the lot about traveling alone. 302 p.

Organizations

Connecting: Solo Travel Network. www.cstn.org
This not-for-profit, international organization publishes a newsletter with complementary ads for those seeking fellow travelers, and it has singles information about tours, cruises, tips and other items. Examined website: 2008

Students
Closely allied to budget travel, the subject of travel for students invariably produces titles that showcase matter designed for this group. In addition, there are a number of organizations that cater to students and the young. Their assistance includes issuing international student id's, arranging for cheap accommodations, providing air tickets, and perhaps offering tours. Note that the organizations may be for-profit and need not be associated with an educational institution.

Many relevant sources in **Study and Travel** could as easily have fitted into this section.

Titles

Let's Go (series) (St. Martin's Press)
Around for decades and written by young adults for their peers, this series has been a standard for the student and budget traveler. Individual volumes cover countries, regions, or cities, with each having a descriptive list of cheaper accommodations and eateries, along with other practicalities of traveling, plus a recommendation of sights and the occasional presence of a shaded city map. Time sensitive data includes prices and hours, which are more likely to be realistic for those titles in this series that are updated annually. The presentation is orderly and plain. Not so closely identified with students but likely to appeal to them and other young travelers are the *Lonely Planet* and *Rough Guides* series. Examined: *Let's Go: Eastern Europe* (2006; 798 p.)

Businesses

Contiki Holidays. www.contiki.com
This long-established company offers budget tours for travelers from eighteen to thirty-five. Examined website: 2008

Women
Travel advice books for women assume they are solo or on business. While the books aim at a female audience, much advice will benefit either sex. As for women who do not wish to travel alone but prefer to go with other women, tours are available to them.
Several titles that are relevant to women are in the above sections **Business**, **Gays and Lesbians**, and **Singles**. Not included below are personal narratives by women, such as *Women Travel: First-Hand Accounts from More Than 60 Countries* (Rough Guides, 1999).
Subject Heading: Women travelers

Titles

Active Woman Vacation Guide: True Stories by Women Travelers Plus 1001 Exciting Adventure Trips / Evelyn Kaye (Blue Panda Publications, 1997).
While nearly two-thirds of the book is first-person accounts, an "A-Z Where to Find Adventure Vacations" has single-page descriptions of

select companies, many of which do not specialize in women clientele. 236 p.

50 Best Girlfriends Getaways in North America / Marybeth Bond (National Geographic, 2007).
   The ten themes of "Big City Getaways," "Spirit Boosters," "Birthday Blowouts," etc. group under each of them five localities, most being in the United States, with the others in Mexico, Canada, and the Caribbean (just one). For each getaway it is common to find section headings with the word "best," whether for day trip, sunset, or dining. Various women contribute personal travel stories related to the appropriate themes, and one is constantly reminded throughout that the perspective and audience is that of and for women. A newer edition is available. (From the same author and publisher is *Best Girlfriends Getaways Worldwide* [2008]). 263 p.

Fly Solo: The 50 Best Places on Earth for a Girl to Travel Alone / Teresa Rodriguez Williamson (Perigee Book, 2007).
   Written in a self-consciously cute and contemporary manner (as in the recurring heading "Why This Place Rocks for Flying Solo"), the work has an arrangement that is by region of the world, then by city or, a few times, by country. After an introduction, the destination is first categorized into paragraphs dealing with cultural opportunities, chances to be active, weather, and the likelihood of social interaction, each receiving a rating of from one to five. The brief advice about preparing for a trip may touch on what to read and what to pack. "The Top 10 Extraordinary Experiences" is an annotated list of things for women to enjoy; for example, in the case of Vienna there is sipping wine at a local tavern, seeing an opera, visiting a historic estate, people-watching in a park, etc. Throughout the volume a majority of the pages have graphic boxes with either tips or facts of interest. 347 p.

Handbook for Women Travellers / Maggie and Gemma Moss. Revised ed. (Piatkus, 1995).
   The double "l" in *Travellers* flags this perspective as British, and so there's a British vocabulary (e.g., "knickers") and perhaps an earthier approach than in the book's American equivalents. Since it references traveling on a budget in Third World countries, the advice is often plain and practical, as it examines such issues as what clothes to bring and how to dress in a foreign culture, health situations unique to women, the presence of poverty, making contact with native people, and personal

safety. Throughout the chapters there are brief quotes by unidentified women travelers. 288 p.

The Independent Woman's Guide to Europe / Linda White (Fulcrum Publishing, 1991).

Based on the author's experience of traveling alone, the discussions concern finding a room, meeting people, being secure, observing customs, how to look good and feel fit, and other matters, all of which come with her anecdotes from European countries. Unlike the earlier subject advice approach, the final four chapters are arranged by country (accommodations, transportation, shopping, and "additional information"), though only the first of them can be said to be aimed at women through its listing of select hotels, etc. 220 p.

A Journey of One's Own: Uncommon Advice for the Independent Woman Traveler / Thalia Zepatos. 3rd ed. (The Eighth Mountain Press, 2003).

Based on her experiences in countries around the world, the author offers thoughtful opinions on both typical and less common travel subjects. The book opens with a consideration of the advantages of traveling solo or with a partner (or one's children) and suggests purposes for a journey, such as genealogy research or volunteering. There is also one chapter about varieties of cultural interaction (e.g., bargaining), another about dealing with sexual harassment and with safety issues, and a final one that focuses on the planning involved in an extended trip. The chapter order is unusual, with the discussion about packing, choosing a camera and guidebooks, researching the best season to go, etc., toward the end. There is the occasional mini-essay related to particular experiences of Zepatos and other women travelers. 349 p.

Safety and Security for Women Who Travel / Sheila Swan and Peter Laufer. 2nd ed. (Travelers' Tales, 2004).

Besides more usual matter, chapters reflect an interesting range of subjects: driving, having the right attitude, encountering strangers, etc. There are suggestions about precautions to take in the matter of seeing a doctor before a trip, home security, things to bring on a journey, solving situations abroad, and the like. The authors fill the book with personal travel anecdotes and follow them with a battery of various tips. Thus, in a chapter about interaction with officials, a story of a traffic accident in Germany precedes a number of compact remarks, among them handling rogue cops and dealing with cash bribes. Though some of the episodes discussed are very serious, it is noted at book's end that they are also unlikely to befall most travelers. Advice from others appears in boxes throughout. 153 p.

The Single Woman's Travel Guide / Jacqueline Simenauer and Doris Walfield (Citadel Press, 2001).
Oddly, the woman traveler doesn't strongly figure in the perspective. The first fifth of the work resembles a typical travel advice guide for any new traveler, while the remainder gathers packaged tours and trips, with themes including the best of Europe and the South Pacific, women only, families, adventure outings, spas, and cruises. Entries for packages may have company name and address, places on the itinerary, a profile of a particular trip, number of meals and kinds of accommodations, characteristics of fellow travelers (e.g., single), the price, and the authors' opinions about the experience. The chapter on spas has a section on facilities, and for the handful of cruise lines mentioned there are references to single accommodations. Several remarks about finding romance can lead the reader to unfulfilled expectations. 194 p.

Travel Tips for the Sophisticated Woman: Over 1,000 Practical Tips on Enjoying Museums, Shopping, Performances, Dining, Chocolate, Looking Great, and More while Traveling in Europe and North America / Laura Vestanen (Xlibris Corporation, 2001).
A wide range of topics comes amid a mixture of both advice and facts. The former is evidenced by the paragraphs on the pros and cons of tours; how to pack and the clothes to take (that together gets nearly fifty pages); plane travel; being secure (complete with a multiple answer quiz); staying healthy; eating on one's own and finding the right food; manners; tipping; bringing gifts; and using cybercafés. Among the facts are lists of tourist offices, definitions of travel terms, museums to visit, and an architectural glossary. The title's word "sophisticated" might suggest an emphasis on how one dresses or finesses social situations as well as the appreciation of creature comforts, but the word "intelligent" could have fairly replaced it. Having a more judicious use of personal anecdotes than in some related titles, this work also appears to have a soft cover version. 349 p.

The Traveling Woman: Great Tips for Safe and Healthy Trips / Catherine Comer and Lavon Swaim (Impact Publications, 2001).
The woman's view is chiefly evident here through its high regard for safety and taking care of oneself, particularly the former. Otherwise there is a good deal of basic advice about traveling abroad for someone who wants to go on her own, rather than traveling with her family, a partner, or in a group. Among the topics discussed are what resources to use in

researching a destination, choosing safe transportation, and booking accommodations with security in mind. Throughout the authors' experiences are used as examples. The work concludes with an annotated list of favorite websites for women travelers. 173 p.

Wanderlust and Lipstick: The Essential Guide for Women Traveling Solo / Beth Whitman (Globe Trekker Press, 2007).

Omitting destination descriptions, this is concerned solely with doling out travel advice for the woman traveling on her own, though much is non-gender-specific. The assumption appears to be that the traveler is inexperienced, so the observations that fill up the text are basic and try to incorporate as much as could be expected. The opening chapters explore reasons to travel solo, what to do on a trip, and overcoming the different excuses that hold someone back. Further on are discussions about forms of transportation—not excluding bicycles and motorcycles—plus handling red tape, what to pack, keeping safe and healthy, making acquaintances, dealing with language barriers, and the like. Now and again the author's or another woman's personal story is introduced as a warning or suggestion. 258 p.

Women Going Places 1996/1997: A Women's Complete Guide to International Travel. 2nd ed. (Women Going Places, 1996).

A bit larger than a paperback, the directory has two-column pages packing a lot of names, addresses, and telephones numbers, which are arranged by country and city, then by type of business or concern (publication, bookstore, café, religious group, etc.), many of which are lesbian-related. A majority of the entries have short descriptions, frequently with recommendations, and there are some ads. Localities in the United States account for one-half of this work's bulk. 713 p.

Businesses

AdventureWomen, Inc. www.adventurewomen.com
This company provides active adventure trips for women over thirty. Examined website: 2008

VIDEO, DVDs, AND TELEVISION

Travel videos and DVDs conventionally serve as travelogues, although practical advice may occasionally supplement the pleasing pictures that boost their product in the possible hope of converting viewers into visitors. Some are used for promotion by travel agencies, tourist organizations, cruise lines, and other groups. But however much they publicize and propagandize, they do present a vivid sense of place that a guidebook cannot match.

Buy videos and DVDs from bookstores (both brick and online), borrow them from libraries, and watch the images at websites.

There are several comprehensive catalogs of current audio-visual material, with "travel" one among a variety of subject groups indexed. Media distributors and publishers also have their catalogs. Videos and DVDs which are part of a series may list these titles on the container, and at any rate the publisher should list them.

Television occasionally touches on a travel concern through news, documentaries, or perhaps a drama set in an eye-catching locale. In particular PBS has regularly, if indirectly, dealt with travel through its nature programs and has had an occasional series whose theme is travel, as those hosted by Michael Palin or Rick Steves. Coming across a news show segment on travel is usually a matter of serendipity, whereas documentaries and dramas may, at least, have their contents described in *TV Guide* and similar magazines. Through some websites that offer television schedules a search may result in listings related to travel.

Among the special interest cable channels that have developed, the Travel Channel takes an exclusive but mostly uncritical examination of places and services for its audience of potential travelers. Another development is hotel televisions that have a channel set aside to advertise local shopping and other attractions.

Subject Heading: DVD—Video discs—Catalogs; Video recordings—Catalogs

Titles

Spencer's Complete Guide to Special Interest Videos: More Than 12,000 Videos You've Never Seen / James R. Spencer. 4th ed. (James-Robert Publishing, 1998).

This general mail-order catalog for videos has one chapter on "Travel & Adventure," which is arranged into geographical and topical sections. Each travel video listed has an order number, length in minutes, price, title, and copyright date; occasional information is the ISBN number and whether the video is available in PAL, which is the technical format in much of Europe and other areas. The short summary of a video's contents uses travel brochure rhetoric ("unique," "magnificent," etc.). There are many series titles, which are set off by red banners at their beginning and end. 746 p.

The Video Source Book. Annual (Thomson Gale).

For those who might be interested in watching travel programs, three large volumes list them as well as a multitude of currently available videos. A subject index in the final volume has a heading for "Travel," under which is gathered a list of titles that are found alphabetized in the main part of the catalog, where title and year of release are followed by a summary of the contents, the intended audience, the distributor, the item's cost, and other facts. A video catalog with a similar purpose, *Bowker's Complete Video Directory,* also has an index heading for travel. Examined: 37th ed. (2006; 3 vol. [4375 p.])

Businesses

Pilot Productions. www.pilotguides.com

Among it travel series, the company offers for sale episodes of *Globe Trekker* (broadcast on PBS), where travelers visit worldwide destinations. Examined website: 2008

Questar. www.questar1.com

The producer and distributor has many individual and series travel titles, including *Video Visits* (typical titles begin with the word *Discovering* followed by a country name) and *Reader's Digest Classic Collection.* Examined website: 2008

WALKS AND HIKES

See the landscape from a pair of walking shoes on a ramble through the countryside for several hours or several days. From a travel guide the walker or hiker should obtain details about the route, the length and time of the trip, and the type of terrain. Since the guide is to be taken in the field, its size should be compact enough to fit in an accessible pocket.

Adventure and outdoor companies arrange group walks and hikes, which are publicized in walking and outdoor magazines. Visit camping supply stores for footwear, compasses, ordinance maps, and whatever else is appropriate.

See also **Adventure Travel** and **Recreation, Sports, and Ranch Vacations**.

Subject Heading: Hiking; Walking

Titles

America's Greatest Walks: A Traveler's Guide to 100 Scenic Adventures / Gary Yanker and Carol Tarlow (Addison-Wesley, 1986).

Walks are through both cities and state and national parks. Each walk has directions where to begin it, the best season to enjoy oneself, a length in distance and amount of time taken, the degree of difficulty affected by ruggedness and steepness, and the sights that are seen. Divided into geographical areas of the United States, the arrangement allots at least one walk for each state as well as for Washington, D.C., and the Virgin Islands. A plain map traces each route. Although the scope of this title is national, numerous guides by state have also been published, as an online library catalog search can reveal when using such terms as "hiking" plus the state name. 257 p.

Backpacker. 9 per year (Active Interest Media). www.backpacker.com

The magazine has articles about backpacking, equipment, outdoor activities, fitness, trails to take, safety, climbing, etc. Examined: issues from 2008

Classic Walks in Western Europe / Gillian & John Souter (Wilderness Press, 2001).

With its large size and color photos, its design is reminiscent more of a coffee table book, and it is better suited to be consulted before or after a walk rather than during one. Whether it is returning to a single base or going a single direction for several overnights, each walk is broken down by the daily distance to be covered and the time it takes, scenery for that day, and in italics the directions along the route. Maps are in several colors and are cartoonish in general; there are representations of routes, mountains, buildings, overnight stops, and other objects. A "notes" section at the end of each major walk has public transportation, where to leave excess luggage, names of maps, accommodations, useful addresses, etc. 160 p.

Climber's and Hiker's Guide to the World's Mountains and Volcanos / Michael R. Kelsey. 4th ed. (Kelsey Publishing, 2001).

In this thick volume with its prodigious array of entries for mountains and volcanoes, arrangement is by five continents, with separate treatments for the Pacific and (in one grouping) for Mexico, Central America, and the Caribbean. Following no standard pattern, the collection of paragraphs for an entry may discuss a place's location, means of getting there prior to the climb, where to stock up, camping issues, charges, the route and the length of time it takes, and more. There are 650 black-and-white photos, and the 584 maps that have wriggly lines and scales in kilometers may display any of dozens of symbols for both manmade structures and natural features, such as peaks and ridges. If the author has climbed a peak, he writes about it. 1248 p.

The Essential Guide to Nature Walking in the United States / Charles Cook (Henry Holt, 1997).

This concentrates chiefly on national and state parks, of which ten are described for every state, and they come with outline maps. The brief description gives physical features (hills, vistas, etc.), kinds of flora and fauna, and whether there are nature centers or guided walks. This is followed just by the names of several nature trails and their distance. The end of each chapter suggests a few addresses for discovering other suitable nature walks in that state. 274 p.

Fodor's Short Escapes (series) (Fodor's Travel Publications).

There's a history and natural history for each country walk, a how to get there by car, and "walk directions," which has the number of hours that the walk takes, its distance, its difficulty, means of access (car, etc.), and the directions themselves arranged in numbered steps. Black-and-white shaded maps point out the route, and there are observations on stops to see, to dine at, and to stay at. The same size of a paperback book, for each walk it also has tourist office addresses and a short "For Serious Walkers." Occasional bolded text warns about problem flora and fauna, weather difficulties, or trail steepness. Britain, France, and New York City are some of the places described within this series. Examined: *Short Escapes Near Boston* (1999; 264 p.)

The Independent Walker's Guide (series) (Interlink Books).

This is a series from a publisher who has produced a number of walking guides, chiefly for European localities. In the case of France, day hikes measure between five and six miles. A general review of the surroundings is followed by headings that cover optional maps available; time and distance of the walk; any climbs; toilet facilities and amount of privacy; refreshments; getting to the walk by train or bus; notes for guidance on the trail; and suggestions for more walking. Additionally there are simple maps, advice for walkers, and walks arranged thematically. Examined: *The Independent Walker's Guide to France* / Frank W. Booth (1996; 206 p.)

Lonely Planet Walking Guide (series) (Lonely Planet).

Front material offers facts about the country, about traveling, and about walking and hiking. The polished layout of double columns, headings, occasional use of colors, and marked edges provide for ready reference when the book is being consulted on the trail. Before narrative details and directions, countryside walks are encapsulated in terms of duration and distance of walks, level of difficulty (easy, moderate, demanding), start and finish locales, nearest town, any public transportation, and an evaluative summary. Also having remarks about places to stay and eat as well as about culture, natural history, etc., the work is punctuated by illustrations and boxed asides on individual regions, and it supplements its text through route maps with heights and general contours of each area covered. Lonely Planet is one of the major publishers of travel guidebooks. Examined: *Walking in France* / Sandra Bardwell and others. 2nd ed. (2004; 368 p.)

Sunflower Landscapes (series) (Sunflower Books).

After a rundown of picnic spots and a guide to eight driving tours, the remaining two-thirds of the work shows numerous walks, identifying their distance in kilometers and miles, describing the grades of difficulty, listing equipment that should be taken, and giving driving directions to the start, and accommodation possibilities. Entries also have paragraphs with directions and sights, color route maps, and color photographs of the area. The book offers a fold-out road map of the area and is narrow enough to fit in a back jeans pocket, though it may stick out. The series is also known as *The Landscapes Series* and *A Sunflower Countryside Guide*. Examined: *Landscapes of Sicily: A Countryside Guide* / Peter Amann (2001; 136 p.)

Walking America: The 1993-94 Guide to More Than 400 Walking Trails /
Judith Galas and Cindy West (West Press, 1993).

Arrangement is by state. An entry opens with a section that has the
town or other location where the self-directed walk begins, name of the
walk, dates when it is available (many are January 1-December 31), and
the (likely outdated) name with phone number of the person to call for
more information. There are three bolded headings with text. The first
provides the numeric level of difficulty, from 1 (suitable for wheelchairs,
etc.) and 1+ (not for wheelchairs) to 5 (demanding); and follows with a
description of sights. The second has suggestions for other sights and
activities, such as bicycling. The third offers brief directions on where to
start the walk, plus driving directions to the town or spot. There are no
maps, and the odd photo is in black-and-white. Despite its year of
publication, the book does have a convenient collection of walks available
through the continental United States. 232 p.

Organizations and Publishers

American Hiking Society. www.americanhiking.org

Producer of the magazine *American Hiker,* this conservation and
recreation group has a link, "Volunteer Vacations," that provides a list of
opportunities to build or maintain trails on public lands. Examined
website: 2008

American Volkssport Association. www.ava.org/index.htm

Allied to the International Volkssport Federation, the network of non-
competitive walking clubs offers organized events. Its official publication
is the bimonthly *The American Wanderer* which has features, a list of
clubs, and a calendar of events. Examined website: 2008

Mountaineers Books. www.mountaineersbooks.org

The publishing arm of the Mountaineers organization, Mountaineers
Books offers works that concentrate on the Northwest and the West,
though it also covers other regions where there is mountaineering,
trekking, and outdoor-related topics. Examined website: 2008

WALKS (CITY)

Walking through a city is the best way to see it in detail and experience its everyday life. Rather than wander around without aim, discover a route so thought-out that it goes to the important tourist sites in the most efficient way. This has been accomplished by city and town walking guides, which combine directions, site descriptions, and maps. There are also guidebooks that, while not advertising themselves as walking guides, plan much of their text around walks, as in the *Michelin Green Guides* series for cities or in certain *Eyewitness Travel Guides* (DK).

Since a proper walking guidebook is designed to be brought along, it should be compact and pocketable, able to be pulled out and read as needed. Route maps should be visually clear in defining the streets to be passed and correlate with the text both in how to get to each sight and identify where it is. The text must be clear on use of landmarks and other permanent cues as it points out left and right turns. Distance, time of the walk, and its physical demand are important knowledge for a participant.

In choosing a guide with walks determine the amount and kind of information it offers, and if it visits sights worth viewing. There are a handful of cities that attract walking guides, London probably the most, but also New York, Paris, and others.

A city's tourist information centers may sell or give away pamphlets containing self-guided walks. At any rate obtain maps there and ask the staff about possible routes.

Both non-profit organizations and for-profit companies offer short walking tours. If willing to invest a few hours in one, check about it either online, at tourist centers or, for schedules, the activities calendar of a local newspaper. In addition, tourist magazines for specific cities may list walks along with a variety of cultural events.

A type of self-guided walking tour uses audio to supply instructions on where to go and what to see. (Whether the format is cassette, CD, or mp3, the tourist will have to carry a player, which could add a slight encumbrance to a walk.) The format may be rented or sold at museums, historic sites, and similar attractions. Also, order titles from audio catalogs.

Subject Heading: Walking—[plus geographic name]

Titles

Frommer's Memorable Walks (series) (Wiley Publishing).
If this edition of the London volume were somewhat smaller it might have fit in a back pocket. It is arranged by neighborhoods, with each chapter beginning with a brief layout of important facts (the underground stations where the walk starts and finishes, its duration, and the best and worst times of the day to take it). After delving into a local area's past and significance, the text gives directions to perhaps two dozen numbered stops of interest, such as churches, pubs, shops, and streets whose historic associations are discussed. For each walk there is one recommended refreshment stop whose treats are mentioned. Separate shaded street maps trace the paths traveled, and the attractions along the way are distinguished by the numbers next to them in the text. The tube (metro) map on the inside back cover is without color and difficult to read. Examined: *Frommer's Memorable Walks in London* / Richard Jones. 5th ed. (2003; 178 p.)

Henry Holt Walks Series (series) (Henry Holt).
Two inches taller than a regular paperback, the volume in this series of smooshed titles (*Pariswalks*, *Jerusalemwalks*, etc.) has a brief front section of general city information and a brief back section noting some museums, hotels, restaurants, and shops, which may also be mentioned in the separate walks' chapters. Gray-shaded maps for each of the four individual walks in *Berlinwalks* use arrows for waymarks, but omit highlighting of the stops that are discussed in the accompanying text, where names are bolded. While CD titles that begin *Walk & Talk* (Recorded Books) are based on volumes from this series, there have been few updated text editions after the 1990s. Examined: *Berlinwalks* (1994; 221 p.)

Rick Steves' Best European City Walks & Museums / Rick Steves & Gene Openshaw (Avalon Travel, 2005).
Although in this mixture of walking and museum tours the latter outnumber the former, it is the walks that are the focus of this review. Each of the featured cities of London, Paris, Amsterdam, Venice, Florence, Rome, and Madrid is allocated a single walk that covers an interesting route. Drawn black-and-white maps highlight the position of numbered stopping points, which the text discusses in terms of their history and importance; inconveniently, their names are not numbered as they are on the map (except for the London tour), and the directions might have been more detailed. Recognizing there might be a packing issue with

the book's bulk (eight inches tall and slightly more than half as wide), the authors suggest ripping out the unneeded chapters, and offer conditions for replacement. Those seeking more European walks in a volume might consider *Turn Right at the Fountain* (below). 473 p.

Tapeguide (series) (Penton Overseas).
Each cassette describes a European city. The voice of a man and woman alternate in giving histories at sites and what to look for along the walker's route. As if obeying the tape instructions in museum self-guided tours, the listener is told when to turn on and off the cassette player. An accompanying color map traces the route clearly, but gives few names to streets, which are graphically lacking in details. Examined: *Triumphant Paris* (1990; approximately 45 minutes)

Turn Right at the Fountain: Fifty-Three Walking Tours through Europe's Most Enchanting Cities / George W. Oakes, with new and additional research material by Alexandra Chapman. 5th revised ed. (Henry Holt and Company, 1996).
The classic guide presents twenty-one cities in Western Europe, plus the Czech Republic and Hungary, and save for a few smaller cities each comes with at least two walks. Narrative paragraphs have facts and appreciations about the museums, monuments, churches, and other sights as they are encountered; the sight names are bolded, allowing them to be readily found. Usually extending to two pages, a city walking map is in clear black-and-white and typically bristles with several routes, though it would have been better for every route to have its own map. The book is too large for a pocket, but a walker could carry it by hand to more easily consult it. For a slicker work that also contains photos (and is more compact despite having a bigger page count) see *Rick Steves' Best European City Walks & Museums* (above). 380 p.

WEATHER

Unfortunately too few places on the globe have claim to perfect weather. The intrusion of rain, heat, humidity or cold can mess up a trip. Then there is the matter of having the wrong clothes for a climate. Defensive strategies are to time a visit when the weather is most agreeable or have handy a jacket, umbrella, or whatever else is appropriate.

Learn what to expect. Reliable predictions on country weather patterns are in several books. They have data on daily temperatures (high, low, and average), rainfall, wind chill, relative humidity, and more, all of which greatly amplify the brief summaries that occur in country guidebooks.

A ready way to find current weather conditions and forecasts is to go to online sources. Consult websites of cities or countries. Or do a search for the words "weather" and the name of the destination. Or visit a weather website, say www.wunderground.com or the Weather Channel's www. weather.com.

Hear up-to-date weather news through the telephone (check under "Weather Forecast Service" in various telephone directory yellow pages) or through radio and television channels. Television broadcasts range from local news programs with a weather segment to the Weather Channel, which is all weather.

It may be online or in print, but a common source for weather forecasts is the newspaper. To find print newspapers from elsewhere, try a library, which may have subscriptions from out of state and other countries. Some newspapers are not limited by location. For example, *USA Today* has weather reports for different spots in the United States and temperatures for world cities.

Subject Headings: Weather; Climatology

Titles

Fodor's World Weather Guide / E. A. Pearce and C. G. Smith (Random House, 1998).

There is a lot in digestible format. In the alphabetical arrangement, a country is compactly discussed in terms of its location, altitude, geography, and climate. However, most of the easy-to-scan facts are presented through a chart or charts of rows and columns for one or more cities in the country. Next to every month are figures for daily hours of sunshine, and the centigrade and Fahrenheit for average temperatures, as well as those that have been the highest and lowest recorded. Relative humidity is given as a percentage while average monthly precipitation is in millimeters and inches, as are wet days, which must be over a certain amount of moisture to be listed. One column without figures is "Discomfort from heat and humidity," and if it is not left blank shows terms beginning with "moderate" and ending in "extreme," according to month. At the beginning are shaded maps, each representing large sections of the world. 453 p.

The Traveler's Weather Guide / Tom Loffman (Ten Speed Press, 1996).

The arrangement is geographical, and short introductions have suggestions about the best time to visit regions of the contiguous United States, Alaska, Hawaii, Canada, Mexico, parts of Europe, Africa, and other areas throughout the world. Following each introduction are several city charts containing per-month average high and low temperatures, amount of humidity, precipitation by number of days and inches, and snowfall in inches. 119 p.

The Weather Almanac: A Reference Guide to Weather, Climate, and Related Issues in the United States and Its Key Cities. 10th ed. (Gale Group, Thomson Learning, 2001)

The traveler who is searching for casual approximations of the kind of weather to expect in a certain month could be swallowed up in the commotion of meteorological data. An encyclopedic first half explains about weather extremes (heat and humidity, thunderstorms, floods, etc.). Following this are climate overviews and detailed tables of monthly normals, means, and extremes for certain U.S. cities. Besides high and low temperatures, there is the percent of daily sunshine, the mean number of cloudy days in a month, average wind speed and prevailing direction, maximum and minimum of precipitation, etc.; and historic tables show weather trends through the years. Foreign countries receive a little recognition from tables limited to temperature and precipitation. A later edition is available. 786 p.

World Traveler: What's the Climate? What to Wear? (Advantage Quest, 1989).

The work is convenient for bringing together in easy-to-find format simple weather information about select world cities, arranged by country. A table on each page gives, by month, a city's maximum and minimum temperatures in both Fahrenheit and Centigrade, humidity percentage, and the number of its rain or snow days. Then follows a brief description of its climate with subsections about each season and the suitable clothing that should be worn. A "dress notes" suggests what to wear in the city for the business or touring traveler. U.S. cities are by far the most numerous, and not every country is represented. 210 p.

Organizations

National Oceanic and Atmospheric Administration. National Weather Service. www.nws.noaa.gov
    The site offers forecasts for towns and cities in the United States and has links to other weather related information. Examined website: 2008

WORK

Combine work and travel. Books, periodicals, and organizations tell how to find a job or volunteer overseas. In the former case, defray the expenses of traveling by earning money on the road, commonly through such entry level employment as food services, migrant labor, and domestic help. Picking up a language or discovering new attitudes may be two of the educational benefits that accrue.

There are also the types of jobs that require travel—the air courier, the car transporter, and the buyer abroad (see **Air Travel, Automobile and Recreational Vehicle Travel**, and **Shopping**). Then there are jobs within the vast travel industry itself which, though outside the scope of *Travel Resources*, are discussed in such a volume as *Inside Secrets to Finding a Career in Travel* (JIST Works, 2001) by Karen Rubin. (To perform a library subject search for books of this nature, use the terms "Travel agents—Vocational guidance.")

The right kinds of skills are pivotal to land jobs, either in your own hometown or half-way across the earth. It also helps to be lucky. Those who go into professions that target working overseas can check such an online site as International Jobs Center (www.internationaljobs.org), whose publications include *International Career Employment Weekly*.

Work-for-profit travel books may have sections on unpaid volunteering, while another category of works devote themselves exclusively to volunteer opportunities.

There are those who volunteer to work for science or society. Science projects welcome helpers, whether in digging up prehistory or studying animals. To join a team of scientists, find addresses in the volunteer directories below or contact such an organization as Earthwatch (likewise below). Universities, institutes, and similar groups are also sources. Checking science magazines written for non-professionals can be productive; for example, some archaeology publications advertise for non-paid participants.

Volunteers in social services may find themselves helping the American Hiking Society build a trail, working with Habitat for Humanity to raise a house, or joining with others at a work camp, which is a way of meeting people from other countries. As with the previous advice on science work, for opportunities see volunteer directories and contact the appropriate organizations.

A job exchange is another means to work elsewhere. Switch places with someone or see if an exchange can be one way. A number of professional organizations have programs to implement exchanges for their own members. Those who belong to one might wish to look into this.

Also be aware of job exchange organizations.

An obvious source of assistance is commercial ventures. Placement agencies may be able to locate openings for their clients abroad.

Paid Work

Subject Headings: Employment in foreign countries; Americans— Employment—Foreign countries

Titles

American Jobs Abroad / edited by Victoria Harlow, Edward W. Knappman (Gale Research, 1994).

Advice on living and working abroad is followed by an alphabetical order of companies, descriptions lay out their total U.S. employees abroad, where offices are, any language requirements, etc. The next largest section is a discussion of what it is like to live and work in a number of countries, with the pros and cons. 882 p.

The Back Door Guide to Short-Term Job Adventures: Internships, Summer Jobs, Seasonal Work, Volunteer Vacations, and Transitions Abroad / Michael Landes. 4th ed. (Ten Speed Press, 2005).

The bodies listed and described are not big businesses, but socially involved organizations, foundations, public service institutions, and related groups, and these are categorized under "adventure jobs," "camps, ranches, and resort jobs," "artistic and learning pursuits," and so forth. An entry is in three parts, beginning with name, category, location, duration, web address, and several icons (e.g., whether pay is given). A central section, sometimes divided through subheadings, provides a description of the organization's purpose, work expectations, and the like, while a block of contact information completes everything. With a good deal of self-help encouragement and remarks designed to inspire, the directory's front section offers advice about finding the right job fit. Among the indexes in back are those by category, geographical location, and program length. 584 p.

Culture Shock! Living and Working Abroad / Monica Rabe (Graphics Arts Center Publishing, 1997).

The work furnishes details about adjustments to living abroad, whether as a temporary or as an expatriate. It starts with the move from home, goes into the familiarization process for people and their family to a new place, looks at such challenges as language and communication, and examines the special psychological pressures on those living abroad, pressures that continue with the return home. 150 p.

The Daily Telegraph Guide to Working Abroad / Godfrey Golzen, Helen Kogan. 22nd ed. (Kogan Page, 2000).

An audience of businesspeople will receive less help on finding a job than consideration of how living abroad affects the family and health, how to manage finance, and how to move back home when the time comes. One-third of the book deals with individual countries, which have brief sections on their economy, personal finance and taxation, working conditions, and useful information (climate, driving, etc.). 358 p.

The Directory of Websites for International Jobs: The Click and Easy Guide / Ronald L. Krannich, Caryl Rae Krannich (Impact Publications, 2002).

The Krannichs have staked out the subject of the internet and travel (see their *Travel Planning on the Internet* under **Computers and the Internet**). Like *International Job Finder* (below), *Directory* is a collection of websites, but while the former work is arranged geographically, here only one chapter (though the largest) is by country and region, the rest being categorized by the subjects of executive recruiters, expatriates, publishers, non-profits, education, etc. Another difference is that in this directory, relatively few websites are described, with the majority presented as name and address only, so such factors as coverage, design, and navigation remain unexplored. As with any book listing internet sites, some of the latter will have changed, disappeared, or died by the time of publication. 150 p.

The Directory of Work & Study in Developing Countries / edited by Toby Milner. 3rd ed. (Vacation Work, 1997).

With the focus on Africa, Asia, the Caribbean, and other parts of the Third World, the arrangement is geographical, starting from worldwide. Receiving a substantial description of what they are and offer, the associations in this collection provide opportunities in paid employment, helping through volunteer work, and study. The first two categories are generally broken down into various types of work such as those involved with agriculture, health care, religion, and teaching; while one grouping consists of entities that are sources for information. There is also special attention to government organizations, commercial and non-governmental organizations, and the United Nations. In the smallest section, "study," universities and formal groups related to education make up the entries. Throughout is a strong British flavor. 253 p.

Great Jobs Abroad / Arthur H. Bell (McGraw-Hill, 1997).

There is advice on what job hunting skills are necessary, preparing for an international interview, legalities, and other subjects. A list of types of jobs available abroad (e.g., cook, tutor) comes with a line or so about them. The chapters containing company descriptions and contacts omit websites, which were hardly pervasive when compared with today. Time also catches up with the longest section (at almost one hundred pages), "An Entrepreneur's Directory to Foreign Service Officers," which has outdated lists of people. (However, a partial remedy is the State Department's *Key Officers of Foreign Service Posts* at www.state.gov.) 378 p.

How to Be an Importer and Pay for Your World Travel / Mary Green and Stanley Gillmar (Ten Speed Press, 1993).

This is based on the experience of the authors, who provide advice on where to travel and what to buy, locating an item and bargaining for it, then how to get it home and sell it. There's a look at pitfalls (what if the shipped item never arrives?), who the customers might be, customs, clothing sizes, etc. 221 p.

How to Find an Overseas Job with the U.S. Government: A Complete & Comprehensive Guide / Will Cantrell and Francine Modderno (World-Wise Books, 1992).

The book is arranged by federal agency (Department of State, Department of Defense, and others) and presents an overview of functions; subarrangement is by job, with description, necessary qualifications, the acceptance process, and the career progression or perks. A back part brings attention to the Foreign Service Exam and filling out government forms. An occupational index eases searching by job. (For newer information on this topic contact the agency or its website, or consult the separate chapter "Overseas Employment Opportunities" in *The Book of U.S. Government Jobs* by Dennis V. Damp [10th ed.; Bookhaven Press, 2008]). 421 p.

How to Get a Job in Europe / Cheryl Matherly and Robert Sanborn. 5th ed. (Planning/Communications, 2003).

The first part is concerned with "how to," but is nonetheless filled with helpful publication titles and addresses. Among its chapters are those about a nine-step search for getting a job in Europe, the making of an international resume, the economic trends in Europe, international professional careers, summer and temporary jobs, and teaching English abroad. The substantially larger second part has a profile for each European country that includes introductory facts; a description of the current economic climate; a paragraph or so on employment regulations and the outlook for Americans; and two-column addresses of American and European companies, which are grouped by type. The profile also contains a short, annotated list of internship programs and volunteer opportunities, job seeker websites (also with annotations), more addresses, and business directory titles. 496 p.

International Job Finder: Where the Jobs Are Worldwide / Daniel Lauber with Kraig Rice (Planning/Communications, 2002).

After introductory advice on finding jobs, the collection fills the bulk of its space with abundant entries. Logically, arrangement is geographic, with "worldwide" leading the way. All seven continents receive attention, though Antarctica has only one listing (for jobs with the National Science Foundation). The majority of the sources are associations, companies, and services with websites; after name and URL a description consists of a block of sentences that may include the number of positions available, ways of navigating the site, comments about its features, how to post a resume, and similar. Books from such recognized reference publishers as Gale and Hoover are also described. Especially for the job seeker willing to use a computer, this is an extensive and valuable utility. 348 p.

International Jobs Directory / Ronald L. Krannich, Caryl Rae Krannich. 3rd ed. (Impact Publications, 1999).

After an academic-toned overview, the list of contacts is divided into ten areas: the U.S. federal government, international organizations, businesses with international interests, consulting firms, teaching abroad, internships, etc. The areas' introductory comments to help the job seeker lead to the entries, each consisting of name, address, telephone and fax number, URL and, except in some categories, several lines of description. A closing chapter suggests various sources that will assist in a search for jobs. 323 p.

International Jobs: Where They Are, How to Get Them / Nina Segal, Eric Kocher. 6th ed. (Basic Books, 2003).

With its professional, business-like attitude the text appears aimed at people who plan on a fulltime career in the international market. The first part looks at the preparation for acquiring an international job, and that includes suggestions about getting internships and earning an academic degree, plus there's a presentation of sample resumes. The international job field is examined in the second part which, while sharing with similar works some categories (the federal government, teaching, etc.), has others for the less common subjects of banking, communications, and law. Chapters have introductory commentary before a selection of hiring organizations or companies, and these come with name, address, telephone number, and website, and are usually followed by a solid profile of their background, goals, internships offered, and job openings. 354 p.

Jobs and Careers Abroad / Deborah Penrith. 12th ed. (Vacation Work Publications, 2005).

As with other Vacation Work titles, the outlook is British. The introductory part that includes advice about doing a job search and enhancing employability also provides a rundown of resources and placement organizations. A subsequent range of chapters discusses specific careers (au pair, journalism, mining, transport, voluntary work, etc.) and comes with descriptive lists of places to apply. International organizations and related broad sources are similarly treated. The work's second half is a selection of countries, the majority in Europe, and aside from general facts about them the focus is on those qualities of chief interest to prospective employees. From country to country the amount of attention and subsections vary; some of the more frequent ones deal with immigration, teaching, voluntary work, and short term work. Among the supplementing addresses are those for local embassies and newspapers, where job ads may be placed. A later edition is available. 446 p.

Jobs for People Who Love to Travel: Opportunities at Home and Abroad / Ronald L. Krannich and Caryl Rae Krannich. 3rd ed. (Impact Publications, 1999).

With discerning examination this book reviews getting jobs and the places to get them. It includes a self-test on travel, a discussion of travel motivations, and a list of mistaken expectations many people entertain. Having employment overviews and descriptions of specific jobs, chapters are categorized into the travel and hospitality industry, government, international education, teaching, business, and other areas. A glance at other titles under **Work** demonstrates how prolific the Krannich team is. 291 p.

Opportunities in Overseas Careers / Blythe Camenson. Revised ed. (VGM Career Books, 2005).

Another book of advice, it doesn't go into great depth but broadly considers general types of jobs—private business, medical, etc.—and, too briefly, the experience of living overseas. Among chapters are those concerned with finding a situation, working in the Foreign Service, and enlisting in the Peace Corps. However, there is an emphasis on opportunities in education, with a chapter apiece on teaching English as a foreign language and teaching at Department of Defense and international schools; while the longest of the appendixes is a collection of selected employment contacts for teachers. Additional appendixes have resources with addresses and websites and a list of job-related publications. 172 p.

Summer Jobs Worldwide Annual (Crimson Publishing).

Known as *Summer Jobs Abroad* when it was put out by another British-based publisher, Vacation Work, *Summer Jobs Worldwide* begins with job-hunting advice, but the bulk of the work is a list of organizations and businesses. Arranged geographically throughout, those in European countries fill well over two-thirds of the overall pages, while the rest are either worldwide or occur in a select number of other countries. Grouped by their type of employment, from agricultural and hotel labor to teaching and voluntary work, entries have contact information and bolded headings with descriptions that identify such features as the job, its duration, its requirements, and the application procedure. Information about each country and its employment outlook includes a section on red tape (visas, work permits, etc.). Examined: 39th ed. (2008; 444 p.)

*Transitions Abroad. Bimonthly (Transitions Abroad). www.transitions abroad.com
See description under **Study and Travel**.

Work Abroad: The Complete Guide to Finding a Job Overseas / edited by Clay Hubbs, Susan Griffith, William Nolting. 4th ed. (Transitions Abroad Publishing, 2002).

Here is first-person how-to advice mixed with lists of organizations, print material, and websites that contain descriptive summaries. Aside from a brief introductory collection of key print and electronic sources, there are lists which are frequently arranged geographically and form important parts of the separate chapters that discuss international careers; short-term jobs (with addresses of possible employers) and internships for students and recent graduates; volunteering; teaching English abroad; and K-12 and university teaching. 215 p.

Work Worldwide: International Career Strategies for the Adventurous Job Seeker / Nancy Mueller (John Muir Publications, 2000).
Omitting names and addresses of hiring businesses and organizations,

the work instead is one of advice about how to go about getting a job overseas and adjusting to a new life there. The book recommends ways that the job seeker may do his or her research, learn the art of social networking while obtaining support from others, and pursue other traditional procedures aimed at a position. Several countries are treated in terms of their culture, business basics, courtesies, and the like. There are pointers both about living abroad and becoming reacquainted upon the return home. A relatively short appendix includes internet resources and addresses for American Chambers of Commerce abroad and foreign embassies in the U.S. 231 p.

Work Your Way around the World: A Fresh and Fully Up-to-Date Guide for the Modern Working Traveller / Susan Griffith. 13th ed. (Crimson Publishing, 2007).
    Revised every other year, the title shares similarities with *Jobs and Careers Abroad* (above), since it comes from a related British publisher and has a comparable bias. The book has lots of wordage, opening with an overview, followed by comments about such subjects as working a passage by sea, land, and air (i.e., air courier), identifying local opportunities to earn money, and paying taxes. Jobs involved with tourism, agriculture, teaching English, and other categories receive attention before the bulk of the work, which is an arrangement by areas and countries of the world, with the emphasis on Europe. The space allotted to countries varies, and will likely deal with work regulations, jobs (by categories identified earlier in the book), and volunteer opportunities. Pertinent addresses and first-person anecdotes are scattered throughout the substantial work, whose target audience appears to be the younger traveler on a budget. 596 p.

Organizations

InterExchange. www.interexchange.org
    Services of this non-profit include various job placement programs that are for both young Americans going abroad and foreign students visiting the United States. Examined website: 2008

Volunteer Work

Subject Heading: Voluntarism—Directories; Work camps

Titles

Alternatives to the Peace Corps: A Guide of Global Volunteer Opportunities / edited by Paul Backhurst. 11th ed. (Food First Books, 2005).
After preliminaries about volunteer organizations, reasons for volunteering, and ways of self-finance oneself, the meat of the book appears with an annotated list of organizations—notably those related to social issues such as community development. Broad subject chapters arrange organizations into international and U.S. ones that are dedicated to voluntary service; also there are those involved with alternative travel and overseas study, and those whose principal function is the distribution of information about their area of expertise. An entry consists of a block with name, address, telephone number, e-mail, and website contact, which precedes a paragraph or so describing the purpose of the organization, and it may include references to qualifications required of volunteers, though level of detail varies. A newer edition is available. 144 p.

Archaeological Fieldwork Opportunities Bulletin. Annual (Archaeological Institute of America). www.archaeological.org
Online and in print, find excavations by geographical region, with project name and location, description of duties, minimum age, type of accommodations, academic credits available, costs, etc. Examined website: 2008

Free Vacations & Bargain Adventures in the USA / Evelyn Kaye. 2nd ed. (Blue Panda Publications, 1998).
The book opens with a grab bag of travel advice along with a few firsthand anecdotes on what it is like to volunteer and how to find a cheap vacation, and all of this is on the thin side of usefulness. Its most important and largest part is a directory of alphabetized names of programs and organizations. Each entry sports several paragraphs on activity highlights and background, and three groups of ready reference facts follow, these being contact name, address, telephone, e-mail, and URL; the cost—from free to thousands of dollars—and whatever is supplied; and how time is spent, the age range, and whether children are welcome. In a short section, the aforementioned vacations are re-organized under broad headings, "Absolutely Free Volunteer Vacations," "Archaeology & History," etc. Note that some of the companies identified fit uncomfortably under the

title word "bargain." For a greater number of volunteering opportunities, see *Volunteer Vacations* (below). 222 p.

International Voluntary Work / Victoria Pybus. 9th ed. (Vacation Work Publications, 2005).

Though voluntary work was one of the subjects in the same publisher's *Summer Jobs Abroad* (under **Paid Work**), this list devotes its entire contents to volunteering. Again, arrangement is geographic. Organizations are put in two groups, the first and largest for those that require volunteers to work and live away from home ("residential work"), while in the second volunteers are used to supplement existing services. Among the kinds of projects available are those involving archaeology, youth, conservation, and community development. After an entry's bolded name and contact details, usually several paragraphs explain what the organization does. It would have made matters clearer if the text had been routinely broken down into segments singling out skills required, accommodations, costs, length of time to serve, etc., but instead inclusion of details is arbitrary. Previously called *International Directory of Voluntary Work*, this volume has a later edition available. 351 p.

Invest Yourself: The Catalogue of Volunteer Opportunities: A Guide to Action. Periodically published (Commission on Voluntary Service and Action).

The book is for those interested in entering non-governmental voluntary service in order to help with such issues as poverty or health needs. It begins with personal perspectives on this form of humanitarian assistance, and then takes up the bulk of its contents with a listing of organizations that accept volunteers and, in a smaller group, those that place volunteers. In both categories an entry consists of several parts. After a block of address information that frequently includes e-mail and the URL, there is under a geographic heading the identification of where the service is performed, and whether local or worldwide. A general description explains the organization's purpose and what the volunteers might expect to assist in, while under the "skills" heading is the capabilities the organization needs in its volunteers. Concluding is the name of a contact person. Indexes sort organizations by the location in which they offer work and by skills and interest. In 2006 the title claimed its 60th(!) edition. Examined: 2004; 276 p.

The Peace Corps and More: 175 Ways to Work, Study and Travel at Home & Abroad / Medea Benjamin and Miya Rodolfo-Sioson. Updated, expanded ed. (Global Exchange, 1997).

This directory collects and describes organizations—many of them small—that provide work in the Third World and in the United States and Canada, as well as those involved with study opportunities and socially responsible travel. The emphasis is on social justice, sustainable development, and a healthier planet. A later edition (with "220 ways") is available. 126 p.

Volunteer: A Traveller's Guide to Making a Difference around the World (Lonely Planet, 2007).

Along with detailed observations on the world of volunteering, the first third of the text also gives advice about the practicalities of journeying to out-of-the-way places. The remaining two-thirds is substantially a directory of volunteer programs, and they are grouped into the organized (with such subdivisions as options for the under-thirties), the structured and self-funding, the religious, and do-it-yourself placements. Each group has introductory matter (including its pros and cons) and a breakdown into geographic areas. On two-column pages the entries consist of organization or program name, address, telephone number, electronic access information, and separate fields of commentary—a general view, time commitment for the volunteer, destinations available, costs, eligibility requirements, the selection and interview process, etc. In sum, this is a valuable addition to the subject of volunteering. 271 p.

Volunteer!: The Comprehensive Guide to Voluntary Service in the U.S. and Abroad / edited by Richard Christiano. 5th ed. (Council on International Educational Exchange, 1995).

This directory is split between projects that are short-term and those medium to long-term, many of which are involved in activism, community service, and similar volunteer work. The lay and religious associations are in alphabetical order and are described according to their purpose, program, any special requirements for the volunteer (such as knowing a language), age minimums, acceptance of volunteers with disabilities, costs, etc. The coverage is worldwide. 189 p.

Volunteer Vacations: Short-Term Adventures That Will Benefit You and Others / Bill McMillon, Doug Cutchins, and Anne Geissinger. 9th ed. (Chicago Review Press, 2006).

This is one of the most comprehensive and probably the most approachable directory for volunteer opportunities. A group's name, address, telephone and fax number, e-mail, and URL are in a block preceding sections for project type; mission statement; when founded; number of volunteers the previous year; funding sources; the work done;

project's location; length of time that volunteers are expected to work; cost; enrollment procedure; needed skills; and who may apply. Indexes at the end are by project cost, length, location, season, and type (community development, scientific research, etc.). Narratives of first-person experiences supplement several of the entries for volunteer organizations. 435 p.

World Volunteers: The World Guide to Humanitarian and Development Volunteering / editors Fabio Ausenda, Erin McCloskey (Green Volunteers, 2006).

After advice about volunteering and a list of useful websites, the directory proper commences, providing guidance for potential volunteers. The alphabetical arrangement of organizations gets going with a block of contact data before a breakdown by category of information. There is an overview of what the organization does; its types of activities (e.g., agriculture, construction) and the countries in which it operates; any qualifications for volunteers; acceptance policy on non-professionals; age limits; duration of assignment; languages required; what is provided; the cost; application procedures; and notes for anything not found elsewhere. Concluding charts have organizations according to countries in which they operate and the areas in which they concentrate. A later edition is available. 255 p.

Worldwide Volunteering: Hundreds of Volunteer Opportunities for Gap Year, Holiday or Vacation Projects / compiled by Roger Potter. 4th ed. (How To Books, 2004).

Some 950 volunteer organizations are listed in alphabetical order on two-column pages. While organization headquarters are in numerous countries, Britain contains the most by far, underscoring that the directory throughout is British-centered. After the name and a block of contact information, an entry has a paragraph about the workings of the organization. Rounding it out are an abundance of bolded headings that precede the number of projects (with those for the world and the U.K. separated); starting months; length in weeks; age range; the causes that the volunteer agency serves; its activities; the total of volunteers placed; when to apply; whether work is alone or with others; qualifications (e.g., enthusiasm); equipment or supplies that should be brought; health requirements (e.g., being fit); out of pocket costs; benefits that come as part of the work; job training; if the volunteer is supervised; something about interviews; and where placements are in the world and in the U.K. In the back, organizations are listed twice, first geographically by placement, then by cause and the population (elderly, etc.) that they serve. 628 p.

Organizations

Earthwatch. www.earthwatch.org
The large organization brings volunteers into research work to help scientists and investigators. A list of current projects is available in a catalog as well as online. Examined catalog and website: 2008

Service Civil International. www.sci-ivs.org
Through its U.S. branch—SCI International Voluntary Service USA (SCI IVS USA)—American participants join international group work camps or accept volunteer postings. To find work camps throughout the world use the search engine at its website. Examined website: 2008

Volunteers for Peace. www.vfp.org
To foster peace, the organization is involved with placing volunteers into international projects. The type of project is determined by the local host community. There is an online directory that allows searching by country, date range, project type, term of service, or keyword. Results include a group of facts, such as a designation for location, age, number of spaces for men and women, and cost, plus a block of text that may include in its description the surroundings, the work to be accomplished, accommodations, food, leisure time activities, etc. Examined website: 2008

Title Index

A star (*) indicates a work of particular use or interest.

About the Author

A librarian at the University of Central Missouri since 1979, Steve Walker has combined his interest in nature, history, and the arts with trips to 61 countries (so far), and he has participated in programs run by Earthwatch, Elderhostel, and Outward Bound. He also writes a fanzine dedicated to the writer H. P. Lovecraft.